Ecuador

& the Galápagos Islands

a travel survival kit

Rob Rachowiecki

Ecuador & the Galápagos Islands - a travel survival kit
2nd edition

Published by
Lonely Planet Publications
Head Office: PO Box 617, Hawthorn, Victoria 3122, Australia
US Office: PO Box 2001A, Berkeley, CA 94702, USA

Printed by
Singapore National Printers Ltd, Singapore

Photographs by
Rob Rachowiecki (RR)
Tony Wheeler (TW)
Front cover: Otavaleño woman with traditional weavings (RR)
Back cover: Marine iguana in breeding colours (RR)

First Published
February 1986

This Edition
March 1989

Although the author and publisher have tried to make the information as accurate as possible, they accept no responsibility for any loss, injury or inconvenience sustained by any person using this book.

National Library of Australia Cataloguing in Publication Data

Rachowiecki, Rob, 1954 –
Ecuador & the Galápagos Islands, a travel survival kit.

2nd ed.
Includes index.
ISBN 0 86442 043 9.

1. Ecuador – Description and travel – 1981– - Guide-books. 2. Galápagos Islands – Description and travel – Guide-books. I. Title

918.66'0474
© Copyright Rob Rachowiecki 1989

Rob Rachowiecki

Rob Rachowiecki was born near London and became an avid traveller while still a teenager. He has visited countries as diverse as Greenland and Thailand. He spent several years in Latin America, travelling, mountaineering and teaching English, and he now works there part time for Wilderness Travel, an adventure tour company. His first book, with Hilary Bradt, was *Backpacking in Mexico & Central America* (2nd edition, 1982) and he has also authored *Climbing & Hiking in Ecuador* (2nd printing 1987, Bradt Publications), and Lonely Planet's *Peru – a travel survival kit* (1987). When not travelling, he lives in the USA with his American wife and daughter and studies biology. His dream is to some day sail around the world.

Dedication For Julia Ann, welcome!

From the Author

This edition has been completely updated and revised following my recent visit to Ecuador. The main change is the expansion of the Galápagos section to over three times its original length. Many travellers helped me with information in Ecuador or by letter. Those who contributed are: Irene Billeter (CH), Lisa & Pat McCarthy (UK), Sue Staniforth (C), Michael Jackson (C), Andrea Heckman (USA), Judith Sherman (USA), Ira Leibowitz & Joann Stern (USA), Deirdre Platt (CI), Gareth Griffith (W), Tom McBride (USA), Jeff Holt (USA), Scott & Miriam Latorre (USA), Lynda Sharp (P), Eric Van Dyck (B), a group of 30 schoolboys from Shropshire (UK), Pieter van Bunnigen & Corinne Duhalde (E), Tony Jenkins (C). Jeff Ceaser (US) completely updated the Guaranda section. Special thanks to Wilderness Travel who sent me to the Galápagos twice in 1987 and Miguel Salcedo of the *Sulidae* who has entertained me on many visits to the islands. And heartfelt thanks to Cathy, whose constant

love and encouragement keeps me going when I feel I can't write another word.

Lonely Planet Credits

Editor	Katie Cody
Maps & illustrations	Greg Herriman
Design, cover design & illustrations	Glenn Beanland
Typesetting	Ann Jeffree

Thanks also to LP editor, Lindy Cameron, for proof-reading and indexing and Charlotte Hindle for editorial assistance.

From the Publisher

Thanks must go to the travellers who used the first edition of this book and wrote to Lonely Planet with information, comments and suggestions.

S Braunwalder (CH), Michael Brown (AUS), Pamela Bryant de Wang (E), Colin Churcher (C), Joel Fentin (USA), Kelly Fleming (USA), Marie & Marc Gaudren (C), Simon Hill (AUS), Jonathan Ingram (UK), Nancy Kanwisher (USA), Tom McBride (USA), N McGuinn (USA), John Myerscough (UK), Rebecca Nicholson (UK), Karl G Olson (USA), Alegandro Pastorelli (SAM), Jack Pitman

(UK), Gene Rainone (E), Bruce Silverman (USA), Roy Smith (E), Susan Wolters (NL), Ana Cristina Zapata (E), Mark Zimmerman (CH)

AUS - Australia, B - Belgium, C - Canada, CH - Switzerland, CI - Channel Islands, E - Ecuador, NL - Nederlands, P - Peru, SAM - South America, UK - UK, USA - USA, W - Wales

A Warning & a Request

Things change - prices go up, schedules change, good places go bad and bad places go bankrupt - nothing stays the same. So if you find things better or worse, recently opened or long since closed, please write and tell us and help make the next edition better! All information is greatly appreciated and the best letters will receive a free copy of the next edition, or any other Lonely Planet book of your choice.

Extracts from the best letters are also included in the *Lonely Planet Update*. The *Update* helps us make useful information available to you as soon as possible - it's like reading an up-to-date noticeboard or postcards from a friend. Each edition contains hundreds of useful tips, and advice from the best possible source of information - other travellers. The *Lonely Planet Update* is published quarterly in paperback and is available from bookshops and by subscription. Turn to the back pages of this book for more details.

Contents

Introduction

Ecuador is the smallest of the Andean countries, and in many ways it is the easiest and most pleasant to travel in. From the beautifully preserved colonial capital of Quito, located in the highlands at 2850 metres (9300 feet) above sea level, you can travel by frequent buses to Andean Indian markets, remote jungle towns and warm Pacific beaches. In fact, starting from Quito, you can get to most points in this tropical country in less than a day by public transport.

The highlands have many colourful Indian markets, some world famous and deservedly so, and others which are rarely visited by foreigners but are no less interesting. Any journey in the highlands is dominated by magnificent volcanoes such as Cotopaxi – at 5897 metres (19,348 feet) one of the highest active volcanoes in the world – and many others.

Jungle travel in Ecuador is easier than in most other countries simply because the distances involved are far less, so you can be in the jungle after just a day of bus travel from Quito. There are many exciting opportunities to hire local guides or strike out on your own from jungle villages such as Misahuallí on the Río Napo, a tributary of the Amazon.

The coast, too, has much to offer. Go to a picturesque fishing village and watch the fishermen expertly return their traditional balsa-wood rafts through the ocean breakers to the sandy shore, or help them pull in their nets in return for some of the catch. Laze on the beach in the equatorial sun, swim in the warm seas, and in the evening listen to salsa music in a local bar.

The Galápagos Islands, 1000 km off the Pacific coast of Ecuador, are high on the list of destinations for travellers interested in wildlife. Here you can swim with penguins and sea lions, or walk along beaches while pelicans flap by and huge land iguanas scurry around your feet. The wildlife is so unafraid of humans that at times it's difficult to avoid stepping on the animals.

Ecuador – a travel survival kit tells you everything you'll need to know about travelling around this enchanting country. The most interesting sights, the best-value hotels and restaurants, details on taking all forms of public transport from cheap air flights to dugout canoes, and a host of background details will make this guide an indispensable part of your trip. And you can do it for as little as US$5 a day – or more if you want some comfort.

Finally, Ecuador is one of the safest and most stable countries in Latin America and the problems of pickpockets and revolutions are much less noticeable than in other countries in the region. You really can't go wrong in Ecuador, even if it's your first time travelling in a foreign country. Enjoy it!

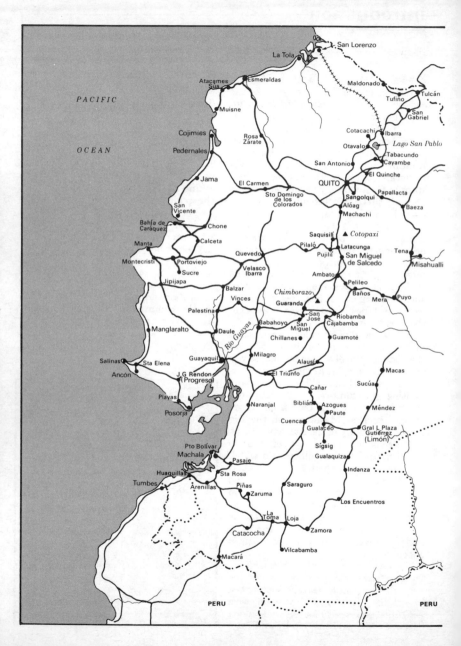

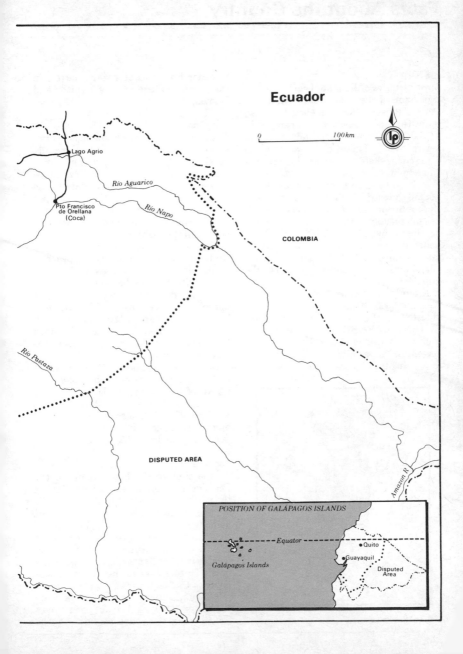

Facts About the Country

HISTORY

Most histories of Ecuador begin with the expansion of the Incas from Peru in the 1400s. Archaeological evidence, however, indicates the presence of people in Ecuador for many thousands of years before then. There are two theories explaining where the earliest inhabitants came from.

It is generally accepted that Asian nomads crossed what is now known as the Bering Strait some 25,000 years ago and began reaching the South American continent by about 12,000 BC. It is believed that several thousand years later, trans-Pacific colonisation by the island dwellers of Polynesia added to the population.

Although stone-age tools have been dated to 9000 BC in the Quito area, the oldest signs of a more developed culture date back to 3200 BC. These belong to the Valdivia period and consist mainly of ceramics, especially small figurines, found in the central coastal area of

Negativo del Carchi

Ecuador. Examples of these can be seen in the major museums of Quito and Guayaquil.

Early Tribes

The history of pre-Inca Ecuador is lost in a tangle of time and legend. Generally speaking, the main populations lived either on the coast or in the highlands. The earliest details we have date to the 11th century AD when there were two dominant tribes; the expansionist Caras in the coastal areas and the peaceful Quitus in the highlands.

The Caras, led by Shyri, conquered the Quitus but it seems to have been a peaceful expansion rather than bloody warfare. The Cara/Quitu peoples became collectively known as the Shyri nation and were the dominant force in the Ecuadorean highlands until about 1300 AD, by which time the Puruhá of the southern highlands had also risen to power under the Duchicela lineage.

Conflict was avoided by the marriage of a Shyri princess, the only child of a King Caran of the Shyris, to Duchicela, the eldest son of the king of the Puruhás. This Duchicela/Shyri alliance proved successful and the Duchicela line ruled more or less peacefully for about 150 years.

The Inca Empire

At the time of the Inca expansion the Duchicela descendants still dominated the north, and the south was in the hands of the Cañari people. The Cañari defended themselves bitterly against the Inca invaders and it was some years before the Inca Tupac-Yupanqui was able to subdue them and turn his attention to the north. During this time he fathered a son, Huayna Capac, by a Cañari princess.

The subjugation of the north took many years and Huayna Capac grew up in Ecuador. He succeeded his father to the

The Moon-God travelling over the sea
in a reed boat

Inca throne and spent years travelling all over his empire, from Bolivia to Ecuador, constantly putting down uprisings from all sides. Wherever possible, he strengthened his position by marriage; and his union with Paccha, the daughter of the defeated Cacha Duchicela, produced a son, Atahualpa.

The year 1526 is a major one in Ecuadorean history. The Inca Huayna Capac died and left his empire, not to one son as was traditional, but to two, thus dividing the Inca empire for the first time. In the same year, on 21 September, the first Spaniards landed near Esmeraldas in northern Ecuador. They were led south by the pilot Bartolomé Ruiz de Andrade on an exploratory mission for Francisco Pizarro, who himself remained further north. Pizarro was not to arrive as conqueror for several years.

Meanwhile, the rivalry of Huayna Capac's two sons grew. The Inca of Cuzco, Huascar, went to war against the Ecuadorean Inca, Atahualpa. After several years of fighting, Atahualpa defeated Huascar near Ambato in central Ecuador and was thus the ruler of a weakened and still divided Inca empire when Pizarro arrived in 1532 with plans to conquer it.

The Spanish Conquest

Pizarro's advance was rapid and dramatic. His horse-riding, armour-wearing and cannon-firing conquistadors were believed to be godlike, and although few in number spread terror among the Indians. In late 1532, a summit meeting was arranged between Pizarro and Atahualpa. Although Atahualpa was prepared to negotiate with the Spaniards, Pizarro had other ideas. When the Inca arrived at the pre-arranged meeting place (Cajamarca in Peru) on 16 November, he was ambushed by the conquistadors who massacred most of his badly armed guards and captured Atahualpa.

Atahualpa was held for ransom, and incalculable quantities of gold, silver and other valuables poured in to Cajamarca. When the ransom was paid the Inca, instead of being released, was put through a sham trial and sentenced to death. His crimes were incest (marrying one's sister was traditional in the Inca heritage), polygamy, worship of false gods, and crimes against the king. He was executed on 29 August 1533, and the Inca empire was effectively at an end.

Despite Atahualpa's death, his general Rumiñahui fought on against the Spaniards in Ecuador for two more years. Pizarro's lieutenant, Sebastián de Benalcázar, finally battled his way to Quito in late 1534, only to find the city razed to the ground by Rumiñahui, who preferred destroying the Inca city to leaving it in the hands of the conquistadors.

Quito was refounded on 6 December 1534, and Rumiñahui was captured, tortured and executed in January of 1535. The only important Inca site in Ecuador which remains more or less intact today is at Ingapirca, near Cuenca.

The Colonial Era

From 1535 onwards the colonial era proceeded with the usual intrigues amongst the Spanish but with no major uprisings by the Ecuadorean Indians. Francisco Pizarro named his brother Gonzalo as governor of Quito in 1540. Gonzalo hoped to conquer the Amazon and find more gold so in 1541 his lieutenant, Francisco de Orellana, left Quito to prospect. He and his force ended up floating all the way to the Atlantic, the first men to descend the Amazon and thus cross the continent. It took them almost a year. This feat is still commemorated in Ecuador and constitutes part of Ecuador's historical claim to a greater part of the Amazon basin than they actually have.

Lima Peru was the seat of the political administration of Ecuador during the first centuries of colonial rule. Ecuador was first known as a *gobernación* (or province) but in 1563 became the *Audiencia de Quito*, a more important political division. In 1739 the *audiencia* was transferred from the viceroyalty of Peru, of which it was a part, to the viceroyalty of Colombia (then known as Nueva Grenada).

Ecuador remained a peaceful colony during these centuries, and agriculture and the arts flourished. Various new agricultural products were introduced from Europe, including cattle and bananas, which still remain important in Ecuador today. There was prolific construction of churches and monasteries which were decorated with unique carvings and paintings resulting from the blend of Spanish and Indian art influences. This so-called 'Quito school of art' has left an indelible stamp on the colonial buildings of the time and is much admired by visitors today.

Life was comfortable for the ruling colonialists but the Indians, and later *mestizos*, were treated abysmally under their rule. A system of forced labour was not only tolerated but encouraged, and it is no surprise that by the 18th century there were several uprisings of the Indians against the Spanish ruling classes. Both poor and rich died in violent fighting.

One of the best-remembered heroes of the early revolutionary period was Eugenio Espejo, born in Quito in 1747 of an Indian father and a mulatto mother. Espejo was a brilliant man who obtained his doctorate by the age of 20 and became a major literary voice for independence. He wrote political satire, founded a liberal newspaper and spoke out strongly against colonialism. He was imprisoned several times and died in jail in 1795.

Independence

The first serious attempt to liberate Ecuador was by a partisan group led by Juan Pío Montúfar on 10 August 1809. The group managed to take Quito and install a government, but this lasted only 24 days before royalist troops were able to regain control.

Independence was finally achieved by Simón Bolívar, the Venezuelan liberator who marched southward from Caracas, freed Colombia in 1819, and supported the people of Guayaquil when they claimed independence on 9 October 1820. It took almost two years before Ecuador was entirely liberated from Spanish rule. The decisive battle was fought on 24 May 1822 when Field Marshal Sucre, one of

Bolívar's best generals, defeated the royalists at the Battle of Pichincha and took Quito.

Bolívar's idealistic dream was to form a United South America and he began by amalgamating Venezuela, Colombia and Ecuador into the independent nation of Gran Colombia. This lasted only eight years and Ecuador became fully independent in 1830. In the same year a treaty was signed with Peru, drawing up a boundary between the two nations. This is the boundary that is marked on all Ecuadorean maps. In 1942, after a war between the two countries, the border was redrawn in Rio de Janeiro and it is this border that is found on non-Ecuadorean maps. However, it is not officially acknowledged by the Ecuadorean authorities.

Independent Ecuador's internal history has been a typically Latin American turmoil of political and open warfare between liberals and conservatives. Quito emerged as the main centre for the church-backed conservatives and Guayaquil has traditionally been considered liberal and socialist. This rivalry continues on a social level today; Quiteños have nicknamed Guayaquileños as *monos* (monkeys) and the lively coastal people think of the highland inhabitants as very staid and dull.

The rivalry between the groups frequently escalated to extreme violence: conservative President García Moreno was shot to death in 1875 and liberal President Eloy Alfaro was killed and burned by a mob in Quito in 1912. The military began to take control and the 20th century has seen more periods of military rule than of civilian.

Ecuador's most recent period of democracy began in 1979 when President Jaime Roldos Aguilera was elected. He was killed in an aeroplane crash in 1981 and his term of office was completed by his vice president, Osvaldo Hurtado Larrea.

In 1984 the conservative León Febres Cordero was elected. On 10 August 1988, following democratic elections, the social democrat Rodrigo Borja became president and the government is now expected to veer sharply left.

Despite intense and bloody rivalry between liberals, conservatives and the military during the earlier part of this century, Ecuador has remained peaceful in recent years and is, at present, one of the safest countries to visit in South America.

GEOGRAPHY

Geographically, Ecuador is one of the world's most varied countries despite its small size, which at 283,520 square km is only a little larger than Great Britain. It straddles the equator on the Pacific coast of South America and is bordered by only two countries, Colombia to the north and Peru to the south.

The country is divided into three regions. The backbone of Ecuador is the Andean range, rising to 6310 metres with Chimborazo its highest peak. The mountains run from north to south and split the country into the western coastal lowlands and the the eastern jungles of the upper Amazonian basin, known in Ecuador as the Oriente. In only 200 km as the condor flies, you can climb from the coast to snowcaps, at over six km above sea level, and descend back down to the steaming rain forest on the eastern side.

The central highlands are two volcanic mountain ranges, about 400 km long, with a valley nestled between them. This valley was appropriately dubbed 'The Avenue of the Volcanoes' by the German explorer Alexander von Humboldt who visited Ecuador in 1802. Within the valley are the capital, Quito – at 2850 metres above sea level the second highest capital in the world – and many other towns and tiny villages often of great interest to the traveller for their Indian markets and fiestas.

CLIMATE

Ecuador's climate follows a pattern very

different from the one travellers from temperate regions are used to. Instead of the four seasons, there are wet and dry seasons. The weather patterns also vary greatly depending on which geographical region you are in.

The Galapagos and coastal areas are influenced by ocean currents. The warm El Niño current from the north causes a hot and rainy season from January through April. It doesn't rain all the time but you can expect torrential downpours which often disrupt communications. Daytime temperatures average about 31°C (88°F) but are often much higher, and this time of year is generally an unpleasant time to be travelling in the coastal regions. From May to December the cool Humboldt current from the south keeps temperatures a few degrees lower and it rarely rains.

If you want to travel in the Oriente, bring your rain gear as it rains during most months. September to December are usually the driest, and June to August are the wettest – with regional variations. It's usually almost as hot as the coast.

The dry season in the highlands is from June through September and a short dry season also occurs during the month around Christmas. It doesn't rain daily in the wet season, however. April, the wettest month, averages one rainy day in two. Daytime temperatures average a high of 20°C to 22°C (68°F to 72°F) and a low of 7°C to 8°C (45°F to 48°F) year round, though you should expect more extreme variations on occasion. These figures are based on climatic data from Quito.

Despite all these statistics, you should remember the Ecuadorean adage that they can experience all four seasons in one day. Without a doubt, the most predictable aspect of Ecuador's weather is its unpredictability.

ECONOMY

Until recently Ecuador was the archetypal 'banana republic'. Until the early 1970s, bananas were the most important export and almost all other exports were agricultural. This changed very rapidly with the discovery of oil. Petroleum exports rose to first place in 1973 and by the 1980s accounted for about half of the total export earnings. Bananas still remain important, accounting for about 7% of the nation's exports, as do shrimp and coffee.

The new-found wealth produced by oil export has definitely improved the standards of living. Nevertheless, Ecuador remains a poor country. Distribution of wealth has been patchy, and much of the rural population continues to live at the same standards it did a decade ago. However, education and medical services have improved.

PEOPLE

The population of Ecuador, according to 1987 figures is 9,120,000. The actual figure is probably tens of thousands higher than this. This is approximately 10 times the number of Indians estimated to have been living in the area at the time of the Spanish conquest.

The population density of about 30 people per square km is the highest of any South American nation. About 40% of this total are Indians and an equal number are *mestizos* (mixed Spanish/Indian stock). About 10% are white and the remainder black or Asian.

Of the Indians, the majority are Quechua-speaking descendants of the people of the Inca empire and live mainly in the highlands. A few other small groups live in the lowlands. About 49% of the population live on the coast (and the Galápagos) and over 47% in the highlands. The remainder live in the jungle region of the Oriente, and colonisation of this area is slowly increasing.

RELIGION

In common with other Latin American countries, the predominant religion is Roman Catholicism. Some of the older towns have splendid 16th and 17th-century Catholic churches. Although churches of other faiths can be found, they form only a small minority. The Indians, while outwardly Roman Catholic, tend to blend Catholicism with their traditional beliefs.

HOLIDAYS & FESTIVALS

Many of the major festivals are oriented to the Roman Catholic liturgical calendar. These are often celebrated with great pageantry, especially in highland Indian villages where a Catholic feast day is often the excuse for a traditional Indian fiesta with much drinking, dancing, rituals and processions. Other holidays are of historical or political interest, for example Columbus Day on 12 October. On the days of the major holidays, banks, offices and other services are closed and transportation is often very crowded, so book ahead if possible.

The following list describes the major holidays, but they may well be celebrated for several days around the actual date.

January
  New Year's Day (1st)
  Epiphany (6th)
March-April
  Carnival Usually held the last few days before Lent, the Carnival is celebrated with water fights. Ambato has its fruit and flowers festival.
April
  Easter Palm Sunday, Holy Thursday, Good Friday, Holy Saturday and Easter Sunday are celebrated with religious processions.
May
  Labour Day (1st) Workers' parades.
  Battle of Pichincha (24th) National holiday celebrates the decisive battle of independence from the Spanish in 1822.
June
  Corpus Christi Religious feast day combined with traditional harvest fiesta in many highland towns. Processions, street dancing.
  St John the Baptist (24th) Fiestas in Otavalo area.
  Sts Peter & Paul (29th) Fiestas in Otavalo area and other northern highland towns.
July
  Simón Bolívar's Birthday (24th) National holiday to celebrate the liberator's birthday.
  Founding of Guayaquil (25th) A major festival for the city of Guayaquil.
August
  Quito's Independence Day (10th)
September
  Fiesta del Yamor (1st-15th) Held in Otavalo.
October

October
Guayaquil's Independence Day (9th)
Columbus Day (12th) National holiday to celebrate the discovery of America (also known as Americas Day).

November
All Saints' Day (1st)
All Souls' Day (Día de Difuntos) (2nd) Celebrated by flower-laying ceremonies in the cemeteries. Especially colourful in rural areas, where entire Indian families show up at the cemeteries to eat, drink, and leave offerings in memory of their departed relatives. The atmosphere often becomes festive rather than sombre.
Cuenca's Independence Day (3rd)

December
Founding of Quito (6th) Celebrated throughout the first week of December with bullfights, parades and street dances.
Christmas Eve, Christmas Day (24-25th)
End-of-year celebrations (28th-31st) Parades and dances culminate in the burning of life-size effigies in the streets on New Year's Eve. In addition to these major festivals, there are many smaller ones. Most towns and villages have their own special day.

LANGUAGE

For the traveller, Spanish is the main language. Most Indians are bilingual, with Quechua being their preferred language and Spanish their second tongue. As well as the Quechua-speaking Indians of the highlands, there are small lowland groups speaking their own languages. These include the Shuar (Jivaro), Auca, Cofan, Secoya, Cayapa and Colorado Indians among others. It is rare to encounter Indians who understand no Spanish at all. Although English is understood in the best hotels, airline offices and tourist agencies, it is of little use elsewhere.

If you don't speak Spanish, take heart. It is an easy language to learn. Courses are available in Quito (see under the Quito section) or you can study books, records and tapes while you are still at home and planning your trip. These study aids are often available for free from many public libraries or you might want to consider taking an evening or college course. Once you have learned the basics, you'll find that you'll be able to travel all over Latin America because, apart from Brazil which is Portuguese-speaking, most of the countries use Spanish.

Spanish is easy to learn for several reasons. First, it uses Roman script, and secondly, with few exceptions, it is spoken as it is written and vice versa. Imagine trying to explain to someone learning English that there are seven different ways of pronouncing 'ough'. This isn't a problem in Spanish. Thirdly, many words are similar enough to English that you can figure them out by guesswork. *Instituto Geográfico Militar* means the Military Geographical Institute, for example.

Even if you don't have time to take a course, at least bring a phrase-book and dictionary. Don't dispense with the dictionary, because the phrase-book limits you to asking where the bus station is and won't help you translate the local newspaper. My favourite dictionary is the paperback *University of Chicago Spanish-English, English-Spanish Dictionary.* It's small enough to travel with, yet has many more entries than most pocket dictionaries and also contains words used in Latin America but not in Spain.

Although the Spanish alphabet looks like the English one, it is in fact different. 'Ch' is considered a separate letter, for example, so *champu'* (which simply means 'shampoo') will be listed in a dictionary after all the words beginning with just 'c'. Similarly, 'll' is a separate letter, so *llama* is listed after all the words beginning with a single 'l'. The letter 'ñ' is listed after the ordinary 'n'. Vowels with an accent are accented for stress and are not considered separate letters.

Pronunciation is generally more straightforward than it is in English, and if you say a word the way it looks like it should be said, the chances are that it will be close enough to be understood. You will get better with practice of course. A few notable exceptions are 'll' which is always pronounced 'y' as in 'yacht,' the 'j' which is pronounced 'h' as in 'happy,' and the 'h' which isn't pronounced at all. Thus the phrase *hojas en la calle* (leaves in the street) would be pronounced 'o-has en la ka-yea.' Finally, the letter 'ñ' is pronounced as the 'ny' sound in 'canyon'.

Grammar

Articles, adjectives and demonstrative pronouns must agree with the noun in both gender and number. Nouns ending in *a* are generally feminine and the corresponding articles are *la* (singular) and *las* (plural). Those ending in *o* are usually masculine and require the articles *el* (singular) and *los* (plural).

There are, however, hundreds of exceptions to these guidelines which can only be memorised or deduced by the meaning of the word. Plurals are formed by adding *s* to words ending in a vowel and *es* to those ending in a consonant.

In addition to using all the familiar English tenses, Spanish also uses the imperfect tense and two subjunctive tenses (past and present). Tenses are formed either by adding a myriad of endings to the root verb or preceding the participle form by some variation of the verb *haber* (to have/to exist).

There are verb endings for first, second and third person singular and plural. Second person singular and plural are divided into formal and familiar modes. If that's not enough, there are three types of verbs – those ending in 'ar', 'er' and 'ir' – which are all conjugated differently. There are also a whole slough of stem-changing rules and irregularities which must be memorised.

Common courtesies

good morning
    buén día
good afternoon (or good evening)
    buenas tardes
yes
    sí

no
    no
hello
    holá
See you later.
    hasta luego Bolivia.
How are you?
    como estás? (familiar) or
    como está? (formal)
please
    por favor
thank you
    gracias
It's a pleasure.
    con mucho gusto

Some useful phrases

Do you speak Spanish?
    habla usted castellano?
Where do you come from?
    de donde es ustéd?
What is your country?
    cual es su país?
Where are you staying?
    donde estás alojado?
What is your profession?
    cuál es su profesión?
What time do you have?
    que hora tiene?
Don't you have smaller change?
    no tiene sencillo?
Do you understand? (casual)
    me entiende?
Where can I change money/travellers' cheques?
    donde se cambia monedas/cheques de viajeros?
Where is the .... ?
    donde está el/la .... ?
How much is this?
    There are fortunately several variations on this well-worn phrase: *a como?*, *cuanto cuesta esto?*, *cuanto vale esto?*
too expensive
    muy caro
cheaper
    más barato
I'll take it.
    lo llevo

What's the weather like?
que tiempo hace?
Buy from me!
comprame!
to the right
a la derecha
to the left
a la izquiereda
Continue straight ahead.
siga derecho
I don't understand.
no entiendo
more or less
más o menos
when?
cuando?
how?
como?
How's that again?
como?
where?
donde?
What time does the next plane/bus/train leave for .... ?
a que hora sale el próximo avión/bús/trén para .... ?
where from?
de donde?
around there
para allá
around here
para acá
It's hot/cold.
hace calor/frío

Some useful words
airport
aeropuerto
bank
banco
block
cuadra
bus station
terminal terrestre
cathedral/church
catedrál, iglesia
city
ciudád
downhill
para abajo

exchange house
casa de cambio
here
amigo/a
here
aquí
husband/wife
marido/esposa
Indian/peasant
campesino (never *indio*)
mother/father
madre/padre
people
la gente
police
policía
post office
correo
rain
lluvia
snow
nieve
there
allí
town square
plaza
train station
estación de ferrocarriles
uphill
para arriba
wind
viento

Time & dates
What time is it?
que hora es? or *que horas son?*
It is one o'clock.
es la una
It is two o'clock.
son las dos
midnight
medianoche
noon
mediodia
in the afternoon
de la tarde
in the morning
de la mañana
at night
de la noche

half past two	2	dos
dos y media	3	tres
quarter past two	4	cuatro
dos y cuarto	5	cinco
two twenty-five	6	seis
dos con veinticinco minutos	7	siete
twenty to two	8	ocho
veinte para las dos	9	nueve
	10	diéz
Sunday	11	once
domingo	12	doce
Monday	13	trece
lunes	14	catorce
Tuesday	15	quince
martes	16	dieciseis
Wednesday	17	diecisiete
miércoles	18	dieciocho
Thursday	19	diecinueve
jueves	20	veinte
Friday	21	veintiuno
viernes	30	treinta
Saturday	40	cuarenta
sábado	50	cincuenta
	60	sesenta
Spring	70	setenta
la primavera	80	ochenta
Summer	90	noventa
el verano	100	cién
Autumn	101	ciento uno
el otoño	200	doscientos
Winter	201	doscientos uno
el invierno	300	trescientos
	400	cuatrocientos
today	500	quinientos
hoy	600	seiscientos
tomorrow	700	setecientos
mañana	800	ochocientos
yesterday	900	novecientos
ayer	1000	mil
	100,000	cien mil
Numbers	1,000,000	un millón
1 uno		

Facts for the Visitor

VISAS & DOCUMENTS

Travellers entering Ecuador as tourists do not require visas. You need your passport (valid for six months or more) and a T-3 tourist card which is obtainable on arrival in Ecuador. There is no charge for this card, but don't lose it as you will need it for stay extensions, passport checks and leaving the country. If you should lose it, you can get another at the immigration office in Quito or Guayaquil, or at the exit point from the country.

On arrival, you are normally asked how long you want to stay. If you're lucky and the duty officer is in a good mood you can get 60 days. You are given an identical stamp on both your passport and tourist card which indicates how long you can stay. The maximum is 90 days, but usually less is given. There is no set pattern in this; during 1983 there was a two-month period when everyone got 30 days irrespective of whether they wanted to stay for three days or three months. Whatever happens, keep cool. If you argue with the official who gave you only 30 days when you wanted 45, he could hassle you further. It's easy and quick to get a stay extension in Quito at Avenida Amazonas 2639.

The main problem with staying in Ecuador is undoubtedly the 90-day rule. This means that you can't stay in the country for more than 90 days in any 12-month period. Ecuador isn't a large country and 90 days is more than enough for most people. A longer stay with a tourist card is flatly refused and the only official way to stay on is with a business, work, student or residence visa. Obtaining one in Ecuador is often a time-consuming, frustrating and costly process, and it's usually better to apply for a visa at your nearest Ecuadorean consul if you are a bona fide businessperson or whatever.

If you don't fall conveniently into one of these categories and you want to stay longer than 90 days, simply leaving the country (across to Peru, for example) and returning a few days later doesn't work. The officials check your passport for entry and exit dates and are quick to notice if your 90 days have been used up. Should you go to Peru and get a new passport at your embassy because your previous one was lost, stolen or expired, then returning to Ecuador is another story. With no Ecuadorean stamps in your brand-new passport you have no problem. If you leave Ecuador with, say only 60 of your 90 days used, you will receive your balance of 30 days upon re-entry with no problem.

In addition to your passport and tourist card, you officially need a ticket out of the country and evidence of sufficient funds for your stay (US$20 per day). This is the law and if you turn up at the border stoned or looking as if you haven't washed or eaten for a week, the law will be enforced. However, in about 10 trips to Ecuador, I was never asked for an onward ticket and was only asked to show sufficient funds once. They didn't count it too carefully – I just waved a bunch of travellers' cheques.

I have heard a story of passengers on an Ecuatoriana flight from Miami to Quito being refused entry without an onward ticket – I don't know the details. If you're flying in, it's safest to buy an onward ticket. It can be refunded if you don't use it. In Ecuador this can take a couple of

NOV 26, 1989 14:40 SALE NO. 172
EARTHLING BOOKSHOP

BOOK NO. 0671660705 1 14.95 14.95
-> UNKNOWN MAN
BOOK NO. 0140097015 1 10.00 10.00
-> MEDIA LAB
BOOK NO. 0864420439 1 7.95   7.95
-> ECUADOR A T GALAPAGOS ISLANDS

TAXABLE: 32.90
NON-TAX: 0.00
SUBTOTAL: 32.90
TAX: 1.97
TOTAL DUE: 34.87

TENDER $ 34.87   CHARGE CARD
^^CHANGE $ 0.00

MCD
805-
649-5107

weeks but they'll give you the money in dollars. Don't worry about an onward ticket at the land borders; it's very unlikely that the rule will be mentioned if you arrive looking reasonably respectable.

You should always carry your passport (or at least a photocopy of the pages with your photo and passport number and your T-3 card) as there are occasional document checks on public transport. You can be arrested if you don't have identification. Another document you can use for identification is a driver's licence (as long as it is of the type with a photo on it) or any similar official-looking document that has a recent photo of you.

If you are carrying a passport photocopy or other document, you may be asked to go to your hotel to produce the passport, so you should always travel from town to town with your passport. Immigration checks go through periodic swings. You can be in Ecuador for three months without anyone asking to see your passport or you can be stopped in the street for no reason and asked for your documents twice in one week. Failure to produce a visa or tourist card can result in deportation.

Colombian Visas

Ecuador is bordered only by Colombia to the north and Peru to the south. To enter Colombia, most nationalities need a visa. Nationals of the following countries do not: Argentina, Austria, Barbados, Belgium, Chile, Costa Rica, Denmark, El Salvador, Finland, Holland, Ireland, Israel, Italy, Japan, Liechtenstein, Luxembourg, Norway, South Korea, Spain, Sweden, Switzerland, Trinidad and Tobago, UK, Uruguay, West Germany.

As of 9 November 1983, all other nationalities require a visa, which costs anywhere from US$5 (for the French) to US$20 for citizens of most other countries. This includes Australians, New Zealanders, Canadians and US citizens, among others. If you don't already have your visa, go to

the Colombian Consul which has offices in Guayaquil, Quito and Tulcán. (See the sections on those cities for further information.)

Peruvian Visas

Most European nationalities – the French being a notable exception – do not require a visa to enter Peru. Most Latins, except Chileans and Venezuelans, do not require visas. Canadians and US citizens do not require visas. Travellers from most communist countries and some African and Asian countries (not Japan) do require visas. Australians and New Zealanders, for some perverse reason, also require visas. If you need a Peruvian visa, you can get one at the consul in Quito, Guayaquil, Macará and Machala. (See the sections on those cities for further information.)

Working

Officially you need a work visa to be allowed to work in Ecuador. You can, however, get a job teaching English in language schools, usually in Quito. They often advertise for teachers on the bulletin board at the almost legendary budget travellers' place, Hotel Gran Casino. They expect you to be a native English speaker, but I know of one Dutchman fluent in English who got a job. Pay is low but enough to live on if you're broke. It's best to start looking soon after you arrive, because it's not easy to get a work visa and you may have to leave in 90 days.

If, in addition to speaking English like a native, you actually have a bona fide teaching credential, so much the better. Schools such as the American School in Quito will often hire teachers of maths, biology and other subjects, and may often help you get a work visa if you want to stay on. They also pay much better than the language schools. I don't know of other jobs which are readily available without a working visa.

Another way of making money, if you're in that unfortunate position of needing it, is by selling good-quality equipment such as camping or camera items. Good gear can be sold for a reasonable though not excessive price – again, use the notice board at the Gran Casino.

Other Paperwork

International vaccination certificates are not required by law, but vaccinations are advisable. See the Health section.

Student cards are of little use, as the number of places that give discounts for students are very limited.

MONEY

The currency in Ecuador is the sucre, usually written as S/. It has nothing to do with sugar; in fact it is named after General Sucre, who defeated the Spanish colonialists at the Battle of Pichincha on 24 May 1824, thus opening the way to independence for Ecuador. There are bills of 1000, 500, 100, 50, 20, 10 and 5 sucres. There is a one-sucre coin which is divided into 100 centavos, but the latter are little used.

There are two rates of exchange; the lower one is used in international business transactions and is of no concern to the traveller. The higher rate is available at all exchange houses. The sucre is frequently devalued, so it is impossible to give accurate exchange rates. The following table gives some idea:

1981	30 sucres per US dollar
1982	65 sucres per US dollar
1983	95 sucres per US dollar
1985	120 sucres per US dollar
1987	200 sucres per US dollar
1988	515 sucres per US dollar

The easiest currency to exchange is the US dollar. Although hard currencies such as other dollars, pounds sterling, French and Swiss francs and German marks are exchangeable in Quito and Guayaquil, outside of these cities you should try to travel with US dollars. It is best to try to exchange as much money as you need in

the major cities, as exchange rates are lower in the smaller towns. In some places, notably the Oriente, it is very difficult to exchange any money at all.

If you are stuck in a small town and are out of sucres, try the banks. Even if they don't officially do foreign exchange, the bank manager may be persuaded to change a small amount of US cash dollars from his personal account, or he may know of someone who will do so. Also ask at the best hotels, restaurants and stores in town. Missionaries, Peace Corps volunteers and other travellers may help you exchange dollars.

Where you should exchange your money varies from month to month. On a recent visit to Ecuador, there was an embargo on foreign exchange at all banks so I had to change at *casas de cambio* (exchange houses). I understand that banks are once again dealing in foreign currency, but you'll have to check the latest situation upon your arrival. *Casas de cambio* usually involve less paperwork and are quicker than banks.

Normally, all exchange rates are within 2% of one another, so it's not worth hassling all day for the best deal unless you're changing a sizable sum. Good places to change money are indicated under each town. There is not very much difference between exchange rates for cash and travellers' cheques. There is no black market and street changers are limited to the borders.

With the lack of a black market, there isn't much advantage in carrying all your money in cash. Travellers' cheques are much safer because they are refunded if they are lost or stolen. I've had no difficulty in exchanging major brands of travellers' cheques in Ecuador. However, I definitely do not recommend using First National Citibank cheques. They took over a year to reimburse me for US$200 in stolen cheques and had the gall to charge me about US$20 for handling. (The theft, I should add, occurred in Peru.) Don't bring all your money in travellers' cheques; it's always useful to have a supply of cash dollars for the occasions when only cash is accepted.

Credit cards are also useful and most major cards are widely accepted. Some transactions are classified as 'business' and you get the lower exchange rate, so check carefully. The best use for credit cards is buying dollars from a bank.

If you run out of money, it is a simple matter to have more sent to you assuming, of course, that there's someone at home kind enough to send you money. A bank transfer is most quickly done by telex, although this will take at least three days. All you need to do is pick an Ecuadorean bank which will cooperate with your bank at home (eg Bank of America, Bank of London & South America) and telex your family, friend or bank manager to deposit the money in your name at the bank of your choice.

Unlike many Latin American countries, Ecuador allows you to receive the money in the currency of your choice (US dollars!). If you are planning on travelling throughout Latin America, you'll find that Ecuador is one of the best countries to have money sent to.

Banks are open for business from 9 am to 1 pm Monday to Friday. In some cities banks are open on Saturday, mainly if Saturday happens to be market day. In some cities, banks may stay open later. *Casas de cambio* are usually open from 9 am to 6 pm Monday to Friday and until noon on Saturday. There is usually a lunch hour, which varies from place to place.

Should you change more money than necessary, you can buy back dollars at international airports when leaving the country. The loss depends on fluctuations of the dollar; sometimes you get back more than you paid but usually you lose a few percent. Airports are good places to change money on Sundays when *casas de cambio* are closed. If you aren't flying out, you can change money at the major land borders.

COSTS

Costs in Ecuador are among the lowest in Latin America. In four years of travelling in Ecuador, I've noticed that the price of travel basics such as hotels, meals and transportation have almost halved. It seems, if anything, to be getting cheaper and you may find that the already low prices in this book are lower still by the time you read this. All good things come to an end, however, so the reverse may also be true. Because of the inflation rate, I've used US dollars in all my price quotes.

If you're on a very tight budget, you'll find that you can easily manage on the classic bare-bones budget of US$5 per day, including the occasional luxury such as a bottle of beer or a movie. If you're really economical, you could manage on less than US$4 per day if you stay in the cheapest US$1 pensiones and eat the meal of the day in restaurants.

If you can afford to spend a little more however, you'll probably enjoy yourself more. The luxury of a simple room with a private hot shower and a table and chair on which to write letters home can be had for as little as US$2.50 per person if you know where to go – this book will show you where.

Saving time and energy by flying back from a remote destination which took you several days of land travel to reach is also recommended. At present, the most expensive internal flight on the Ecuadorean mainland is about US$16 and many flights are much cheaper. A taxi, particularly when you're in a group, isn't expensive and usually costs less than a dollar for short but convenient rides.

Travelling hard, eating well, staying in rooms with a private bath, writing an average of one letter each day to friends/family, buying a daily newspaper, seeing a movie once in a while, and drinking a couple of beers with dinner most nights sounds expensive – almost decadent – to the 'purist' budget traveller. I did that for several months while researching this book, and averaged less than US$10 a day.

Even if you demand the best available, in most parts of Ecuador it will cost much less than wherever home may be.

I sometimes meet travellers who spend most of their time worrying how to make their every penny stretch further. It seems to me that they spend more time looking at their finances than looking at the places they're visiting. Of course many travellers are on a grand tour of South America and want to make their money last, but you can get so burned out on squalid hotels and bad food that the grand tour becomes an endurance test. I'd rather spend eight months travelling comfortably and enjoyably than a full year of strain and sacrifice.

There is one major stumbling block for budget travellers and that is the Galápagos Archipelago. Getting there is very expensive and staying there isn't particularly cheap. I suggest you read the chapter on the Galápagos before you decide whether you want to go.

TOURIST INFORMATION

The government tourist information agency is called DITURIS and they have offices in the major cities; the location of each of these is listed under the appropriate towns. DITURIS seem mostly geared to affluent tourists wishing to see the standard tourist sights and I rarely found them of much help when it came to information about budget hotels, buses to remote villages, or inexpensive nightclubs where the locals go. English was spoken sometimes, but not always. Usually they were friendly and tried to help as much as their limited resources allowed, but at other times I found them bored and disinterested.

It's still worth trying them if you have a problem, because at times they really do go out of their way to be of assistance. I remember complaining to a man at the Esmeraldas tourist office that I couldn't find a bank that would change money for me. He took me to a bank and personally introduced me to a sub-manager he knew,

told him I was a personal friend of his, and made sure that I got some dollars changed. I've never been elevated from the status of complete stranger to personal friend so quickly!

A useful source of information is the telephone directory. You can borrow one from your hotel or the IETEL office. They have a section, usually of green pages, full of useful information and telephone numbers of travel and transport companies, tourist offices, police, airports and other services.

GENERAL INFORMATION
Post

The Ecuadorean postal service is depressingly bad. Most of the letters which I've

sent from Ecuador have arrived at their destinations, sometimes in as little as a week to the US or Europe. Incoming mail is another matter. Some letters have taken as long as two months to arrive. I would estimate that 10% to 20% of my mail never arrived. It has reached the point where I ask that important letters are photocopied and sent twice to lessen the risk of my never receiving them.

Sending Mail I buy aerograms at the post office and use those. Because they contain no enclosure, they're more likely to arrive safely. For a few cents extra, you can send them *certificado*, and although I haven't experienced a loss mailing them this way, there doesn't seem to be much you can do if it doesn't arrive. You'll get some peace of mind, if nothing else.

The post office in each town is marked on the town maps. In some smaller towns it is often just part of a house or a corner of a municipal office. In Quito and Guayaquil there are several post offices dotted around town, but you are advised to go to the central office for greatest efficiency. The hours are usually 9 am to 5 pm Monday to Friday. In the bigger cities they're open a half day on Saturday.

For reasons I don't understand, letters to the same destinations but mailed from different towns are often charged different postage. It appears that some post offices aren't sure what the correct postage is! As a general rule, however, postage costs about two-thirds of what you'd expect to pay in Europe or North America.

Receiving Mail There are several places where you can receive mail but most travellers use either the post office or American Express. Sometimes embassies will hold mail for you, but some embassies refuse to do so and will return it to the sender. Ask before using your embassy. You can also have mail sent c/o your hotel, but it's liable to get lost.

If you have mail sent to the post office, you should know that the mail is filed

alphabetically; so if it's addressed to John Gillis Payson, Esq it could well be filed under 'G' or 'E' instead of the correct 'P.' It should be addressed to John *PAYSON*, Lista de Correos, Correos Central, Quito (or town and province of your choice), Ecuador. Ask your loved ones to clearly print your last name and avoid witticisms such as 'World Traveller Extraordinaire' appended to your name.

American Express will also hold mail for their clients if addressed in the following way: John *PAYSON*, c/o American Express, Aptdo 2605, Quito, Ecuador. Their street address is Avenida Amazonas 339 and they are open from 9.30 am to 12.30 pm and 2.30 to 6 pm Monday to Friday and 9 am to noon on Saturdays. (My sincere thanks to my father-in-law for letting me use his name.)

Telephones

IETEL is the place to go for long-distance national and international telephone, telex and telegram services. The IETEL offices are required by law to be open from 6 am to 10 pm on a daily basis, except in the case of offices in small and remote towns where they can keep shorter hours if they have a dispensation from the government.

I checked on the IETEL office in every town I visited and found that in places of any size, they were indeed open during the specified hours. You will find the IETEL office locations marked on all the street plans in this book. The bigger towns have telex and telegram services; the smaller towns have only the phone.

Even the most remote villages can often communicate with Quito and connect you into an international call. These cost about US$6 for three minutes to the US, and about US$8 to Europe. Waiting time can sometimes be as short as 10 minutes, though it can also take an hour or more to get through. Rates are cheaper on Sundays.

The best hotels can connect international calls to your room at almost any time.

Collect or reverse charge phone calls are possible to a few countries which have reciprocal agreements with Ecuador – these seem to vary from year to year so you should ask at the nearest IETEL office.

Electricity
Ecuador uses 110 volts, 60 cycles, AC.

Time
The Ecuadorean mainland is five hours behind Greenwich Mean Time and the Galápagos are six hours behind. Because of Ecuador's location on the equator, days and nights are of equal length year round and there is no 'daylight savings time'.

It is appropriate to mention here that punctuality is not one of the things that Latin America is famous for.

Weights & Measures
Ecuador uses the metric system, and I have done so throughout this book. For those travellers who still use miles, ounces, bushels, leagues, rods, magnums, stones and other quaint and arcane expressions, there is a metric conversion table at the back of this book.

Laundry
There are no self-service laundry machines in Ecuador. This means that you have to find someone to wash your clothes for you or wash them yourself. Many hotels will have someone to do your laundry; this can cost very little in the cheaper hotels (under a dollar for a full change of clothes). The major problem is that you might not see your clothes again for two or three days, particularly if it is raining and they can't be dried. There are laundromats (*lavanderías*) in Quito and Guayaquil but you still have to leave the clothes for at least 24 hours. Most of these lavanderías only do dry cleaning anyway.

If you wash the clothes yourself, ask the hotel staff where to do this. Most hotels will show you a huge cement sink and scrubbing board which is much easier to use than a bathroom washbasin. Often there is a well-like section next to the scrubbing board and it is full of clean water. Don't dunk your clothes in this water to soak or rinse them as it is often used as an emergency water supply in the case of water failure. Use a bowl or bucket to scoop water out instead, or run water from a tap.

MEDIA
Newspapers & Magazines
Although Ecuador is a small country, there are literally dozens of newspapers available. Most towns of any size publish a local newspaper which is useful for finding out what's screening in the town cinemas or catching up on the local gossip, but has little national news and even less international news. The best newspapers are available in Quito and Guayaquil, although many of these are sensationalist rags which luridly portray traffic-accident victims on the front page while relegating world affairs to a few columns behind the sports section.

There are good newspapers; one of the best is *El Comercio* published in Quito. *Hoy* is also good. In Guayaquil *El Telégrafo* and *El Universo* are recommended. These papers normally cost about 15c each in the city of publication. The further away from the city you are, the more you pay. For example, a day-old *El Comercio* in a small jungle town will be 20c to 25c.

Foreign newspapers and magazines are available at Libri Mundi bookstore, the Hotel Colón shopping mall, and sometimes at the airport. The Hotel Oro Verde in Guayaquil and the airport of that town also have foreign periodicals.

Radio & TV
Ecuador has five television channels, but the programming leaves much to be desired. I remember one evening when Ecuador was playing Peru in a soccer match; every channel was carrying coverage of the match. If you're not much interested in sports, you can watch very bad Latin American soap operas or re-

runs of old and equally bad North American sitcoms. The news broadcasts every evening are quite good, especially for local news. Occasionally, a National Geographic special makes its way to the screen. These kinds of programmes are advertised days ahead in the better newspapers.

If you carry a portable radio when you travel, you'll find plenty of stations to choose from. There is more variety on radio than TV, and you can listen to programmes in Quechua as well as Spanish.

HEALTH
It's true that most people travelling for any length of time in South America are likely to have an occasional mild stomach upset. It's also true that if you take the appropriate precautions before, during and after your trip, it's unlikely that you will become seriously ill. In six years of living and travelling in Latin America, I'm happy to report that I've picked up no major illnesses.

Vaccinations
Vaccinations are the most important of your pre-departure health preparations. Although the Ecuadorean authorities do not, at present, require anyone to have an up-to-date international vaccination card to enter the country, you are strongly advised to read the following list and receive the ones appropriate for your trip. Pregnant women should consult with their doctor before taking these vaccinations.

Yellow fever vaccination is very important if you are planning a trip to the jungles of the Oriente, but not necessary if you intend to avoid the Oriente altogether. This vaccination lasts 10 years.

Typhoid vaccination consists of two injections taken four weeks apart, so you have to think ahead for this one. This vaccine makes some people feel unwell and often gives you a sore arm, so try not to schedule the last shot for the day you're packing. You should get a booster shot every three years, but this doesn't normally feel so bad.

Most people in developed countries get a diphtheria-tetanus injection and oral polio vaccine while they are at school. You should get boosters for these every 10 years.

A cholera vaccination is only necessary if an epidemic has been declared in Latin America. Protection only lasts six months.

Smallpox was eradicated worldwide in 1978 and protection is no longer necessary.

Travel Insurance
However fit and healthy you are, *do* take out medical insurance, preferably one with provisions for flying you home in the event of a medical emergency. Even if you don't get sick, you might be involved in an accident.

First-Aid Kit
How large or small your first-aid kit should be depends on your knowledge of first-aid procedures, where and how far off the beaten track you are going, how long you will need the kit for, and how many people will be sharing it. The following is a suggested checklist which you should amend as you require.

Antiseptic cream
Aspirin
Lomotil for diarrhoea
Antibiotics such as ampicillin and tetracycline
Throat lozenges
Ear and eye drops
Antacid tablets
Motion-sickness medication
Alcohol swabs
Water purification tablets or iodine
Lip salve
Foot and groin powder
Thermometer in a case
Surgical tape, assorted sticky plasters (band-aids), gauze, bandages, butterfly closures
Scissors
First-aid booklet

A convenient way of carrying your first-aid kit so that it doesn't get crushed is in a small plastic container with a sealing lid, such as Tupperware.

Water Purification

If you use tap water for drinking or washing fruits and vegetables, you should purify it first. The most effective method is to boil it continuously for 20 minutes, which is obviously inconvenient. Various water-purifying tablets are available but most of them aren't wholly effective – the hepatitis virus often survives. Also, they make the water taste strange and are not recommended for frequent and long-term use.

The most effective method, and one that doesn't make the water taste as bad, is to use iodine. You can use a few drops of prepared iodine solution but the problem is that it's difficult to know exactly how strong the solution is in the first place and how many drops you should use. The following method is one that I learnt at the South American Explorer's Club in Lima. I find it eliminates these problems and works very well.

Get hold of a small, one-oz glass bottle and put about two to three mm of iodine crystals in it. Don't use a plastic bottle as the iodine will make it brittle and cause it to crack. Both iodine crystals and suitable glass bottles can be obtained from pharmacies. When you need a purifying solution, fill the glass bottle with water and shake it well for about a minute, and then let the crystals settle to the bottom. Only a minute amount of the crystals actually dissolve in the ounce of water and you now have one oz of saturated (not concentrated) iodine solution which is always the same (saturated) strength. Carefully pour the ounce of saturated iodine solution into a quart (or litre) of water and leave it for 15 minutes to produce clean drinking water.

The advantage of this method is that only the iodine solution is used to purify your drinking water and the crystals are left at the bottom of the bottle; they can be used and reused hundreds of times. This is a safe and recommended method except for people who have been treated for thyroid problems and for pregnant women. Also you should be extremely careful not to transfer any of the actual crystals to the drinking water. The saturated solution is quite safe but accidentally swallowing a whole iodine crystal would not do you any good at all.

Health Precautions

Several other things must be thought about before leaving home. If you wear prescription glasses, make sure you have a spare pair and the prescription. The tropical sun is strong, so you may want to have a prescription pair of sunglasses made.

Also buy sunblock lotion, as the lotions available in Ecuador are not very effective. A minimum sunblocking factor of 10 is recommended, or 15 if you are fair or burn easily.

Ensure that you have an adequate supply of the prescription medicines you use on a regular basis. If you haven't had a dental examination for a long time, you should have one rather than risk a dental problem in Ecuador.

Diarrhoea

The drastic change in diet experienced by travellers means that they are often susceptible to minor stomach ailments, such as diarrhoea. After you've been travelling in South America for a while you seem to build up some sort of immunity, which just goes to show that most of the stomach problems you get when you first arrive aren't serious.

The major problem when you have diarrhoea is fluid loss leading to severe dehydration – you can actually dry out to the point of death if you go for several days without replacing the fluids you're losing – so drink plenty of liquids. Caffeine is a stomach irritant, so the best drinks are weak tea, mineral water and caffeine-free soft drinks. Avoid milk and if you can, fast. By giving your body plenty of fluids and no food, you can often get rid of diarrhoea naturally in about 24 to 36 hours. Rest as much as you can.

If you need to make a long journey you can stop the symptoms of diarrhoea by taking Lomotil or Imodium. These pills will not cure you, however, and it is likely that your diarrhoea will recur after the drug wears off. Rest, fast and drink plenty of fluids.

Dysentery
If your diarrhoea continues for several days and is accompanied by nausea, severe abdominal pain and fever, and you find blood in your stool, it's likely that you have contracted dysentery. Although many travellers suffer from an occasional bout of diarrhoea, dysentery is fortunately not very common. There are two types: amoebic and bacillary. It is not always obvious which kind you have. Although bacillary responds well to antibiotics, amoebic – which is rarer – involves more complex treatment. If you contract dysentery, you should seek medical advice.

Hepatitis
The diseases mentioned are dangerous but relatively uncommon. A depressingly common disease is hepatitis A, which is caused by ingesting contaminated food or water. Salads, uncooked or unpeeled fruit, unboiled drinks, and dirty syringes (even in hospitals) are the worst offenders. Infection risks are minimised by using bottled drinks, washing your own salads with purified water, and paying scrupulous attention to your toilet habits.

If you get the disease you'll know it. Your skin and especially the whites of your eyes turn yellow, and you literally feel so tired that it takes all your effort to go to the toilet. There is no cure except bed rest. If you're lucky, you'll be on your feet in a couple of weeks; if you're not, expect to stay in bed for a couple of months.

Research is currently underway to find a 100% effective prophylactic; meanwhile you are strongly advised to get a gamma globulin shot as close to departure as possible. Although it is not 100% effective, your chances of getting hepatitis A are minimised. The shot should be repeated every six months, although some authorities recommend more frequent shots.

If you do get hepatitis A, it's not the end of the world. You may feel deathly ill but people almost never suffer from permanent ill effects. If you're on a long trip, you don't have to give up and go home. Find a hotel that has a decent restaurant and get a room which isn't two flights of stairs and three hallways away from the nearest bathroom. Arrange with the hotel staff to bring you meals and drinks as you need them, and go to bed. Chances are that you'll be fit enough to travel again within a month.

Malaria
This is another disease to think about before leaving. Malarial mosquitoes don't live above 2500 metres, so if you plan on staying in the highlands you needn't worry about them. If you plan on visiting the lowlands, you should purchase anti-malarial pills in advance because they have to be taken from two weeks before until six weeks after your visit. Dosage and frequency of pill-taking varies from brand to brand, so check this carefully.

Chloroquine is recommended for short term protection. Long term use of Chloroquine *may* cause side effects and travellers planning a long trip into the lowlands should discuss this risk against the value of protection with their doctor. Pregnant women are at a higher risk when taking anti-malarials. Fansidar is now known to cause sometimes fatal side effects and use of this drug should be only under medical supervision.

People who are going to spend a great deal of time in tropical lowlands and prefer not to take anti-malarial pills on a semi-permanent basis should remember that malarial mosquitoes bite at night. You should wear long-sleeved shirts and long trousers from dusk till dawn, use frequent applications of an insect repellent, and sleep under a mosquito net. Sleeping under a fan is also effective; mosquitoes don't like wind.

The most effective ingredient in insect repellents is *diethyl-metatoluamide*, also known as 'Deet.' You should buy repellent with 90% or more of this ingredient; many brands, including those available in Ecuador, contain less than 15%, so buy it ahead of time. I find that the rub-on lotions are the most effective, and sprays are good for spraying clothes, especially at the neck, wrist, waist and ankle openings.

Altitude Sickness

This occurs when you ascend to high altitude quickly, for example if you fly into Quito (2850 metres) from sea level. The best way to prevent altitude sickness is to spend a day or two travelling slowly to high altitudes, thus allowing your body time to adjust. Even if you don't do this, it is unlikely that you will suffer greatly in Quito because it is still relatively low. A very few people do become seriously ill, but most travellers experience no more than some shortness of breath and headache. If, however, you travel higher than Quito you may experience much more severe symptoms, including vomiting, fatigue, insomnia, loss of appetite, a rapid pulse and irregular or Cheyne-Stokes breathing during sleep.

The best thing you can do upon arriving at high altitude is to take it easy for the first day, and to avoid cigarettes and alcohol. This will go a long way to helping you acclimatise. If you feel sick, the best treatment is rest, deep breathing, an adequate fluid intake and a mild pain killer such as Tylenol to alleviate headaches. If symptoms are very severe, the only effective cure is oxygen. The best way to obtain this is to descend to a lower elevation.

Heat & Sun

The heat and humidity of the tropics

make you sweat profusely and can also make you feel apathetic. It is important to maintain a high fluid intake and to ensure that your food is well salted. If fluids and salts lost through perspiration are not replaced, heat exhaustion and cramps frequently result. The feeling of apathy that some people experience usually fades after a week or two.

If you're arriving in the tropics with a great desire to improve your tan, you've certainly come to the right place. The tropical sun will not only improve your tan, it will also burn you to a crisp. I know several travellers who have enjoyed themselves in the sun for an afternoon, and then spent the next couple of days with severe sunburn. An effective way of immobilising yourself is to cover yourself with suntan lotion, walk down to the beach, remove your shoes and badly burn your feet, which you forgot to put lotion on and which are especially white.

The power of the tropical sun cannot be overemphasised. Don't spoil your trip by trying to tan too quickly; use strong suntan lotion frequently and put it on all exposed skin. Ecuador doesn't sell strong suntan lotion – bring it from home. Wearing a wide-brimmed sun hat is also a good idea.

Insect Problems

Insect repellents go a long way in preventing bites but if you do get bitten, avoid scratching. Unfortunately this is easier said than done. To alleviate itching, try applying Hydrocortisone cream, Calamine lotion, or soaking in baking soda. Scratching will quickly open bites and cause them to become infected. Skin infections are slow to heal in the heat of the tropics and all infected bites as well as cuts and grazes should be kept scrupulously clean, treated with antiseptic creams, and covered with dressings on a daily basis.

Another insect problem is infestation by lice (including crabs) and scabies. Lice or crabs crawl around in your body hair and make you itch. To get rid of them, wash with a shampoo which contains benzene hexachloride, or shave the affected area. To avoid being re-infected, wash all your clothes and bedding in hot water and the shampoo. It's probably best to just throw away your underwear if you had body lice or crabs. Lice thrive on body warmth; clothing which isn't worn will cause the beasties lurking within to die in about 72 hours.

Scabies are mites which burrow into your skin and cause it to become red and itchy. To kill scabies, wash yourself with a benzene benzoate solution, and wash your clothes too. Both benzene hexachloride and benzoate are obtainable from pharmacies in Ecuador.

Scorpions and spiders can give severely painful – but rarely fatal – stings or bites. A common way to get bitten is to put on your clothes and shoes in the morning without checking them first. Develop the habit of shaking out your clothing before putting it on, especially in the lowlands. Check your bedding before going to sleep. Don't walk barefoot, and look where you place your hands when reaching to a shelf or branch. It's extremely unlikely that you will get stung, so don't worry too much about it.

Snakebite

This is also extremely unlikely. Should you be bitten, the snake may be a non-venomous one. In any event, follow this procedure: first, try and kill the offending creature for identification. Second, don't try the slash-and-suck routine. One of the world's deadliest snakes is the fer-de-lance, and it has an anti-coagulating agent in its venom. If you're bitten by a fer-de-lance, your blood coagulates twice as slowly as the average haemophiliac's and so slashing at the wound with a razor is a good way to help you bleed to death. The slash-and-suck routine does work in some cases, but this should be done only by someone who knows what they are doing. Third, get the victim to a doctor as soon as possible. Fourth, keep calm and

reassure the victim. Even the deadly fer-de-lance only succeeds in killing a small percentage of its victims. Fifth, while reassuring and evacuating the victim, apply a tourniquet just above the bite if it is on a limb. Release pressure for 90 seconds every 10 minutes, and make sure that the tourniquet is never so tight that you can't slide a finger underneath it. If circulation is cut off completely, worse damage will result.

In Australia, which has a fair amount of snake bite experience, a new method of treatment is now recommended. This is to simply immobilise the limb where the bite took place and bandage it tightly (but not like a tourniquet) and completely. Then with the minimum of disturbance, particularly of the bound limb, get the victim to medical attention.

Rabies

Rabid dogs are more common in Latin America than in more developed nations. If you are bitten by a dog, try and have it captured for tests. If you are unable to test the dog, you must assume that you have rabies, which is invariably fatal (if untreated) so you cannot take the risk of hoping that the dog was not infected. Treatment consists of a long series of injections which used to be painful but modern techniques are quicker and less painful. Rabies doesn't develop for several weeks, so if you are bitten, don't panic. You've got plenty of time to get treated.

Rabies is also carried by vampire bats, who actually prefer to bite the toes of their sleeping human victims rather than necks as in popular folklore. So don't stick your toes out from your mosquito net or blanket if you're sleeping in an area where there are bats.

Medical Attention

If you've taken the precautions mentioned in the previous sections you can look forward to a generally healthy trip. Should something go wrong, however, you can get good medical advice and treatment in the major cities. In Quito the Hospital Vozandes is at Vallalengua 263, next to the radio station of the same name. The No 1 Iñaquito bus passes it. They have some English-speaking staff and both outpatient and emergency rooms. A small fee is charged. In Guayaquil, the best hospital where the staff speak English is the Clínica Kennedy.

Many prescription drugs are available in Ecuador, some of which are sold over the counter. If you need to buy any, make sure that they haven't expired and that they have been kept in a cool or refrigerated storage area.

DANGERS & ANNOYANCES

Although rip-offs are a fact of life in Latin America, you'll find Ecuador is safe compared with the worst offenders, Peru and Colombia. You should, nevertheless, take some simple precautions to avoid being robbed.

Armed robbery is still very rare in Ecuador, although parts of Guayaquil and some coastal areas do have a reputation for being dangerous. Sneak theft is more common, and you should remember that crowded places are the haunts of pickpockets. This means badly lit bus stations or bustling markets.

Thieves look for easy targets. Tourists who carry a wallet or passport in a hip pocket are asking for trouble. Leave your wallet at home; it's an easy mark for a pickpocket. Carrying a roll of bills loosely wadded under a handkerchief in your front pocket is as safe a way as any of carrying your daily spending money. The rest should be hidden. Always use at least an inside pocket or preferably a body pouch, money belt or leg pouch to protect your money and passport.

Don't accept food from strangers. I know of one person who ate some cookies given him by some smooth-talking 'friends' on a bus – he woke up two days later in an alley with just his shirt and trousers. I've heard of several reports of this; Ecuadorean authorities claim that it's Colombians who do it. Unopened packages of cookies and other foods are injected with horse tranquilisers using hypodermic syringes. I know it sounds weird, but it's true.

Every year or so, you hear of a couple of night bus robberies in the Guayaquil area. Night buses are simply held up at a road block and robbed by armed men. These are always long-distance buses, so you should avoid taking night buses that go through Guayas province unless you have to. It happens to one bus in many thousands so don't get paranoid if your schedule demands a night bus through the area.

You should carry the greater proportion of your money in the form of travellers' cheques. These can be refunded if lost or stolen. Some airlines will also reissue your ticket if it is lost. You have to give them details such as where and when you got it, the ticket number and which flight was involved. Sometimes a reissuing fee – about US$20 – is charged, but that's much better than buying a new ticket.

It is a good idea to carry an emergency packet somewhere separate from all your other valuables. This emergency packet could be sewn into a jacket (don't lose the jacket!) or even carried in your shoe. It should contain a photocopy of the important pages of your passport in case it is lost or stolen. On the back of the photocopy you should list important numbers such as all your travellers' cheques serial numbers, airline ticket numbers, credit card or bank account numbers, telephone numbers. Also keep one high-denomination bill in with this emergency stash. You will probably never have to use it, but it's a good idea not to put all your eggs into one basket.

Take out travellers' insurance if you're carrying really valuable gear such as a good camera. But don't get paranoid; Ecuador really is a safe country and in almost two years of travelling there I didn't get robbed at all.

If you are robbed, you should get a police report as soon as possible. This is a

Top: Giant Tropical Snail, Western Lowlands (RR)
Left: Scarlet Macaw (RR)
Right: Land Iguana, Plaza Island, Galápagos Islands (TW)

Top: 'Cuy' or roast Guinea-pig, a traditional Inca delicacy (RR)
Bottom: The Extraterrestrial Chicken Restaurant, Quito (RR)

requirement for any insurance claims, although it is unlikely that the police will be able to recover the property. In Quito you should go to the *Servicio de Investigaciones Criminales de Pichincha* (SICP) which is at the intersection of Montufar and Esmeraldas in the old town. In other towns go to the main police headquarters.

FILM & PHOTOGRAPHY

Definitely bring everything you'll need. Camera gear is very expensive in Ecuador and film choice is limited. Some good films are unavailable, such as Kodachrome slide film. Others are kept in hot storage cabinets and are sometimes sold outdated, so if you do buy any film in Ecuador, check its expiry date.

Don't have film developed in Ecuador if you can help it, as processing is shoddy. On the other hand, carrying around exposed film for months is asking for washed-out results. It is best to send it home as soon after it's exposed as possible. The Ecuadorean mail service isn't very reliable so what I normally do is send it home with a friend. You'll often meet people heading back to whichever continent you're from and they can usually be persuaded to do you this favour, particularly if you offer to take them out to dinner. I always buy either process-paid film or prepaid film mailers so I can place the exposed film in the mailer and not worry about the costs. The last thing you want to do on your return from a trip is worry about how you're going to find the money to develop a few dozen rolls of film.

Equatorial shadows are very strong and come out almost black on photographs. Often a bright but hazy day makes for better photographs than a very sunny one. Photography in open shade or using fill-in flash will help. The best time for shooting is when the sun is low – the first and last two hours of the day. If you are heading into the Oriente you will need high-speed film, flash, a tripod, or a combination of these if you want to take photographs within the jungle. The amount of light penetrating the layers of vegetation is surprisingly very low.

The Ecuadorean people make wonderful subjects for photos. From an Indian child to the handsomely uniformed presidential guard – the possibilities of 'people pictures' are endless. However, most people resent having a camera thrust in their faces and people in markets will often proudly turn their backs on pushy photographers. Ask for permission with a smile or a joke and if this is refused don't become offended. Some people believe that bad luck can be brought upon them by the eye of the camera. Others, more sophisticated, are just fed up with seeing their pictures used in books, magazines and postcards. Somebody is making money at their expense. Sometimes a 'tip' is asked. Be aware and sensitive of people's feelings – it is not worth upsetting someone to get your photograph.

ACCOMMODATION
Hotels

There is much variety and no shortage of places to stay in Ecuador. It is almost unheard of to arrive in a town and not be able to find somewhere to sleep, but during major fiestas or the night before market day, accommodation can be rather tight. For this reason, I have marked as many hotels as possible on the town maps. Most of the time, many of these hotels will be superfluous, but once in a while you'll be glad to have the option of as many hotels as possible.

The fact that a hotel is marked on a city map does not necessarily imply that I recommend it – read the 'Places to Stay' sections for descriptions of the hotels. If you are going to a town specifically for a market or fiesta, try and arrive a day early if possible, or at least arrive by early afternoon of the day before the market.

Sometimes it's a little difficult to find single rooms, and you may get a room with two or even three beds. In most cases, though, you are only charged for one bed and don't have to share, unless the hotel is full. You should ensure in advance that you won't be asked to pay for all the beds or share with a stranger if you don't want to. This is no problem 90% of the time.

If you are travelling as a couple, or in a group, you can't automatically assume that a room with two or three beds will be cheaper per person than a room with one bed. Sometimes it is and sometimes it isn't. If I give a price per person, per night, or both, then usually a double or triple room will cost two or three times a single. If more than one price is given, this indicates that double and triples are cheaper per person than singles.

Couples sharing one bed (*cama matrimonial*) are usually, though not always, charged the same as a double room with people in separate beds. To avoid making my figures instantly obsolete because of inflation, I have used US dollars for costs.

Look around the hotel if possible. The same prices are often charged for rooms of widely differing quality. Even in the dollar-a-night cheapies, it's worth looking around. If you get shown into a horrible airless box with just a bed and a bare light bulb, you can ask to see a better room without giving offence simply by asking if they have a room with a window, or explaining that you have to write some letters home and is there a room with a table and chair. You'll often be amazed at the results.

Never rent a room without looking at it first. In most hotels, even the cheapest, they'll be happy to let you see the room. If they aren't, then it usually means that the room is filthy anyway. Also ask to see the bathroom and make sure that the toilet flushes and the water runs if you want a wash. If the shower looks and smells as if someone threw up in it, the staff obviously don't do a very good job of looking after the place. There's probably a better hotel at the same price a few blocks away.

Bathroom facilities are rarely what you may be used to at home. The cheapest hotels don't always have hot water. Even if they do, it might not work or it may only be turned on at certain hours of the day. Ask about this if you're planning on a hot shower before going out to dinner - often there's only hot water in the morning.

Another intriguing device you should know about is the electric shower. This consists of a single cold-water shower head hooked up to an electric heating element which is switched on when you want a hot (more likely tepid) shower. Don't touch anything metal while you're in the shower or you may discover what an electric shock feels like. The power is never high enough to actually throw you across the room, but it's unpleasant nevertheless. I managed to shock myself by simply picking up the soap which I had balanced on a horizontal water pipe (there wasn't a soap dish).

Some hotels charge extra for hot showers and some simply don't have any showers at all. You can always use the public hot baths - there's one in every town.

As you have probably gathered by now, Ecuadorean plumbing leaves something to be desired. Flushing a toilet creates another hazard - overflow. Putting toilet paper into the bowl seems to clog up the system, so a waste receptacle is often provided for the paper. This may not seem particularly sanitary, but it is much better than clogged bowls and water on the floor. A well-run hotel, even if it is cheap, will ensure that the receptacle is emptied and the toilet cleaned every day.

Most hotels will give you a key to lock your room, and theft from your hotel room is not as frequent as it is in some other countries. Nevertheless, carrying your own padlock is a good idea if you plan on staying in the cheaper hotels. Once in a while you'll find that a room doesn't look very secure - perhaps there's a window that doesn't close or the wall doesn't come to the ceiling and can be climbed over. It's worth finding another room. This is another reason why it's good to look at a room before you rent it.

You should never leave valuables lying around the room. It's just too tempting for a maid who makes US$2 a day. Money and passport should be in a secure body pouch; other valuables can usually be kept in the hotel strongbox. (Some cheaper hotels might not want to take this responsibility.) Don't get paranoid though. I haven't had anything stolen from my room in years of travelling in Ecuador, and rarely hear of people who have.

In smaller towns, I usually lump the accommodation together in one section. In larger towns, however, I separate them into groups. 'Bottom-end' hotels are the cheapest, but not necessarily the worst. Although they are usually quite basic, with just a bed and four walls, they can nevertheless be well looked after, very clean, and amazing value for money. They are often good places to meet other travellers, both Ecuadorean and foreign. Prices in this section range from just under US$1 to about US$3 per person. Every town has hotels in this price range and in smaller towns there aren't any more expensive hotels. Although you'll usually have to use communal bathrooms in the cheapest hotels, you can sometimes find rooms with a private bathroom for as little as US$2 each.

Hotels in the 'middle' category usually cost from about US$3 to US$8 per person, but are not always better than the best hotels in the bottom end price range. On the whole, however, you can find some very good bargains here. My wife and I stayed in some really pleasant places in this range. For example, a huge carpeted room with a beautiful countryside view, large and comfortable bed, plenty of furniture, and a clean private bathroom (with twin sinks!) cost a princely US$9 for the two of us. Even if you're travelling on a budget, there are always special occasions (your birthday?) when you can indulge in comparative luxury for a day or two.

'Top-end' hotels are still very cheap by western standards. There is some overlap in prices with the top of the middle-range hotels because often the best place in town costs less than US$8 each. Again, there are some good bargains to be found here if you demand some comfort. Luxury hotels are only to be found in the major cities.

Youth Hostels & Camping

Youth hostels as we know them in other parts of the world aren't found in Ecuador. The cheaper hotels make up for this lack anyway. There are climbers' refuges on some of the major mountains and you can camp in the countryside. If you're carrying a tent or want to hike up to a mountaineering refuge, I suggest you get a copy of my *Climbing & Hiking in Ecuador*. There are rarely campsites in the towns; again, the constant availability of cheap hotels makes town campsites redundant.

Staying in Villages

If you're really travelling far off the beaten track, you may end up in a village that doesn't have even a basic pensión. You can usually find somewhere to sleep by asking around, but it might be just a roof over your head rather than a bed, so carry a sleeping bag or at least a blanket.

The place to ask at first would probably be a village store – the store owner usually knows everyone in the village and would know who is in the habit of renting rooms or floor space. If that fails, you can ask for the *alcalde* or mayor or at the *policía*. You may end up sleeping on the floor of the schoolhouse, the jail or the village community centre, but you'll probably find somewhere if you persevere. People in remote areas are generally hospitable.

FOOD

If you're on a tight budget, food is the most important part of your trip expenses. You can stay in rock-bottom hotels, travel 2nd class, and never consider buying a souvenir, but you've got to eat well. This doesn't mean expensively, but it does mean that you want to avoid spending half your trip sitting on the toilet.

The worst culprits for making you sick are salads and unpeeled fruit. With the fruit, stick to bananas, oranges, pineapples and other fruit that you can peel yourself. With unpeeled fruit or salads, wash them yourself in water which you can trust (see Health section). It actually can be a lot of fun getting a group of you together and heading out to the market to buy salad veggies and preparing a huge salad. You can often persuade someone in the hotel to lend you a suitable bowl, or you could buy a large plastic bowl quite inexpensively and sell or give it away afterwards.

As long as you take heed of the salad warning, you'll find plenty of good things to eat at reasonable prices. You certainly don't have to eat at a fancy restaurant; their kitchen facilities may not be as clean as their white tablecloths. A good sign for any restaurant is if the locals eat there – restaurants aren't empty if the food is delicious and healthy.

If you're on a tight budget you can eat from street and market stalls if the food looks freshly cooked, though watch to see if your plate is going to be 'washed' in a bowl of cold, greasy water and wiped with a filthy rag (it's worth carrying your own bowl and spoon). Alternatively, try food that can be wrapped in paper, such as pancakes.

Markets

Good local dishes to try at markets and street stands (and restaurants too, of course) are the following:

Caldo Soups and stews are very popular and are often served in markets for breakfasts. Soups are known as *caldos, sopas,* or *locro*. Chicken soup, or *caldo de gallina*, is the most popular. *Caldo de patas* is soup made by boiling cattle hooves and, to my taste, is as bad as it sounds.

Cuy Whole roasted guinea pig. This is a traditional food dating back to Inca times. It tastes rather like a cross between rabbit and chicken. The sight of the little paws and teeth sticking out and eyes tightly closed is a little unnerving, but cuy is supposed to be a delicacy and some people love it.

Lechón Suckling pig. Pigs are often roasted whole and are a common sight at Ecuadorean food markets. Pork is also called *chancho*.

Llapingachos Mashed-potato-and-cheese pancakes that are fried – these are my favourite. They are often served with *fritada* – scraps of fried or roast pork.

Seco Stew. The word literally means 'dry' (as opposed to a 'wet' soup). The stew is usually meat served with rice and can be *seco de gallina* (chicken stew), *de res* (beef), *de chivo* (goat), or *de cordero* (lamb).

Tostadas de maíz Tasty fried corn pancakes.

Yaguarlocro Potato soup with chunks of barely congealed blood sausage floating in it. I happen to like blood sausage and find this soup very tasty; many people prefer just straight *locro* which usually has potatoes, corn and an avocado or cheese topping.

Restaurants

In a restaurant, there'll be other dishes to choose from. For breakfast, the usual eggs and bread rolls or toast are available. *Huevos fritos* are fried eggs, *revueltos* are scrambled, and *pasados* or *a la copa* are boiled or poached. These last two are usually semi-raw, so ask for *bien cocidos* (well cooked) or *duros* (hard) if you don't like your eggs too runny. *Tostadas* are toast and *panes* are bread rolls which you can have with butter and jam *mantequilla y mermelada*. A good local change from eggs are sweet corn tamales called *humitas*, often served for breakfast with coffee.

Lunch is the biggest meal of the day for many Ecuadoreans. If you walk into a cheap restaurant and ask for the *almuerzo* or lunch of the day, you'll get a decent meal for well under a dollar – highly recommended for the economy minded. An *almuerzo* always consists of a *sopa* and a *segundo* or 'second dish,' which is usually a *seco* (stew) with plenty of rice. Sometimes the *segundo* is *pescado* (fish) or a kind of lentil or pea stew (*lenteja, arveja*), but there's always rice. Many, but not all, restaurants will give you a salad (often cooked), juice and *postre* (dessert) as well as the two main courses.

The supper of the day is usually similar to lunch. Ask for the *merienda*. If you don't want the *almuerzo* or *merienda*, you can choose from the menu, but this is always more expensive. However, the set meals do tend to get a little repetitious after a while and most people try out other dishes – which can still cost little over a dollar.

A *churrasco* is a hearty plate with a slice of fried beef, one or two fried eggs, vegetables (usually boiled beet slices, carrots and beans), fried potatoes, a slice of avocado and tomato, and the inevitable rice. If you get *arroz con pollo* then you'll be served a mountain of rice with little bits of chicken mixed in. If you're fed up with rice, go to a *Pollo a la Brasa* restaurant where you can get fried chicken, often with fried potatoes on the side. *Gallina* is usually boiled chicken as in soups, and *pollo* is more often spit-roasted or fried. *Pollo* tends to be underdone but you can always send it back to get it cooked longer.

Parrilladas are steak houses or grills. These are recommended places to eat if you like meat and a complete loss if you don't. Steaks, pork chops, chicken breasts, blood sausages, liver and tripe are all served on a grill which is placed on the table. Every time I order a parrillada for two people, I find there's enough for three but they'll give you a plastic bag for the leftovers. If you don't want the whole thing you can choose just a chop or a steak. Although parrilladas aren't particularly

cheap, they are reasonably priced and very good value.

Seafood is very good, even in the highlands, as it is brought in fresh from the coast and iced. The most common types of fish are a white sea bass called *corvina* and trout or *trucha*. *Ceviche* is popular throughout Ecuador; this is seafood marinated in lemon and served with popcorn and sliced onions, and it's delicious. Ceviche can be *de pescado* (fish), *de camarones* (shrimp) or *de concha* (shellfish, such as clams or mussels). You can go the whole hog (if you pardon the expression) and get a *ceviche mixto*. A *langosta* (lobster dinner) costs about US$6 – a bargain by western standards.

Most Ecuadorean meals come with *arroz* (rice), and some travellers get fed up with it. Surprisingly, one of the best places to go for a change from rice is a Chinese restaurant. These are known as *chifas* and are generally inexpensive and good value. Apart from rice, they serve *tallarines*, which are noodles mixed with your choice of pork, chicken, beef or vegetables (*legumbres, verduras*). Portions tend to be filling.

Vegetarians will find that *chifas* offer the best choice for non-meat dishes, or you can go to a *cevichería* if you don't consider seafood to be meat. Vegetarian restaurants are rare in Ecuador. If you have any kind of strict diet, you would be advised to bring a camping stove with you and cook your own. Most hotels don't mind this, especially the cheapest ones. Just don't burn the place down.

If you want inexpensive luxury, go for breakfast at the fanciest hotel in town (assuming they have a restaurant or cafeteria). You can relax with coffee and rolls and the morning paper, or get a window seat and watch the world go by. Despite the elegant surroundings and the bow-tied waiter, you are only charged an extra 10c for your coffee. Makes a nice change and the coffee is often very good.

Cities big enough to have first-class

hotels also have good but expensive (by Ecuadorean standards) international restaurants. These are often right in the hotels themselves.

DRINKS

Water

I don't recommend drinking tap water anywhere in Latin America. *Agua potable* means that the water comes from the tap but it's not necessarily healthy. Even if it comes from a chlorination or filtration plant, the plumbing is often old, cracked and full of crud. Salads washed in this water aren't necessarily clean. One suggestion is to carry a water bottle and purify your own water. (For more about this see the Health section.)

If you don't want to go through the hassle of constantly purifying water, you can buy bottled mineral water very cheaply. Don't ask for mineral water, ask for *Güitig* (pronounced Weetig) which is the best known brand. Another brand is *Manantial* but everyone still asks for *Güitig*. A large 650 ml bottle costs about 25c in most restaurants and less in a store.

Soft Drinks

The advantage of buying a bottled drink in a store is that it is very cheap; the disadvantage is that you have to drink it at the store because the bottle is usually worth more than the drink inside. (Canned drinks cost up to three times more than bottles.) You can pay a deposit, but you have to return the bottle to the store you bought it from; a different store won't give you any money for it. What many travellers do is pay a deposit on, or effectively buy, a bottle of pop, beer or mineral water and then trade it in every time they want to buy a drink in a different place.

All the usual soft drinks are available, as are some local ones with such endearing names as Bimbo or Lulu. Soft drinks are collectively known as *colas* and the local brands are very sweet. Seven-up is simply

called *seven*, so don't try calling it 'siete arriba' as no one will have any idea what you're talking about. You can also buy Coca Cola, Pepsi Cola, Orange Fanta or Crush (called *croosh*) and Sprite - the latter pronounced *essprite*!

Ask for your drink *helada* if you want it out of the refrigerator or *al clima* if you don't. Remember to say *sin hielo* (without ice) unless you really trust the water supply. Diet soft drinks aren't available - the concept of Third World countries paying for a drink with no calories is a little absurd.

Fruit Juices

Juices (*jugos*) are available everywhere and are usually better than colas to my taste, but they cost more. Make sure you get *jugo puro* and not *con agua*. The most common kinds are *mora* (blackberry), *naranja* (orange), *toronja* (grapefruit), *piña* (pineapple), *maracuya* (passion fruit), *sandía* (watermelon), *naranjilla* (a local fruit tasting like bitter orange), or *papaya*.

Coffee & Tea

Coffee is available almost everywhere but is often disappointing. A favourite Ecuadorean way of making coffee is to boil it for hours until only a thick syrup remains. This is then poured into cruets and diluted down with milk or water. It doesn't taste that great and it looks very much like soy sauce, so always check before pouring it into your milk (or over your rice)! Instant coffee is also served. Expresso is available only in the better restaurants. *Café con leche* is milk with coffee, and *café con agua* or *café negro* is black coffee.

Tea, or *té*, is served black with lemon and sugar. If you ask for tea with milk, British style, you'll get a cup of hot milk with a tea bag to dunk in it. Hot chocolate is also popular.

Alcohol

Finally we come to those beverages which

can loosely be labelled 'libations'. The selection of beers is limited, but they are quite palatable and inexpensive. Pilsener usually comes in large 650 ml bottles and is my drink of choice. Club is slightly more expensive, has a slightly higher alcohol content (3.9% as opposed to 3.5% if you're interested), and comes in small 330 ml bottles. Malta is a sweet, dark beer and is sometimes mixed in a blender with eggs and sugar to make a breakfast drink at the markets. I have never been able to bring myself to try it. Lowenbrau is made in Ecuador and tastes like Club. All other beers are imported and available only in the most expensive of restaurants or at speciality liquor stores.

Local wines are truly terrible and should not be experimented with. Imported wines from Chile, Argentina or Peru are good but cost much more than they do in their country of origin – I suggest you wait till you visit them. Californian and European wines are available but are more expensive still, and Australian wines haven't made it to Ecuador yet.

Spirits are expensive if imported and not very good if made locally, with some notable exceptions. Rum is cheap and good. The local firewater, *aguardiente* or sugar cane alcohol, is an acquired taste but is also good. It's very cheap; you can get a half bottle of Cristal aguardiente for about 75c. If you're desperate for gin, vodka or whisky, try the Larios brand – probably the best of a bad bunch.

BOOKS & BOOKSHOPS

There are only two good bookshops in Ecuador which sell books in English (French and German too). One is in Guayaquil and one is in Quito. In Guayaquil go to the Librería Científica on Luque 223. In Quito there is Libri Mundi, the best-known bookshop in Ecuador. They have a branch at Juan León Mera 851 and on the ground floor of the Hotel Colón. Both shops also have a good selection of Spanish books.

Guidebooks

Apart from months of legwork, I used a great many books in compiling the information in this guidebook. I hope you like it, because I couldn't find any other comprehensive guidebooks on Ecuador. There are, however, some good general books on South America which have a chapter on Ecuador, but they are mainly recommended for the traveller who wants one book for a 'grand tour' of Latin America.

For the budget traveller, *South America on a Shoestring* by Geoff Crowther (Lonely Planet, Melb, Australia) is recommended for its many maps and money-saving information, as well as its interesting synopses of the historical/political situation in Latin countries. It is updated regularly.

A broader approach is available in *The South American Handbook*, edited by John Brooks (Trade & Travel Publications, Bath, UK). It has been referred to as the 'South American Bible' by some travellers and it weighs about as much as one and is quite pricey. Its main drawbacks are sometimes overdue updates and paucity of good city maps. It is suitable for everyone from penurious budget travellers to expense-accounted business people, so there is a lot of extraneous information for most readers. Nevertheless, it is the best general guide to the continent.

Another book which I enjoyed is Lynn Meisch's *A Traveler's Guide to El Dorado & the Inca Empire* (Penguin Books). It's full of interesting details on the crafts, cultures, markets, fiestas and archaeology of Colombia, Ecuador, Peru and Bolivia, and has good background information for the traveller. However, it doesn't set out to help with specific information on hotels, restaurants or transport.

Various other guidebooks are available in Ecuador. One is Arthur Weilbauer's booklet *A Guide for Excursions by Car in Ecuador*. This is available in Spanish, German and English although the English translation is entertainingly garbled – 'There are hotels of all denominations, but luckily no high-rise damage the aspect'. Only the Spanish version has maps. Most of the other books available are of the coffee-table variety – fun to look through in the store and suitable as a souvenir or present rather than as a travel guide.

There are also 'mainstream' guides by Frommer, Waldo, Birnbaum, Fodor and others, which seem to cater to the 'today's Tuesday, so it must be Rio' crowd, and are fine if that's what you're looking for.

The Outdoors

My first two years in Ecuador were spent trying to climb as many of its mountains as I could. At that time, there was only one climbers' guide available: *The Fool's Climbing Guide to Ecuador & Peru* by Michael Koerner, Buzzard Mountaineering, USA – now out of print as far as I know. It was a whimsical little booklet from which I derived a great deal of pleasure, and although its mountain descriptions were not very detailed it remains a great favourite of mine.

More favourite still, though I must admit to a certain prejudice because I wrote it, is *Climbing & Hiking in Ecuador* (Bradt Publications). It is a detailed guide to climbing Ecuador's mountains and also describes many beautiful hikes, some of which are simple day hikes suitable for the beginner.

My favourite of all is Edward Whymper's *Travels Amongst the Great Andes of the Equator*, first published in Britain in 1891 and now quite rare, although a good public library might be able to get it for you. This exceptional book describes an 1880 mountaineering expedition which made eight first ascents of Ecuadorean peaks, including the highest, Chimborazo. There are also fascinating descriptions of travel in Ecuador a century ago and the woodcut engravings are pure delight.

Backpacking in Venezuela, Colombia & Ecuador by George and Hilary Bradt describes more Ecuadorean hikes. It is

published by Bradt Publications, 41 Nortoft Road, Chalfont St Peter, Bucks SL9 0LA, UK. (Also Hunter Publishing, 300 Raritan Centre Parkway, NJ 08818, USA.) Bradt Publications sells or produces an excellent and varied collection of outdoor guides and maps to various regions of the world, including eight books and many maps of Latin America.

Books on Ecuador's wildlife are sadly few. *The Birds of Ecuador & the Galápagos Archipelago* by Thomas Butler is merely a check list. A proper field guide by Ridgely and Greenfield will be available in the late 1980s; meanwhile ornithologists have to avail themselves of either guides to the whole continent, or to nearby countries. The best of these is Hilty and Brown's *A Guide to the Birds of Colombia* which covers most of Ecuador's species. *A Guide to the Birds of Venezuela* by de Schauensee and Phelps is also useful.

The only books on plants and animals I know of are *Fauna del Ecuador* (Quito, 1978) and *Flora de Ecuador* (Quito, 1985) both by Erwin Patzelt, in Spanish, and now out of print (though there is frequent talk of new editions). There are however, several excellent books on South American natural history which contain some information on Ecuador. My favourite is Michael Andrews' *Flight of the Condor*. Tony Morrison's *Land Above the Clouds* and *The Andes* are also very good.

Galápagos

The handiest small guide to the history, geology and plant and animal life of these islands is the *Galápagos Guide* by Epler and White, available at the Libri Mundi bookstore in Quito. It costs only about US$2.50.

Somewhat more expensive but much more thorough and highly recommended is *Galápagos: A Natural History Guide* by Michael H Jackson, himself a Galápagos Park guide (University of Calgary Press).

Other useful guides are *A Field Guide to*

the Birds of the Galápagos by Michael Harris (Collins, London). This excellent handbook illustrates and fully describes every Galápagos bird species.

Amateur botanists will want Eileen Schofield's booklet *Plants of the Galápagos Islands* (Universe Books, New York). This describes 87 common plants and is much more convenient than the classic, but encyclopaedic, *Flora of the Galápagos Islands* by Wiggins and Porter (Stanford University Press, USA).

In addition to these guides, there are several good books of a general nature about the Galápagos. The following are particularly recommended: *Islands Lost in Time* by Tui de Roi Moore; *Galápagos – Islands of Birds* by Bryan Nelson; and *Darwin's Islands: A Natural History of the Galápagos* by Ian Thornton. There are many others.

The most famous of the visitors to the Galápagos was Charles Darwin in 1835 and you can read his *On the Origin of Species by Means of Natural Selection* or his accounts of *The Voyage of the Beagle*. These 19th century books are rather dated and make heavy reading today. You may prefer one of the various modern biographies such as Irving Stone's excellent *The Origin* or Alan Moorehead's illustrated *Darwin & the Beagle*. Readers interested in a layman's introduction to evolutionary theory can try the amusingly written but accurate *Darwin for Beginners* by Jonathan Miller and Borin Van Loon.

Miscellaneous

One of my favourite books about travel in Ecuador is Henri Michaux' prose/poetry account of his 1928 visit. Michaux was a Belgian poet and mystic and his *Ecuador – A Travel Journal* is an intriguing look at his impressions of the country more than half a century ago. It was republished by Peter Owen in 1970 and is available in the Libri Mundi bookstore.

Various good books are available about the Indian populations of Ecuador. *The Awakening Valley* by Collier and Buitron (University of Chicago Press, 1949) is a photographic anthropological study of the people of the Otavalo region. The Shuar are studied by Michael Harner using their old name, *The Jivaro: People of the Sacred Waterfall* (Doubleday/Anchor, 1973). A well-illustrated multilingual book available in Quito is *The Lost World of the Aucas* by K D Gertelmann. Other books about Ecuador's and South America's Indian peoples are available at Libri Mundi.

Books about the history or politics of Ecuador are hard to find. Going back to the arrival of the Spanish conquistadors, the best book is undoubtedly John Hemming's excellent *The Conquest of the Incas*. Although this mainly deals with Peru (the heart of the Inca Empire) there are several sections on Ecuador. I have yet to find a readable book about the more recent history or politics of the country.

MAPS

The bookstores have a limited selection of Ecuadorean maps. The best selection is to be had from the *Instituto Geográfico Militar* (IGM), which is on top of a hill on Avenida T Paz y Miño, off Avenida Colombia in Quito. The building can be recognised by a map of Ecuador painted on one of its outside walls. There are no buses; walk or take a taxi (about a dollar). A permit to enter the building is given to you at the main gate in exchange for your passport. Opening hours are from 8 am to 3 pm Monday to Thursday and 8 am to 12 noon on Friday.

Few city maps are published, and except for perhaps a detailed map of the whole of Quito, you'll find the city maps in this book are generally the best available. The IGM does have some excellent large-scale maps of the whole country, ranging from a 1:1,000,000 one-sheet Ecuador map to 1:50,000 topographical maps. Most maps are freely available for reference. Some areas, especially the Oriente and parts of the western lowlands, are inadequately mapped. Bradt Publications has Ecuadorean maps for sale.

THINGS TO BUY

Souvenirs are good, varied and cheap. Although going to villages and markets is fun, you won't necessarily save a great deal of money. Similar items for sale in the main cities are often not much more expensive, so if you're limited on time you can shop in Quito or Guayaquil. If you only have the time or inclination to go on one big shopping expedition, I definitely recommend the Saturday market at Otavalo as being both full of variety and convenient.

In markets and smaller stores, bargaining is acceptable, indeed expected, though don't expect to reduce the price by more than about 20%. In 'tourist stores' in Quito, prices are usually fixed. Some of the best stores are quite expensive; on the other hand, the quality of their products is often superior.

Clothing

Woollen goods are popular and are often made of a pleasantly coarse homespun wool. Otavalo is good for these and you can find sweaters, scarves, hats, gloves and vests. A thick sweater will cost US$5 to US$10 depending on size and quality, so if you're planning trips high into the mountains you can get some good warm clothes in Ecuador. Wool is also spun into a much finer and tighter textile which is used for making ponchos. Otavaleño Indian ponchos are amongst the best anywhere.

Clothing made from orlon is also to be found. It's cheaper than wool but looks garish and unattractive. It's easy to tell the difference just by looking at it, but if you're not sure, you can try the match trick. Take a tiny piece of lint from the material and set light to it. If it melts, it's orlon; if it burns, it's wool. Many people think that only woollen items are traditional, earthy, cool, ethnic, etc. While that may be true, if you see an orlon sweater that you like, there's nothing to stop you buying it and it'll be one of the cheapest sweaters you've ever bought.

Hand-embroidered clothes are also attractive but it's worth getting them from a reputable shop; otherwise they may shrink or run. Cotton blouses, shirts, skirts, dresses and shawls are available.

Ecuadorean T-shirts are among the best I've seen anywhere. If you're a T-shirt collector you'll find all sizes and colours to choose from. The most popular designs are of Galápagos animals, but many others are available. The best designs are by Peter Mussfeldt and the shirts cost about US$4 each.

Panama hats are worth buying. A good panama is so finely made that it can be rolled up and passed through a man's ring, though it's unlikely that you'll find many of that quality. They are made from a palmlike bush which grows abundantly in the coastal province of Manabi. Montecristi and Jipijapa are major centres. Their name dates back to the 1849 Californian gold rush, when prospectors travelling through the Panama Canal bought the hats, but they are originally Ecuadorean.

Weavings

A large variety of mainly woollen weavings are to be found all over the country, with Otavalo as usual having a good selection. They range from foot-square weavings which can be sewn together to make throw cushions or shoulder bags, to weavings large enough to be used as floor rugs or wall hangings. Designs range from traditional to modern; Escher styles are popular.

Bags

Apart from bags made from two small weavings stitched together, you can buy *shigras*, shoulder bags made from agave fibre that are strong, colourful and eminently practical. They come in a variety of sizes and are expandable. Agave fibre is also used to make macramé bags.

Leather

A famous centre for leatherwork is Cotacachi, north of Otavalo. Prices are cheap in comparison to those in more developed countries, but quality is very variable, so examine possible purchases carefully. Although the best leatherwork in Ecuador is supposedly done in the Ambato area, it's difficult to find any for sale. Leatherwork items range from full suits to coin purses, and wide-brimmed hats to luggage bags.

Woodwork

The major woodworking centre of Ecuador is San Antonio de Ibarra, and any items bought elsewhere are likely to have been carved there. Items range from the utilitarian (bowls, salad utensils, chess sets, candlesticks) to the decorative (crucifixes, statues, wall plaques). Again, prices are very low, but quality varies.

Balsa wood models are also popular. They are made in the jungles of the Oriente and sold in many of Quito's gift stores. Brightly painted birds are the most frequently seen items, but other animals and boxes are also sold.

Tagua nut carvings are typical of Ecuador. The tagua nut is actually the seed of a coastal palm. The egg-sized seed is carved into a variety of novelty items such as napkin rings, egg cups and chess pieces. Riobamba is a well-known tagua nut centre.

Jewellery

Ecuador isn't famous for its gemstones but it does have good silver and gold work. Chordeleg near Cuenca is a major jewellery centre. Beautifully filigreed work can be obtained here.

Other

Baskets made of straw, reeds, or agave fibres are common everywhere. Painted and varnished ornaments made of bread dough are unique to Ecuador and are best obtained in Calderón, a village just north of Quito. Onyx (a pale, translucent quartz with parallel layers of different colours) is carved into chess sets and other objects.

WHAT TO BRING

As an inveterate traveller and guidebook writer, I've naturally read many guidebooks. I always find the What to Bring section depressing, as I'm always told to bring as little as possible; I look around at my huge backpack, my two beat-up duffel bags bursting at the seams, and I wonder sadly where I went wrong. I enjoy camping and climbing, so I carry tent, ice axe, heavy boots and so on. I'm an avid birdwatcher, and I'd feel naked without my binoculars and field guides. And of course I want to photograph these mountains and birds, which adds a camera, lenses, tripod, and other paraphernalia. In addition, I enjoy relaxing just as much as leaping around mountains taking photographs of birds so I always have at least two books to read as well as all my indispensable guides and maps. Luckily, I'm not a music addict so I'm able to live without a guitar, a portable tape player or a shortwave radio.

It appears that I'm not the only one afflicted with the kitchen-sink disease. In Latin America alone, I've met an Australian surfer who travelled the length of the Pacific coast with his board looking for the world's longest left-handed wave; a couple of Canadian skiers complete with those skinny boards; a black man from Chicago who travelled with a pair of three-foot-high bongo drums; an Italian with a saxophone (a memorable night when those two got together); a Danish journalist with a portable typewriter; a French freak with a ghetto blaster and (by my count) 32 tapes; and an American woman with several hundred weavings which she was planning on selling. All of these were budget travellers staying for at least 1½ months and using public transport.

After confessing to the amount of stuff I travel with, I can't very well give the time-honoured advice of 'travel as lightly as possible.' I suggest you bring anything that is important to you; if you're interested in photography, you'll only curse every time you see a good shot (if only you'd brought your telephoto lens), and if you're a musician you won't enjoy the trip if you constantly worry about how out of practice your fingers are getting.

A good idea once you're in Quito is to divide your gear into two piles. One is what you need for the next section of your trip, the rest you can stash in the storage room at your hotel (most hotels have one). Ecuador is a small country so you can use Quito as a base and divide your travelling into, say, coastal, highland and jungle portions, easily returning to Quito between sections and picking up the gear you need for the next.

There's no denying, however, that travelling light is much less of a hassle, so don't bring things you can do without. Travelling on buses and trains is bound to make you slightly grubby, so bring one change of dark clothes that don't show the dirt, rather than seven changes of nice clothes for a six-week trip. Many people go overboard with changes of clothes, but one change to wash and the other to wear is the best idea. Bring clothes that wash and dry easily. (Jeans take forever to dry.)

The highlands are often cold, so bring a wind-proof jacket and a warm layer to wear beneath, or plan on buying a thick sweater in Otavalo. A hat is indispensable; it'll keep you warm when it's cold, shade your eyes when it's sunny, and keep your head dry when it rains (a great deal!). A collapsible umbrella is great protection against sun and rain as well.

You can buy clothes of almost any size if you need them, but shoes are limited to size 43 Ecuadorean, which is about 10½ North American. Suffice it to say that I have US size 12 feet (don't laugh, they're not that big!) and I can't buy any footgear at all in Ecuador. This is also true of most Latin countries, so bring a spare pair of shoes if you're planning a long trip.

The following is a checklist of small items you will find useful and probably need:

Pocket torch (flashlight) with spare bulb and batteries
Travel alarm clock
Swiss Army-style penknife
Sewing and repairs kit (dental floss makes excellent, strong and colourless emergency thread)
A few metres of cord (also useful for clothesline and spare shoelaces)
Sunglasses
Plastic bags
Soap and dish, shampoo, tooth brush and paste, shaving gear, towel
Toilet paper (rarely found in cheaper hotels and restaurants)
Ear plugs for sleeping in noisy hotels or buses
Insect repellent
Suntan lotion (strong blocking lotions are not available in Ecuador)
Address book
Notebook
Pens and pencils
Paperback book (easily exchanged with other travellers when you've finished)
Spanish-English dictionary
Small padlock
Large folding nylon bag to leave things in storage
Water bottle
First-aid kit (see Health section)

Tampons are available in Ecuador, but only in the major cities and in regular sizes, so make sure you stock up with an adequate supply before visiting smaller towns, the jungle or the Galápagos. If you use contraceptives, then you'll also find them available in the major cities. Choice of oral contraceptives is limited, however, so if you use a preferred brand, you should bring it from home.

A sleeping bag is useful if you plan on travelling on a budget (or camping), because some of the cheaper hotels don't supply enough blankets and it can get cold at night. Most hotels will give you another blanket if you ask, however, so a sleeping bag is useful but not indispensable if you're planning on staying mainly in the major tourist areas.

You need something to carry everything around in. A backpack is recommended because carrying your baggage on your back is less exhausting than carrying it in your hands, which are left free. On the other hand, it's often more difficult to get at things inside a pack, so some travellers prefer a duffel bag with a full-length zipper.

Whichever you choose, ensure that it is a good, strongly made piece of luggage, or you'll find that you spend much of your trip replacing zippers, straps and buckles. Hard travelling is notoriously hard on your luggage, and if you bring a backpack, I suggest one with an internal frame. External frames snag on bus doors, luggage racks and airline baggage belts, and are liable to be twisted, cracked or broken.

Getting There

There are three ways of getting to Ecuador: air, land and sea. However, very few people even consider the ocean route these days as it is more expensive and less convenient than flying.

AIR

There are two international airports serving Ecuador – Guayaquil on the coast and Quito in the highlands. Remember that an internal flight between these two cities only costs about US$15 if you buy the internal ticket in Ecuador.

If you fly to Ecuador, bear in mind that the main hub for flights to and from western South America is Lima, Peru. You can often fly more cheaply to Lima and finish your journey to Ecuador by land. Bus travel from Lima to the Ecuadorean border takes about 30 hours and costs about US$20. If you prefer to travel direct to Ecuador, frequent international flights arrive and depart from either Quito or Guayaquil.

The ordinary tourist or economy-class fare is not the most economical way to go.

It is convenient, however, because it enables you to fly on the next plane out and your ticket is valid for 12 months. If you want to economise further, there are several options. Students and those under 26 can get discounts with most airlines.

Whatever age you are, if you can purchase your ticket well in advance and stay a minimum length of time, you can buy a ticket which is usually about 30% or 40% cheaper than the full economy fare. These are often called APEX, excursion or promotional fares depending on the country you are flying from and the rules and fare structures that apply there.

Normally the following restrictions apply. You must purchase your ticket at least 21 days (sometimes more) in advance and you must stay away a minimum period (about 14 days on average) and return within 180 days (sometimes less). Individual airlines have different requirements and these change from time to time. Most of these tickets do not allow stopovers and there are extra charges if you change your dates of travel or destinations. These tickets are often

sold out well in advance of departure so try and book early if possible.

Stand-by fares are another possibility from some countries, such as the USA. Some airlines will let you travel at the last minute if they have available seats just before the flight. These stand-by tickets cost less than an economy fare but are not usually as cheap as other discounted tickets.

The cheapest way to go is via the so-called 'bucket shops,' which are legally allowed to sell discounted tickets to help airlines fill their flights. These tickets are usually the cheapest of all, particularly in the low seasons, but they often sell out fast and you may be limited to only a few available dates.

While discounted tickets, economy and student flights are available direct from the airlines or from a travel agency (there is no extra charge for any of these flights if you buy them from an agent rather than direct from the airline), discount bucket shop tickets are available only from the bucket shops themselves. Most of them are good and reputable companies, but once in a while a fly-by-night operator comes along and takes your money for a super-cheap flight and gives you an invalid or unusable ticket, so check what you are buying carefully before handing over your money.

Bucket shops often advertise in newspapers and magazines; there is much competition and a variety of fares and schedules are available. Fares to South America have traditionally been relatively expensive, but bucket shops have recently been able to offer increasingly economical fares to that continent.

It is worth bearing in mind that round-trip fares are always much cheaper than two one-way tickets. They are also cheaper than 'open jaws' fares – an 'open jaws' ticket enables you to fly into one city (say Quito) and leave via another (say Caracas).

From the USA

Generally speaking, the US does not have such a strong bucket shop tradition as Europe or Asia, so it's harder getting cheap flights from the US to South America. Sometimes the Sunday travel sections in the major newspapers (*The Los Angeles Times* on the west coast and *The New York Times* on the east coast) advertise cheap fares to South America although these are sometimes no cheaper than the APEX fares with one of the several airlines serving Ecuador.

One travel agency which can find you the best deal to Ecuador (and anywhere else in the world) is Council Travel Services which is affiliated with the Council on International Educational Exchange (CIEE). You can find their addresses and telephone numbers in the telephone directories of Berkeley, La Jolla, Long Beach, Los Angeles, San Diego and San Francisco (all in California), Amherst, Boston and Cambridge (in Massachusetts), New York City, Portland (Oregon), Providence (Rhode Island), Austin (Texas) and Seattle (Washington).

There are three major departure cities from the US to Ecuador. Typical round-trip APEX fares to Quito are US$520 from Miami, US$620 from New York, and US$750 from Los Angeles. People are often surprised that fares from Los Angeles in southern California are so much higher than from northerly New York. A glance at the world map soon shows why. New York at 74° west is almost due north of Miami at 80° and Quito at 78°30. Thus planes can fly a shorter, faster and cheaper north-south route. Los Angeles, on the other hand, is 118° west and therefore much further away from Quito than New York is.

The national Ecuadorean airline is Ecuatoriana and they fly from the US to Ecuador and other Latin American countries. I flew Ecuatoriana four times in 1987. My four flights were six, twelve, eight and two hours late respectively. In addition, Ecuatoriana change their schedules with maddening frequency. This means that a flight which you expect to leave the US at midnight and arrive in Ecuador early the next morning may be rescheduled a few weeks before departure to leave at 7 am, thus forcing you to overnight in the airport (or find a hotel) and also causing you to lose the first day of your trip. There is no such thing as a perfect airline, but Ecuatoriana has generally provided the most unreliable service of any airline with which I have flown to South America.

If, because of a late flight (but not a rescheduled one) you lose a connection or are forced to overnight, the carrier is responsible for providing you with help in making the earliest possible connection and paying for a room in a hotel of their choice. They should also provide you with meal vouchers. If you are seriously delayed on an international flight, ask for these services.

From Europe

Bucket shops generally provide the cheapest fares from Europe to South America. Fares from London are often cheaper than from other European cities and there are also more bucket shops. For this reason some European budget travellers buy their tickets from London bucket shops. This is especially true of travellers from Scandinavian countries, where cheap fares are difficult to find.

In London competition is fierce. Bucket shops advertise in the classifieds of newspapers ranging from *The Times* to *Time Out*. I have heard consistently good reports about Journey Latin America (JLA), 16 Devonshire Rd, Chiswick, London W4 2HD (tel 01 747 3108) who specialise in cheap fares to the entire continent as well as arranging itineraries for both independent and escorted travel. They will make arrangements for you over the phone. Another reputable budget travel agency is Trailfinders, 42-48 Earl's Court Rd, London W8 6EJ (tel 01 937 9631). The useful travel newspaper

Trailfinder is available from them for free. Typical round trip fares from London are about £500.

From Australia

There is no real choice of routes between Australia and South America and there are certainly no bargain fares available. The only direct route is to fly from Australia to Tahiti and connect from there with the weekly Lan Chile flight to Santiago in Chile.

If you buy your ticket direct from Lan Chile one way costs A$1530 while a return ticket is around $2495. However, you can get considerable discounts through travel agents. From Chile you could then fly or travel overland through Peru to Ecuador.

The other alternative is to fly to the US west coast and from there either fly to South America or make your way overland through Mexico and Central America. The one-way fare from Australia to Los Angeles or San Francisco is A$1013, the return fare again varies with season – from A$1446 in the low season, A$1786 in the shoulder, A$1966 in the high. You won't find any special deals offered on the Lan Chile flight but, by shopping around you should be able to knock the fares to the USA down by a reasonable amount. Check the ads in the travel pages of papers like the Melbourne *Age* or the *Sydney Morning Herald*.

From Asia

There is also very little choice of direct flights between Asia and South America apart from Japan and there certainly won't be any bargains there. The cheapest way will be to fly to the US west coast and connect from there.

Departing Ecuador

There is a hefty US$20 departure tax on international flights from Ecuador. This is payable in cash dollars or sucres at the exchange rate of the day.

Top: Basketware, Saquisilí (RR)
Left: Pottery Market (RR)
Right: Inspecting weavings in Otavalo market (RR)

Top: Río Cuchipamba raft ferry near Gualaquiza (RR)
Left: Bus and buggy, Saquisilí (RR)
Right: Isla Bartolomé, Galápagos Islands (TW)

OVERLAND

If you live in the Americas, it is possible to travel overland. However, if you start from North or Central America, the Pan American highway stops in Panama and begins again in Colombia, leaving a 200-km roadless section of jungle known as the Darien Gap. This takes about a week to cross on foot and by canoe in the dry season (January to mid-April) but is much heavier going in the wet season.

Most travellers going by land fly around the Darien Gap. From South America it is straightforward to travel by public transport from Peru or Colombia into Ecuador.

SEA

It may occasionally be possible to find a ship going to Guayaquil, the main port for Ecuador.

Getting Around

Ecuador has a more efficient transport system than most Andean countries. Also, it is a small country, which means you can usually get anywhere and everywhere quickly and easily. The bus is the most frequently used method of transportation; you can take buses from the Colombian border to the Peruvian border in 18 hours if you want to. Aeroplanes and boats (especially in the Oriente) are also frequently used, but trains less so.

Whichever form of transport you use, remember to have your passport with you and not leave it in the hotel safe or packed in your luggage. To board most planes and boats, you need to show your passport.

Buses have to go through a transit police check upon entering any town and although passports are infrequently asked for, it's as well to have it handy for the one time in 20 that you are asked to show it. If your passport is in order, these procedures are no more than cursory. If you're travelling anywhere near the borders or in the Oriente, you can expect more frequent passport checks.

AIR
Even the budget traveller should consider the occasional internal flight. With the exception of flying to the Galápagos, internal flights are comparatively cheap, and even the most expensive flight is currently only US$16. Almost all flights originate or terminate in Quito or Guayaquil, so the most useful way for the traveller to utilise these services is by taking a long overland journey from one of

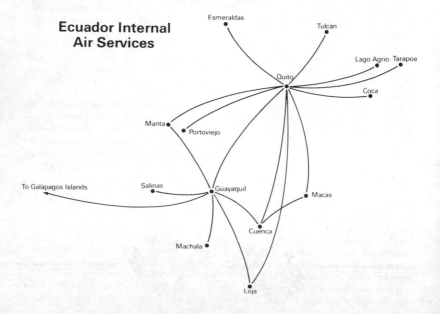

Ecuador Internal Air Services

Esmeraldas
Tulcán
Lago Agrio Tarapoa
Quito
Coca
Manta
Portoviejo
To Galápagos Islands
Salinas
Guayaquil
Macas
Cuenca
Machala
Loja

these cities and then returning quickly by air.

Ecuador's most important domestic airline is TAME, which flies to almost all the destinations in the country. Their closest competitor is SAN-Saeta (formerly two airlines) who have a good schedule of flights between Quito, Guayaquil and Cuenca. Prices from both companies are the same so, if travelling between these major cities, use the one whose schedule most closely matches yours. A third airline is TAO, which flies small aircraft between Puyo and Macas in the Oriente.

There are other small local airlines. The military have been known to provide flights, as have the missions and the oil companies, however, you hear about this less and less. These days, with improving air services, it's usually easier to pay a few dollars for a scheduled flight than to spend several days lining up a flight with someone else.

TAME flies from Quito to and from Guayaquil, Cuenca, Loja, Macas, Coca, Tarapoa, Lago Agrio, Tulcán, Esmeraldas, Manta, Portoviejo and the Galápagos. TAME also flies from Guayaquil to and from Quito, Cuenca, Loja, Machala, Manta and the Galápagos. Cuenca and Loja are also linked by scheduled flights. There are sometimes TAME flights between Guayaquil and Macará and seasonal flights to Salinas. Except for the major cities, flights usually operate several times a week but not on a daily basis. For more details, see the Air sections under the appropriate cities.

Flights are frequently late, but not very much so. Flights first thing in the morning are more likely to be on time but by the afternoon things tend to have slid half an hour behind schedule. You should show up about an hour early for domestic flights, as baggage handling and check-in procedures tend to be rather chaotic. There are about eight flights a day both ways between Quito and Guayaquil.

If you show up early for your flight, you can often get on the earlier flight if there is room. If you paid for your ticket with cash (not credit card) then TAME will accept your SAN-Saeta ticket and vice versa.

There are no seating assignments on domestic flights so you choose your seat aboard on a first-come, first-served basis. There are no separate sections for smokers and non-smokers. Many of the flights give extraordinarily good views of the snow-capped Andes and it is worth getting a window seat even if the weather is bad because the plane often rises above the clouds, giving spectacular views of volcanoes riding on a sea of cloud.

Once in a while you may get treated to a special mountain fly-by. This happened to me once on the flight from Macas to Quito. We flew by Cotopaxi and the pilot decided to give us a closer look so he banked sharply and did a complete circuit of the volcano. For over a minute we were able to have wonderful views of the top of the mountain with a rare look directly down into the crater. TAME scored a lot of points that day! So try to get on the plane early and study a topographical map to see which side of the plane will be best for you.

Flying from Quito to Guayaquil, you will get the most spectacular mountain views on the left-hand side; flying to Macas the view is on the right-hand side. Many of the other flights have mountains on either side. You should decide which specific peaks you would prefer to have a good look at and also consider the time of day so that you won't be looking into the sun. Good views are to be had about half the time so make an effort to plan your trip and get good seats.

Flights on the mainland cost the same whether you're an Ecuadorean or foreigner. Flights to the Galápagos are a different matter, however. Although Ecuadoreans pay only about US$40 for the round trip from Guayaquil, all foreigners have to pay about US$324 for the same flight, and they are not treated to better in-flight service. There is nothing you can do about this except be thankful that the rest of the internal flights cost the same for all nationalities.

Wherever you want to fly, don't despair if you can't get a ticket. It's always worth going to the airport in the hopes of someone not turning up for the flight. Make sure that you're there early and get yourself on a waiting list if there is one. If you do have a reservation, make sure you confirm it. And reconfirm it. And reconfirm it again. As a general rule, I would confirm flights both 72 and 24 hours in advance, as well as when you arrive in Ecuador. Ecuadoreans are notorious for bumping you off your flight if you don't reconfirm. If it's impossible for you to reconfirm because you're in the middle of nowhere, tell them so that they know. Try to have it on the computer if possible. And try to find someone to reconfirm for you.

A final point about air travel from Ecuador. You can't buy international charter or other economy flights in Ecuador. You have to pay full first-class or full tourist-class fare. In addition to the fare you must pay a 10% tax, so it is best to buy your international ticket ahead of time in your home country. There is a US$20 international departure tax but no taxes for domestic flights.

BOAT

Boat transportation is commonly used in Ecuador and can be divided into four different types.

The most commonly used is the motorised dugout canoe, which acts as a water taxi or bus on the major rivers of the Oriente and parts of the coast. In the Galápagos you find medium-sized motor cruisers or motor sailboats which are used by small groups to visit the different islands of the archipelago, either on day trips or for trips of several days duration. Thirdly, there are large vessels used either for carrying cargo and a few passengers or as cruise ships for many passengers. Finally, many rivers are crossed by ferries which vary from a paddled dugout taking one passenger at a time to a car ferry capable of taking half a dozen vehicles across the river. These are sometimes makeshift transportation to replace a bridge which has been washed out, is being repaired or is still in the planning stages.

Dugout Canoes

Dugout canoes often carry as many as three dozen passengers and are the only way to get around many roadless areas. Although you can hire one yourself to take you anywhere, but this is very expensive. If you take a regularly scheduled one with other passengers, however, it is quite affordable, though not as cheap as a bus for a similar distance. This is simply because an outboard engine uses more fuel per km than a bus engine, and because a dugout travels more slowly than a bus.

The most likely places that you will travel any distance in dugouts are Misahuallí to Coca in the jungles of the Oriente and San Lorenzo to La Tola on the north-west coast.

Most of the boats used are literally dugouts, with maybe a splashboard added to the gunwales. They are long in shape and short on comfort. Seating is normally on hard, low, uncomfortable wooden benches which accommodate two people each. Luggage is stashed forward under a tarpaulin, so carry hand baggage containing essentials for the journey. You will be miserable for hours if you don't take the following advice, which is worth the cost of this book! *Bring seat padding.* A folded sweater or towel will make a world of difference on the trip.

Pelting rain or glaring sun are major hazards and an umbrella is excellent defence against both. Bring suntan cream and wear long sleeves, long pants and a sun hat – I have seen people literally unable to walk because of second-degree burns on their legs from a six-hour exposure to the tropical sun. The breeze as the boat motors along tends to keep insects away, and it also tends to cool you so you don't notice the burning effect of the sun. If the sun should disappear or the rain begin, you can get quite chilled, so bring a light jacket.

Insect repellent is useful during stops along the river. A water bottle and food will complete your hand baggage. Remember to stash your spare clothes in plastic bags or they'll get soaked by rain or spray.

A final word about dugout canoes: they feel very unstable! Until you get used to the motion of them, you might worry about the whole thing just rolling over and tipping everybody into the shark, piranha or boa constrictor-infested waters. Clenching the side of the canoe and wondering what madness possessed you to board the flimsy contraption in the first place doesn't seem to help. I've ridden many dugouts and never had a problem, even in rapids and ocean waves. Nor have I met anyone who was actually dunked in. Dugouts feel much more unstable than they really are, so don't worry about a disaster; it almost never happens.

Other Boats

In the Galápagos, you have the choice of travelling in anything from a small sailboat taking four passengers to a large cruise ship complete with 48 air-conditioned double cabins with private baths. The choice is yours. More information on these boats is given in the chapter on the Galápagos.

In addition to the dugout canoes of the Oriente, there is one cruise ship which makes leisurely luxurious passages down the Río Napo. This is the *Flotel*, based in Coca. More information about it is given under the Coca section in the Northern Oriente chapter.

There are a few ratty steamers plying coastal routes. These are mainly cargo boats and are rarely used by travellers. A few boats go out to the Galápagos from Guayaquil, but it's better to fly there and sail around the islands themselves. Otherwise you could get stuck in

Guayaquil for weeks. Again, there is more information under the appropriate coastal towns.

Your Own Boat The idea of sailing your own yacht to the Galápagos sounds romantic. Unfortunately, to sail in the Galápagos you need a licence and these are all limited to Galápagos boats. If you arrive in the islands in your own boat, you will have to moor the boat in Puerto Ayora and hire one of the local boats to take you around. The Ecuadorean authorities give transit permits of only 72 hours for sailors on their own boats.

TRAIN

Ecuador's rail system was severely damaged by landslides and flooding during the extremely heavy rains of the 1982/83 El Niño wet season. Many km of track were totally destroyed. Roads and bridges were also badly damaged so available repair money has been channelled into the more important road network; the railway system has to wait until funds become available.

Since the 1982/83 disaster (when thousands of families had their homes and fields flooded) Ecuador has noticed a decline in the amount of tourist revenue entering the country. This has been attributed to the loss of the Quito-Guayaquil railway line, which is one of the most spectacular train rides in the world and was one of the main reasons some tourists visited Guayaquil. The section from Riobamba in the mountains to Guayaquil on the coast is a dramatic descent which has been made famous in a British TV series on the world's greatest train journeys. Although I've heard rumours that the railway system will be in action again by late 1988, don't be surprised if it's not.

There are two railway networks in Ecuador. Before 1982 the northern lines ran from Quito to Ibarra and from there to San Lorenzo on the coast. The southern lines ran from Quito to Guayaquil with a branch to Cuenca. Neither of these lines are working in their entirety at this time. The northern train runs only between Ibarra and San Lorenzo. The southern runs from Quito only as far as Riobamba.

Ordinary trains are not normally used, with the exception of Metropolitan Touring's expensive tour train from Quito to Riobamba. Instead, an *autoferro*, which is like a bus mounted on a railway chassis, is used. Space is limited, so you are advised to buy tickets ahead of time if you wish to travel by autoferro. It is not as comfortable as a normal train. Departure times and other details are given under the appropriate town headings.

BUS
Long Distance

Ecuador is developing a system of central bus terminals in each city – especially in the highlands and increasingly in the lowlands – which means that if you have to change buses you don't have to go looking for different terminals. All buses arrive and depart from the same place. Once you have located the central bus terminal, often referred to as the Terminal Terrestre, it is a simple matter to find a bus to take you where you want to go. Some towns still haven't completed their main bus terminals, however, so they still have several smaller ones.

Throughout this book, I have indicated where the bus terminals are located on the city maps. The accompanying text will tell you the most important destinations served by the terminal, the approximate cost of the journey, about how long it will take to get there, and how frequently buses leave.

I have refrained from giving exact schedules, as that is a sure way of making this book obsolete before it is published. Timetables change frequently and are not necessarily adhered to. If a bus is full, it might leave early. Conversely, an almost-empty bus will usually spend half an hour giving *vueltas* or just driving from the terminal to the main plaza and back again

with the driver's assistant yelling out of the door in the hopes of attracting more passengers.

Various types of buses are used; they can be roughly grouped into two types. *Busetas* (small buses) usually hold 22 passengers and are fast and efficient. Although standing passengers are not normally allowed, the seats can be rather cramped. Larger coaches have more space, but they often allow standing passengers and so can get rather crowded. They are generally slower than the busetas and at times can take almost twice as long to reach their destinations because they drop off and pick up so many standing passengers.

Although they're slow, the big old coaches are sometimes more fun because there's more activity going on with passengers getting on and off all the time, perhaps accompanied by chickens or a couple of hundredweight of potatoes. If you're in any hurry, make sure that you get a buseta. The approximate times given for most of the journeys in this book tend to lean towards the faster times.

Getting around Ecuador by bus is easy, but here are some tips to make your travels more enjoyable. If you go to the terminal the day before your bus trip, you can usually buy tickets in advance. This means you can choose your approximate time of departure, and often you can choose your seat number too. I'm over six feet tall, and one of my pet hates is being squished in a tiny back seat of a bus. I think it's worth buying tickets in advance so that I can get a front-row seat, which generally means more leg room, much better views and a more exciting trip.

Some people prefer second-row seats, to avoid being jostled by passengers getting on and off. Try to avoid those rows over the wheels – usually the third row from the front and the third from the back in the *busetas*, and the fourth or fifth rows from the front and back in larger buses. Ask about the position of the wheels when buying your ticket. Also remember that

RIOBAMBA - QUITO

3,30 am.	2,30 pm.
5 am.	4,15 pm.
8 am.	7,45 pm.

TELEFONO GUAYAQUIL 513616

RIOBAMBA - GUAYAQUIL

3,15 pm.	1,45 pm.
5 am.	2,30 pm.
8 am.	4,30 pm.
9,30 am.	7,15 pm.
10,45 am.	7,45 pm.

GRANCOLOMBIANA DE TURISMO

DE GUAYAQUIL A

NOMBRE

ASIENTO Nº   CARRO Nº

FECHA MAR 2 6 1985   DIA

HORA DE SALIDA

Eficiencia - Comodidad - Seguridad y buen trato es el lema de nuestra Empresa

VALOR DEL PASAJE $ 220

TOTAL 660

NOTA: Al comprar este boleto Ud. acepta las disposiciones de esta Empresa, siendo el mismo válido en la fecha y hasta la hora máxima que debe llegar al terminal. El pasajero tiene que estar ¼ de hora antes de salida del carro.

the suspension at the back of a bus is usually far worse than anywhere else, so try and avoid the back rows.

Some bus companies don't sell tickets in advance. This is usually when they have frequent departures (about twice an hour or even more often). You just arrive and get on the next bus that's going your way.

If travelling during long holiday weekends or special fiestas, you may find that buses are booked up for several days in advance, so book early if you can.

If you're travelling very light, it's best to keep your luggage inside the bus with you. If I'm off on a trip for a few days, I often leave much of my luggage in a hotel storage room and travel with a bag small enough to fit under the seat. Local people get away with taking fairly large pieces of luggage aboard so you don't have to put yours on the luggage rack, even if the driver tells you to.

If your luggage is too big to fit under the seat, it will have to go on top or in a luggage compartment. Sometimes the top is covered with a tarpaulin, but not always, so pack your gear in large plastic bags (garbage bags are good) to avoid getting everything wet if it rains. The luggage compartment is sometimes filthy, and your luggage can get covered with grease or mud. Placing your luggage in a large protective sack is a good idea. Most of the Indians use grain sacks as luggage; you can buy them for a few cents in general stores or markets.

Every time a bus stops on the main routes, vendors selling fruit, rolls, ice cream or drinks suddenly appear – so you won't starve. Long-distance buses usually stop for a 20-minute meal break at the appropriate times. The food in the terminal restaurants may be somewhat basic, so if you're a picky eater you should bring food with you on longer trips.

Fares for tickets bought in bus terminals are a set price. The larger terminals often have traveller information booths which can advise you about this, but normally I find that you get charged the correct fare. The booths can give you information on all the routes available from the larger terminals. If you're only going part of the way, or you get on a bus in a small town as it comes by between larger towns, the bus driver will charge you appropriately. About 90% of the time you are charged honestly, although once in a while they try and overcharge you.

Once I was charged 50c for a ride that I paid 20c for going the other way. I pointed this out to the driver who was adamant that the fare was 50c. The Latin American machismo meant that he didn't want to admit that he was wrong. Although there's little point in getting uptight about a few cents, this particular example was too blatant for me to just ignore. I told him he could have 20c or we could go talk to the transit police; he didn't want to talk to the transit police. This sort of thing doesn't happen very often; the only way to guard against it is to know roughly the correct fare beforehand.

If you want to travel somewhere immediately, just go to the terminal and you'll usually find the driver's assistant running around trying to hustle up some passengers for his bus. Often you'll be on a bus going your way within a few minutes of arriving at the terminal. Before boarding a bus, make sure it's going where you want to go. Occasionally drivers will say that they are going where you want to go and then take you only part of the way and expect you to change buses. If you want a direct bus, make sure you ask for it. Also make sure that it is leaving soon, and not in two hours. Finally, if the bus looks too slow, or too fast, or too old, or too cramped, or you just don't like it for some reason, you can usually find another bus leaving soon if you're going to a major destination. Most places are served by several bus companies and you can make the choice that's best for you.

One last word about Ecuadorean buses: toilets – there aren't any. Long-distance buses have rest stops every three or four hours – try not to get onto a bus with a full bladder or you may join the famous traveller who had to pee in his boot.

Local

These are usually slow and crowded, but very cheap. You can get around most towns for about 5c. Local buses often go out to a nearby village and this is a good way to see an area. Just stay on the bus to the end of the line, pay another 5c, and head back again, usually sitting in the best seat on the bus. If you make friends with the driver, you may end up with an entertaining tour as he points out the local sights in between collecting other passengers' fares.

When you want to get off a local bus, yell *Baja!*, which means 'Down!' Telling the driver to stop will make him think you're trying to be a back-seat driver, and you will be ignored. He's only interested if you're getting off, or down from the bus. Another way of getting him to stop is to yell *Esquina!*, which means 'Corner!' He'll stop at the next one.

Trucks

In remote areas, trucks often double as buses. Sometimes they are flatbed trucks with a tin roof, open sides and uncomfortable wooden plank seats. These curious-looking buses are called *rancheros* and are especially common on the coast.

In the highlands, ordinary trucks are used to carry passengers; you just climb in the back. If the weather is OK, you get fabulous views and can feel the wind blow refreshingly by (dress warmly!). If the weather is bad you hunker down underneath a dark tarpaulin with the other passengers. It certainly isn't the height of luxury, but it may be the only way of getting to some areas, and if you're open minded about the minor discomforts, you may find that these rides are among the best you have in Ecuador.

Payment for these rides is usually determined by the driver and is a standard fare depending on the distance. You can ask other passengers how much they are paying; usually you'll find that the trucks double as buses and charge almost as much.

TAXI

Ecuador is a petroleum-producing country and it keeps down the price of petrol for domestic consumption. It's a low 40-50c a gallon (for some reason petrol is not dispensed in litres). This price combined with low wages means that taxis in Ecuador are very cheap.

The main rule for taking taxis is to ask the fare beforehand, or you'll be overcharged more often than not. A long ride in a large city (Quito or Guayaquil) shouldn't go over US$3 and short hops can cost as little as 50c. In smaller towns fares vary from 30c to about a dollar. Meters are rarely seen, with the exception of in Quito where they are obligatory. Even if there is a meter, the driver may not want to use it. This can be to your advantage, because with the meter off the driver can avoid interminable downtown traffic jams by taking a longer route. This saves both you and him time and the extra cost in petrol is negligible. At weekends and at night fares are always about 25-50% higher.

You can hire a taxi for several hours. A half day might cost about US$10 if you bargain. You can also hire pickup trucks which act as taxis to take you to remote areas (such as a climbers' refuge). If you hire a taxi to take you to another town, a rough rule of thumb is about US$1 for every 10 km. Remember to count the driver's return trip, even if you're not returning. A longer trip may average a little less. If you split the cost between four passengers, you'll each be paying between two and three times the bus fare for a round trip.

CAR RENTAL

This is as expensive as full-price car rental in Europe or the US. Cheap car rentals aren't found. If the price seems reasonable, check to see for what extras you have to pay; often there is a per km charge and you

have to buy insurance. Some cars are not in very good condition (perhaps that's being overly euphemistic).

It is difficult to find any kind of car rental outside of Guayaquil and Quito. I checked several places in Quito and was told that I had to have a credit card to be able to rent, as they wouldn't accept a cash deposit. Expect to pay at least US$30 per day.

HITCHING

As mentioned earlier, trucks are used as public transport in remote areas, so trying to hitch a free ride on one is the same as trying to hitch a free ride on a bus. Private cars are not as common in Ecuador as in more developed nations, so hitch-hiking generally is not as easy or successful. It can be done, however.

I have hitched several times on secondary roads in Ecuador and generally I offer to pay the driver. If the driver is stopping to drop off and pick up other passengers, then you can assume that he will expect payment. Talk to other passengers to find out what the going rate is. If you are the only passenger, the driver may have picked you up just to talk to a foreigner, and he may wave aside your offer of payment. This was the case in almost half my rides. I have never hitched on roads with good bus services, however, because buses are so cheap. Hitch-hiking isn't normally done and if you want to try, make sure in advance of your ride that you and the driver agree on the subject of payment.

Quito

Quito is my favourite Latin American capital. At about 2850 metres above sea level it has a wonderful spring-like climate despite the fact that it is only 22 km south of the equator. It is in a valley flanked by mountains and, on a clear day, several snow-capped volcanoes are visible from the capital. As well as being in a beautiful location, it is rich in history and much of the old colonial town is well preserved.

The site of the capital dates from pre-Columbian times. Early inhabitants of the area were the peaceful Quitu people, who gave their name to the capital. The Quitus integrated with the expansionist coastal Caras to give rise to the Indian group known as the Shyris. About 1300 AD the Shyris joined with the Puruhás through marriage, and their descendants fought against the Incas in the late 1400s.

By the time of the Spanish arrival, Quito was a major Inca city but it was totally destroyed by Atahualpa's general Rumiñahui shortly before the arrival of the Spanish conquerors in Quito. There are no Inca remains. The present capital was founded on top of the ruins of the Inca city by Sebastián de Benalcázar on 6 December 1534, and many old colonial buildings survive in the old town.

In 1978 UNESCO declared Quito one of the world's cultural heritage sites, and now Quito's old town development and other changes are strictly controlled. This does not mean that progress has stopped. On the contrary, the old centre is extremely bustling and full of traffic. The buildings haven't changed, however, and a walk down colonial Quito's streets late at night, after the rush hour traffic has finished, is a step into a past era. There are no modern buildings discordantly built next to centuries-old architecture and no flashing neon signs to disrupt the ambience of the past.

Quito has a population of nearly 900,000 and is thus the second largest city in Ecuador. (Guayaquil is the largest.) It is located along the central valley in a roughly north-south direction and is approximately 17 km long and four km wide. It can conveniently be divided into three segments.

The centre (*el centro*) is the site of the old town with its whitewashed and red-tiled houses and colonial churches; this is the area of greatest interest to the traveller. The north is modern Quito with its major businesses, airline offices, embassies, shopping centres and banks. It also contains the airport and middle and upper-class residential areas. This area is of importance to the traveller who needs to get some business done. Finally, the south consists mainly of working-class housing areas and is of less interest.

Information

DITURIS runs three tourist information offices. The main one is in the new town at Calle Reina Victoria 514 and Roca (tel 239044). They can provide you with brochures, maps and tourist information, and there is often someone available who speaks English. There is a branch in the old town, in the Municipal Palace on the south-east side of the Plaza Independencia. This branch is frequently closed. Finally, there is a branch at the airport but it keeps irregular hours.

Warning The elevation of about 2850 metres will make you feel somewhat breathless when you first arrive from sea level. This is a mild symptom of altitude sickness and will disappear after a day or two. It is best to take things easy on arrival. Don't over-exert yourself, eat lightly and cut back on cigarettes and alcohol to minimise altitude-sickness symptoms.

Although Quito is a safe city, you should be aware that pickpockets work crowded areas such as public buses, markets and church plazas. Keep money and other valuables in inside pockets and cameras firmly strapped across your body, and you won't have any problems.

Should you be unfortunate enough to be robbed, you should file a police report, particularly if you wish to make an insurance claim. The place to go is the SICP (El Servicio de Investigacion Criminal de Pichincha) at the intersection of Montufar and Esmeraldas in the old town.

Immigration There are two offices. One is for tourist card extensions and the other is for visas. Most travellers will only need the tourist card extension but if you want to stay longer than 90 days you will need a student, business, work or residence visa. Visas are usually expensive and complicated, while the tourist card extension is free and straightforward as long as you haven't used up your 90 days.

For tourist card extensions go to Avenida Amazonas 2639 (also numbered 3149 for some strange reason) and República from 8 am to noon and 2.30 to 6 pm Monday to Friday. It takes anywhere from 10 minutes to two hours depending on how busy they are on the day you go. Although onward tickets out of Ecuador and 'sufficient funds' are legally required, they are rarely asked for. It's still worth bringing any airline tickets or travellers' cheques you may have, just in case.

For visas go to the Extranjería at Calle Reina Victoria and Colón. They are open mornings only, Monday to Thursday.

Embassies Most nationalities require visas to enter Colombia and some to enter Peru (see Visas section in Facts for the Visitor). The Colombian consulate is at Avenida Amazonas 353 and Robles and is open 8.30 am to 12.30 pm and 2.30 to 4 pm Monday through Friday. The Peruvian

consulate is in the Edificio España at Avenida Amazonas 1429 and Colón.

A US embassy official sent me a letter recently, suggesting that if you plan on travelling to the US you would find it easier to obtain a tourist visa in your home country. According to my nameless source, 'young, single, rootless people, such as the travellers who would normally be expected to use the book, might get turned down' The US embassy is at Avenida Doce de Octubre and Patria. All visitors to the US require a tourist visa.

Money Banks are open from 9 am to 1.30 pm but do not normally change money unless you have an account with them. They will handle money wired from your home bank and pay you in US dollars. Most bank offices are on Avenida Amazonas.

Exchange houses, or *casas de cambio*, are the best places to exchange money. Rates vary, but usually not by very much. Rodrigo Paz is the best-known place. They have several branches. Their old town office is at Calle Venezuela 659 and Sucre. In the new town they have an office at Avenida Amazonas 370 and Robles. Their offices are normally open from 9.30 am to 12.30 pm and 3 to 6 pm Monday to Friday, and mornings only on Saturday. These offices do a lot of business and you may have to stand in line for 15 minutes.

Other companies have offices near these locations. If you want to change money on Sunday, you will find the Rodrigo Paz airport office open. Also, the office at the Hotel Colón is open on Sunday and they are often open until 7 pm on weekdays.

If you change more money than you need, it is easy to buy back dollars at a rate about 2% below what you sold them for.

Post There are several post offices but the best one for receiving and sending letters is the central office on Calle Benalcázar behind the Plaza Independencia. They are open from 9 am to 5 pm on weekdays and booths selling stamps are usually

1 Hotel Gran Casino (Old)
2 Hotel Gran Casino II
3 Hotel Monasterio
4 Hotel Sucre
5 Plaza San Francisco
6 Monastery of San Francisco
7 Ecuahotel
8 Mitad del Mundo Bus
9 Church of La Merced
10 Museum of Colonial Art
11 Pensión Astoria & Hotel Minerva
12 Hotel Venecia
13 Church of La Compañia
14 Central Post Office
15 Hotel Felix
16 Caspicara Hotel
17 Hotel Real Audiencia
18 Cine Atahualpa
19 House of Sucre
20 Rodrigo Paz Casa de Cambio; Auca Hotel; Cine Metro
21 Cathedral
22 Church of El Sagrario
23 Plaza de la Independencia
24 Government Palace
25 Casa de Benalcázar
26 Hotel Colonial
27 Hotels Capitalino & Zulia
28 Hotel Interamericano
29 Hotel Juana del Arco
30 Hotel Roma
31 Plaza Santo Domingo
32 Municipality & Tourist Office
33 Hotel Los Andes
34 Hotel Indoamericano & Residencial Los Andes
35 Hotel Restaurant Ingatur

36 Hotel Guayaquil
37 Church of Santo Domingo
38 Hotel Huasi Continental
39 Residenciales Bolivar & Quitumbe; Cine Bolivar
40 Monastery of San Agustin
41 Taberna Quiteña
42 Hotel Viena
43 Hotels Viena Internacional & San Agustin
44 Hotel Los Canarios
45 Plaza del Teatro & Teatro Sucre
46 Chifa Hong Kong
47 Church of La Basilica
48 Banco Central
49 Simón Bolivar Monument
50 SAN-Saeta airline
51 Residencial Marsella
52 Cine Capital
53 Church of El Belén
54 Instituto PRALI
55 Legislative Palace
56 Instituto Geográfico Militar
57 Ñucanchi Peña
58 To: Casa Paxi (800 m)
59 Cine Universitario
60 Parcel Post
61 Hotel Residencial Florida
62 Buses to Otavalo, Ibarra & Tulcán
63 Residencial Carrión
64 Hotel Versalles
65 Cine Majestic
66 Residencial Santa Clara
67 Quito Spanish School
68 Cine Colón
69 Casa Familiar
70 Bailey's Restaurant

71 Hotel Nueve de Octubre
72 Hotel Embajador
73 American Express & Airlines
74 Hotel Colón
75 Rodrigo Paz Casa de Cambio
76 Manolos Pavement Restaurant
77 Teatro Prometeo
78 Tourist Information (DITURIS)
79 Libri Mundi Bookshop & Galeria Latina
80 Residencial Cumbes Baqueadano
81 Taberna Quiteña
82 Colombus Steak House
83 Casa de Cultura (museums)
84 Hotel Tambo Real
85 US Embassy
86 Churrascaria Tropeiro
87 Hotel Embassy
88 Mama Chlorindas Restaurant
89 Restaurant Excalibur
90 TAME airline
91 Catholic University & Museo Jijón y Caamaño
92 Museo Shuar
93 Ecuatoriana airline & Post Office branch
94 La Jaiba Mariscos Restaurant
95 SAN-Saeta airline
96 IETEL
97 Restaurant La Choza
98 Olga Fisch Crafts
99 To: Hotel Quito & British Embassy (400 m)

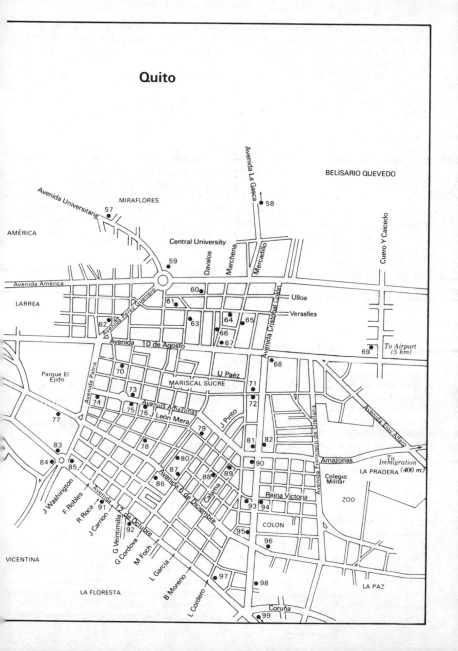

Quito

BELISARIO QUEVEDO

Avenida Universitaria

MIRAFLORES

57

AMÉRICA

Avenida La Gasca

58

Central University

Cuero Y Caicedo

59

Davalos

Marchena

Mercadillo

Avenida América

60

Ulloa

LARREA

61

Versalles

Avenida Pérez Guerrero

62

63

64

65

66

67

Avenida Cristóbal Colón

Avenida   10 de Agosto

69

To Airport
(5 km)

Parque El
Ejido

70

68

Avenida Patria

U Paéz

MARISCAL SUCRE

71

73

72

Avenida Amazonas

74

75

76 J León Mera

77

J Pinto

Avenida Eloy Alfaro

Avenida Francisco de Orellana

78

79

81

82

83

80

Amazonas

To
Immigration
(400 m)

84

85

87

88

89

90

LA PRADERA

J Washington

86

Colegio
Militar

F Robles

Avenida 6 de Diciembre

Calama

ZOO

R Roca

91

Reina Victoria

92

93 94

COLON

LA PAZ

VICENTINA

J Carrion

G Ventimilla

12 de Octubre

G Cordova

M Foch

L Garcia

B Moreno

95

96

97

98

LA FLORESTA

L Cordero

Coruña

99

open from about 8 am to 6 pm. There is a branch post office in the new town at Colón and Reina Victoria. If you want to mail a package of over a kilogram you have to use the office at Calle Ulloa 943 and Ramirez Dávalos.

If you are an American Express client you can receive mail sent to you c/o Amex, Aptdo 2605, Quito, Ecuador. Their street address is Avenida Amazonas 339 at the Ecuadorean Tours office, which is open from 9.30 am to 12.30 pm and 2.30 to 6 pm Monday through Friday and mornings only on Saturday.

Phone The central IETEL office by the Plaza de la Independencia is now closed. The main office for long distance calls is open from 6 am to 10 pm (last call at 9.30 pm) daily and is on Avenida 6 de Diciembre near Avenida Colón. There is a smaller IETEL office at the central bus station which is open 8 am to 10 pm. There are both IETEL and post offices at the airport. Cheap rates for international calls are after 7 pm.

Bookshops Libri Mundi is the best, with a good selection of books in English, German, French and Spanish. They have books about Ecuador as well as books of a more general nature. Their main shop is at Calle Juan León Mera 851 near Veintimilla and is open from 9 am to 7 pm Monday to Friday, and 9 am to 1 pm on Saturday. A smaller branch is open until 8 pm in the Hotel Colón shopping mall (same prices). The other bookshops in Quito mainly sell books in Spanish.

Foreign Newspapers You can read British newspapers and magazines at the British Council, Amazonas 1615 and Orellana. They also have a library. Up-to-date newspapers from all over the world are available for guests at the Hotel Colón reading room on the ground floor. If you're reasonably dressed you could go in there.

Maps The best maps are available from the Instituto Geográfico Militar (IGM), which is on top of a hill at the end of Calle T Paz y Miño. This small street is off Avenida Colombia a few blocks southeast of Parque El Ejido in the new town. There are no buses, so walk or take a taxi. The IGM is open from 8 am to 3 pm Monday through Friday. You need to leave your passport at the gate to be allowed in.

They have a good selection of country and topographical maps to look at or buy, but their selection of city maps is very limited and you'll be better off with the city maps in this book. Country maps are also available from street vendors and the Libri Mundi bookstore, but they are more expensive than at the IGM.

Medical An American run hospital with an outpatient department and emergency room is Hospital Voz Andes, Juan Villalengua 263 (tel 241540) near the intersection of Avenidas América and 10 de Agosto. The No 1 Iñaquito bus passes close by. Fees are about US$4.

Spanish Courses There are two places which will teach you Spanish. Classes are available at various levels. The Quito Spanish School (Academia de Español Quito) is at Marchena 130 and 10 de Agosto, 3rd floor (tel 553647). Their mailing address is PO Box 39-C, Quito, Ecuador and they will send you information in English.

They offer two and four-week courses and provide accommodation with a local family so that you can practice your Spanish out of the classroom. Each student has a private tutor at the school for seven hours a day. Cost for a four-week course including tuition, family accommodation and all meals is US$578 and can be arranged in advance from your home country. You can take either the tuition or the family accommodation only if you wish. Cheaper rates can be obtained by making arrangements after you arrive in Quito and paying in sucres.

If you prefer group classes and providing your own accommodation, then try the Catholic University (Universidad Católica) at Avenida 12 de Octubre and Robles. They have six-week classes for about US$100. They will also provide you with a student card. Although there are few price reductions for students in Ecuador, the card is very useful in Peru. The university also has classes in Quechua.

Signing up for these classes may be a way of helping you get a student visa.

Student Cards If you sign up for a Spanish course at the university you can get a student card there. Otherwise, you can get one from the Student Travel Office on the 6th floor of Edificio Parlamento, corner of 6 de Diciembre and Pazmiño by the Parque La Alameda. There is a US$10 fee and they don't verify your student status. Whilst a student card does not save you much money in Ecuador, if you're heading south to Peru you'll find it entitles you to substantial discounts there.

Teaching English This is the most usual way in which travellers are able to earn money in Ecuador. The British Council pays the best wages but accepts only bona-fide qualified teachers and usually only if they apply in advance from England. The best bet is at one of the local 'English as a second language' schools such as Instituto PRALI at Luis Sodiro and Colombia. Schools occasionally advertise in the 'gringo' hotels or in the newspapers when they need teachers.

Laundry There are no laundromats where you can wash and dry your own clothes. Instead, clothes must be left with a *lavandería* and picked up later, usually the following day. Most hotels will wash and dry your clothes – this gets quite expensive in the first class hotels but is less expensive in the more modest establishments. There are not many public *lavanderías* and many of those that are available are for dry cleaning only. Ask at your hotel about the nearest one. Most of the cheaper hotels provide facilities for hand washing laundry.

Guides Guided trips to hike in the mountains, climb the snow-capped volcanoes, explore the jungle or visit the Galápagos can be arranged in Quito but be warned that most guide services are not cheap.

Especially recommended for mountaineering and hiking expeditions is the very experienced multilingual guide Pieter Jan Van Bunningen and the anthropologist/mountaineer Corinne Duhalde at Casa Paxi, Navarro 364 y La Gasca (tel 542 663). (Casa Paxi is a hostal – see the Places to Stay section.)

The manager of the Hotel Gran Casino, César Gavela Jr, has information about cheap tours to the Galápagos and the jungle. These trips are only cheap with full groups and César can help bring individual travellers together. Because of the need for groups, individuals may have to wait some time before their desired trip becomes available – on the other hand you may be lucky and find the trip you want is leaving the next day and has one space left to fill.

The most convenient and inexpensive starting point for jungle excursions is Misahuallí and detailed information is in that section.

There are several travel agencies which organise tours or provide guides for expeditions. The biggest and best known (also the most expensive) is Metropolitan Touring which employs the well known Ecuadorean mountaineer Marco Cruz as a climbing guide and also runs luxurious trips to both the jungle and the Galápagos. Further information on Galápagos tours is in the last chapter.

Construction Most of Avenida 24 de Mayo

has been torn up while it is being remodelled to form tunnel entrances to the new Cumanda bus terminal. It is impassable by vehicle at this time. The project is due to be completed in 1989 but don't bank on it!

Things to See
The DITURIS information office told me that churches are open from 9 to 11 am and 3 to 5 pm daily except Sunday, and that museums are open from 9 am to 5 pm daily except Monday. This is not true. Hours are haphazard to say the least. Museums can change hours for reasons varying from a national holiday to staff sickness, so the opening hours in the following sections are meant only as guidelines. Generally speaking, however, Monday is the worst day to visit museums, as many of them are closed.

Churches are open every day but are crowded with worshippers on Sunday. Early morning seems to be a good time to visit churches. They are usually closed for a long lunch hour and in the afternoons sometimes remain open until after 6 pm. It's unpredictable. Good luck!

Museums
Casa de Cultura Ecuatoriana If you want to kill several birds with one stone, you should head for the Casa de Cultura Ecuatoriana, the large circular glass building at the corner of Avenidas Patria and 12 de Octubre, to the east of the Parque El Ejido. They have an art museum, open from 9 am to 6 pm Tuesday to Saturday and 10 am to 2 pm on Sunday, which contains more than just an excellent art collection.

There is a fascinating display of traditional musical instruments, many several centuries old. The instruments are mainly Ecuadorean, but there are also Asian, African and European oddities. Also on display are examples of traditional Ecuadorean regional dress. The art collection contains both contemporary Ecuadorean work and 19th-century pieces. The contemporary work includes canvases by Ecuador's most famous artists, Guayasamín and Kingman among others.

Also in the Casa de Cultura is a small natural history museum open from 9 am to 6 pm Monday to Friday, and 9 am to 1 pm on Saturday. Here you can see condor and giant tortoise skeletons and a variety of other exhibits. All the museums in the Casa de Cultura are free.

Museo de Jacinto Jijón y Caamaño Across the traffic circle from the Casa de Cultura and north-east along Avenida 12 de Octubre is the Catholic University, which has an interesting private archaeology museum on the third floor of the library. The entrance to the Museo Jijón y Caamaño is near the intersection with Calle J Carrión.

Hours are from 9 am to noon and 3 to 6 pm Monday through Friday. Admission is 20c and you can get a guided tour (sometimes available in English) of the small archaeological collection. There is also a collection of colonial art.

Museo de Banco Central The best archaeology museum is that of the Banco Central, on the 5th floor. It houses well-displayed pottery, gold ornaments (including the gold mask that is the symbol of the Museo del Banco Central), skulls showing deformaties and early surgical methods, a mummy and many other objects of interest. On the floor above is a display of colonial furniture and religious art and carving.

The bank is at the beginning of Avenida 10 de Agosto in front of the apex of the Parque La Alameda. Outside of working hours, the entrance is through the gate to the right of the bank and then through a side door. There is an elevator. Hours are from 2.30 to 6 pm Tuesday through Friday, and 10.30 am to 5 pm on Saturday and Sunday.

Entrance is about 30c but is free on Sundays and evenings from 6 to 8 pm –

Top: Monastery of San Francisco, Quito (RR)
Left: Presidential Palace guard, Quito (RR)
Right: Independence Plaza, Quito (RR)

Top: Author researching Quito nightlife in Taberna Quiteña (RR)
Left: Old Quito and Mt Cayambe (RR)
Right: Virgin of Quito, Panecillo (RR)

though it can be crowded then. Tours in English can be arranged in advance for free.

Museo de Arte y Historia This museum is in an old building in the centre. It used to be a Jesuit house until 1767, when it became an army barracks. The present museum contains a wealth of early colonial art dating from the 16th and 17th centuries. The building is at Espejo 1147, just off the Plaza Independencia. It is open from 8.30 am to 6.30 pm Tuesday to Friday and 10 am to 3 pm on Saturday and Sunday. Admission is 10c.

Casa de Sucre Several other historical buildings in the centre are now museums. A good one to visit is Casa de Sucre, which is well restored and contains period (1820s) furniture and a small museum. It is on Calle Venezuela 573 and Sucre. Hours are from 9 am to noon and 3 to 6 pm daily, and entrance is free. They have a small gift shop with books about Ecuador.

Casa de Benalcázar An older house is the Casa de Benalcázar, dating from 1534. It was restored by Spain in 1967 and entrance here is also free. It's on Calle Olmedo 962 and Benalcázar. There are sometimes classical piano recitals here and it is a delightful site for such entertainment. Check the newspapers or enquire at the house.

Museo de Arte Colonial This museum is on the corner of Calle Cuenca and Mejía and has recently reopened after a long period of restoration. The building dates from the 17th century and houses what many consider to be Quito's best collection of colonial art. Hours are from 10 am to 1 pm and 3 to 6 pm Mondays to Fridays, and from 10 am to 12 noon and 3 to 5 pm on Saturdays.

Museo Guayasamín Modern art can be seen at the Museo Guayasamín, the home of Oswaldo Guayasamín, an Ecuadorean Indian painter born in 1919 and now famous throughout the world. The museum is at Calle José Bosmediano 543 in the residencial district of Bellavista to the north-east of Quito. It's an uphill walk and the No 3 Colmena-Batan bus goes near the museum. Make sure the bus has a Bellavista placard, or ask the driver. It is open from 9 am to 12.30 pm and 3 to 6 pm Monday to Saturday, and entrance is free. You can buy original artwork here.

Museo Camilo Egas Another Ecuadorean painter who has a museum in his name is Camilo Egas (1889-1962). Some 40 of his works are displayed in the Museo Camilo Egas, now under the auspices of the Banco Central. The collection has been recently restored. The museum is open 9 am to 1 pm and 3 to 6 pm Tuesday to Friday, and 9 am to 2 pm on Saturday. Admission is 20c. The address is Calle Venezuela 1302 and Esmeraldas.

Museo Shuar There is a small collection of jungle Indian artefacts at this museum run by the Salesian Mission. Indian cultural publications (in Spanish) are also available for sale. The museum is at 1436, 12 de Octubre and is open from 3 to 5 pm on Mondays to Thursdays. Admission is 20c.

Churches
There is a wealth of churches, chapels, convents, monasteries, cathedrals and basilicas in Quito. The old town especially has so many of them that you can hardly walk two blocks without passing a church. Photography is not normally permitted because the intensity of the flash has a detrimental effect on the pigment in the many valuable religious paintings. Slides and postcards can be bought at the post office.

Monastery of San Francisco The oldest church is the Monastery of San Francisco, on the plaza of the same name. Construction began only a few days after the founding of Quito in 1534, but it was not finished until

70 years later. It is the largest colonial structure in Quito. The founder is commemorated by a statue at the far right of the raised terrace in front of the church. He is the Franciscan missionary Joedco Ricke, who is also credited with being the first man to sow wheat in Ecuador.

Although much of the church has been rebuilt because of earthquake damage, some of it is still original. Go to the chapel of Señor Jesus de Gran Poder to the right of the main altar to see original tilework. The main altar itself is a spectacular example of baroque carving, and the roof and walls are also wonderfully carved and richly covered in gold leaf. Much of the roof shows Moorish influence.

The church contains excellent examples of early religious art and sculpture; unfortunately it is often too dark to see them properly. Tour guides turn lights on periodically so keep your eyes open for this. The bells are rung every hour, and often on the quarter hour. You can see the bell-ringer at work in his cubbyhole just to the right of the main door. Visiting hours are from 8 to 11 am and from 3 to 6 pm; admission is free.

To the right of the main entrance is the Franciscan Museum, which contains some of the monastery's finest artwork. Here you can see paintings, sculpture and furniture dating back to the 16th century. One of the oldest signed paintings is a Mateo Mejía canvas dated 1615. Some of the woodcarvings are even older and are covered with gold leaf, paint, period clothing or a fine porcelain flesh finish. Some of the furniture is fantastically wrought and inlaid with literally thousands of pieces of mother-of-pearl.

The museum costs 50c to visit, and Spanish-speaking guides are available. It is open from 3 to 6 pm Monday to Saturday. Morning hours are erratic: 9 to 11 am on most weekdays except Tuesday and Friday, when they are open from 9 to 10 am.

La Compañía Looking out across the plain, cobblestoned plaza of San Francisco, you see the ornate green and gold domes of the church of La Compañía de Jesus, just two blocks away. The construction of this Jesuit church began in 1605, the year that San Francisco was completed, and it took 163 years to build. The church is famous as the most ornate in Ecuador; it has been claimed that seven tons of gold were used to gild the walls, ceilings and altars. Note the Arab (Moorish) influence in the intricate designs carved on the magnificent red-and-gold columns and ceilings. There is a beautiful cupola over the main altar. The remains of the Quiteño saint, Mariana de Jesus, who died in 1645, are kept here.

A sign just inside the door gives visiting hours as 9.30 to 11 am and 4 to 6.30 pm on weekdays, 9.30 to 11 am, 3.30 to 4.30 pm, and 5.15 to 6.15 pm on Saturdays, and 3.30 to 4.30 pm and 5.30 to 6.30 pm on Sundays – but don't rely on it.

The Cathedral One block away from the ornate Jesuit church is the Plaza de la Independencia with the stark cathedral. Although not as rich in decoration as some of the other churches, the cathedral has several points of historical interest. Plaques on the outside walls commemorate Quito's founders and General Sucre, the leading figure of Quito's independence, is buried in the cathedral. To the left of the main altar is a statue of Juan José Flores, Ecuador's first president. Behind the main altar is the smaller altar of Nuestra Señora de los Dolores; the plaque there shows where President Gabriel García Moreno died on 6 August 1875. He was shot outside the Presidential Palace (just across the plaza) and was carried, dying, to the cathedral.

El Sagrario The main chapel of the cathedral was begun in 1657 and was finished 49 years later, but it is now a separate church, El Sagrario. This church is being renovated by Poland's University of Warsaw and is interesting to visit if you want to see how restoration work is done.

El Sagrario is on García Moreno, next to the cathedral.

San Agustín Two blocks away from the Plaza de la Independencia is the church where many of the heroes of the battles for Ecuador's independence are buried. This is the church of San Agustín, site of the signing of Ecuador's declaration of independence on 10 August 1809. The church is another fine example of 17th century architecture.

The historical museum where you can see various Independence mementoes as well as colonial art is in the convent to the right of the church. It is open from 9 am to noon and 3 to 6 pm Monday to Saturday and costs 10c to get in.

Santo Domingo The church of Santo Domingo is especially attractive in the evening, when its domes are floodlit. It too dates back to early Quito. Construction began in 1581 and continued until 1650. An exquisite statue of the Virgen del Rosario, a gift from King Charles V of Spain, is now one of the church's main showpieces. The statue is in an ornately carved baroque-style side chapel. In the busy Plaza Santo Domingo in front of the church is a statue of General Sucre pointing in the direction of Pichincha, where he won the decisive battle for independence on 24 May 1822.

La Merced One of colonial Quito's most recent churches is that of La Merced, which was begun in 1700 and completed in 1742. Its tower has the distinction of being the highest (47 metres) in colonial Quito and it contains the largest bell of Quito's churches.

The church has a wealth of fascinating art. Paintings show volcanoes glowing and erupting over the church roofs of colonial Quito, the capital covered with ashes, General Sucre going into battle, and many other scenes. The stained-glass windows also show various scenes of colonial life such as early priests and conquistadors among the Indians of the Oriente. It is a surprising and intriguing collection.

Other Churches Moving out of the old town, you can still find several interesting churches. High on a hill on Calle Venezuela is the new basilica, which is still unfinished though work on it began in 1926. Obviously, the tradition of taking decades to construct a church is still alive. At the north end of the Parque La Alameda is the small church of El Belén, which was built on the site of the first Catholic mass to be held in Quito.

Finally, in a precipitous valley on the east side of town, is the Sanctuary of Guápulo, built between 1644 and 1688. The best views of this delightful-looking colonial church are from behind the Hotel Quito at the end of Avenida 12 de Octubre. There is a steep footpath that leads down to the Guápulo and it's a pleasant walk, though somewhat strenuous coming back.

This is just a selection of Quito's most interesting and frequently visited churches. There are dozens more, some of which are closed to the public.

Other Sights
Virgin of Quito The small, rounded hill which dominates the old town is called El Panecillo or 'the little bread loaf' and is a major Quito landmark. It is topped by a huge statue of the Virgin of Quito. There are marvellous views of the whole city stretching out below, as well as views of the surrounding volcanoes. You can get there from the old town by climbing the stairs at the end of Calle García Moreno – it takes about half an hour.

Unfortunately, I have recently received a report of travellers being robbed on the climb – but a lot of people walk anyway. A taxi from the old town costs about US$2 and they will wait and bring you back or you can ride up and make the easier downhill stroll.

Statue of Virgin of Quito

Markets At the bottom of the Panecillo is Avenida 24 de Mayo. This used to be a major open-air Indian market. An indoor market was opened in 1981 at the upper end of 24 de Mayo. Nonetheless, some outdoor selling still takes place, especially on Calle Cuenca and the streets to the north-west of it.

La Ronda Just off Avenida 24 de Mayo between Calles García Moreno and Venezuela and on to Maldonado is the historic alley now called Calle Juan de Dios Morales, but known to most people by its traditional name of La Ronda. This street is perhaps the best preserved in colonial Quito and is narrow enough so cars rarely drive along it, which adds to its charm. It is full of old, balconied houses and you can enter several of them. Just walk along the street and you'll see which ones are open to visitors; they usually have handicrafts for sale.

Plaza de la Independencia While wandering around the churches of colonial Quito you'll probably pass through the Plaza de la Independencia several times. Apart from

the cathedral you can visit the Palacio de Gobierno, also known as the Palacio Presidencial. It is the low white building on the north-west side of the plaza and has the national flag flying atop it. The entrance is flanked by a pair of handsomely uniformed presidential guards.

Inside you can see a mural depicting Francisco Orellana's descent of the Amazon. The president does indeed carry out business in this building, so sightseeing is limited to the mural and lower courtyard – if you are allowed in at all.

Plaza del Teatro At the junction of Calles Guayaquil and Flores is the tiny Plaza del Teatro, where you'll find Teatro Sucre, built in 1878. This is Quito's most sophisticated theatre with frequent concerts and plays.

Parque La Alameda Leaving the old town, you'll see the long, triangular Parque La Alameda with an impressive monument of Simón Bolívar at the apex. There are several other interesting monuments in the park. To the right is a relief map of Ecuador and further in there are statues of the members of the 1736-1744 French Académie des Sciences expedition which surveyed Ecuador and made the equatorial measurements which gave rise to the metric system of weights and measures.

In the centre of the park is the Quito observatory, which was opened by President García Moreno in 1864 and is the oldest in the continent. It is used both for meteorology and astronomy and can be visited on Saturday mornings.

At the base of the park are a pair of ornamental lakes where rowboats can be hired for a few sucres. It is filled with picnicking families on weekends.

Parque El Ejido A few blocks beyond Parque La Alameda is the biggest park in downtown Quito, the pleasant, tree-filled Parque El Ejido. This is a popular venue for ball games and you can usually see impromptu games of soccer and volleyball, as well as a strange, giant marbles game typical to Ecuador. It is played with golf ball sized steel balls.

Avenida Amazonas From the centre of the north end of the park runs modern Quito's showpiece street, Avenida Amazonas. Here are modern hotels and airline offices, banks and restaurants. It is a wide avenue with plenty of room for pedestrians. Buses and trucks are prohibited (except for blue double-decker London buses). There are several outdoor pavement restaurants where you can have a coffee or a snack and watch modern Quito go by.

Palacio Legislativo On the edge of the new town is the legislative palace where the government works. The modern building is distinguished by a huge outdoor mural depicting the history of Ecuador.

Quito Zoo Continuing down Avenida Amazonas, you cross Avenida Francisco de Orellana about 1½ km from Parque El Ejido. Here there is a military college which, for some reason, runs the Quito Zoo. The entrance is around the back on Calle La Pradera. It costs 20c to get in and you can see various Ecuadorean species such as giant Galápagos tortoises, Andean condors and monkeys. Some of the cages are quite good, but a few leave much to be desired and are far too small for the comfort of the animals.

Places to Stay
As befits a capital city, Quito has well over a hundred hotels and it would be pointless to list every one. The following selection will give you plenty of choice. As a general guideline, hotels in the old town tend to be less comfortable, older and much cheaper than those in the new town. That is not to say that there are no cheap hotels in the new town.

Places to Stay - bottom end
When I first arrived in Quito in 1981 with a backpack full of climbing gear, no ticket home and about US$150 in my pocket, I went straight to the legendary *Hotel Gran Casino* at Calle García Moreno 330 and Ambato. There is no hotel quite like it in any Latin American capital. If you travel to meet the locals and get away from other travellers, this is not the place to stay. It is always full of budget travellers and is a great place to pick up on the latest travel news. If you've been travelling in Ecuador (or Latin America) for any length of time you often meet someone you know staying here. Its popularity is such that it's been nicknamed the 'Gran Gringo'.

They have a cheap restaurant that serves reasonable meals and is usually crowded. There is a notice board, laundry facilities (they'll do it for you in about two days or you can wash it yourself), left-luggage facilities (25c per week and you are given a claim check), and an excellent view from the roof (don't miss it). The notice board often lists teaching jobs, 'wanted to buy' and 'for sale', as well as notes from travellers looking for partners to travel with.

The rooms are very basic, usually just a bed and a chair, but they vary in quality. If you don't like the first one you see, ask to see another one. A few rooms have excellent views and others have only a door onto the hallway. Singles cost about US$1.40 and tend to go fast. Rooms with two to six beds are about US$1 per person. If you arrive alone, you can share a room if you want to economise. Shared rooms are usually available until fairly late in the evening. There are a few rooms with a private shower for US$2 per person.

If you use the communal showers, hot water is available only from 7 am to 3 pm – so if you arrive in the evening you're out of luck. The showers are on the ground floor and there are only three of them so expect to wait in line at about 7.30 am. A bench is provided for waiting. Next door to the hotel are some Turkish baths and sauna where you can soak away your travel grime and tensions for about US$1. It's open from about 9 am to 9 pm and you can spend as long as you want in there.

As you can gather, I've spent a lot of nights here and have developed quite a soft spot for this hotel. There are many other budget hotels to choose from, some of which may well be better, but somehow I always end up staying here when I'm on a tight budget. The hotel has been criticised by some travellers who have lost laundry from the washing lines and by others who find the hotel too basic. They should try the new *Gran Casino II* which is two blocks away on Avenida 24 de Mayo and Bahía de Caraquez and run by the same people. Prices are about twice that of the first hotel and rooms are better with private showers and often good views of the old town.

If the *Gran Casino* is full, the nearest hotels are the *Monasterio* on Avenida 24 de Mayo and García Moreno, and the *Pensión Astoria* at Loja 630 and Venezuela. Neither of them is particularly good but they are cheap at US$1.20 each.

A good place to go looking for cheap hotels is the Plaza Santo Domingo area, and Avenida Maldonado and Calle Flores running off the plaza. Here you'll find a score or more of cheap hotels within a few blocks of one another but some of them are not very good. Now that the new Cumandá bus terminal has opened, this is a convenient place to look for budget hotels close to the terminal. New hotels are opening with the recent influx of travellers to the immediate area.

On the Plaza Santo Domingo is the *Hotel Roma* at Rocafuerte 1331 and at the corner of the plaza is the *Caspicara Hotel* at Rocafuerte 1415. Both charge about US$1.60 per person, are basic but clean, and have hot water. The nearby *Hotel Venecia* charges about US$2 each. The attractive *Hotel Juana del Arco* has hot water and pleasant but noisy rooms (good views) for US$2.50 per person or more with private bath. Just off the plaza at Guayaquil 431 is the *Hotel Felix*, which has pretty flowers on the balconies though the rooms are still basic. It has hot water and it's secure – ring the bell to get in. They charge about US$1 each – good value.

As you head down Avenida Maldonado you'll encounter many hotels. In the first block on the right are the hotels *Interamericano, Capitalino* and *Zulia*. The *Interamericano* charges US$1.70 to US$3 each depending on whether or not you have a private bathroom. The *Capitalino* is US$1.60 each and looks basic but clean. They have hot water all day long. The *Zulia* is a very basic cold-water hotel charging US$1 each.

On the left side of the first block of Maldonado are the hotels *Guayaquil* and *Ingatur*. The *Ingatur* has hot water, is clean and charges US$1.50 each. It has a simple restaurant with cheap *almuerzos* and *meriendas* available. The *Guayaquil* charges US$1.40 to US$2.80 per person depending on whether you have a single or double and whether you have a private bathroom or not. There is hot water and the rooms vary; some are good and spacious, others less so.

There are several more cheap hotels further down Maldonado. One of the best is the *Hotel Colonial*, which is down an alley from Maldonado 3035, is quiet and has hot water. Basic but clean rooms are US$1.20 per person; or if you want a private bath the rooms are US$2.75 single and US$5 double. On the other side of Maldonado are several more hotels which cost about US$1.20 but look grimy and have only cold water. These include the hotels *Caribe* and *Los Andes*, and *Residencial Los Andes*. A little better is the *Hotel Indoamericano*, which charges US$1.50 and has hot water in the mornings.

Going in the opposite direction from Plaza Santo Domingo along Calle Flores, you'll find more hotels to choose from. *Huasi Continental* at Flores 330 and Sucre is recommended. It has spartan but clean rooms with private bathrooms and hot water for US$3 per person – but ask for a room away from the street. A reader writes that the nearby *Hotel Montufar* at Sucre 160 is quiet and good for US$1.75 per person. *Residencial Bolívar* at Espejo 832 and Flores has clean, basic rooms for US$1.30 per person but their hot water supply is erratic. *Quitumbe* opposite at Espejo 815 is very clean and secure and has hot water but no private bathrooms. They charge US$3 each. *Hotel Viena* at Flores and Chile charges US$1.75 and has hot water; the *Viena Internacional* on the other corner is in the middle price category following. Further down is the *Hotel San Agustín* and *Los Canarios*, which charge US$2 to US$4 per person depending on the rooms. Both hotels have hot water and are clean and good.

Other budget hotels in the old town include the *Hotel Sucre* on the corner of Plaza San Francisco, which looks very good from the outside, but has only basic rooms although some have good views. They will provide you with hot water if you ask, and charge only 80c per person. The rather charming *Ecuahotel* at Chile 1427 near Cuenca has a few rooms with good views and charges US$5 for a double room with a private bath.

A good budget hotel closer to the new part of town is the *Residencial Marsella* at Los Rios and Castro just east of the Parque La Alameda. It charges about US$4 for a double room with bath, is clean, has hot water, a roof with a view, is family run, and is well recommended. A few singles are available.

Casapaxi is a small, quiet and clean hostal run by guides Pieter Van Bunningen and Corinne Duhalde. They charge US$3 per person and hot showers, kitchen facilities, living room, luggage storage, a notice board and information are available in a friendly and relaxed environment. It is a good place to meet travellers interested in hiking or off the beaten track travel. There is a good view of the city from the rooftop terrace.

The hostal is at Navarro 364 and Avenida La Gasca which is about one km north and uphill of Avenida América – the No 19 bus passes by. Only 12 guests can be accommodated so it is best to call ahead on tel 542663. They have just opened a bigger place called *Casa Familiar* at Ulloa 1710 and Cuero y Caicedo (tel 237195).

Places to Stay – middle
Directly opposite the new bus terminal is the newly built *Hotel Cumanda* which charges US$4.50 single and US$8 double in clean, comfortable rooms with private hot shower and telephone. There are a few mid-range hotels in the old town, of which the *Viena Internacional* at the corner of Flores and Chile is one of the best. They charge about US$6 per person in very pleasant rooms with private bath, hot water, telephone and carpeting.

Also good is the *Hotel Juana del Arco*, which has rooms with private showers for US$5 a single and US$8 a double – rooms overlooking the Plaza Santo Domingo have nice views but are noisy. The *Auca Hotel* looks spartan and grim but has clean, small rooms with private bathrooms for US$7 single and US$10 double.

The nearby and new *Hotel Real Audiencia* is the best hotel in the old town and has clean rooms with private bath, phone, TV, and a restaurant. Rooms are US$11.50 a single and US$15 a double.

The best choice of mid-range hotels is in the new town. Most of them will provide full board if you ask them to. There are several good ones in the area between Avenida 10 de Agosto and the university. One of the cheapest is the *Hotel Versalles* at Versalles 1442 and Marchena. They charge US$3.50 per person in rooms with a private bathroom. It's OK but nothing fancy.

Better is the *Residencial Santa Clara* at Darquea Teran 1578 and 10 de Agosto. The residencial is a pleasant-looking house and it's clean, comfortable and friendly. Rooms are available both with (US$5 per person) and without (US$4 per person) private bathrooms. Meals are available.

The *Residencial Florida* at Versalles 1083 and Carrión is excellent value at US$6.50 a single and US$10 a double in rooms with private bath. Cheaper rooms with shared bath are also available. The residencial is spotlessly clean and good food is served. Around the corner is the slightly more expensive but highly recommended *Residencial Carrión*, which is geared to long-staying guests.

Hotel Majestic at Mercadillo 366 and Versalles has pleasant, clean rooms with private baths for US$8 a single, US$13 a double and US$17 a triple. They have friendly staff but their hot water supply is sometimes erratic. (Isn't it everywhere?) Most of the hotels in this section are excellent value and highly popular. They are often full so try early in the day.

Two good hotels close to one another and large enough that they usually have rooms available are *Hotel Nueve de Octubre* at 1047 and the *Embajador* at 1046 Calle 9 de Octubre and Colón. They are both friendly and recommended. Rooms are about US$5 a single and US$9 a double with private showers. The *Nueve de Octubre* has some slightly more expensive rooms with carpets and telephones.

Finally, *Hotel Embassy*, in the heart of a quiet residential district at Presidente Wilson 441 and 6 de Diciembre, is highly recommended as being very good value – it could almost be called a top-end hotel. It is motel-like and rather lacks character, but the comfortable rooms are spotless and complete with carpeting, telephone and private bathroom. Their restaurant is recommended and they charge around US$9 a single and US$13 a double, depending on the room.

Places to Stay - top end

The fanciest places in town are *Hotel Colón* on Avenida Amazonas at Patria, complete with shopping mall, casino, swimming pool, three restaurants, two bars, sauna, discotheque, etc, etc; *Hotel Quito*, similar but quieter and smaller on the end of Avenida 12 de Octubre with pleasant gardens; and the *Alameda Real*, which is on Amazonas at Roca and has rooms with private kitchens which can be rented by the week. These hotels charge roughly US$50 to US$60 for a double room.

There are several 1st class hotels which are much more economical. They are often booked up well ahead. One of the best is *Residencia Los Alpes*, in a beautiful old house at Tamayo 223 and Jorge Washington. Comfortable carpeted rooms with spotless bathrooms and a telephone are about US$14 a single and US$21 a double.

Also good and recommended is *Residencial Cumbes Baqueadano* at Baqueadano 164 near 6 de Diciembre. It has clean rooms with private bathrooms for US$10 a single and US$16 a double. Breakfast is included. Opposite the Casa de Cultura is the *Hotel Tambo Real* which is good value for about US$22 for a double room.

Places to Eat

If you are economising, it is best to stick to the standard *almuerzos* or *meriendas*. If you're staying at the *Hotel Gran Casino* then you'll find the prices there as cheap as anywhere although the helpings aren't very big. There are several cheap restaurants on the 1400 block of Rocafuerte near the Plaza Santa Domingo.

The good *Chifa Hong Kong* is at Guayaquil 1384 near the Plaza Sucre. They serve large and inexpensive portions. The *Oasis* opposite the Hotel Quitumbe has also been recommended for cheap and filling meals. There are many other simple and inexpensive restaurants in the old town but most of them are unremarkable. The best restaurants are generally in the new town and cost a little more.

Quito is famous for its *cebiches* made of marinated seafood. One of the best *cebicherías* is *Las Redes* at Amazonas 845 and Veintimilla. Have the *cebiche mixta*;

it's huge and delicious and costs about US$4. There are cheaper dishes. Other excellent seafood restaurants are *El Cebiche* at Juan León Mera 1232 and Calama, and *La Jaiba Mariscos* at Avenida Colón and Reina Victoria. Expect to pay about US$4 for a full meal.

Avenida Amazonas is a good place to come and watch the world go by. *Manolo's* pavement café is one of the most popular places and it isn't exorbitant. They serve a decent cup of coffee and don't hassle you if you sit there for hours. It's an extremely popular meeting place. Manolo's is at Amazonas 420 and Robles and there are several similar places nearby.

The cafeterias on the 500 block of Amazonas are inexpensive. The *Colón Cafeteria*, which is not very expensive considering that it is in one of the capital's most luxurious hotels, serves reasonable food and is open 24 hours.

Good, typical Ecuadorean food in elegant surroundings can be eaten at *La Choza* at 12 de Octubre and Cordero. You can eat well here for about US$4. Of course it's much cheaper at a market, but if you have a delicate stomach you can eat here and not get sick. Another place to try 'safe' Ecuadorean food is the *Taberna Quiteña*. There are two locations and they have entertainment at weekends (see Entertainment section). A good cheap place to try local food, particularly at lunch time, is *Mama Chlorindas* at Reina Victoria and Calama – meals are only about US$1.

For dining with a view of the city you can go to the *Panecillo* restaurant. It's quite elegant and medium priced rather than expensive. The food is OK but the service slow. Better service and a superb view is had at *La Terraza del Tartaro* on the top floor of the Edificio Amazonas building at Avenida Amazonas and Veintimilla. An elevator at the back of the lobby will take you up (press button 2 and you automatically get taken to the top floor). This is a classy place and you can

expect to pay about US$7 to US$8 each for a meal with a view.

If you like steak, the *Casa de Mi Abuela* at Luis Cordero 1922 and 10 de Agosto is excellent. Steaks are about US$4. Cheaper and locally popular is the *Columbus Steak House* on Avenida Colón at Amazonas. It's good, but don't expect anything but meat. Their *parrilladas* are recommended.

A good place to go if you are hungry, especially for meat, is the Brazilian *Churrascaria Tropeiro* at Veintimilla and 6 de Diciembre. US$5 buys an 'all-you-can-eat' meal. Waiters keep coming round with steak, roast pork and lamb, chicken, and other goodies and there is a help yourself salad bar. The food is good.

If you want to treat yourself to a good meal in elegant surroundings I recommend the *Excalibur* at Calama 380 and Juan León Mera. There are several other fancy restaurants on Calama. Also good is the British run *Bailey's* at Páez 232 and 18 de Septiembre – they have a pleasant pub-like bar where you can sit while you wait for your meal.

Even the most expensive restaurants in Quito are inexpensive by European standards. You can get a lobster dinner for US$7 in the best restaurants. The most expensive part of any meal will be wine. Ecuadorean wine is not good and imported wine is expensive. While a full meal including hors d'oeuvres and dessert will cost under US$15 in even the most expensive restaurant, a single bottle of mediocre wine can be more expensive than the meal.

Finally, the *Hotel Colón* serves a delicious and varied all-you-can-eat lunch buffet in the lobby every Sunday from 12 noon till 2 pm. It costs US$5 and is well worth it if you are looking for a luxurious splurge.

Entertainment

Quito is not the world's most exciting capital for nightlife. Read the newspapers for exact details of what is going on. *El Comercio* has the most thorough coverage.

Entertainment reaches its height during the various fiestas. The founding of Quito is celebrated throughout the first week of December and there are bullfights at the Plaza de Toros, just beyond the intersection of Avenida América and 10 de Agosto. There is also street-dancing on the night of 6 December.

New Year's Eve is celebrated by erecting life-sized puppets in the streets and burning them at midnight. These puppets are often very elaborate and usually represent politicians. Carnival, which is a moveable Catholic feast, is celebrated by intense water fights – no one is spared. Colourful religious processions are held during Easter week.

On a day-to-day basis, films provide cheap and good entertainment. There are some 20 cinemas and at least some of them show good English-language films with Spanish subtitles. The cinemas which consistently show the best films seem to be the *Cine Colón* at the intersection of Avenida Colón and 10 de Agosto, and the *Universitario* at the Indoamerican Plaza on Avenida América at Perez Guerrero. Other cinemas also show good films once in a while. For their addresses look in the white pages of the telephone directory under 'Cine' or 'Teatro'. Entrance is only about 80c.

If your Spanish is up to it, you can see a play at the *Teatro Sucre* on Guayaquil in the old town, or the *Teatro Prometeo* on Avenida 6 de Diciembre behind the Casa de Cultura in the new town. The Prometeo is the cheapest and sometimes has mime performances which anyone can understand.

Nightlife is usually expensive. Often there is a cover charge or a minimum consumption and you may be expected to wear a jacket or skirt. To listen to local music inexpensively you can go to the *Taberna Quiteña*, which has music on weekends and has no cover charge. They serve typical Ecuadorean food and aren't cheap but you don't have to order much. They have two locations. In the old town

they are at Calle Manabí and Luis Vargas and in the new town at Avenida Amazonas 1259 and Colón. Both have a 'cellar bar' atmosphere. The one in the old town usually has a greater variety of musicians. They often wander from table to table and ask you if you want to hear your request in Spanish. The evening entertainment doesn't normally get underway until after 9 pm.

At Avenida Universitaria 496 and Armero in front of the university is the *Ñucanchi Peña*, also good for local music (tel 540967). Other places advertise in the newspaper and are more expensive.

There are several British or American bars which have a pub-like atmosphere. They are not cheap by Ecuadorean standards. One is *El Pub*, next to the British Embassy on Avenida Suarez at the end of Avenida 12 de Octubre. Another bar you might want to try is the *Reina Victoria* on the street of the same name near Calle Roca. It's American-run and a place to meet some of the local English-speaking community. They have a dart board.

The best hotels have expensive nightclubs and discotheques.

Shopping

The main shopping street in the old town is Calle Guayaquil. Here you can buy most kinds of Ecuadorean handicrafts. There are also handicraft shops around the main plazas and along La Ronda. Bargaining is acceptable and expected.

There are many good stores for souvenir hunters in the new town along and near Avenida Amazonas. If buying on the streets (there are street stalls and ambulatory vendors) you should bargain. In the fancier stores, prices are normally fixed. The better stores are usually more expensive but not necessarily exorbitant, and the items for sale are often top quality.

The best, and definitely the most expensive, is the store of designer Olga Fisch, at Avenida Colón 260. At Calle

Quito street scene

Urbina 111 and Cordero (near the intersection of Avenidas Colón and 6 de Diciembre) is the much cheaper, and highly recommended, Productos Andinos Indian cooperative. Somewhere between the two in price range is the fairly new and excellent *Galería Latina* next to the Libri Mundi bookstore on Juan León Mera.

Looking in these three shops will give you a good idea of prices and quality. The best place to buy the colourful T-shirts popularly called 'Galápagos T-shirts' – but in fact decorated with various Ecuadorean motifs – is Cosas at Calle Juan León Mera 838.

Getting There & Away

Air There is an international airport departure tax of US$20 payable in either US dollars or sucres. If you are flying internationally, confirm 72 hours in advance, reconfirm 24 hours in advance, and arrive at the airport two hours before your flight. You will probably take off several hours late, but at least you'll be on

the flight. The local representatives of international airlines are notorious for bumping you off their frequently over-booked flights – 'Sorry, señor, you're not on the computer'.

There is no departure tax for internal flights, most of which are run by TAME (although flights to Guayaquil and Cuenca are also operated by SAN-Saeta). The two airlines will accept one another's tickets if their flights aren't full and if you paid for the ticket with cash. Internal flights (except for the Galápagos) are inexpensive – prices and schedules change frequently and the following are approximate. Flights to Guayaquil (US$15) leave from six to 14 times a day, most frequently on weekdays. Flights to Cuenca (US$16) leave one to three times a day.

Only TAME operates services to the following cities: Tulcán (US$8) Monday to Friday at noon; Esmeraldas (US$10) Monday to Saturday mornings and Friday afternoons; Portoviejo (US$13)

Monday to Friday afternoons and Sunday mornings; Manta (US$13) Monday to Saturday mornings and Sunday afternoons; Macas (US$10) Monday, Wednesday and Friday mornings; Coca (US$11) Monday to Friday mornings; Lago Agrio (US$10) daily (several a day until the road destroyed by the March 1987 earthquake is rebuilt); Tarapoa (US$10) Wednesday and Friday mornings; Loja (US$10) Monday to Saturday mornings. Other cities which can be reached from Quito with connections at Guayaquil are Machala and Macará.

The Galápagos are reached from Quito by TAME flights every morning except Sunday. There is usually a change at Guayaquil but your luggage is transferred. The return cost is about US$360 for non-Ecuadorean residents. These flights go to Baltra airport and are the normal way to go for travellers heading to the main port of Puerto Ayora on Santa Cruz Island. SAN-Saeta also have morning flights on Monday, Wednesday and Friday to San Cristobal Island – same price.

TAME has several ticket offices – unfortunately they seem to change address quite frequently so check before you go. In the old town TAME is at Manabí 635 and Venezuela (tel 512988) and in the new town at Avenida Colón 1001. SAN-Saeta has an office at Avenida Colón 535 and 6 de Diciembre (tel 561995), at Avenida Colombia 610 (tel 527555) and at Guayaquil 1228 and Olmedo in the old town (tel 211431). In addition, you can buy domestic air tickets from most reputable travel agents at the same cost as direct from the airlines.

Several international airlines have offices in Quito. Almost all of them are on or near Avenida Amazonas, and many – including Ecuatoriana, Aeroperu, KLM, Eastern and Avianca – are at Amazonas and Jorge Washington.

Rail The famous Quito-Guayaquil train has been suspended since the 1982/83 El Niño floods which destroyed about 80 km of track. It is not known when, if ever, services will resume. Meanwhile there is a daily *autoferro* to Riobamba. It leaves Quito at 3 pm and goes via Latacunga (40c, two hours) and Ambato (60c, 3½ hours), to Riobamba (90c, five hours).

Monday to Wednesday is the best time to go as the train is often crowded towards the end of the week. You should try and buy tickets in advance. The ticket booth is open from 10 am to 12 noon and from 2 to 3 pm. Tickets for the next day's train are sold only reluctantly and with persuasion.

The train station is on Avenida Sincholagua and Vicente Maldonado about two km south of the old town. The No 2 Colon-Camal bus from the Plaza Santo Domingo goes there. There is a railway booking office in the old town on Calle Bolívar 443 and Benalcázar, but it remains closed while the line to Guayaquil is down.

Metropolitan Touring (Avenida Amazonas 239) operates a very expensive tourist train trip which includes an overnight at a first-class Riobamba hotel.

Bus The new modern bus station known as *Terminal Terrestre de Cumanda* became fully operational in 1987 although not all the access roads have yet been built, causing some congestion in the Avenida 24 de Mayo area. There are several dozen bus companies with offices at the terminal. They serve most destinations to the south, east and west of Quito. There is an information window which will tell you which company goes where, although it's fairly obvious. Walk around and compare departures.

Usually there are several companies serving the same destination at different times. For the most popular destinations you'll find driver's assistants hustling passengers for their bus. Only buses departing within a few minutes are allowed to park outside the terminal so you can often be on your way within minutes of arriving. If you do find you have to wait, there is a snack bar. Usually it is easy enough to get onto the bus you want, but if you plan on travelling during holiday periods and just before the weekend it's best to go to the terminal and book in advance.

With literally hundreds of buses departing during the day, it is impossible to give accurate timetables. There are several buses a day to most destinations, and some places – such as Ambato – may have several departures an hour. Here is a list of the major destinations served and the approximate cost and length of a journey.

The bus ride to Cuenca is over poor roads, and service is erratic.

to	cost	hours
Ambato	US$1.10	2½
Bahía de Caráquez	US$3.80	8
Baños	US$1.50	3½
Coca	US$3.30	13
Cuenca	US$3-4	9-14
Guaranda	US$1.70	5
Guayaquil	US$2.80	8
Lago Agrio	US$3.00	10
Latacunga	US$0.80	1½
Loja	US$4.90	18
Machala	US$3.70	11
Manta	US$3.90	8
Portoviejo	US$3.90	8
Puyo	US$2.00	8
Riobamba	US$1.60	4
Santo Domingo	US$1.10	2½
Tena	US$2.90	9

For other destinations, you may have to go to the nearest major city and change. Enquire at the bus offices.

Northbound buses do not leave from the Terminal Terrestre. There are several terminals for the north; the majority of them are clustered together in three or four blocks of the streets to the north-west of the Parque El Ejido. Calles 18 de Septiembre and Manuel Larrea are the places to go to find frequent buses for Otavalo (85c, 2½ hours), Ibarra (US$1, three hours) and Tulcán (US$2, 5½ hours). Buses often leave as soon as they are full and few companies will sell tickets

in advance. Some buses from here also go to Santo Domingo and Esmeraldas (US$2.50, six hours).

There are companies (for example TEPSA) which will sell international bus tickets to Peru or Colombia. Avoid these. The tickets are very expensive and you still have to change buses at the border. Once across the border you often find that only one company will accept your ticket and you can wait for hours until they depart. It's much cheaper and far more convenient to buy tickets as you go.

Getting Around
Airport Quito International Airport terminal is on Avenida de la Prensa about 10 km north of the old town centre. The easiest way to get there by public transport is aboard the blue double-decker London buses which begin from the Casa de Cultura and run along Avenida Amazonas to the airport. The journey in either direction costs only 10c but the bus does not run after dark.

Other buses which go to the airport tend to be more crowded. They are usually marked by an 'Aeropuerto' placard. The No 1 Villa Flora-Iñaquito bus runs from Plaza Santo Domingo in the old town to the airport. A taxi costs about US$2.50.

Services at the airport terminal include tourist information, money exchange, cafeteria/bar, post office, IETEL international telephone office and gift shops. The telephone number for airport information is 241580.

Bus The crowded local buses have a flat fare of 5c which you pay as you board. Generally speaking, buses run north-south and have a fixed route. The drivers are usually helpful and will tell you which bus to take if they are not going to your destination. Traffic in the old town is very heavy and you may often find it faster to walk than to take a bus, especially during the rush hours. Buses have both a name and a number, and although they usually have a fixed route, this may vary because of heavy traffic, road repair or the whim of the driver.

The narrow streets of downtown are usually one-way. Calles Guayaquil and Venezuela are one-way into the old town towards the Panecillo, and Calles García Moreno and Flores are one-way out of the old town and away from the Panecillo. There are about 40 different routes. A selection of the ones you might use follows:

1 Iñaquito-Villa Flora
   Airport-10 de Agosto-Guayaquil-Santo Domingo-Maldonado-Villa Flora
2 Colón-Camal
   Coruña-Colón-10 de Agosto-Guayaquil-Santo Domingo-Maldonado-Terminal Terrestre
3 Colmena-Batan
   La Colmena-24 de Mayo-García Moreno-Vargas Torres-Manuel Larrea-Patria-Juan León Mera-Colón-6 de Diciembre-El Batan
7 Marin-Cotocollao
   Plaza Marin-10 de Agosto-Airport-Cotocollao
9 Ermita-Las Casas
   Ermita-24 de Mayo-García Moreno-América-University-La Gasca-Las Casas
10 San Bartolo-Miraflores
   San Bartolo-Maldonado-Santo Domingo-10 de Agosto-18 de Septiembre-Miraflores
11 El Tejar-El Inca
   El Tejar-Mejía-La Alameda-6 de Diciembre-El Inca (end of 6 de Diciembre)
15 Marin-Quito Norte
   Plaza Marin-10 de Agosto-Airport-North Quito
19 Camal-La Gasca
   Patria-Perez Guerrero-América-La Gasca
Blue Airport Bus
   Airport-Avenida Amazonas-Patria

Some minibuses cost a few cents extra.

Taxi A law was passed in 1984 requiring Quito cabs to have meters and almost all drivers now use them, although occasionally they will ask to arrange a price with you beforehand. Sometimes this is to your advantage as it enables the driver to take a roundabout route to avoid traffic, thus saving both of you time.

Taxi cabs are all yellow. They can be hired for several hours or for a day. If you bargain hard, you could hire a cab for a day for about US$25 if you don't plan on going very far. Short journeys downtown cost from about 50c. To the airport is about US$2 to US$4 depending on how far south you are.

Car Rental Car rental in Quito, as elsewhere in Ecuador, is expensive. There are car rental offices at the airport. Expect to pay at least US$30 per day and make sure that mileage and adequate insurance are included.

AROUND QUITO

The most famous excursion is to the equator at Mitad del Mundo about 22 km north of Quito. Here there is a large stone monument and a museum which was recently closed for restoration but should be open soon. En route to the equator, the road passes an intriguing highway art gallery. Famous Latin American artists have painted roadside billboards with weatherproof paint; the works, some two dozen of them, are stretched out along the highway.

To get there, take a Mitad del Mundo bus, which leaves about every half hour from the street market by Imbabura and Mejía in the old town. It's not an obvious bus stop so ask. The journey takes about an hour and costs about 15c. A taxi, including waiting time at the monument, will cost less than US$10.

The Indian market nearest the capital is the Sangolquí Sunday morning market. Frequent local buses go there from Plaza Marin at Calle Chile and M de Solanda.

North of Quito

The Andean highlands north of Quito are one of the most popular destinations in Ecuador. Few travellers spend any time in the country without visiting the famous Indian market at the small town of Otavalo, where you can buy a wide variety of weavings, clothing and handicrafts. Though many travellers limit their visit to just Otavalo, there is much more to see in the region.

The dramatic mountain scenery is dotted with shining white churches set in tiny villages, and includes views of Cayambe, the third highest peak in the country, as well as a beautiful lake district. Several small towns are noted for speciality handicrafts such as woodcarving or leatherwork.

Ibarra is a small, charmingly somnolent colonial city worth visiting, both in its own right and as the beginning of the Ibarra-San Lorenzo railway linking the northern highlands with the coast. If you are travelling overland to or from Colombia, it's almost impossible to avoid this region.

CALDERÓN

About 10 km north of Quito on the Pan American highway is the village of Calderón, famous as the best centre of a unique Ecuadorean folk art. Here they make decorations of bread dough ranging from small statuettes to colourful Christmas tree ornaments, such as stars, parrots, angels and tortoises. The ornaments make practical gifts as they are small, unusual and cheap (about 10c each).

Some figurines are used for All Soul's Day ceremonies in Calderón and many other Andean villages. It is thought that the figurines represented animal or human sacrifices in pre-conquest times. These are decorative figures and are inedible; preservatives are added to them and they'll last some years.

Calderón is a small village so you won't have any difficulty finding stores on the one main street. There is nowhere to stay and no proper restaurants.

If you wanted to visit just Calderón from Quito, you could hire a cab for about US$5 including some waiting time for you to shop.

NORTH TO CAYAMBE

Beyond Calderón the road descends in a series of magnificent sweeps towards the village of Guayllabamba, in a fertile river valley of the same name and famous for its produce. Roadside stalls offer huge avocados and that strangely reptilian-looking Andean fruit, the *chirimoya*. It's a member of the custard apple family, and perhaps the nearest translation is the 'sweetsop' – I prefer the Spanish name. Its knobbly green skin is discarded and you eat the white pulp inside. The chirimoya definitely tastes better than it looks or sounds.

Some three km beyond Guayllabamba, the road forks and you can take either fork as they both end at Cayambe. About 10 km along the right-hand road you pass a turnoff to the right which leads back to Quito via a roundabout route. (This takes you through Quinche, famous for the Virgin and paintings inside the church, and on through pretty countryside and tiny hamlets to Pifo. Here you turn right and return to Quito via Tumbaco.)

A few km further you cross the equator, marked by a monument consisting of a large concrete globe which is much less visited than the ever popular 'Mitad del Mundo' monument north of Quito. Soon you cross the railway tracks of the now defunct Quito-Ibarra train, and 60 km from Quito you reach Cayambe.

The left-hand route, although a little shorter, is somewhat more twisting and slower than the right-hand route; therefore some drivers avoid it. It also crosses the equator but there is no marker. It is generally less inhabited and has more barren countryside than the other road. I prefer it for the exciting drive and wild scenery. The only village of any size on this road is Tabacundo.

A few km before Tabacundo is a turnoff to the left which leads to Tocachi and the ruins of Cochasquí. These were built by the Cara Indians before the Inca conquest and had been largely forgotten until recently. The area was declared a national archaeological site in 1977 and is currently being excavated and investigated. There are thought to be 15 pyramids, some of which are almost 100 metres long, but there is little to see for the casual visitor and there are no facilities or public transport.

CAYAMBE

Cayambe (population 14,000) is the most important town on the way to Otavalo. It is famous for its dairy industry and there are many stores and restaurants selling a variety of local cheeses and cheese products. Although this is the nearest town of any size to the equator, few people stay here, preferring instead to buy some cheese and continue to Otavalo. Accommodation is limited to the brand new *Hostería Mitad del Mundo* at the south end of town – it looks medium priced.

It is a further 50 km to Otavalo. The snow-capped mountain to the right of the road is the extinct volcano of Cayambe, which at 5790 metres is Ecuador's third highest peak. For trivia buffs it is the highest point in the world through which the equator directly passes – at about 4600 metres on the south side. The road climbs and crosses the provincial line from Pichincha to Imbabura, a province known for its lake district. Soon you see the largest of these lakes, Lago San Pablo, stretching away to your right with the high peak of Imbabura (4609 metres) behind it. The area is dotted with many simple villages inhabited by the Otavaleño Indians.

OTAVALO

This small town of some 17,500 inhabitants is justly famous for its friendly people and their Saturday market. The market dates back to pre-Inca times when jungle products were brought up from the eastern lowlands and traded for highland goods. Today's market has two different functions: the local market for buying and bartering animals, food and other essentials, and the crafts market for the tourists.

The story of the phenomenal success of the Otavaleño weavers is an intriguing one. Their ability as weavers was harshly exploited by the colonialists and later the Ecuadorean landowners who forced them to labour in *obrajes* or sweatshops, often for 14 or more hours a day. Miserable though this was, it did have the effect of instilling a great knowledge of weaving in the Otavaleño people.

In 1917 a local weaver had the idea of copying the Scottish tweeds that were then in vogue and this was so successful that it led to recognition of the ability of the Otavaleño weavers. This ability, combined with a shrewd business sense, has made the Otavaleños the most prosperous Indian group in Ecuador and perhaps on the continent. It is difficult to find a town of any size which does not have an Otavaleño store. They also make frequent business trips to neighbouring countries and even to North America and Europe.

The goods they sell are undeniably oriented towards the tourist market and this has led to recent complaints from 'real travellers' that the market is too 'touristified'. This seems to me a kind of inverse snobbism that reveals a lack of concern for the well-being of the weavers. Their prosperity in a changing and difficult world is only to be applauded, but a truer measure of their success is perhaps not only their prosperity but their continuing sense of tribal identity and tradition.

One of the most evident features of the Otavaleños' cultural integrity is the traditional way of dress. This is not just put on specially for the tourists at the Saturday market, but is worn on normal workdays in their houses, villages and fields. The men are immediately noticeable because of their long single pigtails, calf-length white pants, rope sandals, reversible grey or blue ponchos and dark felt hats. The women are very striking with beautifully embroidered blouses, long black skirts and shawls, and interesting head cloths whose colour and style of folding denotes marital status. The women also wear bright jewellery; the most obvious are the many strings of gold-coloured blown glass beads around their necks, and bracelets consisting of long strands of red beads.

Of the 17,500 inhabitants of Otavalo, the majority are whites or mestizos. There are about 35,000 Indians, most of whom live in the many nearby villages and come into Otavalo for market day. Quite a few Indians own stores in Otavalo, however, and you can buy most items here if you are unable to visit on market day.

Money
You are strongly advised to bring as much as you think you'll need from Quito. If you must change money, try the Banco del Pichincha on the main plaza. They usually accept cash dollars and travellers' cheques at about 5% below the Quito rate, but it's difficult to negotiate many other currencies (though Colombian pesos are accepted). Some of the better hotels will exchange dollars at an unfavourable rate but normally you have to stay there. It's worth trying to buy souvenirs with cash dollars – often the Indians like to have a little stash of hard currency.

Post & Phone
The post office is in the Municipalidad on the García Moreno side of the main plaza.

(It has changed location several times over the past few years so don't be surprised if it has moved again.) There are two IETEL offices – the old one is on Garcia Moreno and Roca and should close by 1988 when the new one at Calderon and Sucre opens.

Tourist Information An excellent information and guided tour office has recently opened. This is *Zulaytour* run by the friendly and knowledgeable Señor Rodrigo Mora, at Sucre y Colón 10-14, Otavalo, Ecuador. Messages can be left at tel 920008.

A variety of inexpensive guided tours are available which enable you to visit local Indian homes, learn about the entire weaving process, buy products off the loom, and take photographs. An emphasis on anthropological and sociological background information makes these tours very worthwhile.

The most popular tour visits several local villages and takes all day. Transportation is included and a tour costs about US$30 with a maximum of six passengers. That means US$5 per person with a full group or US$15 per person if there are just two people. Lunch is extra. Other tours are available, for example to visit the beautiful Andean lakes around Otavalo (all day, US$45 for six people). Ask at Zulaytour for more information.

If you have a reasonably large sized group, an informative slide presentation of the area can be arranged. At appropriate times of year, visits to some of the local fiestas may be possible (although not all fiestas are open to outsiders). General tourist information is always available.

The Market
The main market day is Saturday. There are three main plazas, with the overflow spilling out onto the streets linking them. The Poncho Plaza is where the goods of most appeal to tourists are sold. Here you can buy woollen goods such as ponchos, blankets, scarves, sweaters, tapestries

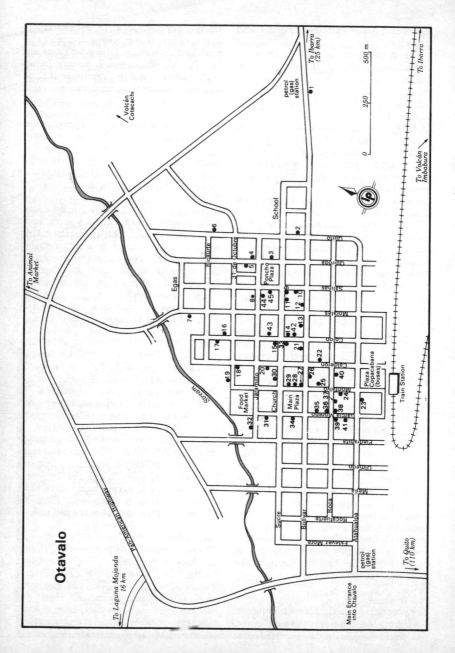

Otavalo

and gloves as well as a variety of embroidered blouses and shirts, shawls, string bags, rope sandals.

Bargaining for every purchase is expected. If you buy several items from the same person, you can easily expect a discount of 20% or even more if you are good at bargaining. Some people aren't good at it and feel uncomfortable trying to knock a few sucres off an already cheaply priced item. Just remember that it is expected and make an offer a little below the first asking price (assuming you want to buy the thing).

This market gets underway soon after dawn and continues until about noon. It can get rather crowded in mid-morning when the big tour groups arrive. If you come in the early morning there's a greater selection.

The food market sells produce and household goods for the locals, and there is an animal market beginning in the pre-dawn hours (4 to 8 am) on the outskirts of town. These are not designed for tourists but you are welcome to visit them; many people find the sight of poncho-clad Indians quietly bartering for a string of screaming piglets much more interesting than the Poncho Plaza. The animal market is over by early morning, however, so you should plan on an early arrival. It lies over a km out of town – cross the bridge at the end of Morales and follow the crowds to get there.

Fiestas

Some small village fiestas date back to pre-Columbian rituals and can last as long as two weeks, with much drinking and dancing. They are not much visited by outsiders and, in some cases, it would be dangerous for tourists to just show up. One little-known annual event involves ritual battle between rival villages – locals may be killed – the authorities turn a blind eye and outsiders are not tolerated.

24 June is St John the Baptist Day, and 29 June is the Day of Sts Peter and Paul. These and the intervening days are an

1	Hotel Yamor Continental
2	Fire Station
3	Peña de los Chaskis
4	Ali Micui
5	Residencial Centenario
6	Bahai Institute
7	Parenthese Restaurant
8	Residencial Samar-Huasy
9	Public Toilet
10	Hat Shop
11	Residencial El Indio
12	Pensión Vaca 2
13	Residencial La Herradura
14	Pollo Koko Rico Chicken Restaurant
15	El Mesón del Arrayan
16	Residencial Santa Ana
17	Residencial Colón
18	Buses to local villages
19	Cockfight Stadium
20	IETEL (new)
21	Cine Bolívar
22	Transportes Otavalo
23	Bar Huasipungo
24	Pensión Residencial Los Andes
25	Residencial Otavalo
26	Camba Huasy Chicken Restaurant
27	Restaurant Copacabana
28	Banco del Pichincha
29	Royal Cafeteria & Camba Huasy Fuente de Soda
30	Mama Rosita Restaurant
31	Café El Triunfo
32	Police Station
33	Zulaytour
34	Municipalidad & Post Office
35	Chifa Tien An Men
36	Chifa Casa de Korea
37	Hotel Otavalo & Golden Eagle Restaurant
38	Hotel Riviera-Sucre
39	Apollo Theatre
40	Santo Domingo Church
41	IETEL (old)
42	Pensión Los Angeles
43	Pensión Imbabura
44	Peña Amauta
45	Shenandoah Café

important fiesta for Otavalo and the surrounding villages. There is a bullfight in Otavalo and a boating regatta on Lago San Pablo, as well as celebrations in nearby Ilumán.

A few km south of Otavalo, on the southern shores of Lago San Pablo, in the villages around San Rafael, there is a fiesta called *Corazas* on 19 August. Also in some of the south shore villages is the *Pendoneros* fiesta on 15 October.

Otavalo's best-known fiesta is held in the first two weeks of September. The *Fiesta del Yamor*, as it is known, consists of plenty of music, processions and dancing as well as firework displays, cockfights and election of the Queen of the Fiesta.

Precise dates of these can vary from year to year but they are usually well publicised and you can find out what's going on from posters. In addition, there are the usual feast days celebrated throughout the land.

Places to Stay - bottom end

Because Otavalo is such a popular destination, there are many more places to stay than in other, bigger, but less interesting towns. Despite this, it can get rather crowded on Friday nights so arrive early for the best choice. Most places are quite cheap, and new hotels open frequently. If you arrive midweek and plan to stay a few days, a cheaper price can often be negotiated – but late Friday night isn't a good time to expect any favours.

One of the most popular cheapies is the friendly *Residencias Santa Ana*, which is small and tends to fill up quickly. Beds are about US$1 each in quads, and a few cents more in the singles and doubles – but these go really fast. Most of the rooms are large, there's a pretty courtyard, and there are hot (or tepid) showers.

A rather larger and also friendly place is the *Pensión Otavalo*. Actually, it's not that much bigger but the rooms are smaller so there's more of them. There's

hot water most of the time and prices are from US$1 to US$1.50 per person, depending on the room and when you arrive.

The *Residencia Samar-Huasy* is conveniently half a block from the Poncho Plaza and seems to be gaining popularity recently. The management is friendly and there are many clean, though small, rooms. Hot showers are available at certain times of day. Rooms (shared showers) are US$1.25 per person.

The *Pensión Vaca No 2* has been recommended as good, cheap, clean and with hot water, but I've never visited it. The *Residencial La Herradura* is pretty good, with clean rooms, friendly staff, hot showers, and a restaurant for about US$1.50 each.

Also good and clean is the *Hotel Riviera-Sucre* which is US$1.50 per person and has hot water. The best room is No 4 which is a corner room and has three beds – US$4.50 for the room. Also clean and in this price range is the *Residencial Centenario*.

The *Residencial El Indio* is a brand-new hotel which has recently opened just off the Poncho Plaza. It's clean, has hot water, and there's a restaurant. It is very popular and always full of gringos at weekends, and even midweek rooms are often not available. Rooms with shared baths are about US$3.50 double and with private bath about US$6.50 a double.

If there's no room at any of these hotels you can try the *Pensións Los Andes, Imbabura, Los Angeles* or *Residencial Colón*, all of which are cheap and basic – I haven't heard any rave reviews about them.

Places to Stay - middle

There's only one better hotel in the town centre, the *Hotel Otavalo* (as opposed to the cheap *Pensión Otavalo*). It's clean – in fact last time I was in there it smelt overpoweringly of wax polish – and has rooms with private baths for about US$12 a double and half that price for rooms with shared baths, and breakfast is included. There's a good restaurant. They recommend reservations for the weekend and you can telephone them on Otavalo 416.

I prefer the *Hotel Yamor Continental* (tel Otavalo 451), which has clean and spacious rooms in a hacienda-like building set in charming flower-filled gardens at the north-east end of town. Supposedly there is a pool – but it's more like an ornamental pond. There's a good restaurant and bar. Rooms with private bath are about US$10 single and US$15 double. Hot water only runs in the evening and early mornings and you have to make sure that they turn it on; it can take half an hour to warm up.

Taxis from the bus station are about 75c or you can walk in 20 minutes. They are only 10 minutes from the Poncho Plaza.

Places to Stay – top end

Although there aren't any top-notch hotels in Otavalo, there are three good hotels in San Pablo (about 10 km away) either by the lake or near the village. On the southern outskirts of the village is the very popular *Hostería Cusín*, which is in a beautiful converted 17th-century hacienda with all the old trimmings. They are only open at weekends and usually booked well ahead. It costs about US$25 for a double with bath, delicious home-cooked set meals in the restaurant, a charming bar and beautiful gardens.

For reservations call the San Pablo operator and ask to be connected to the Cusín or write to Señora Crichton at the hotel, San Pablo, Imbabura. English is spoken at the hotel.

Note that telephone service can be inconsistent and there isn't any on Sunday. It is a three km walk to the nearest main crossroads for buses into Otavalo.

In addition, there are the slightly more expensive *Hostal Chicapan* and *Cabañas del Lago*, whose main attraction is their location by the lake. They are modern and comfortable.

Places to Eat

Ali Micui's, on the corner of the Poncho Plaza, is undoubtedly the favourite gringo hangout. They serve both vegetarian and non-vegetarian food. The selection is excellent, the prices reasonable, and the service usually very slow. The restaurant serves dishes made with *quinua*, an Andean grain with a very high protein content and an important traditional food of the Incas. It's rarely found these days. Their banana bread is excellent. Micui's is also a good place to meet people. They will not sell beer.

If you're on a really tight budget, *Mama Rosita's* is basic and cheap and has been recommended for pancakes. Another cheapie you might try is the *Copacabana* on the main plaza. During the day the stalls at the market are probably the cheapest of all.

If you just want a snack, there's the *Royal Cafetería* and *Camba Huasy Fuente de Soda* for ice cream. They are next door to one another on the main plaza. The *Shenandoah* on the Poncho Plaza is good for snacks and dessert – they have a wide selection of fruit pies and juices.

The *chifas* are, as usual, excellent value and there are several in town. The best is the excellent *Casa de Korea. Tien An Men* is also good. If you're after fried chicken, you'll find a few chicken restaurants marked on the map. None of them seem especially noteworthy.

Out on the road to the animal market is *Parenthese* which seems to change owners about once a year and has been variously French, American and Ecuadorean run. In the past it has been good for drinks, meals, soup and salads, desserts, and meeting people – but not all at the same time! It's always worth checking out the latest reincarnation of this place. They are usually open only from Thursdays to Saturdays.

The most expensive and fanciest restaurant is *El Mesón del Arrayan*, but it's not always open mid-week. The restaurants at the better hotels are also worth bearing in mind.

Entertainment

Otavalo is a quiet place during the week but gets livelier on the weekend. There are two movie theatres (see map) with some English-language films. Many people like to hang out at *Ali Micui's* restaurant where you can meet other travellers and read the bulletin board to see what's going on.

On Friday and Saturday nights there's the popular *Amauta Peña* which doesn't get under way until after 10 pm and costs about US$1. The music and ambience can vary from abysmal to quite good but there's not much else to do anyway. Another peña, *Los Chaskis*, has been recently closed but may reopen.

Finally, there's the weekly cockfight which costs a few cents and is held in the ring at the end of 31 de Octubre every Saturday afternoon about 3 pm.

Getting There & Around

Train There is a railway station, though trains have not run to Quito for many years. Trains to Ibarra stopped running in 1986 but it is possible that they'll start again. Fares were cheaper than the already cheap buses.

Bus From Quito to Otavalo is totally straightforward. There are several companies and the buses leave frequently. Go to the area underneath the flyover at Avenida Perez Guerrero and Avenida 10 de Agosto, at the corner of Parque El Ejido in the new town. There are four or five companies within two blocks. They all charge about 80c for the two or three-hour ride. If you don't like the departure schedule of one company, go around the corner to the next.

They won't sell you tickets in advance. Just turn up when you want to travel and you'll be on your way within an hour.

From the northern towns of Ibarra or Tulcán you'll find buses leaving for Otavalo every hour or so from the respective terminal terrestres.

In Otavalo, the main bus terminal area is near the strangely named Plaza Copacabana, where you'll probably arrive from Quito. There is a taxi rank if you need it; 50c will take you to most hotels. This is where you catch return buses to Quito and also old local buses to some of the villages south of Otavalo such as San Pablo del Lago.

A couple of blocks away, on Avenida Calderón, you'll find Transportes Otavalo, which has frequent buses to Ibarra (about 20c) where you change for buses further north. There are no buses direct to Tulcán at this time. Transportes Otavalo also has many Quito-bound buses.

Further down Avenida Calderón, at the intersection with Avenida 31 de Octubre, you'll find a bunch of rather decrepit buses with people waiting hopefully in them. This is a good place to find out about bus services to Cotacachi, Apuela and many of the remoter towns and villages. There is no strict schedule and prices are low. Adventurous travellers might just want to get aboard and see what happens – but leave yourself enough time to get back to a hotel, as most of these villages have absolutely no accommodation.

Reaching the villages of Calderón, Guayllabamba and Cayambe mentioned earlier in this section is not straightforward. The bus companies running between Quito and Otavalo normally don't sell tickets to intermediate points. You can buy a full-price ticket to or from Otavalo and get off where you want, assuming that you know where to get off or speak enough Spanish to explain to the driver. You'll be dropped off at the turnoff from the main road and will have to walk several hundred metres to the village.

Some buses run to these villages direct from Quito but they don't leave from the main bus terminals. It's best to catch one of these by standing on the side of the road. A good place to stand is on Avenida 10 de Agosto where it intersects with

Avenida Juan de Ascaray near the bull ring in Quito. Flag down any bus that has a sign indicating it's going where you want to go or that looks like it could use some passengers. Start early enough in the day so that you won't get stuck somewhere at nightfall and you'll probably have plenty of adventures.

Taxi You can always hire a taxi from Quito for a few hours and have them take you exactly where you want to go. A taxi for the day can easily be had for US$50 or less if you have any bargaining ability – not too bad if you split it three or four ways.

AROUND OTAVALO
Many of the Indians live and work in the nearby villages of Peguche, Quinchuqui and Ilumán, which are loosely strung together on the north-east side of the Pan American highway a few km away from Otavalo. There are many other Otavaleño villages in the area and a visit to

Zulaytour in Otavalo will yield much information. The villages to the south-west of Lago San Pablo are known for the manufacture of fireworks and tortora reed mats and other reed objects.

Peguche
A popular walk is out of Otavalo to the north and then east off the main highway – you'll be in Peguche in about an hour. Some people go in the hopes of being invited into the Indians' houses and buying the best weavings direct from the loom at bargain prices. That's wishful thinking. Prices aren't much (if at all) lower than Otavalo's, and people have better things to do than invite curious gringos into their houses. On the other hand, the locals are friendly and you might be lucky – especially if you speak Spanish. You can continue north-east on foot to Quinchuqui and Ilumán, about four and seven km away from Peguche respectively.

Otavalo market

Agato

Another possible village to visit is Agato about four km north of Lago San Pablo or three km south-east of Peguche. Here you can find Co-operativa Tahuantisuyo. They make traditional weavings on backstrap looms and use only natural dyes and products. These weavings are much more expensive than the market weavings, however, and are mainly for those seriously interested in textiles. They are rarely available for sale in the market but the weavers tend to go to the *Hostería Cusín* at weekends.

Lago San Pablo

The easiest way to reach the lake on foot from Otavalo is to head roughly south-east on any of the paths heading over the hill behind the railway station. When you get to the lake you'll find a paved road goes all the way around it, with beautiful views of both the lake and Volcán Imbabura behind it. You pass through the village of San Pablo del Lago and end up on the Pan American highway. Although people are generally friendly, you should bear in mind that on Saturday afternoons after the market and on Sundays, some of the Indians get blind drunk (as happens throughout the Andes) and you may find this an inopportune time for visiting.

High Mountain Forest Retreat

This retreat is a working farm which lies at 1900 metres in the western Andes. It is a two hour ride followed by a one hour hike from Otavalo. The surrounding forest is rich in flora and fauna and the scenery is lovely. Orchids bloom from July to September, which is the dry season. The rainy season is from October to May with most rain in the afternoons and evenings – mornings are often sunny. Bird life is prolific.

Food and accommodation is provided by an American family. Rooms are clean, simple (no electricity) and may be shared. Food is mainly local produce, with an emphasis on vegetarian food – though chicken is also available.

A maximum of 10 guests can be accommodated at US$25 per person per day with all meals included. Information is available from Bill Oliver, Academia Cotopaxi, Casilla 199, Quito or from Hacienda La Florida, Casilla 18, Otavalo. Zulaytour also knows this place.

COTACACHI

This small village, some 15 km north of Otavalo, is famous for its leatherwork. Stores are strung out all along the main street and you can find almost anything you might want in the way of leather goods. Market day is Saturday. Most tourists just pay a quick visit to the stores and return to Ibarra or Otavalo but if you wander around to the right of the main street you'll find an attractive main plaza.

Places to Stay & Eat

The hotel *El Mesón de las Flores* charges about US$15 for a double with private bath. It's at the corners of García Moreno and Sucre, tel Cotacachi 101. The building is over two centuries old and there is a bar/restaurant.

A brand new hotel which opened in 1987 is the *Hostería La Mirage*, tel Cotacachi 237, reservations at PO Box 11365, CCNU, Quito. It is an attractive country hotel with antique furniture, bar, restaurant, fireplace, sauna, tennis, horseriding, and tame birds. There are only 12 rooms charging US$15 single, US$22 double and US$30 for a suite and it has been well recommended.

There's also a cheaper restaurant at the corner of the small plaza on the main road. The *Restaurant La Estancia* is next to the hospital and open at weekends. You can eat *cuy* (guinea-pig) here. There are no cheap hotels.

Getting There & Away

From Otavalo there are buses about every hour.

LAGUNA CUICOCHA

Driving east some 18 km from Cotacachi, you come to an ancient, eroded volcano famous for the deep lake found in the crater. Cheap boat rides (30c) are available to take you on a half-hour trip around the islands on the lake. On sunny weekends it is often popular with some of the poorer locals. Just watching everyone hanging around waiting for a boat can be more interesting than the ride itself. The view of the lake and the extinct volcano Cotacachi (at 4939 metres Ecuador's 11th highest peak) behind it is quite impressive.

Places to Stay & Eat

There is a *Hotel Cuicocha* on the lakeshore. There is a restaurant here too but both the hotel and restaurant are only open intermittently. Prices are medium to high.

Getting There & Away

A group can hire a taxi or pickup from Cotacachi for about US$10. Buses from Otavalo to Apuela pass by Laguna Cuicocha, or you can hitch-hike.

APUELA

Soon after Laguna Cuicocha the road reaches its highest point and begins to drop down the western slopes of the Andes. The scenery is rugged and this is an opportunity to see some of the remoter and less-visited parts of the highlands. Some 40 km beyond Cuicocha by dirt road, you reach the village of Apuela where there are thermal springs, a very cheap and basic pensión and a simple restaurant.

Getting There & Away

There are five buses a day from Otavalo and more on Saturday. Beyond Apuela there are more remote villages – ask in Apuela about transportation.

IBARRA

Just 22 km north of Otavalo and 135 km north of Quito is the attractive colonial town of Ibarra (population 53,000), which is the provincial capital of Imbabura. One of the main reasons for coming here is to take the train from Ibarra to San Lorenzo on the coast.

There's not much to do in Ibarra but I enjoy it because it's so old-fashioned. Horse-drawn carts clatter along cobbled streets flanked by colonial buildings, dark-suited old gentlemen sit in the shady parks discussing the day's events, and most good folks are in bed by 10 pm. It's a relaxing sort of place.

Ibarra can be roughly divided into two areas. The south-east around the railway station is the busiest and has the bulk of the cheap hotels, while to the west are the main plazas and the older buildings in a generally quieter and more pleasant area.

Information

The DITURIS information office is now at 4-52 Calle Elias Libaria, as is the post office. The IETEL office is half a block from the park. There are no exchange houses and the banks were unwilling to change money when I was last there. Bring enough with you.

Streets in Ibarra are both numbered and named. Roughly, north-south streets are numbered *calles*, and west-east streets are numbered *carreteras*. Both names and numbers are used on the street signs but the names seem more widely accepted. I use names throughout this section.

Things to See

Plazas Parque La Merced (also known as Peñaherra) has a small museum and a church with a famous image of the Virgin of La Merced. The larger, tree-filled Parque Pedro Moncayo is dominated by the cathedral. Pedro Moncayo (1807-1888) was an Ibarra-born journalist and diplomat.

Out at the end of Bolívar is the quaint little Plazoleta Boyaca with a monument to Simón Bolívar to commemorate his

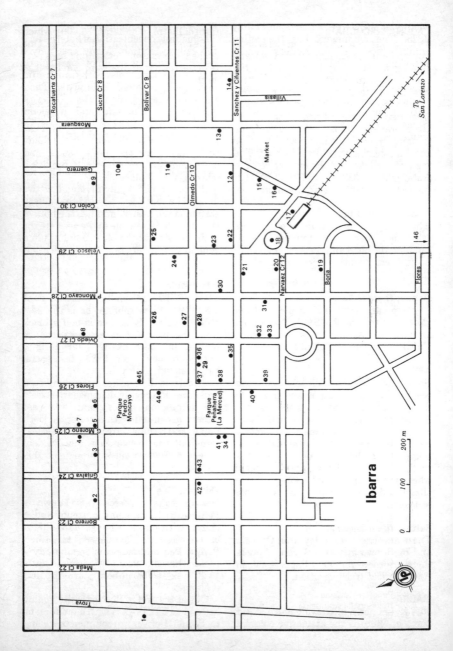

Ibarra

victory at the Battle of Ibarra on 17 July 1823. The monument has the rather unlikely scene of an Andean condor attacking an African lion.

Behind the plazoleta is the modern concrete block church of Santo Domingo topped by a huge statue of St Dominic with a giant rosary swinging in the wind. Some people may enjoy viewing the paintings in the rather garish interior. A few of the paintings seem rather tongue-in-cheek: an old-fashioned representation of the Jesus throwing the moneylenders out of the temple depicts one of the throng clutching a bag marked '$1000 Petroleo'.

Other Sights Apart from visiting these plazas, there's not much to do. The small, private archaeological museum costs 20c and is closed on Sundays and Mondays. There are two movie theatres. Ibarra is a good base from which to visit some of the surrounding villages and to wait for the train to the coast.

Places to Stay - bottom end
The highest concentration of hotels is near the railway station. Many cost only a dollar or so but are not particularly attractive - basic, noisy with train traffic, and usually with only cold water. These include the residenciales *Guayas, Atahualpa, Tahuando* and pensiones *Olmedo 1 & 2* and *Varsovia*. For a little more money you can find better places nearby.

The *Residencial Colón* charges US$1.60 per person, is clean, friendly, and has hot water. Rooms with a private bath are US$2.50 per person and they'll do your laundry for you. This hotel is often full by mid afternoon.

As you head away from the train station you'll find quieter hotels. *Hotel Berlin* is US$1.20 each, and they have tepid showers and clean and spacious rooms. It's worth staying here if you get a front room, some of which have with little balconies and views of Parque La Merced.

1	Plazoleta Boyaca & Church of Santo Domingo	24	Residencial Los Alpes
2	Residencial Yaguarcocha	25	Hostal El Ejecutivo
3	IETEL	26	Residencial Vaca
4	Cine Gran Colombia	27	Residencial Imperio
5	Luchino Pizza & Bar	28	Residencial Madrid
6	DITURIS	29	Café Pushkin
7	Cafeteria del Diablo	30	Residencial Madrid
8	Bar Restaurant El Dorado	31	Residencial Guayas
9	Hot Baths	32	Hotel Imbabura
10	Buses 28 de Septiembre	33	Residencial Los Ceibos
11	Buses San Miguel de Ibarra	34	Restaurant La Estancia
12	Buses 28 de Septiembre & San Miguel de Ibarra	35	Residencial El Principe
13	Hotel Ibarra	36	Residencial Majestic
14	Buses to La Esperanza	37	Several chifas on this block
15	Residencial Tahuando	38	Hotel Berlin
16	Pensión Olmedo 2	39	Residencial Imbabura
17	Railway Station	40	Taxis Lagos
18	Obelisk	41	Residencial La Merced & Museum
19	Cine Popular	42	Pensión Descanso
20	Residencial Colón	43	Hostal Nueva Colonia
21	Pensión Varsovia	44	Post Office
22	Residencial Atahualpa	45	Residencial Imperial
23	Pensión Olmedo 2	46	To: Hotel Agavi (300 m), Terminal Terrestre (750 m), Otavalo (21 km)

Also on the park is *Residencial La Merced*, which has hot water and the added attraction of being in the same building as the archaeological museum. The rooms at the front aren't bad but the back rooms are just plywood boxes – about US$1.50 each. The *Residencial Majestic* is reasonable for US$1.80 per person or US$2.20 in rooms with private bath and hot water.

A popular place with travellers is *Hotel Imbabura*, which is run by a friendly old lady and has a delightful little courtyard with flowers, a fish pond and birds. The best rooms are on the quiet street, at US$1.50 each. The rather dark inside rooms are US$1.20 per person. There's hot water. Don't confuse this with the *Residencial Imbabura*, which is US$1 each and quite clean but has only cold water. Similar is the *Residencial Yaguarcocha*. Next door to the *Hotel Imbabura* is the rather dark and uninviting-looking *Residencial Los Ceibos*, which also charges US$1 and has only cold water.

The cheapest cold-water place in town is the *Pensión Descanso*, which is clean and only 80c each. At the other end of the cheapies price range is the *Residencial Vaca*, which looks pretty good – they charge US$2/3 per person with/without private bath. Hot water provided.

Other hotels in the US$1 to US$2 range include the residenciales *El Principe*, *Imperial* and *Los Alpes*. If you stay in a place with cold water and you want a hot shower you can always go to the public baths which are open from 6 am to 9 pm daily.

Places to Stay – middle
There's several reasonably priced hotels which provide you with a little luxury if you're getting fed up with always slumming it. For example, the *Residencial Imperio* (not to be confused with the *Imperial*) charges only US$3 each for rooms with a private bath and sometimes a TV! The *Hostal Nueva Colonia* is new

and clean and charges US$5 per person in carpeted rooms with private bath and telephone.

For some reason there are two residencials *Madrid*. The one on Olmedo charges US$3.50 a single and US$6 a double for rooms with private bath; many of the rooms are carpeted and have TV. Around the corner on P Moncayo, the other *Madrid* charges about US$1 more and offers phones in the rooms. The most elegant of the mid-range hotels is the new *Hostal El Ejecutivo*, which is good value at US$5.50/8.50 a single/double with private bath.

Places to Stay – top end
There is one fancy hotel in town and it is conveniently located three blocks from the railway station. This is the *Hotel Ibarra* (tel 950091), which has modern, comfortable rooms with private bath for US$8/11 a single/double.

More expensive still are three hotels on the road south out of town. The first-class *Hotel Ajaví* (tel 951221) is halfway between town and the bus terminal, and boasts a good restaurant and bar, swimming pool and relatively luxurious rooms for about US$25 double. A km beyond the bus terminal heading south is the slightly cheaper but still good *Hostería San Agustín* (tel 951888).

A further km south is the best hotel in the Ibarra area, the *Hostería Chorlaví* (tel 950777). This has old-world charm; it is in a converted hacienda and has pretty gardens, a swimming pool and an excellent restaurant/bar. They have a famous buffet-style lunch with folk music on weekends, which is very popular with well-off Ecuadoreans and tour groups after the Otavalo market – perhaps a bit too touristy for many travellers' tastes.

The good hotels are often booked well in advance, particularly at weekends. You may want to call them.

Places to Eat
A good place to start the day off is *Café*

Pushkin, which has decent breakfasts and fresh home-made bread. *Chifas* are good and cheap; there are several near the Parque La Merced. I haven't eaten at the *Luchino Pizza & Bar* on the Parque Pedro Moncayo – you could investigate if you have a sudden craving for Italian food.

Two blocks away, the new *Bar Restaurant El Dorado* is trying to be the best place in town, judging by the white tablecloths and shining silverware. The food is good and reasonably priced.

Traditionally, the 'best' in town is the *Restaurant La Estancia* which has old world atmosphere and is reasonably priced although the food is not as good as the *El Dorado*. You could also try the better hotels.

Getting There & Away

Rail It used to be that you could get from Quito to Ibarra by train, but this service has been discontinued for some years now. The train service of most interest is the Ibarra-San Lorenzo railway which links the highlands with the coast (this is the only coastal train running).

The train is actually a converted school bus mounted onto a railway chassis. There is usually only one departure a day (6.30 am, 90c) so seats are limited, although a second and even a third train may sometimes be added. It is best to make a reservation on the previous day, although normally you are told that you must buy tickets on the day of departure. This is notoriously difficult – huge crowds of people push and shove to try and get their money into the tiny opening in the ticket grille and you have to be pretty obnoxious to obtain a ticket. It's much better to persuade the official that you really would prefer to buy a ticket in advance. Plead, insist, or tell them you'll pay a 'reservation fee' (about 25c should do it) but whatever you do, keep smiling and don't lose your cool or you won't get anywhere.

The journey is scheduled to take about seven hours but in reality often takes twice as long. Delays caused by landslides, breakdowns and cows on the track are the norm. If there are two trains leaving, try and get on the first one because most of the line is single track and so a broken down train will block the train behind it. Every few weeks, a landslide will close the track for a few days and getting tickets for the next available train isn't easy. In short, it can be an exciting trip.

The scenery en route is quite spectacular. You drop from Ibarra at 2225 metres to San Lorenzo at sea level 293 km away. Thus you see a good cross-section of Ecuador. Most of the drop occurs during the first half of the trip as you descend along the Río Mira valley with good whitewater views on the right of the train. At several stops fruit and other food can be purchased but a water bottle and some emergency food is advised. Once in San Lorenzo you can return the way you came or continue along the north coast by boat – there are no roads.

Bus Buses from Quito leave from several terminals located near the flyover at Avenida Perez Guerrero and Avenida 10 de Agosto at the corner of Parque El Ejido in the new town. Buses leave all day long, once or twice an hour. The trip can take from 2½ to four hours, depending on the company. The fastest is Transportes Andinos at Avenida 18 de Septiembre 801 and Avenida Perez Guerrero, but the buses are small and uncomfortable and you feel like the driver has suicidal tendencies. Other companies within two blocks will take you more slowly and safely. They all charge about US$1. There are also frequent buses from Otavalo and Tulcán.

In Ibarra, the main Terminal Terrestre for buses is about 1½ km south of the town centre. Buses from Quito and Otavalo will drop you here. If you are arriving from Tulcán you could get off before the terminal to save backtracking. There's little in the way of accommodation near the terminal. A taxi to the centre will cost well under a dollar. There are local buses for about 5c which leave from outside the terminal. They all go within a couple of blocks of the railway station where there are plenty of hotels.

From the bus terminal there are frequent departures for Quito, Tulcán (US$1.10, 2½ hours) and Otavalo (20c, 30 minutes). Two or three times a day there are buses direct to several other major towns – these trips usually involve a stop in Quito but save you having to look for another bus terminal in the capital. There are four daily buses to Esmeraldas, for example, if you can't get on the train to San Lorenzo.

Taxi If you are in a real hurry to get back to Quito you could use Taxis Lagos on the Parque La Merced. They charge about US$3 and cram six passengers into a large taxi. The taxis leave five or six times a day for the 2¼ hour ride.

Getting Around
Bus Local buses leave for the main terminal three or four times an hour near the railway station. They run along Calle Guerrero and are usually marked – if in doubt ask the driver. Two companies run this route: 28 de Septiembre and San Miguel de Ibarra. Some of their buses continue to San Antonio de Ibarra. Different buses leave from the same street for several other local destinations. An exception is the bus to La Esperanza, which leaves about once an hour near the east end of Avenida Sánchez y Cifuentes.

Note that Calle Guerrero was being torn up and rebuilt during 1987-88 causing some temporary disruption of local service.

SAN ANTONIO DE IBARRA
This village, which is almost a suburb of Ibarra, is famous for its woodcarving. It has a pleasant main square around which are found a number of stores, poorly disguised as 'workshops'. The most

famous is the *Galería Luís Potosí*, which has some of the best carvings.

Señor Potosí is famous throughout Ecuador and sells his work all over the world. Some of his pieces are really beautiful and sell for hundreds of dollars – the best carvings are to be seen in the upstairs section of his gallery. The atmosphere is totally relaxed; there's no high-pressure salesperson breathing down your neck while you inspect the work.

A warning though – should you decide to purchase a large carving and have it shipped home, it's best to arrange for the shipping yourself. Some friends of mine bought a carving, left a deposit for it to be shipped back, and found out many months later that their carving had been sold to someone else a few days later. They received their deposit back but were very disappointed – their once-in-a-lifetime art investment had been sold to someone who paid cash and carried it out. That's Latin America!

There's little wood found in the Ibarra area so most of it comes from the Ecuadorean jungles. A type of cedar and walnut are among the more frequently used woods. Various subjects are depicted but the favourites seem to be beggars, religious statues and nude women – again, that's Latin America!

Not all the pieces are expensive and you can buy small, mass-produced carvings for a couple of dollars if you like that sort of thing. Some people recommend that the best deals and selections are to be found on the streets away from the main square. Frankly, I couldn't see any difference.

Places to Stay & Eat
The *Hostería Los Nogales* has rooms for US$2.50 per person and they told me that you could get meals in the bar. There was only cold water – and signs of construction. Maybe it'll be fully functional by the time you read this.

There's nowhere else to stay, staying in Ibarra is best, nor are there any proper restaurants in San Antonio de Ibarra.

There is one place, a block off the main plaza, which serves horribly greasy hamburgers and hot dogs.

Getting There & Away
Transportation from Ibarra is frequent during daylight hours. Buses drop you off at the main plaza. The 15-minute ride costs just a few cents. Or you could walk the five km or so south on the Pan American from Ibarra.

LA ESPERANZA
This is a pretty little village some 10 km south of Ibarra and has recently become a popular place to stay for budget travellers looking for peace and quiet. There's nothing to do except talk to the locals and take walks in the surrounding countryside. It's supposed to be a good place to look for the San Pedro cactus.

Places to Stay & Eat
There is only one very basic but friendly hotel which costs US$1 per person – the *Casa Aida*. You can get good, simple and cheap meals here. There is also the small *Restaurant María* which can rent you a basic room.

Getting There & Away
Buses serve the village frequently along a cobbled country road from Ibarra (see city map) and irregularly continue further south through Olmedo to Cayambe.

SAN GABRIEL
This is the next town of any size north of Ibarra on the Pan American highway. It's almost 90 km away from Ibarra but only 38 km from the border town of Tulcán. It's not a particularly interesting place but I mention it here because Tulcán hotels can occasionally be full and this is the nearest place to stay. It's also a good place to go if you want to be the only gringo in town.

As you drive north from Ibarra you soon pass the highly touted tourist site of Lake Yaguarcocha – Quechua for 'lake of blood'. It was so called after a battle between the Incas and the Caras, when the latter's bodies were supposedly thrown into the lake, turning the water red. There's not much to see except for a race track around the lake.

The Pan American drops quite steeply to the Chota River valley at about 1600 metres before beginning the long climb to San Gabriel at almost 2900 metres. En route it crosses the provincial line from Imbabura into Carchi and passes the little village of La Paz. Near La Paz are thermal springs and waterfalls; there are buses to the springs from Tulcán. The road north of Ibarra is steep, winding and rather slow, and the scenery is wild.

At San Gabriel there is a bus stop on the Pan American highway; many buses don't enter the town. Walk up the hill on Calle Montalvo for two blocks, then turn right onto Calle Bolívar, which is the main street. Walk three blocks, passing the church, until you reach the Plaza Central, where there is a startling nude statue of Bolívar, the liberator. (Imagine a nude George Washington in a small US town!)

Places to Stay & Eat
On the plaza is the *Residencial Montufar*, which costs US$1.25 and doesn't have water. Better is the *Residencial Ideal*, which costs only US$1 and has hot water in the mornings. It's on Calle Montufar 8-26, half a block from the plaza. Also on the plaza are two or three simple restaurants, the IETEL office and a movie theatre.

Getting There & Away
The Ciudad de San Gabriel bus company is also on the plaza and has buses to Quito every 45 minutes from 3 am to 6.30 pm. The five-hour ride is about US$1.30. For buses to Tulcán it's best to wait on the Pan American highway.

TULCÁN
This small city of 32,000 inhabitants is the provincial capital of Carchi. As you drive through this, the northernmost province

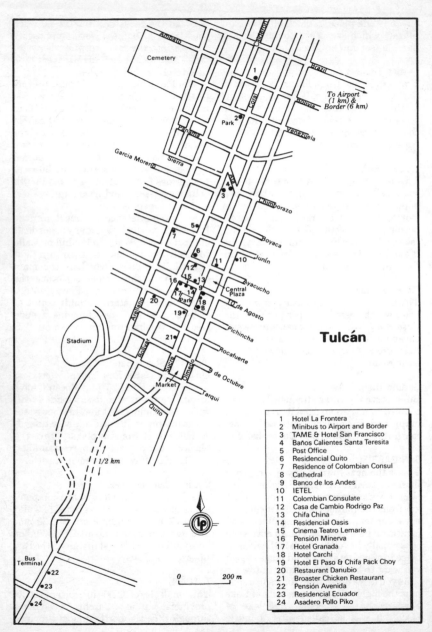

Tulcán

1   Hotel La Frontera
2   Minibus to Airport and Border
3   TAME & Hotel San Francisco
4   Baños Calientes Santa Teresita
5   Post Office
6   Residencial Quito
7   Residence of Colombian Consul
8   Cathedral
9   Banco de los Andes
10 IETEL
11 Colombian Consulate
12 Casa de Cambio Rodrigo Paz
13 Chifa China
14 Residencial Oasis
15 Cinema Teatro Lemarie
16 Pensión Minerva
17 Hotel Granada
18 Hotel Carchi
19 Hotel El Paso & Chifa Pack Choy
20 Restaurant Danubio
21 Broaster Chicken Restaurant
22 Pensión Avenida
23 Residencial Ecuador
24 Asadero Pollo Piko

0   200 m

Top: San Lorenzo Autoferro, Ibarra (RR)
Left: Church door in Otavalo (RR)
Right: Topiary at Tulcán Cemetery (RR)

Top: Town of Baños (TW)
Left: Aerial view of Cotopaxi crater (RR)
Right: Private Chapel at 400-year old Hacienda La Cienga, Central Highlands (RR)

of the Ecuadorean highlands, you see plenty of farms and ranches, particularly as you get close to Tulcán. It is therefore an important market town, but for most travellers its importance is mainly as the gateway city into Ecuador from Colombia, some seven km away.

With the present favourable rate of exchange of the Colombian peso against the Ecuadorean sucre, it has become very popular for Colombian weekend bargain hunters. There is a Sunday street market (no tourist items) and the hotels are often full of Colombian shoppers on Saturday nights.

Tulcán lies about 3000 metres above sea level and hence has a rather cold climate. It is the highest provincial capital or town of its size in the country.

Money

Money exchange is best in Tulcán rather than at the border. The bus running between Tulcán and the border will accept both Colombian and Ecuadorean currency. Banco de los Andes is reputedly the only bank doing foreign exchange, but for some reason they are not always able to do so.

There are several exchange houses which pay about 4% less than you can get in Quito. The best known is Casa de Cambio Rodrigo Paz, which will exchange both pesos and dollars (including travellers' cheques at a 1% discount). There are several others nearby; most give rates within 1% of one another.

There are also street changers with their little black attaché cases full of money. They hang out around the border, the banks and the bus terminal. Because there is no real black market, you won't get much better rates from them than from the exchange houses.

If leaving Ecuador, it is best to try and change sucres to dollars and then dollars to pesos when you get to Colombia. If arriving, cash dollars are your strongest currency.

Things to See

The big tourist attraction in town is the topiary garden in the cemetery. Behind the cemetery the locals play paddle-ball at weekends. It's a strange game played with a small soft ball and large spiked paddles that look like medieval torture implements. I couldn't figure it out. Parque Isidro Ayora has a rather striking white statue of Abdón Calderón riding a horse. There's one movie theatre. If that's not enough to keep you enthralled, you can call home from the IETEL office or send your first/last postcards from Ecuador through the post office. Both are on the map.

Places to Stay

There aren't any fancy hotels in Tulcán. The best is the *Residencial Oasis*, which costs US$2.50, US$5 and US$7.50 for single, double and triple rooms with shared bathrooms. If you want a room with a private bathroom you'll pay about US$1 extra per room. The next best is the *Hotel El Paso*, which has good clean rooms for US$2.50 each (shared baths) or US$3 (private baths). They have hot water and fill up very fast, especially at weekends.

The downtown *Pensión Minerva* is basic, unfriendly, has only cold water and costs US$1.80 per person. Similarly priced, and cold and dingy, is the *Hotel Granada*. *Hotel Carchi* is US$1.60 each and also has only cold water. The nearest hotel to the minibus stop for border buses is the *Hotel La Frontera* but it looks run down and has a 'for sale' sign outside. The *Residencial Quito* charges about US$2 per person and is quite good – hot water is available at times. Similar is the *Hotel San Francisco* which charges US$1.75 per person.

There are two hotels out by the main bus terminal. The *Pensión Avenida* is the cheapest place in town at US$1.20 each. Although it has only cold water, the staff are friendly. The *Residencial Ecuador* has quite nice rooms but a very erratic water supply. It costs US$1.80 and US$3 per person for rooms without and with private baths. There's supposed to be hot water but I once stayed there and they didn't even have cold, so check the bathrooms before accepting the room.

As usual in highland towns, there are public hot showers (*Baños Calientes Santa Teresita*) if you can't face a freezing cold one and the hot water hotels are all full.

Saturday evening is a rotten time to arrive in Tulcán, as many hotels are completely full. The next town is San Gabriel, some 40 minutes away. There are two basic hotels there.

Border There is only one place to stay at the border and it is pricey but good. The *Complejo Turístico Rumicacha* is half a km away from the border and offers a swimming pool (50c for non-residents), restaurant, bar, discotheque and supposedly a casino if you can find someone to open it. Prices are US$10/$14 single/double with private bath.

Llama

Places to Eat

Tulcán is not one of the world's great culinary centres. In the town centre there are the usual *chifas*, of which the *Pack Choy* beneath the Hotel El Paso isn't bad at all. A block away is the *Broaster Chicken Restaurant*, which is new and clean and serves, well, chicken. For more Ecuadorean style food, the *Restaurant Danubio* is OK but has a limited menu. There's a restaurant at the main bus terminal which is not always open and is nothing to write home about when it is, but at least it's cheap. Nearby is a basic chicken restaurant, the *Asadero Pollo Piko*.

Out by the border there are a bunch of stalls selling snacks, but no restaurants. Many restaurants only open for lunch and supper and close in mid-afternoon.

Crossing the Colombian Border

You don't need to obtain an exit or entry stamp in Tulcán. All formalities are taken care of at the Ecuador-Colombia border, 6½ km away at Rumicacha. Fourteen-seater minibuses to the border leave all

day long from Parque Isidro Ayora as soon as they are full. They cost about 20c (Ecuadorean or Colombian currency).

Return buses from the border will charge the same to the town centre but you can usually persuade the driver to charge double and take you to the Tulcán bus terminal some 3½ km away if you are in a hurry to head south. Taxis between Tulcán and the border are about US$1.80.

The border is open daily from 8 am to 5.45 pm. It is closed for lunch from noon to 1 pm. There is a lot of traffic from Colombia, and entrance formalities (into Ecuador) are usually no problem. Almost nobody needs a visa, and tourist cards (which you must keep until you leave) are issued at the border. An exit ticket or sufficient funds are rarely asked for unless you look like a bum. They often won't give you the full 90 days that you are allowed, but don't hassle over it – extensions in Quito are normally fast and straightforward.

If leaving Ecuador, you have to get an exit stamp in your passport and hand in your tourist card. If you've lost it they should give you another one free if your passport is in order but it's best not to lose it. Keep it tucked in your passport. If your documents aren't in order, several things could happen. If you've merely overstayed the time allowed by a few days you can pay a fine which is usually about US$10 - this really is a fine, not a bribe. If you've overstayed by several months you may well have to pay a hefty fine or get sent back to Quito. And if you don't have an entry stamp you also get sent back.

Visas Australians, New Zealanders, US citizens and citizens of some 'socialist' Latin American countries need a visa for Colombia. Most western Europeans don't. Whichever category you fall into, you should check in case regulations change. There is a Colombian Consul in office 204/5, in the Delegación de Tulcán building near the Parque La Independencia. They are open from 8.30 am to 12.30 pm and 2.30 to 4 pm Monday through Friday.

Supposedly the secretary of the Colombian Consul lives at Junín 441 and he may be able to help you out of business hours if you approach him the 'right way'. To get a Colombian visa you officially need a ticket out of Colombia, two photos and sufficient funds (US$10 per day for students, double for others) but this is not always asked for. If you don't need a visa you can get the necessary tourist card at the border.

Getting There & Around

Air San-Saeta used to operate flights but no longer do. TAME has flights to Quito which save you five or six hours on the bus. It operates Monday to Friday but it's best to check at the TAME office for the latest schedules. The flight takes 30 minutes and costs US$8. That's not a misprint – internal flights are inexpensive in Ecuador.

To get to the airport you can take the border-crossing bus, which will leave you there for the same price as going to the border. A taxi will cost about 75c. Or it's a two km walk. If flying into Tulcán, you have to take a taxi or walk because there are no airport buses.

Bus Buses to and from Ibarra (two to three hours, US$1.10) and Quito (five to six hours, US$2.10) leave and arrive from the main Terminal Terrestre. There are frequent departures but there is a better selection of times in the mornings. There are also a few daily departures direct for Santo Domingo or Guayaquil if you enjoy the slow form of torture provided by cramped Ecuadorean buses during journeys taking 10 hours or longer.

The main bus terminal is inconveniently located 3½ km uphill from the town centre. City buses (5c) run along Avenida Bolívar and will deposit you at the terminal. If arriving at Tulcán, you have to cross the street in front of the terminal and take the bus from the other side to get to the town centre.

If you wish to travel west of Tulcán along the border to Tufino and Maldonado, you have to take the Co-operativa Transportes Norte buses. There is a bus to Tufino about every hour until mid-afternoon (one hour, 25c). There is also one daily bus which leaves about 11 am and continues on to Maldonado, some four hours and US$1 away.

There are also weekend excursion buses leaving from a bus stop in front of the cathedral for day trips to nearby thermal springs. The La Paz hot springs, seven km from the village of that name, are visited on a Saturday excursion leaving at 8 am for US$1 round trip. The Aguas Hediondas (literally 'stinking waters') thermal baths, beyond Tufino, are visited on the 8 am Sunday-morning trip and costs 50c.

TUFINO & MALDONADO

These small villages are right on the border to the west of Tulcán and are rarely visited by gringos. A road is planned, which will continue from Maldonado on to the coast at San Lorenzo, but this won't be completed for many years yet. Meanwhile, Maldonado is the end of the road and adventurous travellers may be intrigued to see what's there – it certainly is a remote area.

At Tufino there are several thermal springs, most of them on the Colombian side of the border. It is easy enough to cross over to Colombia on a day pass to soak in the pools, but you are sent back to Tulcán if you want to enter Colombia properly. However, regulations may have changed.

There is a basic restaurant in the village but no hotels. If you ask around, you could probably find someone to rent you a bed or floor space, but it's probably easiest to visit Tufino in the morning and return to Tulcán on an afternoon bus.

The drive beyond Tufino takes you over the Páramos de El Angel, famous for their strange highland vegetation, especially the giant *frailejones*. The dirt road climbs to over 4000 metres before beginning the long descent down the western slopes of the Andes. Maldonado is in the San Juan River valley at just over 2000 metres. The climate is reportedly pleasant and swimming in the river invigorating, although I've never been there. There are a couple of small pensiónes.

South of Quito

A glance at a relief map of Ecuador shows the Pan American highway heading almost due south of Quito along a long valley flanked by two parallel ranges of high mountains. These two ranges consist for the most part of volcanoes, and several of them are still active. It was this feature that prompted the famous German explorer Alexander von Humboldt, who visited the country in 1802, to name Ecuador's central valley 'The Avenue of the Volcanoes'. This name is still used today.

The central valley is only a tiny fraction of Ecuador's land surface, yet it contains almost half of its population. Traditionally Ecuador's Andean Indians farmed the relatively rich volcanic soils found here, and after the conquest the Spanish found that the central valley made a good communication route between north and south. Today the same route is used for the Pan American highway, and a string of towns stretches south from the capital to Ecuador's third largest city, Cuenca, some 300 km away.

In between lies some of Ecuador's wildest scenery, with nine of the country's 10 highest peaks and scores of tiny villages of Andean Indians leading lives little changed in centuries. Many of these villages are so remote that access is only on foot; some are easier to get to and provide a fascinating glimpse of Andean life. The larger towns are well connected with one another by road, and travel is generally easy with superb views.

MACHACHI

This small town of 7000 inhabitants is 35 km away from Quito and the first place you arrive at on the way south from the capital. Its main attraction is the Güitig mineral-water bottling plant which you can visit. There's not much else to do.

There is one basic hotel in the centre, the *Hotel Residencial Mejía*. Some travellers told me it was a quiet place in which to get away from Quito for a while without having to travel far.

LATACUNGA

It's worth coming here just for the drive from Quito, which is magnificent. Cotopaxi is the ice-cream cone-shaped mountain looming to the left of the Pan American highway. At 5897 metres, it is the second highest peak in Ecuador and the highest active volcano in the world. The two Ilinizas, also snow capped, are on your right, and several other peaks are visible during the 90-km drive.

About 50 km south of Quito the highway crosses a pass at over 3500 metres, and soon after there is an entrance road to Cotopaxi National Park. The road drops and crosses the railway at the small village of Lasso and then continues to Latacunga at about 2800 metres above sea level.

Latacunga (population 29,000) is the capital of Cotopaxi province. Although not a particularly exciting town, it has an interesting history and is a good base for several excellent excursions. It was an important centre for the Puruhá Indians who lived here before the Incas.

The town's name originates from the Indian words 'Llacta cunani' which translates rather charmingly into 'land of my choice'. It became an important colonial centre immediately after the conquest but today there is little evidence of this long and varied history.

The reason is Cotopaxi, which dominates the town on a clear day. A major eruption in 1742 destroyed the town and it had to be rebuilt. Another eruption 26 years later wiped it out again but the indomitable (or foolhardy) survivors rebuilt it a second time. An immense eruption in 1877 destroyed it a third time – and yet again it

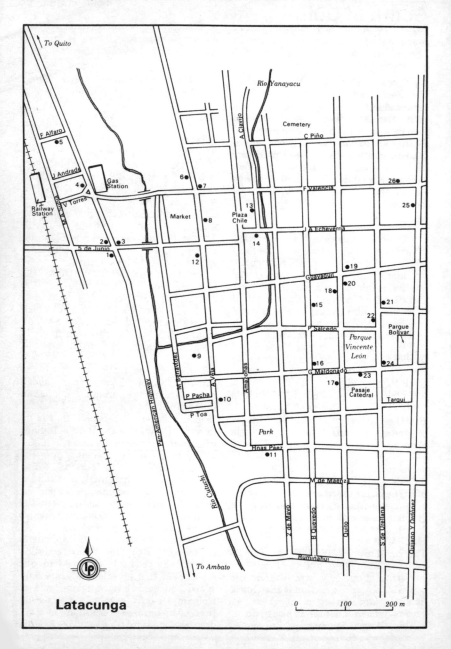

Latacunga

0   100   200 m

was rebuilt on the same site. At present the volcano's activity is minor and it is extremely unlikely that an eruption will occur within the next several years.

Information

The post office and IETEL office are marked on the map. Banks will not change money but *Cambios Salguero* will change cash dollars. It is best to change money in Quito. The town closes down early – most restaurants stop serving by 9 pm.

Things to See

Latacunga is a good centre for several excursions, which will be described at the end of this section. In the town itself, there's little to do. A small ethnography museum, the Molinos de Monserrat, is run by the Casa de Cultura Ecuatoriana and is open from 10 am to 5 pm Tuesday through Saturday.

There are several plazas, of which Parque Vicente León is the most attractive with a well-tended garden. At the southeast corner of this plaza is the town hall topped by a pair of stone condors, and on the south side is the cathedral. Behind the cathedral is a little arcade which includes an art gallery. Many of the buildings are light grey and have been built from the local volcanic rock. There is one tiny theatre which shows bad movies.

Fiestas

Latacunga's major annual fiesta is La Virgen de las Mercedes, held 23-24 September. This is more popularly known as the Fiesta de la Mama Negra, and there are processions, costumes, street dancing, Andean music and fireworks. This is one of those festivals which, although outwardly Christian, has much pagan Indian influence and is worth seeing.

There is also a weekly market on Saturday and a smaller one on Tuesdays. The markets are colourful, but of no special interest.

Places to Stay

There are six hotels open in Latacunga at this time. The newest and most expensive is the *Residencial Los Andes* on the Pan American highway. For US$4 per person you get a clean room with private bathroom and hot water. In the town centre is the rather older *Hotel Cotopaxi* which has rooms with private baths and hot water at US$3.50 each. Some of the rooms have pretty views of Parque Vicente León and are good value.

A good and economical hotel which has clean rooms and hot water in the communal showers is the *Hotel Estambul*, also in the town centre, at US$2 per person. There are three basic hotels at US$1.10 each. The *Hong Kong Internacional* and the *Costa Azul* are both over restaurants of the same name, close to where you get off the bus on the Pan American highway. (The nearby *Hotel Turismo* is closed.) All three are none too clean and the cold showers work only irregularly.

The *Hostal Residencial Jackeline* just across the river is cleaner and friendlier, but the last time I was there the showers didn't work – though the manager will show you a place across the street for a wash.

Some 20 km north of Latacunga is the excellent *Hostería La Cienega*, which is in a 400-year-old hacienda belonging to the Lasso family, whose land once spread from Quito to Ambato. The grounds are beautiful and you can go horse riding. Their main agents in Quito are Metropolitan Touring who will book you rooms for about US$20 a double, or you can try just arriving, although they are often full. The hotel is a km west of the Pan American highway a little south of Lasso; there is a sign.

Many people stay in Latacunga on Wednesday nights for the Thursday morning Indian market at Saquisilí. Hotels are often full by mid afternoon so try and get there early if you're arriving on Wednesday.

Places to Eat

There are no particularly fine or expensive restaurants in Latacunga. The best are restaurants *Candilejas* and *La Carreta* in the town centre. On the ground floor of the Hotel Cotopaxi you'll find *Parrilladas Los Copihues* which has good food but service was unfriendly and slow when I was there. *Pinguino* is good for ice cream and *Restaurant Los Alpes* is open for breakfasts (and all day). *El Mashca* is a chicken restaurant.

There is also a cluster of cheap and simple restaurants which are open all day at the corner of the Pan American highway and Avenida 5 de Junio. Most restaurants close about 9 pm.

The Latacunga area is famous for its *allullas*, sold by local women at every bus stop or checkpoint. The women's high-pitched cries of *aziuuuzia* become quite familiar. Allullas are rather dry biscuits made of flour, pork fat and a local unpasteurized cheese, and I'm afraid they taste no better than they sound.

Getting There & Away

Air There is a Latacunga airport but it is not used for regularly scheduled flights. On rare occasions a plane may be diverted here if it cannot land at Quito. You hear occasional discussion about expanding the airport into an international one for Quito traffic – I can't see it happening this century.

Rail The railway station is on the west side of the Pan American highway and a km from the town centre. At this time there is no Quito-Guayaquil train; the service goes only as far as Riobamba. The autoferro train leaves at 7.30 am for Quito (40c, two hours) and at 5 pm for Riobamba (60c, three hours). The train is very crowded and it's best to book in advance.

Bus There is no main bus terminal. Buses from Quito's Terminal Terrestre will usually drop you on the Pan American highway at the corner with Avenida 5 de Junio before continuing to Ambato. This corner is a good place to stand if you're wanting to catch any north or southbound bus – they pass every few minutes. This may be difficult on holiday weekends, as many buses are full and tend to do the Quito-Ambato-Riobamba run without picking up passengers at Latacunga. Be patient or try to avoid leaving Latacunga on holiday weekends.

Occasionally a bus will leave from Quito's terminal direct for Latacunga. Approximate fares and times: Quito, 80c, two hours; Ambato, 40c, one hour; Riobamba, US$1, 2¼ hours; and Baños, 75c, 1¾ hours.

Just half a block from the Pan American highway on Avenida 5 de Junio is the bus stop for westbound buses. For Pujilí there are buses several times an hour costing 10c. Beyond Pujilí the road deteriorates but continues down through the western slopes of the Andes to Quevedo in the lowlands.

This is the roughest, least-travelled, and perhaps most spectacular bus route joining the highlands with the western lowlands. If you're not pressed for time and don't mind the discomfort, riding a beat-up crowded old bus on this dirt road may be the most interesting way of leaving the highlands.

The bus climbs to Zumbagua at 3500 metres (60c, two hours) and then drops to Quevedo at only 150 metres above sea level. Transportes Cotopaxi run this route in six hours at an average speed of less than 30 km an hour and charge about US$1.60. They have departures every two hours, all day long.

Buses departing for various nearby villages leave from the Plaza Chile (also known as El Salto) near the market. Refer to the city map for locations of each stop. The bus most frequently used by travellers is the Saquisilí bus, which costs 15c for the half-hour ride. Departures are every few minutes on market-day mornings, and every hour or so at other times. Other destinations served by buses from this plaza are Sigchos, Chugchilán and Mulaló – ask around for other villages.

Plaza Chile is also the place to go to hire pickup trucks for visits to Cotopaxi National Park.

COTOPAXI NATIONAL PARK

This is mainland Ecuador's most popular and frequently visited national park. That is not to say it is crowded – indeed, it can be almost deserted midweek. There is a small museum, a domesticated llama

herd, a climbers' refuge and camping and picnicking areas.

The entrance fee to the park is about 20c. Sleeping in the climbers' refuge costs about US$2 – bunk beds and cooking facilities are available, but bring a warm sleeping bag. Climbing beyond the refuge requires experience and snow and ice climbing gear.

Apart from Cotopaxi (5897 metres) there are several other peaks within the park of which Rumiñahui, at 4712 metres, is the most important. The park gives you a good look at the *páramo*, as the typical high-altitude plateaus of Ecuador are called, and there are excellent hiking possibilities. (See my *Climbing & Hiking in Ecuador*, Bradt Publications, 1984.)

Getting There & Away

Pickup trucks from Latacunga will cost about US$20 but you should bargain. Mountaineers wishing to reach the climbers' refuge must clearly specify that they want to go to the parking lot under the *refugio* at the end of the road. Most pickups will make it; a few can't. You can arrange for the pickup to return for you on a particular day – another US$20. It is almost an hour's walk uphill from the parking lot to the refuge. Any car will get you into the park to visit the museum, see the llamas, and picnic by Lake Limpiopungo from where excellent views of the mountain are obtained.

You can walk or hitchhike into the park. There are two entrances on the Pan-American highway about 20 and 25 km north of Latacunga respectively. Ask the bus driver to put you down at either entrance. Both have signs and you follow the main dirt roads (also signed) to the administration building and museum, about 15 km away from either entrance.

The Lake Limpiopungo area for camping and picnicking is about 4 km beyond the museum and the climbers' refuge about a further 12 km. The lake is at 3800 metres and the refuge is a thousand metres higher – it is very hard work walking at this altitude if you are not used to it.

Altitude sickness is a very real danger – acclimatise for several days in Quito before attempting to walk in. At weekends a fair number of local tourists visit the park and there is a very good chance of getting a lift. Mid week the park is almost deserted and you'll probably end up walking.

SAQUISILÍ

For many people, the Thursday morning market of Saquisilí is the main reason for coming to Latacunga. It is definitely not a tourist-oriented market, though there are the usual few Otavalo Indians selling their sweaters and weavings. This market is for the inhabitants of remote Indian villages who flood into town to buy (or sell) everything from bananas to homemade shotguns, and herbal remedies to strings of piglets. The majority of the Indians from the area are recognised by their little felt 'pork pie' hats and red ponchos.

There are eight different plazas, each of which sells specific goods. One of my favourites is the animal market, a cacophonous affair with screaming pigs playing a major role. Cattle, sheep and a few llamas are also seen. Ecuadorean economists consider this to be the most important Indian village market in the country and many travellers rate it as the best they've seen in Ecuador.

The bus from Latacunga drops you off near the Plaza La Concordia, which is recognised by its many trees surrounded by an iron railing. On Thursdays this becomes the plaza selling clothes, hats, hardware and homemade shotguns.

Places to Stay

On the Plaza La Concordia at Bolívar 4-88 and Sucre is the *Pensión La Chabela* (also known as La Chabelita), which provides basic accommodation. There is no sign. A bed can also be found at *Salón Pichincha* a couple of blocks away at Bolívar 2-06 and Pichincha. They are likely to be full

the night before the market and most travellers find it best to stay in Latacunga – the bus service begins at dawn and you don't miss anything.

Places to Eat

There are no restaurants but plenty of places to eat. I enjoyed breakfast in an unnamed place at Sucre 7-66 and Bolívar. Inside there's a large smoky kitchen full of Indians and an Elvis Presley poster on the wall. A huge woman supervises the cooking of breakfast over a charcoal brazier and it's a good opportunity to try dishes such as *llapingachos, fritada, caldo de gallina, tortillas de maíz* and *moté* cooked in traditional style. Makes a change from bacon and eggs!

There are similar places nearby and also plenty of street stands. One plaza seems to be nothing but food stalls – if you stick to cooked food and don't have a delicate stomach you'll enjoy it.

Getting There & Away

There are buses returning to Latacunga several times an hour after the market; there are also trucks and buses going to many of the remote villages in the interior such as Sigchos and Chugchilán.

OTHER VILLAGES

Pujilí has a basic unmarked pensión and a couple of simple restaurants on the main plaza. Market day is Sunday. This is a good town for the All Souls Day festivities of 2 November. Further west is **Zumbagua**, a very small village which has an unspoilt and interesting market on Saturdays. Food is available but accommodation is extremely basic (one pensión, no water) and it is best to stay in Latacunga.

North of Zumbagua is the famous volcanic lake of Quilotoa but transportation is both infrequent and irregular. You could hire a vehicle or walk there in three or four hours, but carry water – the lake is alkaline. North of the lake on a deteriorating road you can reach **Chugchilán**. This is five more hours on foot. The daily bus from Latacunga arrives via a different, more northern road.

At Chugchilán you can sleep in one of the houses on the square. North of Chugchilán is the bigger village of **Sigchos** on a better road and with two or three buses a day to Latacunga. These are all in a very remote area of the Ecuadorean highlands; still more remote communities can be found on foot.

The scenery is quite splendid and the Andean Indian inhabitants somewhat withdrawn and not used to seeing strangers. Travellers wishing to spend any time here should be self-sufficient and have some experience in rough travel in strange areas.

SAN MIGUEL DE SALCEDO

This small town is normally called Salcedo and is the next town south of Latacunga on the Pan American highway. It has a Sunday market. In mid-March they have an important Agricultural and Industrial Fair. Otherwise it's of little interest.

Places to Stay

There are a couple of basic hotels in the town centre. On the northern outskirts of the town is the *Hostería Rumibamba de las Rosas*, a fairly modern hotel with 'log cabin' bungalows which are furnished and decorated with antiques. There is a small private zoo, duck pond, pony rides (and a saddled llama for children!), swimming pool, tennis courts, and games rooms. The whole place has a Disneyland atmosphere – rather corny but clean and well run and the management is very friendly and anxious to please.

There is a good restaurant and bar on the premises and rooms start at about US$15. It is a popular place for Ecuadoreans on family outings.

AMBATO

Forty km south of Latacunga is the important town of Ambato, the capital of Tungurahua province. It was badly damaged in a 1949 earthquake but a modern city was soon rebuilt. It is prosperous and growing; a population of about 101,000 makes it Ecuador's sixth largest city.

Ambato is famous for its flower festival (Fiesta de Frutas y Flores) which is supposed to coincide with Carnaval, but usually is held during the last two weeks in February. Hotels tend to be full at this time so plan ahead. Otherwise, most travellers just pass through Ambato on their way to Baños, which is one of the more popular destinations in the country. It is, however, worth staying here for a night to see the museum, which is little known but interesting.

Information

The DITURIS office may have more tourist information – they are in the process of moving and are temporarily located in the Government Office at Sucre and Castillo. The IETEL and post office are on or near the main plaza, or Parque Juan Montalvo. Banks won't change foreign currency but Cambiato will change both US$ travellers' cheques and cash at rates a little below Quito's.

Things to See

The museum in the Colegio Bolívar on the Parque Cevallos is well worth a visit. Entrance is 25c from 7.30 am to 12.30 pm and 2 to 5 pm, Monday through Friday. It has a variety of exhibits. Primarily there are hundreds of stuffed birds, mammals and reptiles, some of which are quite well done and others rather ratty.

In the absence of comprehensive field guides to Ecuadorean wildlife, this is a good museum to visit if you wish to identify species you may have seen in the wild. (There's also a rather gruesome display of freaks such as two-headed calves and six-legged lambs.)

I particularly enjoyed the fine display of photographs taken around 1910 by the famous Ecuadorean mountaineer Nicolás Martínez. There are period street and

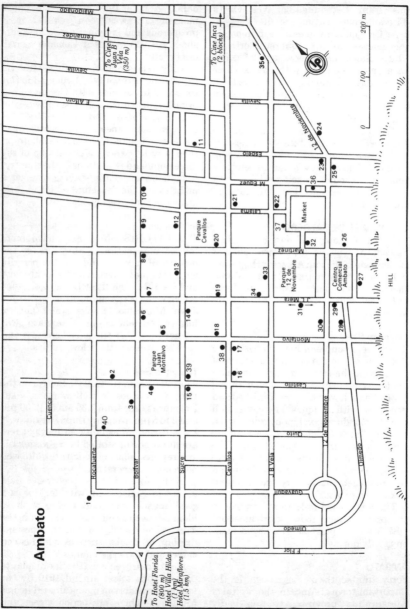

Ambato

countryside scenes, as well as photographs of early mountaineering expeditions and Cotopaxi in eruption. The museum curator, Señor Héctor Vásquez, is also a mountaineer with ascents of the highest peaks of Argentina, Peru and Ecuador to his credit. He is knowledgeable and

1	Hotel Ambato
2	IETEL
3	Teatro Roxi & Parrilladas El Gaucho
4	Post Office
5	Cathedral
6	Cambiato (Money Changer)
7	PasteliQuito
8	Chifa Nueva Hong Kong
9	Teatro Lalama
10	Ecuatoriana Airlines
11	Residencial Europa 2
12	Museum
13	Cine Sucre
14	Restaurant El Alamo
15	DITURIS
16	Chifa Jao Fua
17	El Alamo Junior Caferteria
18	Restaurant El Gran Alamo
19	Hotel Vivero
20	Local Buses
21	Hotel Tungurahua
22	Hotel Nacional
23	Residencial La Unión
24	Hotel Asia
25	Cine Bolívar & Taberna Disco Bar
26	Peña Tungurahua Bar
27	Mama Miche Restaurant
28	Residencial Guayas
29	Residencial Estrella
30	Residenciales Loja & Napo
31	Residenciales Laurita & 9 de Octobre, Hotel Guayaquil
32	Residencial Ambato
33	Residenciales América & Europa
34	Panadería Enripan
35	To Residencial Pichincha (600m), Hotel Cumanda & Chifa Hong Kong (700m), Bus Terminal & Train Station (1200m)
36	Residencial Amazonas
37	Residencial Ambato
38	Hotel La Liria
39	Banco Central
40	Chambord Restaurant

helpful with the exhibits. There are also numismatic, geological, archaeological and other displays.

Because of the recent reconstruction, most of the buildings are new and of no great interest. The main plaza is attractively laid out and dedicated to the famous Ambateño writer Juan Montalvo (1833-1889), of whom there is a statue. On this plaza is the modern and rather bleak cathedral with some good stained-glass windows. The walk to the pleasant modern suburb of Miraflores has been recommended.

The market is held in and around the main market on Mondays, with smaller markets on Wednesdays and Fridays. It is a huge, bustling affair and was once recommended as one of the best in the country. It's still large but modernised and not as interesting as it used to be.

Places to Stay – bottom end
Hotels tend to be full for the flower festival and during Carnaval.

The place for cheap hotels in the city centre is in the Parque 12 de Noviembre area. For about a dollar you can stay in the basic *Residencial América*, which has one of those showers that provides tepid water and electric shocks if you touch any of the pipes, but is probably the best of the super cheapies.

Similarly priced are the *Residencials Europa*, which claim to have hot water but don't. *Hotel Nacional* at US$1.25 has hot water in the mornings – sometimes. None of these places are particularly clean or highly recommended except for the penurious.

For US$1.60 you can stay at the *Hotel Guayaquil* which is reasonably clean and friendly and has hot water, as does the similarly priced *Residencial La Unión*. *Hotel Asia* has hot water only in the mornings and the *Residencial 9 de Octubre* only has cold water although they also charge about US$1.60.

Several other very basic and rather grungy-looking hotels are shown on the map. They include the residencials *Guayas, Estrella, Loja, Napo, Laurita, Ambato, Astoria* and *Amazonas*.

If you'd rather stay near the bus terminal, there is the *Hotel Carrillo* right above the terminal for US$2 each. They have hot showers but it's noisy. Walking right from the terminal along Avenida de las Américas to the traffic circle and left on Avenida 12 de Noviembre brings you to the friendly *Residencial Pichincha* on the right-hand side (five minutes from the terminal). They have clean rooms for US$1.60 single and US$2.80 double but only cold water.

Places to Stay - middle & top end
Just before Residencial Pichincha is the *Hotel Cumandá*, US$4.50 per person in rooms with private baths and hot water. It's the only hotel in this price range near the bus terminal.

If you want some comfort downtown, the most economical is the clean, pleasant and recommended *Hotel Vivero* at US$4/6.50 per person without/with private bath. Also in the city centre is the fancier *Hotel Tungurahua* for US$9.50 a single and US$13.50 a double. Similarly priced and new, clean and good is the *Hotel La Liria*. The fanciest hotel in town is the *Hotel Ambato* which has casino, restaurant and bar, and charges US$13 and US$18 for singles and doubles.

Out on Avenida Miraflores in the suburb of the same name are three quiet and pleasant hotels. All have restaurants and rooms with private baths and are recommended. The closest and cheapest is the *Hotel Florida* with rooms for about US$7 and US$10 a single and double. Further along is the *Hotel Villa Hilda*, which is set in large and beautiful gardens and costs US$12 and US$16 a single and double. Finally we come to the clean and modern *Hotel Miraflores* with double rooms for US$13.

Places to Eat
The best value is the *Chifa Jao Fua* where a good meal can be had for about US$1. Cheaper and almost as good is the *Chifa Nueva Hong Kong*. For breakfast the best bet is one of the cake shops for coffee, juice and rolls or sandwiches. Try the *Panadería Enripan* or the *Pastelería Quito*.

There are three good Swiss-run *El Alamo* restaurants. *Restaurant El Gran Alamo* is quite fancy and comparatively expensive. *Restaurant El Alamo* is lower priced and good, and *El Alamo Junior* is a self-service-style cafeteria. If you're in the mood for steak, try the Argentine style *Parrilladas El Gaucho* which is good and medium priced. The *Chambord Restaurant* which is open from Tuesday to Saturday and for lunch only on Sunday is recommended for its very pleasant atmosphere. *Mama Miche Restaurant* is quite good value considering it's open so late (supposedly 24 hours). You can get super-cheap meals around the market.

If you're staying near the bus station there's a basic restaurant in the terminal and food stalls outside. Also there's the *Chifa Hong Kong* opposite the Hotel Cumandá.

All the best hotels have good restaurants.

Entertainment
There is some nightlife – but not much. The *Peña Tungurahua Bar* has *música folklórica* evenings on Fridays and Saturdays but it doesn't get underway until about 11 pm. No cover is charged. There is a casino at the new *Hotel Ambato*. You can try the *Taberna Disco Bar* in the Cine Bolívar building.

Ambato has six movie theatres, of which one may well be showing a decent film. Consult the map for locations and the local newspaper *El Heraldo* for what's playing.

Getting There & Away
Air There is a small airstrip nearby for emergency and military use only. Ecuatoriana airlines has an office downtown if you need to reconfirm an international flight with them.

Rail The train station is near the main bus terminal, two km away from the town centre. *Autoferros* leave for Quito at 6.30 am (70c, 3½ hours) and at 5.30 pm for Riobamba (30c, 1½ hours). As usual it's crowded and advance ticket purchase is recommended.

Bus The Terminal Terrestre is two km away from the town centre and buses to all destinations leave from here. The most frequent departures are for Quito (US$1.10, three hours), Baños (40c, 45 minutes), Riobamba (60c, one hour), and Guayaquil (US$2.40, six hours). There are also several buses a day to Guaranda (90c, 2½ hours), some of which continue to Babahoyo and a couple to Chillanes. Several companies run a bus to Tena in the Oriente (US$2.25, six hours depending on road conditions).

For northern destinations it's usually best to take a bus to Quito and change. Cuenca buses are erratic; the road is very bad beyond Riobamba and at this time it's best to travel via Guayaquil and change buses. This is also true for most destinations south of Riobamba.

There is frequent talk of resurfacing the highland road to Cuenca and by the time you read this there may be better bus services to the south. Check at the terminal for the most up-to-date information; there is an information office.

Getting Around
Bus The most important local bus service for the traveller is the route from the town centre to the terminal. Buses marked 'Terminal' leave from the Calle Martínez side of Parque Cevallos – many buses leave from this park so if in doubt, ask. From the terminal, climb the exit ramp to the Avenida de las Americas, which crosses the railway line on a bridge. On this bridge is a bus stop where a westbound (to your right) bus, often signed 'Centro', will take you to the Parque Cevallos for 5c. A block away from this park is Calle Bolívar, with buses to Miraflores running along it.

Taxi Taxis to the centre will cost about 50c and to Miraflores about US$1.

SALASACA
As you head south-east from Ambato on the Baños road, the first place of interest is Salasaca about 14 km away. The village and its environs are inhabited by some 2000 Salasaca Indians who are famous for their tapestries. They are less well known for their history, which is particularly interesting. Originally they came from Bolivia but were conquered by the Incas in the 1400s.

One of the ways in which the Incas controlled the peoples they had conquered was to move them en masse to an area which the Incas had long dominated and where there was less chance of an uprising. This is what happened to the Salasacas. After the Spanish conquest, they remained where they were but retained an unusually high degree of independence and were almost unknown by outsiders until about 40 years ago.

The villagers are recognised by their typical dress, especially the men who are normally seen wearing broad-brimmed white hats, black ponchos, and white shirts and trousers. Traditionally they are farmers and raise their own sheep to obtain wool for their weavings which are a secondary source of income. Their tapestries are all made by hand and are different from work done by other Indian groups (though telling the difference is difficult unless you know something about weaving).

There is no local produce market in Salasaca; the villagers use the nearby Pelileo Saturday market or go to Ambato. There is a small crafts market held every Sunday morning around the village store which is by the church on the Ambato-Banos road. You can buy their tapestries here and in craft stores in Quito and Cuenca. They make and sell tapestries

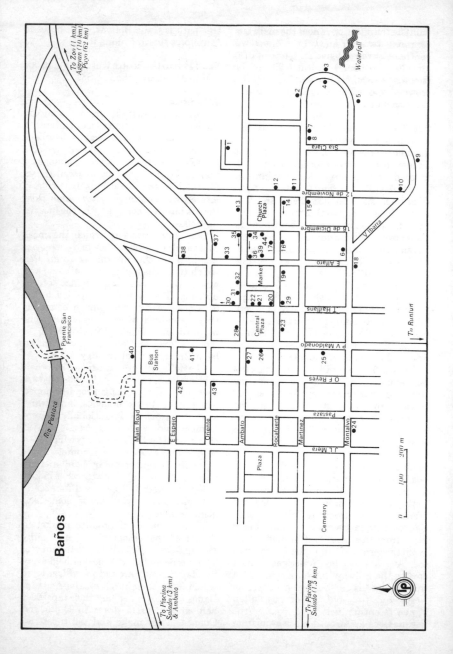

Baños

almost exclusively. There are no restaurants or hotels – stay in Ambato or Baños.

There are many Indian fiestas in the Salasaca area which are worth looking out for. May and June are good months for fiestas all over the highlands. On the Sunday after Easter there is a street dance between Salasaca and Pelileo. On 15 June the Salasacas dress up in animal costumes for Santo Vintio. Corpus Cristi (movable date in June) is celebrated in Salasaca and Pelileo. Saint Anthony is celebrated at the end of November. All the usual dates (Christmas, Easter, etc) also offer interesting fiesta possibilities.

PELILEO

Some six km beyond Salasaca on the Baños road is the rather bigger village of Pelileo. Despite its 400-year history, today's Pelileo is a very modern village. It was founded by the colonialist Antonio Clavijo in 1570 but destroyed by earthquakes in 1698, 1797, 1840 and 1949. The present site is about two km away from the ruins of the old town. It is the market town for nearby villages including Salasaca. Saturday is market day.

Baños is only 24 km away but the road drops some 850 metres from Pelileo. The descent along the Pastaza River gorge is spectacular and some of the best views of the snow-capped volcano Tungurahua are to be seen on this drive. At 5016 metres, it is Ecuador's 10th highest peak and gives its name to the province.

BAÑOS

The most recent census places the population of this small town at only some 11,000 people, yet there are almost 50 hotels in Baños and its outskirts. It is one of the most important tourist spots in the country, popular with Ecuadoreans and foreigners alike. Surprisingly, it is very pleasant and unspoilt and its popularity

1	La Burbuja Disco	25	Residencial Timara
2	New Swimmimg Pool & Baths	26	Residencial La Delicia 2
3	Piscina de la Virgen (Hot Baths)	27	Residencial Viena
4	Hotel Sangay	28	Residencial La Delicia 1 &
5	Hotel Palace		Bus Stop for El Salado
6	Rique's Cafe Alemán	29	Hostal Los Helechos &
7	Restaurant El Paisano		Restaurant Vegeteriano y Carnes
8	Hostal El Castillo	30	Pensión Jota & Residencial Dumay
9	Santa Clara Swimming Pool	31	Hotel Humboldt/Paraiso
10	Residencial Villa Santa Clara	32	Chifa Central
11	Hotel Americano	33	Pensión Patty
12	Residencial Santa Teresita	34	Pensións Luisita, San Martín,
13	Santuario & Museum		Ecuador & Residencial Cordillera
14	Hotel Guayaquil, Hostal Agoyan,	35	Residenciales Irmita & Guadalupe,
	Residencial Acapulco		Hostals Guayas & Bolívar,
15	Banco Pacifico		Residencial Baños
16	Residencial Anita	36	Bus Stop to Zoo and Agoyan
17	Residenciales Mercedes & Lucy	37	Residenciales Cecilia & Magdalena
	& Rincon de Suecia Pizzeria	38	Restaurant Monica
18	Villa Gertrudis	39	Chifa Oriental
19	Hotel Danubio	40	Sugar Cane Stalls
20	Town Hall & Clock Tower	41	Fluvial Tours Gift Shop
21	IETEL	42	Residencial Julia
22	Post Office	43	Residencial El Rey
23	Residenciales Olguita & Los Piños	44	Hotel Achupalla
24	Hospital		

remains undiminished despite the many thousands of visitors annually.

Unless you've only just arrived in Latin America, you'll know that Baños means 'baths' and that is precisely what the town is famous for. Some of them are fed by thermal springs from the base of the active volcano Tungurahua, which means 'little hell' in Quechua. Other baths have melt water running into them from Tungurahua's icy flanks. Locals swear that the baths are great for your health. While that is a debatable point, it is true that the casual atmosphere of this pretty resort town makes it an excellent place to unwind after some hard travelling, and few travellers can resist the opportunity to relax here for a few days.

The baths are not the only attraction. Baños' elevation of 1800 metres gives it an extremely agreeable climate and the surroundings are green and attractive. There are good opportunities for both short walks and ambitious climbs of Tungurahua, and El Altar an even higher extinct volcano some 25 km south of Tungurahua.

Baños is also the gateway town into the jungle via Puyo and Misahuallí. East of Baños the road drops spectacularly and there are exceptional views of the upper Amazonian basin stretching away before you. In the town itself there are more attractions; an interesting Basilica, a small museum, a zoo, and restaurants selling typical local food.

Baños became the seat of its *cantón* on 16 December 1936, and an annual fiesta is celebrated on this and the preceding day. There are the usual processions, fireworks, music and a great deal of street dancing.

Information

Both IETEL and the post office are on the central plaza. The IETEL sometimes has problems in making connections 'because of the surrounding mountains' and may close early because of this. The Post Office is open only from Tuesday to Saturday.

The *Banco Pacifico* (see map) changes both US$ cash and travellers' cheques at rates only a little lower than Quito's. The streets have numbers as well as names.

Things to See

In the town itself the Santuario de Nuestra Señora de Agua Santa is worth seeing. This Dominican church is dedicated to the Virgin of the Holy Water, who is credited with the performance of several miracles in the Baños area. There is an annual celebration in her honour during October with much street music and many Indian bands playing, but generally she is the object of devout admiration, as exemplified by the many offerings to her and the paintings depicting her miracles.

These paintings are simple but charming, with explanations in Spanish along the lines of 'On January 30th, 1904, Sr X fell off his horse as he was crossing the Río Pastaza bridge. As he fell 70 metres to the torrents below he yelled 'Holy Mother of the Holy Water' and was miraculously saved!' Other paintings show people being miraculously saved from exploding volcanoes, burning hotels, transit accidents and other misfortunes. Reading the explanations is amusing and a great way to practise your Spanish. Please remember however, that this is a place of worship and act accordingly.

Just above the church is a museum with an eclectic display of stuffed animals, religious paintings, church vestments and local handicrafts. It's open daily from 7.30 am to 4 pm and costs 10c. There is also a small gift shop.

Things to Do

First of all, relax. This is a laid-back town and most people take it slowly. You're on vacation in Baños.

Baths There are four baths, three in Baños and a fourth out of town. All the baths have a modest entrance fee for which they provide changing rooms and a safe storage system for your clothes. Towels and

View of Baños

bathing costumes can be rented and soap is for sale. (Nude bathing is prohibited.)

The best-known bath is the Piscina de La Virgen, with hot showers and several pools of different temperatures. They charge 15c, are open before dawn and can be quite busy as early as 7 am. You can't miss them – they're right under the big waterfall at the south-east end of town. You can see it from most parts of Baños.

Next door is another bath which has bigger swimming pools (one cold and one hot) but no hot showers. There is a pleasant garden and they charge 25c. There is also a cold swimming pool at Santa Clara. Most of the better hotels have swimming pools.

If you walk up the hill past the cemetery on Carretera Martínez, you'll end up on a track which crosses a stream (Quebrada de Naguasco) on a small wooden footbridge. The track continues on the other side to a road in front of Cabañas Bascun, where you turn left to reach the Piscina El Salado. Here there are hot and cold showers, several pools of varying temperatures and an ice-cold waterfall to stand under if you're the masochistic sort. A real deal for 20c. Because these are two or three km of out of town, they're not quite so crowded. There are buses too.

Walks Once you've visited all the pools, there are many walks to take. Following are some suggestions.

The walk down to the Río Pastaza is easy and popular. Just behind the sugar cane stalls by the bus station is a short trail which leads to the Puente San Francisco. You can continue up the other side as far as you want.

Going south on Calle Maldonado takes you to a footpath which climbs to a building with a white cross high over Baños, and then continues to the tiny settlement of Runtun some two hours away. Great views!

You can walk out of town east on the main road to get to the zoo a couple of km away. There is a bus as well. The zoo, although small, houses an interesting collection of Ecuadorean species, including tapir and the rare harpy eagle.

Continue a further six or seven km beyond the zoo to the famous Agoyan Falls, now being turned into a major hydroelectric project. Buses go here.

Or continue down to the river just beyond the zoo, cross it on the suspension bridge and follow the trail back round to Baños, crossing the Puente San Francisco. It takes an hour or two.

At the police checkpoint at the west end of town, turn right and visit the Cascada Ines María a km away.

Tungurahua From the check point mentioned above, find a trail climbing to your left and follow it to the village of Pondoa (two hours), the climbers' refuge (six more hours), and the summit of Tungurahua (for experienced climbers with equipment). There is a new dirt road that now goes from Baños to Pondoa and then on to a point about half way to the refuge (the road does not, for the most part, follow the trail).

A taxi can be hired from Baños for about US$6 and a pickup truck can be arranged from the Pensión Patty about four mornings a week. This costs US$1 per person. The Pensión Patty has climbing information and can provide guides and rent equipment. The refuge is very basic – a roof over your head.

For more information on these and other hikes and climbs read my *Climbing & Hiking in Ecuador*, Bradt Publications.

Jungle Tours Because of the proximity of Misahuallí, some information about jungle tours and accommodation can be obtained in Baños. Ask at the *Restaurant El Paisano*, *Residencial Timara* or the *Fluvial Tours Gift Shop*.

Horseback Riding Another possible activity is riding horses. Several hotels have information about renting by the hour or day.

Places to Stay – bottom end

There are literally dozens of hotels to choose from and obviously I couldn't spend a night in each! Therefore many of these descriptions are necessarily brief. Some of the cheap hotels try and charge more than they are worth – check your rooms before accepting them. Others charge double rates for one night but will drop their prices if you spend more than one night. Usually there are plenty of rooms available but choice can become very limited if you arrive on a Friday night or if there is a fiesta underway. Try and arrive early in the day for best rooms.

For rock-bottom costs there are the extremely basic pensión *Jota* and *Residencial Dumay*, both one block from the central plaza on Haiflans; they have little to recommend them. On one block of Ambato near the church plaza are more equally basic hotels – *Pensións Luisita, San Martín, Ecuador, Residenciales Irmita, Baños* and *Hostal Guayas*, none of them very good and mostly charging under US$1 per person. Mixed in with them are the better and cleaner *Hostal Cordillera, Residencial Bolívar* and *Residencial Guadalupe* at US$1.50 per person.

Better cheap hotels are the clean *Hotel Americano* (US$1 each) with spacious rooms and a restaurant, and the *La Delicia 1*, same price, smaller rooms but clean and friendly. La Delicia has only one hot shower for 22 rooms. Its front rooms (Nos 1 and 2, 18 and 19) face the plaza with great views.

There is also the *Residencial Santa Teresita*, which is clean and has hot showers sometimes. The *Residencial Timara* is also about US$1 per person and has hot water and jungle information. They also have a gift store selling balsa birds and other jungle products and advertise guided trips from Misahuallí.

For many years *Pensión Patty* has been very popular with gringos, with basic but clean rooms, friendly management and information on trekking, climbing and horse riding in the area. Rooms are US$1.50 the first night and US$1 for subsequent nights. The pensión has one hot and several cold showers, and a communal kitchen if you want to cook your own food. (You sometimes meet a great group of people – everyone chips in with something to eat or drink, conversations flow, a rum bottle gets opened or a guitar appears.)

Also good is the *Residencial Villa Santa Clara* which offers facilities similar to those at the *Patty* and is set in a garden. On the central plaza the *Residencial Olguita* is also recommended, especially the front rooms with good views. They have hot showers. The new *Residencial La Delicia 2* (not run by the same people as No 1) is also good for a dollar, though they charge US$2 for the first night.

A little more expensive at US$1.50 per person are the following: the *Hostal Agoyan* with only cold water but clean rooms; the *Hostal Residencial Lucy*, also clean and with hot water; the old and run down *Hotel Danubio* with hot showers, large rooms and a cheap restaurant; and the *Residencial Anita*, with spotless rooms and comfortable beds. The *Anita* also has rooms with private bathroom for US$2 per person.

The friendly and pleasant *Hostal El Castillo* provides home cooking in their dining room and it costs US$1.50 per person in rooms with private shower or US$3.50 with meals. For US$2 the *Hotel Guayaquil* has a restaurant and hot showers. Also for US$2 each you can get clean rooms with private bathrooms and hot water at the *Hotel Humboldt/Paraiso* (depending on which sign you read). The mattresses in some rooms look rather lumpy though, so check them first.

There are several more places shown on the map which charge from US$1 to US$2 and are unremarkable.

Places to Stay - middle
There are few mid-priced hotels in Baños. Prices tend to jump from US$2 to US$10.

One new exception is the *Hostal Los Helechos* which has clean carpeted rooms with private showers for US$2 per person – some rooms have balconies. For US$3.50 per person is the new *Hotel Achupalla* which also has private baths in the rooms.

Places to Stay - top end
The *Hotel Palace* is clean and pleasant with a good restaurant attached. Rooms with private baths are US$10 a single, US$13 a double and US$17.50 a triple – suitable for families. The *Hotel Sangay* is considered by many to be the best place in town and is good value. There are squash courts, a swimming pool, restaurant and bar, and prices are about the same as the *Palace* in the main building, or a few dollars more in the bungalows. The most expensive in town is the good *Villa Gertrudis*, which charges US$18 per person including meals.

Houses for Rent
Ask at the *El Paisano* restaurant for simple houses to rent by the week or month.

Places to Stay - El Salado Baths
About two km from town by footpath or four km by road is the *Piscina El Salado*, with three nearby hotels. There are two basic US$1 residencials right by the baths – *El Salado* and the *Puerto del Salado* with good views of Tungurahua. About 10 minutes before getting to the baths are the *Cabañas Bascun* for US$7 per person in bungalows with private baths, restaurant, pool and sauna (US$2 extra).

Places to Eat
If you're staying at the more expensive hotels you may as well eat there, as there are no better restaurants in Baños. The most popular restaurant in town (at least for travellers) is the *Rincón de Suecia* which bills itself as a 'pizzería' but in fact sells more than just Italian food. The meals are good and reasonably priced.

Recently opened is *Rique's Cafe*

Alemán which serves German style potato pancakes and exciting ice-cream shakes. They have a real coffee machine.

Another good restaurant is the simpler and cheaper *El Paisano*, which has some vegetarian dishes. It's friendly and run by the children of the woman who runs the *El Paisano* in Misahuallí. Several travellers recommend the *Restaurant Vegetariano y Carnes* in the *Hostal Los Helechos* for friendly service and inexpensive food.

The *Chifa Oriental* and *Chifa Central* by the market are also good – I preferred the *Oriental*. There are many other cheap restaurants on Ambato and around the market. The *Pan de Casa* bakery next to the market is the first place to have fresh bread in the mornings.

On certain days you can buy *cuy* at some of the market restaurants. *Cuy* is guinea pig which is a traditional food dating to pre-conquest times. They are normally roasted whole and some people find the sight of their little roasted feet sticking up and their tiny teeth poking out a bit disconcerting. Don't say I didn't warn you! Surprisingly, they taste quite good, a little like a cross between a chicken and a rabbit. In fact the local nickname for them in some areas is *conejo*, which means rabbit.

Another local food popular in Baños is toffee. You can see people swinging it onto wooden pegs in the doorways of many of the town's shops – the idea is to blend and soften the toffee. You can try a piece for a couple of cents.

I am no longer able to recommend *Restaurant Monica*, for many years a favourite gringo hangout with menus in 12 languages hanging on the wall. It's still multilingual but the items on the menu are rarely available. A sign on the wall says 'All items home cooked – Please be patient'. This seems to act as an excuse for incredibly poor service – slow and inefficient. Recently the restaurant seems to be used by local workers who come in for a set meal; meeting them may be the best reason to go there.

Entertainment

Nightlife in Baños consists mainly of chatting with new friends in the restaurants after a strenuous day of soaking in the pools. Generally the town closes down early – most restaurants close by 9 pm. The cinema on the central plaza is closed. *La Burbuja* disco is open nights from Tuesday to Saturday but there's rarely much happening except perhaps weekends after 10 pm. (Bring all your friends and make it happen!) There's no cover but they get you for a minimum consumption of about US$1.50.

Getting There & Away

Buses from Ambato's Terminal Terrestre leave about every half hour for Baños. The fare is 40c and the ride is 45 minutes. From Quito and many other towns its sometimes quicker to catch a bus to Ambato and change rather than wait for the less frequent direct buses.

The Baños Terminal Terrestre is within walking distance of most hotels – it's a small town. Buses for Quito (US$1.40, 3½ hours) leave almost every hour or you can take more frequent buses to Ambato and change for other destinations. There are frequent departures for Riobamba (50c, one hour) but most of these buses go to Riobamba's Oriente bus terminal which is several km away from the main bus terminal (if you need to make a connection).

Buses for the Oriente (Puyo or Tena) may be delayed by the road improvement project which has been ongoing for several years. Therefore it is recommended that you buy tickets for the first bus leaving Baños. Find out if the bus is leaving from Baños because buses from Ambato or Quito heading for the Oriente pass by the Baños terminal and are often full.

Ticket offices in Baños will sell you tickets for these buses but usually won't guarantee you a seat nor give you a refund if the bus is full. You can, however, buy a ticket from the driver, so it's best to wait for a bus to pass by and then board if there's room. It's best to buy tickets for buses starting at Baños.

At one time, because of the rebuilding of the Baños to Tena road, you had to take a bus to the construction area, drag your luggage across a km or more of churned-up mud, then catch another bus beyond the construction area. Recently buses have been getting straight through, but don't be too surprised if the *trasbordo* (as the mud-slogging system is euphemistically called) goes into effect again. Assuming no problems with road construction, the ride to Puyo costs US$1 and takes two hours. To Tena costs US$2 and takes five hours.

Getting Around

Buses run along the main street named Ambato. Eastbound buses for the zoo and Agoyan Falls are marked 'Agoyan' and leave every few minutes during daylight hours from the corner of Ambato and Alfaro. Westbound buses leave from the central plaza outside Residencial La Delicia 1. They are marked 'Al Salado' and go to the baths of that name. Fares are about 5c. A taxi to these baths costs about 40c.

GUARANDA

Guaranda is a small town (population 14,000) but nevertheless is the capital of the agricultural province of Bolívar. Its name derives from that of the Indian chief Guarango. Guaranda is a quiet, provincial town which has been described as 'dismal'. I found it dignified rather than dismal, and it is pleasantly located with pretty hills all around. It certainly can't be described as exciting and the main reason you'd want to be here is probably for the bus rides, which are spectacular.

The road from Ambato, which was officially inaugurated in November 1980, is paved and comfortable. The 85 km drive climbs from Ambato at 2550 metres to bleak *páramo* at over 4000 metres before dropping to Guaranda at 2650 metres, making this the highest paved road in the country. It passes within 10 km of Chimborazo (6310 metres) and Carihuairazo (5020 metres), the highest and ninth highest peaks in Ecuador.

For the best views of these giants you should get seats on the left of the bus (if going to Guaranda). In addition to the mountains, you get a good look at the harsh and inhospitable Andean moorlands known as the *páramo*. The bus ride can get cold so remember to carry some warm clothes onto the bus with you.

When you leave Guaranda there are other equally exciting rides. You can continue on down the western slopes of the Andes to Babahoyo and the coast – a route which was once the most important connection between Quito and Guayaquil but which is now infrequently used. Or you can head due east to Riobamba on a dizzying dirt road which skirts the southern flanks of Chimborazo and gives fantastic views that are not for the faint-hearted (sit on the left side of the bus).

Information

Dollars can be changed at the Banco de Pichincha at 5% less than the Quito rate. The bank is open from 9 am to 1.30 pm daily except Sunday. Guaranda has an IETEL and post office.

Things to Do

There is one movie theatre, which doesn't have shows every day. Off the map in the south end of town (*abajo* or lower end) you'll find the *Disco La Chosa* with a bar, restaurant, and music. Admission is 75c and it's frequented by Peace Corps Volunteers on their time off.

Main market days are Saturday and Sunday, with a smaller one on Wednesday. The best place for the market is Plaza 15 de Mayo – even on ordinary days it's worth visiting for its pleasantly quiet, forgotten colonial air (if you ignore the school on one side). The market at Mercado 10 de Noviembre is held in a modern but ugly concrete building.

If you've got nothing to do, go down to

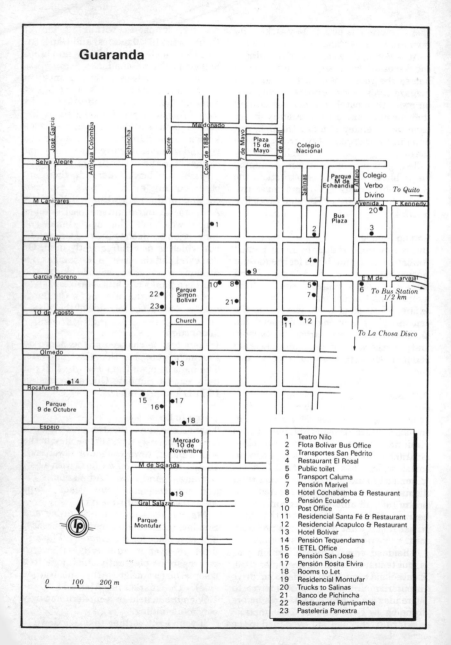

Guaranda

1 Teatro Nilo
2 Flota Bolívar Bus Office
3 Transportes San Pedrito
4 Restaurant El Rosal
5 Public toilet
6 Transport Caluma
7 Pensión Marivel
8 Hotel Cochabamba & Restaurant
9 Pensión Ecuador
10 Post Office
11 Residencial Santa Fé & Restaurant
12 Residencial Acapulco & Restaurant
13 Hotel Bolívar
14 Pensión Tequendama
15 IETEL Office
16 Pensión San José
17 Pensión Rosita Elvira
18 Rooms to Let
19 Residencial Montufar
20 Trucks to Salinas
21 Banco de Pichincha
22 Restaurante Rumipamba
23 Pastelería Panextra

the Parque Montufar and see if one of the statues there still has a bees' nest under its right armpit! Walk the streets for a few hours; you'll end up in the last century.

About three km out of town is a monument called *El Indio de Guaranda* from where you get a good view of Guaranda, Chimborazo and the surrounding countryside. A taxi will take you for US$1.50

Places to Stay

You can probably afford to stay in the best place in town, which is the clean and new *Hotel Cochabamba*. It's good value for US$4.50 a single with private bath or US$3.50 with clean communal showers and hot water. It has a good restaurant downstairs. A bit more run down but still reasonable is the *Hotel Bolívar*, which charges US$3.50/3 per person with/without private bath. It has hot water.

The rest of the hotels in town are mainly cold-water cheapies. *Pensión Tequendama* is US$1.50 per person and has a garage in case you happened to bring your own car. For a dollar each you can stay at the *Pensión Ecuador* which is run by a friendly old woman, or at the *Pensión San José*, also friendly. Both have only cold water.

Residencial Acapulco has a restaurant attached and charges US$1 per person (cold water) and has a few rooms for US$1.50 each with a hot water bathroom next door. The *Residencial Santa Fé* has a rather odd arrangement of rooms with communal hot showers for US$1.50 per person and rooms with private cold shower for US$2 per person. Other places priced at US$1 to US$2 are shown on the map.

Outside of town is the *Hotel Matiavi* at the bus terminal. It advertises rooms with private baths and hot water but was temporarily closed last time I was in Guaranda. A 15-minute walk out of town on the Quito road is a 'tourist complex' called *Hotel La Colina* which is often empty. Located on a hill, it has some

rooms with good views, a restaurant, bar and small swimming pool. They charge US$8 and US$12 single and double with private bath and hot water.

Places to Eat

There are few restaurants and they close early – many by 7.30 pm. The best in town is the reasonably priced *Restaurant Cochabamba* under the hotel of that name, but they don't always have everything on the rather impressive-looking menu.

Cheaper are *Restaurant Acapulco* and *Restaurant Santa Fé* both on the same block and found under the Residenciales of the same name. The *Acapulco* serves a good cheap *chaulafan* (a rice dish).

On Parque Bolívar you'll find the reasonably priced *Restaurante Rumipamba* which the local gringos (mainly Peace Corps Volunteers) term 'the chicken place' because of all the freshly killed chickens hanging in the refrigerator as you enter.

On the same block is the *Pastelería Panextra* which has good pastries. *Restaurant El Rosal* in the bus plaza is OK, and there's a basic place to eat at the main bus terminal.

Getting There & Away

Bus Most buses now leave from the new bus terminal a km out of town. Just head east on García Moreno – you can't miss it. A few buses still leave from the bus plaza in town (locally known as Plaza Roja) and there are several bus company offices there. As a general rule, the old country buses are likely to leave from the plaza, and the main buses for Riobamba, Ambato and Babahoyo will probably leave from the new terminal. Bus departures are from 4 am to 5 pm and no later. Afternoon buses can get booked up in advance so plan ahead.

The most frequent departures are for Ambato (90c, 2½ hours) and Quito (US$1.70, five hours), with buses for these destinations leaving about once an hour with various companies. Almost as frequently there are buses for Babahoyo (US$1.40, four hours) and Guayaquil (US$1.80, five hours). There are about six daily buses to Riobamba (70c, 2½ hours).

There are also several buses a day to Chillanes, a small town at the end of the road some three hours south of Guaranda. I've never been there nor met anyone who has, but I'm told there's a basic pensión. It certainly would be getting off the beaten track if that's what you want. Chillanes is a coffee and *aguardiente* (sugar cane alcohol) producing area. En route to both Babahoyo and Chillanes, you pass through the old town of San Miguel, which still has wooden colonial buildings with carved balconies.

SALINAS

About 35 km north of Guaranda in wild and beautiful countryside is the peaceful community of Salinas. It is known for its excellent cheeses, homemade salamis and roughspun sweaters and you can visit the small 'factories' which produce them. The people are very friendly and not much used to seeing travellers. It's an interesting destination for people who enjoy off the beaten track travel and seeing how people live in a remote rural Ecuadorean community. Definitely very 'tranquilo'.

Information

There is a small store on the plaza which sells the naturally dyed roughspun sweaters for about US$6 to US$7. Prices are fixed and other woollen goods are available. There is also a small restaurant and you can buy cheese in 31 kilo balls! There is no telephone service and little electricity in town.

There are no hotels but you can usually stay in the *Centro de Madres* where there are a few bunks – bring a sleeping bag. Señora Janeth Samariego has the key – everyone knows her. The local priest, Padre Antonio, is very friendly, knows the area, and likes to chat with foreigners.

Getting There & Away

Trucks from near the bus plaza in Guaranda leave on Wednesday, Friday, Saturday and Sunday (to coincide with Guaranda's markets). The fare is 50c. Otherwise take a bus about 10 km north on the Guaranda-Ambato road and get off at Cuatro Esquinas. From here it is about 25 km and you can hitchhike (though expect to pay for the ride). In Salinas, hang out in the main plaza and flag down any vehicle. Most vehicles leaving town are going to Guaranda.

RIOBAMBA

'All roads lead to Riobamba' proclaims a road sign as you enter this city, and it is indeed true that Riobamba is at the heart of an extensive and scenic road network. Whichever way you arrive or leave, you should try and plan your journey for daylight hours so as not to miss the great views.

The usual way to arrive is on the Pan American highway from Ambato, which is 65 km to the north. The road climbs over a 3600-metre-high pass which gives good views of Ecuador's highest peak Chimborazo (6310 metres) as well as Carihuairazo (5020 metres) before dropping to Riobamba at 2750 metres.

Another equally spectacular route is the dirt road arriving from Guaranda. There is also a lower road from Baños which follows the Chambo River valley and passes through numerous small villages. One of these, Penipe, is the entrance to the dirt road climbing towards the rugged peak of El Altar (at 5319 metres it is Ecuador's fifth highest peak). Looking back along this road will also give you views of Tungurahua.

The city itself is fairly important, and with a population of some 73,000 is the capital of Chimborazo province. The area was inhabited long before the Spanish conquest. It was a Puruhá Indian centre before becoming part of the Inca Empire during the late 15th century.

The first Spanish colonialists built a

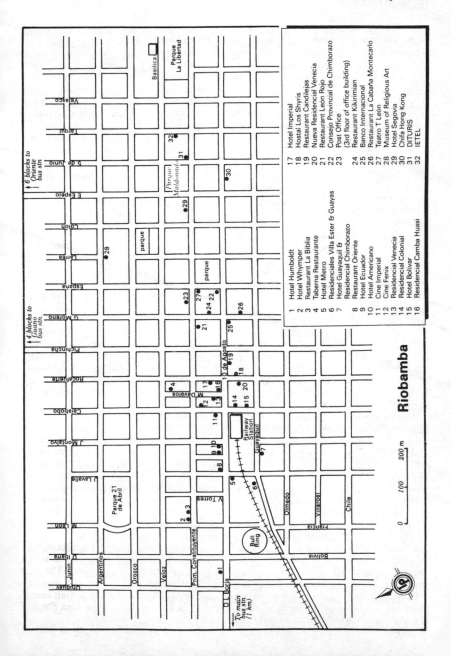

Riobamba

1 Hotel Humboldt
2 Hotel Whymper
3 Restaurant La Biblia
4 Taberna Restaurante
5 Hotel Metro
6 Residenciales Villa Ester & Guayas
7 Hotel Guayaquil &
   Residencial Chimborazo
8 Restaurant Oriente
9 Hotel Ecuador
10 Hotel Americano
11 Cine Imperial
12 Cine Fenix
13 Residencial Venecia
14 Residencial Colonial
15 Hotel Bolivar
16 Residencial Camba Huasi

17 Hotel Imperial
18 Hostal Los Shyris
19 Restaurant Candilejas
20 Nueva Residencial Venecia
21 Restaurant León Rojo
22 Post Office
23 Consejo Provincial de Chimborazo
   (3rd floor of office building)
24 Restaurant Kikirimian
25 Banco Internacional
26 Restaurant La Cabaña Montecarlo
27 Teatro T Leon
28 Museum of Religious Art
29 Hotel Segovia
30 Chifa Hong Kong
31 DITURIS
32 IETEL

city near present-day Cajabamba. This was destroyed in a 1797 earthquake and the survivors moved to the present site on a large plain surrounded by several snow-capped peaks. The flat terrain of Riobamba enabled it to be built in a regular chessboard pattern with wide avenues and imposing stone buildings. It has rather a sedate air and Ecuadoreans call it the 'Sultan of the Andes'.

Information

There is an IETEL office downtown and also at the bus terminal. The post office can be difficult to find as the sign is tiny and the office is on the third floor of an office building (see map). Also marked on the map is the Banco Internacional, which is the only place that will change cash dollars and travellers' cheques. Rates are almost as good as in Quito. Normal banking hours are from 9 am to 1 pm Monday to Friday, but recently they have also been open until noon on Saturdays to cater to market-goers.

There is a DITURIS tourist information office on the corner of Parque Maldonado but, regrettably, I am only able to recommend them for friendliness and not efficiency. There is also an information desk at the bus terminal which has city maps.

A reader writes that there is a British man named Jimmy in the Riobamba prison. He is interesting, likes visitors, makes tea, and will trade English books.

Market

Market day is Saturday and there's much activity in the streets, especially around 5 de Junio and Argentinos. It seems rather incongruous to see a barefooted Indian woman leading a squealing piglet on a string through the streets of a major town. The market certainly is a colourful affair, with thousands of people from many surrounding villages flocking to market.

Unfortunately, new market buildings have been constructed which tend to detract from the *ambiente*, and the

modern market sells mainly food items and plastic consumer goods. If you look hard, you'll still see some crafts for sale but certainly not as many as there used to be.

The most typically Riobambeño handicrafts are the *tagua* nut carvings. These nuts are actually seeds from a type of jungle palm. They are fairly soft until they are carved, but when exposed to the sun and air they become very hard. The seeds are the size of large chicken eggs and are carved into a variety of novelties such as busts, miniature cups and rings. Although the palm grows in many areas, for some reason only Riobamba has become a carving centre for the tagua nut.

Another interesting handicraft from the Riobamba area is the *shigra*, a tough woven bag made from agave or century plant fibres. Their durability and practicality make them very popular souvenirs for many travellers, who often use them as day bags.

There are also baskets and mats made by the Colta Indians. They are woven from the reeds lining the shores of Lake Colta, a few km south of Riobamba. There are many clothing items such as woven belts, fine ponchos and embroidered shawls.

It should be mentioned that the Otavalo market is the most tourist-oriented and convenient place to shop for souvenirs. At the Riobamba market you'll have to do a lot of searching past stalls of potatoes, plastic buckets and polyester pants – less convenient but perhaps more fun!

Museo de Arte Religioso

The museum in the old church of La Concepción is famous and worth a visit. The building has been beautifully restored and there are many rooms with a good variety of paintings, sculptures and religious artefacts. Their major piece is a huge, gem-encrusted gold monstrance said to be priceless. Entrance is 60c from 9 am to 12.30 pm and 3 to 6.30 pm Tuesdays through Saturdays. On Sundays and holidays it's open mornings only; closed Mondays.

Parque 21 de Abril

There is an observation platform here, from which the city and surrounding countryside can be appreciated. There is also a tilework representation of the history of Ecuador. The view of snow-capped Tungurahua rising behind the church of San Antonio is especially impressive.

Parque La Libertad

This is another quiet plaza. Its Basilica is famous as the only round church in Ecuador. Begun in 1883, it took over 30 years to complete and was designed, built and decorated mainly by locals – a source of civic pride. It's often closed; try Sundays and evenings after 6 pm.

There are several other plazas with impressive buildings and churches. A walk along Primera Constituente will take you past some of them.

Places to Stay – bottom end

Most hotels are in the town centre a couple of km away from the main bus terminal. If you want to stay near the terminal, you'll find the clean *Residencial Puruha* across the street behind it. They charge US$1.70 per person and have hot water.

The best selection of cheap hotels is near the train station. The *autoferro* leaves at 5 am, so avoid rooms facing the tracks. The cheapest is probably the *Residencial Colonial* which charges about US$1 and has hot water. Other hotels for a dollar are less attractive. They include the residencials *Villa Ester, Guayas, Chimborazo* and *Hotel Guayaquil*.

I prefer the *Residencial Camba Huasi* for US$1.40 per person. It is a block from the station and hence quieter, and although it doesn't look up to much it has

San Antonio church

friendly staff, spacious rooms and hot showers.

Other places with hot water but facing the station are the hotels *Americano, Bolívar* and *Ecuador* and the *Residencial Venecia*. They are all about US$1.40 each. There is also the *Nueva Residencial Venecia* which has opened recently.

Places to Stay – middle

The *Hotel Metro* charges US$3.50 and US$3 per person for rooms with and without private baths. There's hot water and a restaurant but the staff has been criticised as 'nasty' and won't let you look at the room before you pay for it. At about the same price, the *Hotel Imperial* is friendly and clean and has an interesting glass ceiling/floor between the second and third floor lobbies. New, clean and good is the *Hotel Whymper* at US$10 double with private bath (including breakfast).

The older *Hotel Segovia* charges US$3.50 each for rooms with private bath, but the restaurant *El Cafetal* below is rather expensive for what you get. Two reasonable hotels are the *Humboldt* and the newer *Hostal Los Shyris*, which have comfortable rooms with private baths for US$4 each. Cafeterias are attached.

In front of the main bus terminal is the comfortable and new *Hotel Las Retamas*, which has a restaurant and charges US$5.50 per person in rooms with private baths, hot water and TV.

Places to Stay - top end

The best hotel in town is on Avenida Argentinos and a long way from the centre. It's the *Hotel El Galpón* and is highly recommended for the rich and/or luxury loving. About US$20 and US$28 a single and double.

Places to Eat

Most restaurants in Riobamba are fairly basic and cheap and there are many of them. Budget travellers are recommended to try the four-course lunch for 70c at the simple and homely *Restaurant Kikirimian*. There are several cheap restaurants near the railway station, some of which are rather grimy. Not quite as cheap but excellent value is *Restaurant La Biblia* – they have good meals and you might try their fresh pineapple juice for 20c.

As usual, there are several inexpensive *chifas*, of which the *Hong Kong* is quite reasonable. The new *Taberna Restaurante* is worth a try. For dining with a little style try the restaurants *Candilejas* or *La Cabaña Montecarlo*. They are less expensive than they look and even the most impoverished budget traveller can afford a night out at a place with a clean tablecloth once in a while. One of the fanciest places in town, and very good value, is the good German-run *Restaurant León Rojo*.

Entertainment

Nightlife is extremely limited. There is a *Peña Bar* just off the west end of the map at Avenida D L Borja 37-47. Otherwise, I could find nothing except the three movie theatres on the map. They advertise in *El Libertador*, the local daily paper.

Getting There & Away

Air There is a secondary airport which is used for military and emergency services only.

Rail The service to Guayaquil and Cuenca was disrupted by the 1982/83 El Niño floods which washed out over 80 km of the track beyond Riobamba. It is unlikely that services will resume before 1989 – quite possibly much later. At this time there is only one daily *autoferro* to Quito which leaves at 5 am, costs 90c and takes about five hours. It is usually full and advance booking is recommended. Enquire at the train station in the town centre.

Bus The main bus terminal is almost two km north-west of the town centre. Unfortunately, not all buses leave from there. Northbound buses for Quito (US$1.60, four hours) and intermediate points are frequent. Also frequent are buses for Guayaquil (US$1.95, five hours). There are two buses at 7 and 9 pm for Machala (US$3, 10 hours) and Huaquillas (US$3.50, 12 hours) if you're heading for Peru.

If you're headed south you'll only find three buses a day for Cuenca with the Patria bus company. They leave at 5.30 and 7.30 am and 1 pm and cost about US$2.50 for the ride which can take from seven to 12 hours. The Pan American highway south of Alausi is in terrible condition and there are frequent landslides – buses for Cuenca may well go via the western lowlands (El Triunfo) and then back up into the Sierra. Buses for Alausi leave about every hour with CTA and cost 80c for the 1½ hour ride, but trying to continue from there to Cuenca can be problematical.

Three blocks south of the main bus

terminal (turn left out of the front entrance) is a smaller terminal with frequent local buses for Cajabamba and Balbanera; fare is 15c.

For buses to Baños and the Oriente you have to go to the Oriente bus terminal on Avenidas Espejo and Luz Elisa Borja almost four km away. There is no direct bus linking the two terminals – a taxi should be about 50c.

Once in a while there are buses leaving the main terminal for Baños – it's a matter of luck. If you're arriving in Riobamba from the Oriente, you may find that your bus makes a swing through the centre before ending up at the Oriente terminal.

Getting Around

Bus North of the main bus terminal, behind a church with a blue dome, is a local bus stop for the city centre nearly two km away. These buses run along Avenida León Borges, which turns into 10 de Agosto near the railway station. Here there is a good selection of hotels. To return to the main terminal, take any bus marked 'Terminal' on Avenida Primera Constituente. The fare is 5c.

To visit the villages of Guano and Santa Teresita, take a 10c local bus ride from the stop at Avenidas Pichincha and New York.

CHIMBORAZO

Señor Enrique Veloz of Riobamba (tel 960916) is the president of the Asociación de Andinismo de Chimborazo. He has climbed Chimborazo and the other peaks many times and can guide you himself or arrange a good guide. This is fairly priced but not cheap, and it is not for the beginner mountaineer.

At Riobamba's *Residencial Camba Huasi* you can hire a pickup for about US$25 for a day trip to the climbers' refuge on Chimborazo. The manager of the *Hotel Imperial*, Señor Carlos Morales, has a 4WD jeep and will take you to the refuge for about US$33. (He will also drive you to Ingapirca and other small villages for US$50 for the entire day.)

If you can bargain hard, you can try hiring a pickup truck from near the Riobamba railway station – about US$15-20 depending on the vehicle and your bargaining abilities. It is also possible to get a truck to the village of San Juan (30c) and from this village hire a pickup for about US$7 to the refuge – assuming that all the vehicles in San Juan haven't gone somewhere else!

There are two climbers' refuges. Most vehicles reach the new lower one where you can buy drinks and candy. You can sleep at the upper refuge (about a half hour walk uphill) for US$1.50 per night; there is a fireplace and cooking facilities but bring your own sleeping bag. The refuge is named after Edward Whymper, the British climber who in 1880 made the first ascent with the Swiss guides, the Carrels.

At 5000 metres this is Ecuador's highest refuge, and altitude sickness is a very real danger. It is essential that you spend several days acclimatising at the elevation of Riobamba or higher before going to the refuge. Beyond the refuge, the climb is only for experienced mountaineers with snow and ice climbing gear. For more mountaineering information see my *Climbing & Hiking in Ecuador*, Bradt Publications.

GUANO & SANTA TERESITA

These small villages are a few km north of Riobamba and make an ideal day trip. Guano is an important carpet making centre and although it's unlikely that many travellers will have room in their luggage for a couple of souvenir carpets, it is nevertheless interesting to see this cottage industry. In Guano you should get off the bus at the central plaza, where there are several carpet stores , and then continue down Avenida García Moreno which will take you past several more. There are no hotels or restaurants.

From the main plaza you can continue

with a 5c bus ride to Santa Teresita a few km away. The bus terminates at the end of the road and you turn right and head down the hill for about 20 minutes to the Balneario. Here there are swimming pools fed by natural springs. The water is quite cool (22°C or 71°F) but the views of Tungurahua and El Altar are marvellous. There is a basic cafeteria, and camping is permitted.

The round trip from Riobamba will take about six hours if you take it leisurely and have a swim in the pool. There are frequent buses during daylight hours and it's a good chance to see some of the local countryside.

CAJABAMBA

The southbound Pan American highway actually heads west out of Riobamba until it reaches a cement factory 10 km away. Here the road forks, with the west fork continuing to Guaranda and the main highway heading south-west to Cajabamba about seven km further.

Cajabamba was founded in 1534 and was historically important until it was devastated by the 1797 earthquake which killed several thousands of its inhabitants. Most of the survivors founded nearby Riobamba, but a few remained and their descendants still live here. As you arrive, look up to your right and you'll see a huge scar on the hillside – the only sign of the landslide which caused much of the damage in 1797.

Most of the buses from Riobamba continue down the Pan American highway beyond Cajabamba; if you want to see some of the old town you should get off at the entrance which is at the junction of the main highway and Avenida 2 de Agosto on the right. Most bus drivers stop here. There's little to see; if you head down 2 de Agosto you'll soon come to the History Museum on your right, which contains about a dozen fragments of carved rock dating from before the earthquake. It's not worth seeing, but maybe in the future the museum will have a proper exhibit.

Continuing down the road, you come to the earthquake-damaged town church on your left. There are no hotels.

Returning to the Pan American, you'll see a few food stalls and very basic restaurants. Heading south on the main highway, you soon pass open fields which are the site of the interesting weekly market. There are no permanent buildings; the Indians just lay out their wares in neat rows. Every Sunday morning the bare fields are transformed by a bustling but surprisingly orderly throng who buy, sell and barter produce. Quechua rather than Spanish is spoken and there are no tourist items; this is one of the more traditional markets in the Ecuadorean highlands. Amazingly, it takes place right by the side of the Pan American highway – a measure of just how rural this part of Ecuador is.

Most buses from Riobamba continue about four km beyond Cajabamba to Lake Colta – an interesting place. The road climbs gently to a notch in the hill to the south and the little chapel of La Balbanera. It is built on the site of the earliest church in Ecuador, which dates from 15 August 1534, though only a few stones at the front survived the devastating earthquake of 1797. The church has been almost completely rebuilt and the curious traveller can enter to inspect its simple interior and look at the usual disaster paintings.

In La Balbanera one painting carries the explanation: 'On the 17th of May, 1959, the train derailed, setting the whole convoy on fire. Sr Juan Peñafiel, the brakeman, prayed to the Divine Lady of La Balbanera and her miracle saved the train near Alausí'.

Looking almost due north of the chapel, you can see Chimborazo looming up from 30 km away. Next to the chapel are a few basic restaurants and the more elaborate *La Balbanera* tourist restaurant where you can sample local dishes. A little to the south of the chapel there is a road fork. This is where the decision must be made whether to continue south on the Pan

American or take the 100-km detour to the right via the junction of El Triunfo and then return to the Pan American at Cañar. Frequent road closures caused by landslides sometimes make the detour impossible to avoid.

Opposite the road fork is Lake Colta, which is often choked up by reeds, which form an important crop for the local Colta Indians. Sometimes you can see the Coltas' rafts on the lake; the Indians cut the reeds for use as cattle fodder or for the reed mats and baskets for which they are famous.

Some of the more traditional Colta Indian women can be easily identified, as they dye the fringes of their hair a startling golden colour. If you have the time or inclination you could walk around the lake in a couple of hours.

GUAMOTE

From the Cajabamba region the southbound Pan American highway roughly follows the railway and crosses the tracks quite often. Some 30 km beyond Cajabamba you reach the village Guamote, which has a Thursday market. Until 1982 it had some importance because of its railway station, but the trains haven't run for some years and it's rather forgotten now. There is one basic pensión near the train tracks.

ALAUSÍ

Almost 50 km south of Guamote you reach Alausí, which is near the head of the Chanchán River valley down which the railway used to run to the coast. Just below Alausí begins the famous Nariz del Diablo, where a hair-raising series of railway switchbacks negotiated the steep descent towards the lowlands.

Unfortunately, this is the area where the most damage was done by the landslides caused by the torrential rains of the 1982-1983 El Niño. Alausí used to be a popular highland resort for Guayaquileños wishing to get away from the unpleasant heat and humidity of the coast while experiencing one of the world's great feats of railway engineering.

Although the railway doesn't run, the hotels remain, often empty. Everyone hopes that the railway will reopen – but I'd be very much surprised to see it running before the end of the decade. Forgotten by the tourists, Alausí nevertheless retains some importance as an agricultural centre.

There is a movie theatre that shows badly scratched and distorted kung fu movies and an IETEL office if you need to call your mother.

Places to Stay & Eat

The hotels are all on Avenida 5 de Junio. There are no first-class hotels and the best seems to be the *Hotel Gampala*, which has hot water and charges about US$2 per person. For US$1.60 you can stay at the clean *Hotel Panamericano*, which only has hot water in the mornings and a basic restaurant below.

Hotel Ecuador also has a basic restaurant and can provide hot showers around the back for a fee of 20c if you ask in advance. The rooms are a dollar per person. The *Residencial Tequendama* looks pretty basic but has hot water and charges US$1.20 per person.

Apart from the hotel restaurants, there are a couple of other basic places to eat.

Getting There & Away

Bus Buses from Riobamba (90c, 1½ hours) arrive every hour or so, but to go further south is sometimes impossible and you might get stuck in Alausí. Buses turn off the Pan American highway and drop down into town, arriving on the main street, Avenida 5 de Junio, where they stop near the Hotel Panamericano.

Pickup trucks act as buses for nearby destinations and leave from this street. Some of the rides can be quite spectacular, especially the one to Achupallas about 23 km to the south-east. Make sure that any sightseeing ride you take is coming back to Alausí, as there are few, if any, places to stay in these villages. Buses for Cuenca also leave from the main street.

Cuenca & the Southern Highlands

The three southern Sierra provinces, Cañar, Azuay and Loja, are noticeably different from the seven highland provinces to the north. Geographically they are much lower, with very few peaks reaching 4000 metres. The topography is rugged nevertheless, and communications with the rest of Ecuador have only been developed relatively recently. Cuenca, the major city of the region and Ecuador's third largest, didn't have paved highway connections with Guayaquil and Quito until the 1960s, and even today these highways are often in bad shape. The area is rich in history and the region has a strong flavour of the colonial past, due to its isolation until recent times.

The southern highlands had a colourful history even before the Spanish conquest. These were the lands of the Cañari Indians, an independent culture with exceptional skill in producing gold jewellery and other metalwork, fine weavings and ceramics. In the late 15th century the Cañaris were conquered by the Incas, who built several major centres. These included the city of Tomebamba near present-day Cuenca, and the fortress of Ingapirca – the best-preserved pre-colonial ruin found in Ecuador today. The Inca influence was short lived, however, and the Spaniards under Pizarro were in control by the 1530s. Cuenca was (re)founded relatively late in 1557. Several other important towns of the region were founded earlier, such as Loja in 1548.

Remnants of the colonial era are more likely to be seen here than anywhere else in the country, except Quito. Although progress is slowly catching up with the southern Sierra, this area is still a long way behind the coast and northern highlands. Today's traveller is struck by the paucity of large cities in the southern highlands. Apart from Cuenca and Loja,

there are no towns with a population of over 20,000 inhabitants. There are many villages with old balconied houses and cobbled streets, and there is a strong tradition of handicrafts ranging from jewellery-making to weaving. A journey through the provinces of Cañar, Azuay and Loja is a journey into the past.

CUENCA

Barely half a century before the arrival of the Spaniards, the powerful Inca Tupac (or Topa) Yupanqui was undertaking the difficult conquest of the Cañari Indians, who struggled bravely to stem the expansion of the Inca empire. After several years of bitter fighting, Tupac Yupanqui's forces prevailed.

The Inca began the construction of a major city whose splendour and importance was to rival that of the imperial capital of Cuzco. The Indians told of sun temples covered with gold sheets and palaces built using the finest skill of Cuzqueño stonemasons, but what happened to Tomebamba, as the city was called, is shrouded in mystery.

By the time the Spanish chronicler Cieza de León passed through in 1547, Tomebamba lay largely in ruins, although well-stocked storehouses indicated how great it recently had been. Today it is difficult to imagine Tomebamba's splendour, for all that remains are a few recently excavated Inca walls by the river.

This river bears the name of the Inca city and divides Cuenca in half. South of the river lie fairly recent suburbs and the modern university. To the north is the heart of the colonial city. Although Cuenca has expanded to become Ecuador's third largest town with 151,000 inhabitants, it still retains a pleasantly provincial air and the old centre has churches dating from the 16th and 17th centuries. The earliest building is the original cathedral, construction of which began in 1557, the year Cuenca was founded by the Spanish conquerors. There are cobbled streets and red-tiled roofs, art galleries and flower markets, shady plazas and museums. The majority of the hotels, too, are near the centre, so the traveller can conveniently enjoy a relaxing few days in this colonial city.

Information
The IETEL and post office are next door to one another on the corner of Gran Colombia and Presidente Borrero.

The DITURIS information office is on Benigno Malo, half a block from the main plaza (or Parque Calderón). They are friendly and they do try to help. As usual, though, they seem to be geared mostly to tourists staying in the best hotel in town for one night and wishing to 'see' Cuenca in three hours. Still, they're better than most other tourist offices and should be able to help with up-to-date museum information, etc. It's a good place to go if you want to help someone practise their English.

Almost opposite the DITURIS office is the Municipalidad, where you can buy the best available map of the city. It's a very good, up-to-date map and costs about US$1.50, but don't be surprised if it's sold out.

There are several bookshops but English-language books are almost unavailable. The Monsalve bookstore has a very mediocre selection of English-language magazines and occasionally one of the magazine stalls around the main plaza has a month-old copy of *Newsweek*.

Money When I was last in Cuenca it was impossible to exchange foreign currency in the banks. You had to go to the exchange houses, which paid about the same as the best Quito rate. They were open from 9 am to 6 pm Monday to Friday and from 9 am to noon on Saturday. There wasn't a great difference between places.

Two are shown on the map. Dollars were the easiest to change but other currencies were possible. It is quite possible that banking regulations will change, enabling banks to cash foreign currency in the future.

Things to See
The River Tomebamba is attractively lined with old colonial buildings, and washerwomen still lay out their clothes to dry on its grassy banks. A pleasant walk is along Avenida 3 de Noviembre, which follows the north bank of the river. The following selection of places of interest to the visitor begins near the south-eastern end of the river, moves north-west into the town centre, and finally moves out to the west. All the sites are marked on the city map and the complete walk out along the river and back is about six km.

Padre Crespo Museum If you happen to like museums, the good news is that you'll find quite a selection in Cuenca, although they aren't as good as the museums in Quito or Guayaquil. The bad news is that the most famous Cuenca museum, the wonderful rambling collection of Padre Crespo, has been closed indefinitely since the Padre's death in 1982. The collection has been taken over by the Banco Central but it was not available for viewing when I was last in Cuenca.

Museo del Banco Central This museum is in the south-east part of town near the River Tomebamba and is not very obvious (no sign). The entrance gate is on Calle Larga (see map) and the building is across open grounds. The guard at the gate will indicate the way but you should have your passport.

Entrance is free and the museum is open from 9 am to 4 pm Tuesday to Friday and from 9 am to noon on Saturday. There is a permanent collection of old black-and-white photographs of Cuenca and a changing exhibit which is often very good. When I was last there this was about the

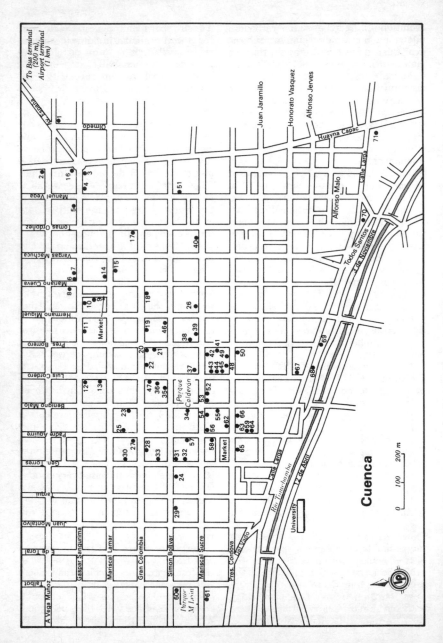

Cuenca

evolution of man and it was most interesting to see this familiar subject explained from an Ecuadorean point of view using local examples. There is also a small exhibit of ancient musical instruments.

Inca Ruins Walking back along Calle Larga and along the river, you come to the ruins on Avenida Todos los Santos. There are some fine niches and walls but most of the stonework was destroyed to build colonial buildings. There are a few explanatory

signs in Spanish. If you're coming from Peru the ruins will seem rather lacklustre.

Municipal Museum Further along Calle Larga you come to the Municipal Museum, which is open from 8 am to 1 pm and 3 to 5 pm Monday to Friday. Religious sculptures, colonial furniture and paintings are on display. They have a fine collection of Indian artefacts but only a few were on show recently. The 1984 canonisation of St Miguel, who came from the Cuenca area, meant that a display of the life of the

1	Residencial La Alborada	36	TAME
2	Hostal Emanuel	37	Old Cathedral
3	Hotel España	38	Cambio Sur Money Exchange
4	Residencial Tito	39	Internacional Hotel Paris
5	Hostel El Galeon	40	Hotel Atahualpa
6	Pensión Taiwan	41	La Cantina Bar Restaurant
7	Residencial Florida	42	Teatro Sucre
8	Pensión Andaluz	43	Cafeteria Roma
9	Residenciales Norte & Colombia	44	Teatro Casa de Cultura
10	Residencial La Ramada	45	Instituto de Folklore
11	Restaurant Balcón Quiteño	46	MAG Office
12	Residencial Atenas	47	Monsalve English magazines
13	Hotel Majestic	48	Chifa Pack How
14	Cine 9 de Octubre	49	Restaurant La Carreta
15	Residencial Niza	50	Restaurant El Jardín
16	Hostal Hurtado de Mendoza	51	San Blas Church
17	El Paráiso Vegetarian Restaurant	52	Cambistral Money Exchange
18	Residencial Siberia & Ecuatoriana Airline	53	Municipal Hall
		54	Casa de Cultura
19	Hotels El Conquistador & Presidente	55	DITURIS
20	Post Office	56	Flower market
21	IETEL	57	Hotel Catedral
22	Hotel El Dorado	58	Pensión Azuay
23	Hotel Internacional	59	Hostals Bellavista and San Francisco
24	Hotel Tomebamba	60	San Sebastián Church
25	Teatro Cuenca	61	Museum of Modern Art
26	Hostal Paredes	62	Hotel Alli Tiana
27	Santo Domingo Church	63	Hotel Milan
28	Hotel Residencial Emperador	64	Restaurant El Inca
29	San Cenáculo Church	65	San Francisco Church
30	Residencial Paris	66	Hotel Cantabri
31	Hotel Pichincha	67	Hotel Crespo Annex
32	Residencial El Inca	68	Hotel Crespo
33	Gran Hotel	69	Municipal Museum
34	New Cathedral	70	Inca ruins
35	Pio Pio Chicken Restaurant	71	Banco Central Museum

saint took up several rooms. Exhibits change frequently.

Instituto Azuaya de Folklore From a block west of the Municipal Museum, head north to Luis Cordero 722 and the institution is on the 3rd floor, up a rather grimy staircase. They are open from 10 am to noon and 3 to 5 pm Monday through Friday. It's free and there is a small but worthwhile exhibit of pottery, traditional musical instruments, native and regional costumes, and various handicrafts. Explanations are in Spanish and a guide is sometimes available. A tip is appreciated.

Parque Calderón The main plaza, or Parque Calderón, is half a block away from the institution. The dominant building is the **new Cathedral** with its huge blue domes. It is particularly attractive when illuminated, although the lighting hours are unpredictable. The interior is rather stark. Almost unnoticed on the other side of the park is the squat **old Cathedral** (also known as El Sagrario) which was renovated for the visit of Pope John Paul to Ecuador in 1985. It is open to the public but hours are variable.

Casa de Cultura At the south-west corner of Parque Calderón is the Casa de Cultura. There is a good art gallery here with frequently changing exhibits. Most paintings are by local artists and are for sale but there is absolutely no pressure to buy. In fact it's hard to find a salesperson if you should happen to see a work that you're seriously interested in. There's also a bookshop of art-oriented Spanish-language books.

Other Attractions At the corner of Sucre and Aguirre is the small **Plaza de Carmen** where there is a colourful daily flower market in front of the church. (Turning left here brings you to the **San Francisco market**). Continuing down Sucre, you come to the **Parque Miguel León**, which is also known as the Plaza San Sebastián.

This is a quiet and pleasant park with the interesting old Church of San Sebastián at the north end. The park seems to be developing into an 'artists' quarter', with a mural of infant art on one wall, a couple of art galleries, and the **Modern Art Museum** at the south end. This is free and open from 9 am to 1 pm and 3 to 6 pm Monday to Friday and on Saturday morning. They plan on opening on Sundays too; it's worth checking if that is your only free day.

You can return back into the centre along Bolívar and look into the colonial **Church of San Cenáculo** as you go. This has recently been cleaned and has had work done on it – it looks very bare in contrast to the opulent churches of Quito. After San Cenáculo, continue into the centre along Gran Colombia, the main handicraft shop street in Cuenca. Soon you pass the **Church of Santo Domingo** on your left, which has some fine carved wooden doors and colonial paintings inside. In the next few blocks you pass by many arts and crafts stores selling a variety of handicrafts. Parque Calderón is only a block to the south. A few blocks north, at Vega Muñoz 9-33, is a hat shop run by Senor Ortega. It has been recommended for panama hats.

Market day is Thursday, with a smaller market on Saturday. There are two main **market areas**: one around the Church of San Francisco and the other at the plaza by Avenidas Mariscal Lamar and Hermano Miguel. The market is mainly for locals rather than tourists, and crafts shoppers will do better to look along Gran Colombia. The markets are nevertheless lively and interesting but watch your belongings – pickpockets have been reported. The market continues on a smaller scale on other days of the week.

Las Cajas National Recreation Area
This recreation area lies about 30 km west of Cuenca and is famous for its many beautiful lakes. It is rugged hiking and camping country. Buses from Cuenca

leave at 6.30 am (except Thursdays) from the Church of San Sebastián for the two-hour ride and there is a return bus in the afternoon. There is a refuge where you can usually sleep for a fee (but don't rely on it) and camping is allowed. A permit costs US$1. The park is administered by the Ministerio de Agricultura y Ganadería. The MAG offices in downtown Cuenca should give you further information, maps and permits – but they have been criticised for being unhelpful and unfriendly. It's worth the hassle though, because the park really is lovely, especially for hiking.

Jungle Trips

A correspondent reports that Daniel Cooperman at the Hotel Crespo arranges jungle trips staying with indians in a remote village. The trips are sensitively organised, and cost about US$20 per day.

Fiestas

3 November is Cuenca Day and combines with 1 and 2 November (All Saints' Day and All Souls' Day) to form an important holiday period for the city. The markets are in full swing and there is music and dancing. Hotel rooms may be rather difficult to find at this time.

Carnaval, as in other parts of Ecuador, is celebrated with boisterous water fights. No one is spared – I saw a whole bucket of water poured from a balcony over an old nun's head! Cuenca seems to be more enamoured of these soggy celebrations than the rest of the country; Easter and New Year's are also popular with water-throwers. Protect your camera gear. There is a colourful city parade on Christmas Eve.

Places to Stay

Hotels are often full for the celebrations 1-3 November and your choice will be limited – though there are so many places listed that you're bound to find somewhere.

Prices tend to rise during the fiestas. For some reason, almost all hotels (except a few of the most desperately cheap) seem to have hot or at least tepid water. So you can assume that hot water is available unless I mention otherwise. I also noticed that several hotels have inexpensive rooms with private baths which cost little more than rooms with shared bathrooms. You might want to consider treating yourself to this luxury, even if travelling on a budget. There are half a dozen hotels within a few hundred metres of the bus terminal, but most are a km or more away in the downtown area.

Places to Stay – bus terminal area

Directly opposite the front of the terminal is the *Residencial Los Alamos*, which has a simple restaurant attached. They charge US$2 and US$4 per person for clean rooms with shared and private baths.

Turning right out of the terminal and heading down Avenida España for about five minutes, you reach the *Residencial La Alborada*, which charges US$2 each. A little further, by the traffic circle, is the friendly *Hotel España*, which is US$1.50 each or US$2.30 with a private bath. Both are clean and good. Also by the traffic circle is the newer *Hostal Hurtado de Mendoza* which has a cafeteria attached and rooms with private bath, carpet and phone for US$4.40 per person.

Within a block of the traffic circle are the *Hostal Emanuel* and *Residencial Tito*, both of which charge US$1.80 each; the *Tito* also has rooms with a private bath for US$3 each and a restaurant below – it has been recommended by several travellers. Also recommended is the modern and clean *Hostal El Galeon*, a block beyond the *Tito*. It has spacious rooms with private bathrooms for US$3.50/US$6 for singles/doubles. *El Galeon* is about 700 metres from the bus terminal; all the hotels in the bottom end category are a km or more from the terminal.

Places to Stay - bottom end

If you're really low on money head for the market area by Cueva and Sangurima. Here you'll find the basic but adequate *Residencial Norte*, which charges just 70c per person for inside rooms and 90c for a room with a window. There are some other similarly priced cheapies nearby but I wouldn't recommend them unless you're desperate. These include the pensiones *Andaluz* and *Taiwan* and the *Residencial Florida*.

Next door to the *Norte* is the *Residencial Colombia*, which is rather better but charges US$1.50 each. Around the corner is the *La Ramada*, which charges from US$1.20 to US$1.50 each depending on the room. The best hotel in this market area is the *Residencial Niza*, which is clean and friendly. The staff always chatted to me when I went in and out and tried to answer my questions when they could. They charge US$2 each in rooms with shared baths or US$3 a single and US$5 a double for a room with a private bath.

There are several good, cheap hotels further into the town centre. For US$1.20 each try the *Residencial Siberia*, which is old but friendly and pleasant - they have lots of flowers at the entrance. One of the best cheap hotels is the friendly *Residencial Inca*, which has long been used by budget travellers and is still only US$1 per person. A simple restaurant is attached (not the *Restaurant El Inca* marked on the map). For US$2 and US$2.20 each there are the clean but unremarkable *Hotel Emperador* and *Pichincha*. The extremely cheap and basic *Pensión Azuay*, *Hotel Cantabri* and Hostals *Bellavista* and *San Francisco* are by the San Francisco market. They have nothing to recommend them except their cheapness.

If you are trying to economise but would like a simple and clean room with a private bath, try the following selection. The *Residencial Atenas* charges US$2.30 and US$4 for comfortable singles and doubles but their left-luggage facilities have been criticised. The old and somewhat run-down *Hotel Majestic* has friendly staff and their spacious rooms go for US$2.50 per person. The recommended, clean and friendly *Hotel Milan* is well worth the US$2.50 single and US$4 double; try to get a room with a balcony - some superb views. The *Gran Hotel* at US$2.80 each has also been recommended - both these last two have good luggage storage facilities. Some of these hotels have cheaper rooms with shared baths.

Places to Stay - middle

For about US$3.50 each you can stay at the oldish and rather stately *Hotel Internacional* or the recently remodelled *Residencial Paris* (not to be confused with the *Internacional Hotel Paris*). Both have private baths and even telephones in the rooms. The *Hostal Paredes* is similarly priced and has a restaurant attached. *Hotel Alli Tiana* charges US$5.50 each and has some rooms with good views.

Places to Stay - top end

Brand new and modern-looking in a quiet part of town is the *Hotel Atahualpa*, which charges US$7.50 a single and US$12 a double. Somewhat more central is the similarly priced *Hotel Tomebamba*. The highly recommended *Hotel Crespo* has a great variety of rooms with an equally great range of prices, from moderate to relatively expensive. They have rooms in their main building and in the annex across the street. Some rooms have inside windows, others have street windows or river views. Prices are US$6 to US$14 single and US$7.50 to US$18 double. There is a good restaurant.

The good *Hotel Catedral* charges about US$9 a single and US$14 a double, and the friendly management gives discounts to Peace Corps workers and similar organisations - use your imagination. They have a good restaurant. The *Internacional Hotel Paris* and *Hotel El Conquistador* are both good, modern, recommended and have restaurants.

They charge about US$11 a single and US$16 a double. A little more expensive is the new *Hotel Presidente* which, apart from having all the usual first class amenities, also has a ninth floor bar with a great view of the city.

The fanciest hotel downtown is the *El Dorado*, which has been criticised for snooty staff (maybe they've changed). Expect to pay US$22 for a single and US$26 a double. Finally, if you want luxury and prefer staying out of town, try the expensive, Swiss-run *Hotel La Laguna* on Avenida Ordoñez Lazo, at the north-western edge of Cuenca.

Places to Eat

The finest restaurant in town is opposite one of the cheapest good ones. *Restaurant El Jardín* has been described as the best restaurant in Ecuador; this is a matter of opinion but it's certainly very good value. You can eat well here for US$5. Almost opposite it is *La Carreta*, which serves good meals for under a dollar.

The areas around the two markets have plenty of cheap restaurants. One of the cheapest near the San Francisco market is *Restaurant El Inca*, where a decent set meal can cost as little as 70c. On Avenida Sangurima you can find several cheap places, of which the *Balcón Quiteño* is recommended. Local people eat here which is always a good sign. On the first block of Avenida Sangurima there are good *chifas* next to and opposite the *Hotel España*. Another *chifa* is shown on the map – the *Chifa Hong Kong* isn't because they made the classic errors of cooking a fly in my food and then overcharging me.

On the main square is the *Pio Pio* chicken restaurant, which has good coffee. Also on the main plaza is the *Raymypampa* restaurant under the new cathedral. It looks quite nice but has the slowest service I've ever encountered anywhere. Turn this to your advantage – order a coffee and write letters home. Just off the plaza is the rather undistinguished

entrance of the *Cafeteria Roma*. Inside it is quite spacious and has a slightly tarnished but nevertheless charming old world decor. Although their prices aren't dirt cheap, they do serve good Italian food and I recommend it.

The recently opened *La Cantina Bar* has a pleasant and elegant patio suitable for a medium priced lunch. If you're looking for vegetarian food try the very simple *El Paraiso*. There is also the Hare Krishna run *Govinda* next to the Hotel Crespo annex on Luis Cordero.

The best hotels in town have good restaurants open to the general public; you can relax inexpensively with coffee and croissants in pleasant surroundings. The *Internacional Hotel Paris* has a good and very moderately priced restaurant, *El Conquistador* has some of the best coffee in town and *El Dorado* can give you breakfast from 6.30 am, though it's somewhat expensive for other meals. Both the Hotels *Presidente* and *El Dorado* have top floor restaurant/bars with good city views. You can just have a drink.

A reader informs me that there is a good Spanish run paella and seafood restaurant in a beautiful residential area about 10 minutes drive from the centre. The address is Cipreses 1-10 and Ordoñez Lazo, tel 824736, and the restaurant is at the back of the house.

If you're leaving town – or arriving, for that matter – you can eat at the main bus terminal. They have a 24-hour snack bar and a decent restaurant open during the day.

Entertainment

Though Cuenca is Ecuador's third largest city, entertainment is minimal. *El Mercurio* is the Cuenca newspaper for listings of movies at the half dozen cinemas. The *Teatro Casa de Cultura* is not the same place as the *Casa de Cultura*, which occasionally also has movies or lectures – both are shown on the map. The expensive *El Dorado Hotel* has a nightclub and there's a discotheque weekends at the *Hotel Alli Tiana*. There are a couple of other disco or show possibilities on the same block – irregular dates. I suggest you bring a good long novel if you need entertainment.

Getting There & Around

Air The Aeropuerto Mariscal Lamar passenger terminal is conveniently only two km from the heart of town, on Avenida España. Taxis are about 50c and city buses pass the terminal frequently, although they tend to be rather full just after a plane arrives. Downtown, buses depart from the stop by the flower market on Padre Aguirre – not all are marked so ask the drivers.

Flight schedules to and from Cuenca change several times a year so you should make local enquiries about these. There are usually daily flights to and from Guayaquil for about US$10 and two or three flights a day to Quito for US$16. There are flights on Mondays, Wednesdays and Fridays for Macas. For flights to cities south of Cuenca you have to fly to Guayaquil and then take another flight back to your final destination. This is expensive and inconvenient but it is possible that there will be direct flights to Loja in future. For flights to cities to the north you must change in Guayaquil or Quito.

Most flights are with TAME, which has its downtown office by the central plaza. Business hours are 9.30 am to 12.30 pm and 2 to 5 pm on weekdays, subject to change. Their airport desk is open for incoming and outgoing flights. SAN-Saeta also has begun services to Quito, and has an office at the Cuenca airport and at Bolívar 539.

There is an Ecuatoriana office downtown for information on international flights. All of these leave from either Guayaquil or Quito.

Rail The railway station is on the south-eastern outskirts of town. There used to be a daily service north to Sibambe with connections to Guayaquil and Quito, but these have been halted because of damage to the track during the 1982/83 El Niño floods. It is unlikely that service will resume before 1989 or later.

Bus A new and well-organised Terminal Terrestre was opened in November 1983 and most long-distance buses now arrive and leave from here. It is on Avenida España on the way to the airport and about 1½ km from the town centre. City buses leave from in front of the terminal for the centre (5c) and buses for the terminal leave from the bus stop on Padre Aguirre by the flower market. Most (but not all) buses are marked 'Terminal' so ask the driver to be sure.

There are literally dozens of different bus companies with offices in the terminal. Some run two or three buses every hour, others run two or three every week. Some run fast, small and cramped minibuses (or *busetas*) with guaranteed seating, others use huge but slow old coaches with more leg room but standing passengers as well. You should check out the various possibilities and find the one most convenient for you.

Buses leave for Guayaquil (US$2.50, five hours) every few minutes. Buses for Azogues (25c, 45 minutes) leave at least every hour, many continuing to Cañar (45c, 1½ hours) and Alausí if the road is open. For Quito (US$3-4, nine to 14 hours depending on route and road conditions) there are buses about every hour. For destinations between Alausí and Quito there are several departures every day but times and costs vary depending on road conditions and routes taken. Buses leave for Machala (US$2, five hours) about every hour; a few continue to Huaquillas but it's usually quicker to change buses in Machala. There are six or seven buses a day to Saraguro (US$1.90, 4½ hours) continuing to Loja (US$2.40, seven hours). For destinations south of Loja it is best to change in Loja. There are three or four buses a day to Macas (US$2.40, 10 hours) and a couple of buses to Gualaquiza (US$2, seven hours) if you want to go into the southern Oriente. There is a passenger information desk at the terminal where you can ask about other unusual destinations.

Buses to Gualacéo for the Sunday market depart from the corner of Avenidas España and Benalcázar about 100 metres south-west of the main terminal. They leave every few minutes on market day and less frequently on weekdays for the 40-minute, 25c ride. Ask in the main terminal for buses continuing to Sígsig; they leave almost hourly with CITES (40c, 1½ hours).

Local buses (5c) for Baños leave from Avenida Gen Torres by the San Francisco market. At Baños you'll find hot springs with public pools and restaurants.

AZOGUES

About 35 km north of Cuenca on the Pan American highway lies Azogues. It is a quiet, small town of only 15,000 inhabitants, yet it is the capital of the province of Cañar. 'Azogues' literally means 'quick-silver' and the name is derived from the mercury-rich ores supposedly found in the area; I could find no evidence of mercury extraction. The town is more important for its panama hat industry and Saturday market, and is worth visiting for its church. It is a possible alternative to Cuenca as a base for visiting Biblian, Cañar and Ingapirca to the north.

Information

The IETEL office is on the main plaza. Filanbanco will reluctantly exchange dollars at a bad rate – it's better to go to Cuenca.

Things to See

The most interesting place to visit is the **Church of San Francisco**, which dominates the town from a hill to the south-east. You can't see it when you arrive at the bus terminal but if you head generally south-

east and then climb up the Avenida de la Virgen, you'll reach it in about half an hour.

From the church there are sweeping views of the town, the surrounding countryside, and several other churches perched on the top of nearby hills. Hilltops seem to be the place to build churches in this region. Inside San Francisco there is a beautiful gilt altar. The building is sometimes illuminated at night and sitting on the dark hill it looks almost as if it were floating in mid-air.

Another church worth visiting is that of Biblian. This village is some nine km north of Azogues on the Pan American; there are plenty of buses from the terminal. The **Santuario de la Virgen del Rocío** (or Sanctuary of the Virgin of the Dew) is highly visible to the right of the main highway on a steep hill dominating Biblian. It is one of the most attractive churches I've seen and looks more like a fairy-tale princess's palace than it does a church. Keep your eyes open for it even if you're just driving straight through Biblian. There is an annual pilgrimage here on 8 September. There's also a weekly market on Sunday.

Both these churches were renovated in late 1984 for the pope's visit in 1985, and buildings on all the main streets in Azogues were whitewashed. Walking the streets of the town and admiring the colonial architecture is very pleasant.

As you stroll, keep your eyes open for signs of the panama hat industry. Avenida 3 de Noviembre is a good street to see hats being blocked and sold. The main market is on this street and is where the bustling Saturday morning market is held. There is also a smaller market on the Plaza San Francisco in front of the church – it's worth going to for the view.

If you spend the night and want something to do, try the movie theatre. There's only one.

Places to Stay & Eat

Despite its provincial capital status,

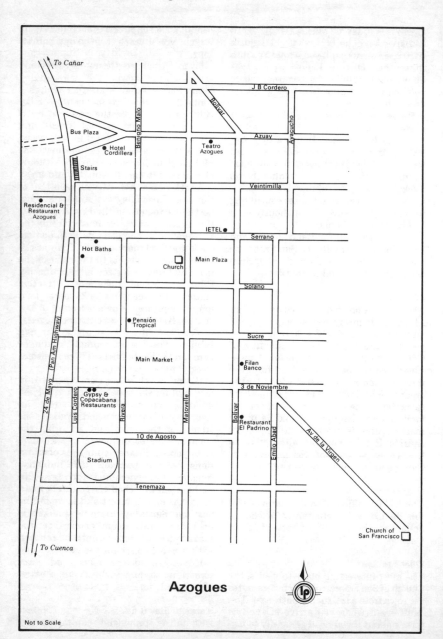

Azogues

Not to Scale

Azogues does not yet have any particularly good hotels. The best place in town is across the highway from the bus terminal and down a small hill. This is the small, clean and family-run *Residencial y Restaurant Azogues*. All the rooms have communal showers and there is hot water. They charge US$2.50 per person and are often full.

At the bus station there is the basic *Hotel Cordillera* for US$2.30 each. Closer to the town centre is the still more basic *Pensión Tropical* at US$1.50 each. They're OK but have no hot showers. Public baths charge 20c for a hot shower and there are two marked on the map.

The best place to eat is at the *Residencial y Restaurant Azogues* but their menu is often limited. Three inexpensive but quite acceptable restaurants are shown on the map: the *Gypsy, Copacabana* and *El Padrino*.

Getting There & Away

Rail There is a train station but, as you've gathered by now, services were indefinitely suspended in 1983.

Bus The bus terminal is right on the Pan American highway, which is renamed 24 de Mayo as it goes through Azogues. For buses to Cuenca or Cañar it is often best to stand on the highway and wait for one to come by – often Cuenca-Cañar buses don't pull into the terminal. The fare to either Cuenca or Cañar shouldn't be more than about 30c although one driver tried to charge me twice that.

There are direct buses from Azogues to Cuenca with Empresa Auto Via but their buses are very old, very slow, and pick up everybody and their chickens – interesting and worthwhile if you're not in any hurry. From the terminal there are several departures a day for Quito, Guayaquil and Machala. For other destinations it is best to go to Cuenca and change buses.

CAÑAR

The small town of Cañar on the Pan American is the nearest place to stay for travellers wishing to visit the Inca ruins of Ingapirca. Market day is Sunday and otherwise there's not much of interest.

Places to Stay & Eat

Cañar has some simple places to stay. The basic *Pensión Guayaquil* on the street of the same name charges US$1.20 per person and 30c extra for hot water. The *Residencial Patricia* is over the store at 3 de Noviembre and Bolívar. They have hot water and charge US$1.50 per person. If these are all full you can find accommodation in unsigned private houses if you ask around. Places to eat are not particularly noteworthy and most close by about 7 pm.

Getting There & Away

Buses from Cuenca's Terminal Terrestre leave for Cañar (45c, 1½ hours) every hour or so.

INGAPIRCA

Although Ingapirca is the major Inca site in Ecuador it is difficult to get to and nobody seems to know much about the ruins. They have never been 'lost', as was Machu Picchu – indeed, the Frenchman Charles-Marie de La Condamine drew accurate plans of them as far back as 1739. The ruins are referred to as a fortress, but its garrison – if there was one – must have been quite small.

Archaeologists think that the main structure, an *usnu* elliptical platform known as the Temple of the Sun, had religious and ceremonial purposes. This building boasts some of the Inca's finest mortarless stonework and has several of the typical trapezoidal niches and doorways which are a hallmark of Inca construction. The less well-preserved buildings were probably storehouses and the complex may have been used as a *tambo* or stopping place for runners carrying imperial messages from Quito to Tomebamba.

At Ingapirca there is a small village with an occasionally open craft shop/

A running Fox God

museum by the church on the plaza. There are no restaurants or accommodation and the few stores sell only the most basic of food items. There is a weekly market on Fridays.

The ruins are about a km away from the village. There is no entrance fee. An on-site museum was recently opened but the exhibit suffers from a lack of interpretive signs. There is a shelter by the entrance with basic toilet facilities and benches, but you can't sleep there.

Getting There & Away

Although Ingapirca is Ecuador's most important Inca ruin, visiting it cheaply is not straightforward as there are no direct bus services. A few tourist agencies in Cuenca organise day trips but charge US$15 per person and need a five-person minimum. It would be better to rent a taxi for the day, which should cost under US$20 – bargain for the best rate.

To make an economical visit, you must first take a bus to Cañar (45c, 1½ hours from Cuenca). About two km before Cañar there is a signed turnoff to Ingapirca on your right. You can wait here for a passing vehicle to take you the 15 km to the ruins; expect to pay about 30c for the ride. You can walk or hitch but still are expected to pay if you get a ride. Vehicles

pass by about once an hour. Leave early or you may get stuck without a ride back. There are no facilities at Ingapirca.

The bus from Cuenca usually continues through Cañar to El Tambo. From here there is a shorter (eight km) road to Ingapirca which is the shortest walk from the Pan American. Pickup trucks travel the road several times a day and act as buses. This route is probably the fastest and most convenient. I'm told that there is a very basic place to stay in El Tambo but I've never tried it.

There is a train station about three or four km from Ingapirca – if they ever reopen it.

Pickup trucks leave Cañar for Ingapirca when they have a load. There are no set departure times or places. Ask around. You could probably hire a truck to take you there for about US$3.

GUALACÉO, CHORDELEG & SÍGSIG

These three villages are all famous for their Sunday markets. If you started from Cuenca early in the morning you could easily visit all three markets and be back in Cuenca in the afternoon. The best-known markets are at Gualacéo and Chordeleg, which are within two or three km of one another.

Gualacéo has the biggest market and

sells mainly produce, animals and household goods. Chordeleg's market is smaller but important for textiles and jewellery – it is one of Ecuador's most famous jewellery centres. Sígsig market is further away from Cuenca and less visited by tourists. All three villages are good examples of colonial towns.

Gualacéo

In addition to being an important market town, Gualacéo has some importance as a tourist resort and has a pretty location by a river. There are several restaurants by the river and the stroll is pleasant. The town is quite progressive and has a large and spacious modern church with good stained-glass windows. There are several restaurants and places to stay as well as an IETEL office and a cinema.

Places to Stay & Eat The best place to stay in town is the *Gran Hostal Gualacéo*, which charged me an incredibly cheap US$1.30 for a room with a private bath and hot water. (No, they didn't know I was researching this book.) I can't believe that these prices will last but it must be the best hotel deal in Ecuador. The other two hotels in town are the residencials *Gualacéo* and *Español*. They both charge US$1 and have hot water sometimes.

About 20 minutes out of town is the new *Hostería La Ribera* (see map), which is by the river and has a restaurant and small swimming pool. They charge US$8 and US$12 for singles and doubles with private bath but are open to bargaining, especiall for stays of more than one night.

Gualacéo has several barely adequate restaurants on the east side of the market. You'll find more restaurants by the river – one of the best is *Los Sauces*. It is designed for weekend relaxation with skittles, volleyball and tennis, as well as food and beer. The tennis courts are a far cry from Wimbledon! Most of the riverside places are closed during midweek.

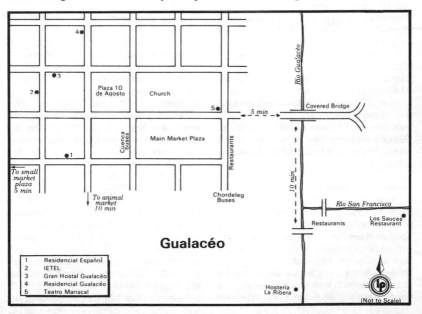

Gualacéo

1	Residencial Español
2	IETEL
3	Gran Hostal Gualacéo
4	Residencial Gualacéo
5	Teatro Mariscal

(Not to Scale)

Chordeleg

Chordeleg has many stores selling a great variety of crafts – some people complain that it is too 'touristy'. Maybe it is; it's especially popular with Guayaquileños looking for highland bargains. On the other hand, if you're shopping for souvenirs or gifts you can choose from gold and silver filigree jewellery, woodcarvings, pottery, textiles, panama hats and embroidered clothing.

There is a pleasant central plaza with a small modern church containing simple but attractive stained-glass windows. Also on the plaza is an excellent museum. It's just a small village museum, yet it manages to pack more into it than many bigger city museums. It's open from 8 am to 5 pm daily except Monday and is free. There are very informative displays about the history and techniques of many of the local handicrafts such as filigreed metalwork, panama hat making and *ikat* weaving. Guides are available. It helps if you understand Spanish.

Places to Eat There is nowhere to stay in Chordeleg but you can find a couple of simple restaurants.

Sígsig

Sígsig is a pleasant, old colonial village where little happens except the Sunday market. There are a couple of restaurants on the main market plaza. A few blocks from the plaza is the CITES bus office. Opposite it is a store that will rent you a room. The ride out here from Cuenca is nice.

Getting There & Away

Buses from Cuenca take about 40 minutes to reach Gualacéo and leave every few minutes on market day and about every hour on weekdays. You can continue the two or three km to Chordeleg on foot or take a local bus (see map for locations). Buses pass the Chordeleg plaza for Sígsig at least once an hour and charge 20c for the 40-minute ride. Sit on the right-hand side of the bus for good views of the river canyon on the way to Sígsig. CITES buses return from Sígsig to Cuenca about every hour for 40c. Three buses a week (Monday, Wednesday and Saturday at 6 am) leave Sígsig for Gualaquiza if the road is passable.

PAUTE

A few km before you reach Gualacéo, the road forks. The left-hand fork takes you up the Paute River valley to the village of the same name. Nearby is the Distilería Uzhupud, which makes several of the local liquors.

Places to Stay

Also near the village is the *Hostería Uzhupud*, an excellent hotel in pleasant countryside. They have a very good restaurant, a swimming pool, tennis courts and an amazing garden which contains hundreds (I've heard thousands) of varieties of flowers, including dozens of species of orchids. They charge about US$15.

OÑA

The Pan American highway heads south from Cuenca to Loja via the towns of Oña and Saraguro. The road climbs steadily from Cuenca and there are good views of *páramo* moorlands and the southern Ecuadorean Andes. Oña is reached after about 2½ hours and the bus sometimes stops here to refuel. The interesting and ancient petrol pump is generator-driven. The attendant has to switch on the generator before he can deliver the fuel, and then he switches it off – a good measure of how frequently vehicles stop in Oña. It's a one-street town with a couple of simple restaurants and a basic pensión – there's not much reason to stop here.

SARAGURO

Just beyond Oña, the road crosses the provincial line into Loja and continues rising and falling through the eerie *páramo* scenery until it reaches Saraguro,

4½ hours, 165 km and US$1.80 south of Cuenca.

The town is named after the Saraguro Indians, who originally came from the Lake Titicaca region in Peru but became colonists in this region under the Incas. They are readily identifiable by their traditional dress. Both men and women wear flat white felt hats with wide brims. The men sport a single pigtail and wear a black poncho but perhaps the most unusual part of their attire is their knee-length black or navy-blue shorts which are sometimes covered with an odd little white apron. They carry double shoulder bags with one pouch in front and one behind for a balanced load. The women wear heavy pleated black skirts and shawls fastened with ornate silver pins. The pins are known as *topos* and are highly prized.

The Saraguros were well known for their jewellery but this craft seems to be dying out. Cattle-raising is their main occupation and they can be seen on foot driving their herds to tropical pastures in the 28 de Mayo area. Wherever they go, they normally wear their traditional clothing and are the most successful Indian group of the southern Ecuadorean highlands. Their market day is Sunday.

Places to Stay & Eat

There are no real hotels, but if you ask around you'll be shown houses where lodgers are taken. There's one next to the *Helados* sign on Calle Loja, just off the main plaza. There are two or three basic restaurants, of which the best is the *Salón Cristal* behind the church.

Getting There & Away

Loja, the provincial capital, is 60 km to the south and CTS buses leave Saraguro six or eight times a day for the two-hour ride, which costs 60c. The CTS bus office is a block from the main plaza. They also have buses leaving for various small villages in the area. For Cuenca, it is best to wait in the plaza for a northbound bus from Loja to pass by.

LOJA

From Saraguro the road drops steadily to Loja at 2225 metres. It was founded by the Spanish captain, Alonso de Mercadillo, on 8 December 1548, and so is one of the oldest towns in Ecuador. None of the earliest buildings survive, although houses from the 18th century can be found. With about 80,000 inhabitants, Loja is both an important provincial capital and a college town, with two universities, a music conservatory and a law school.

Loja is very close to the Oriente and the surrounding countryside is green and pleasant. The people are proud of the great variety of plant species found in the region. They tell the story of the beautiful Countess of Chinchón, wife of an early 17th-century Peruvian viceroy, who was dying of malaria. A Franciscan monk cured her with quinine extracted from the bark of a tree found in the Loja area. After her recovery, fame of the tree's 'miraculous' properties of the tree spread throughout the Spanish empire and the world. Today the tree is called the chinchona after the countess.

Alexander von Humboldt, the German scientist and explorer, visited the area in 1802 and called it 'the garden of Ecuador'. The British botanist Richard Spruce also mounted an expedition here in the mid-19th century. Recently, the area has been recognised for its biological value and a National Park is being set up in the nearby mountains. You could ask around for further information, although the park is still quite inaccessible.

Although the town itself is not exceptionally interesting, travellers on their way to Peru via the border town of Macará find this a convenient place to stop. The highland route to Peru through Loja and Macará is slower and rougher but much more scenic than the more

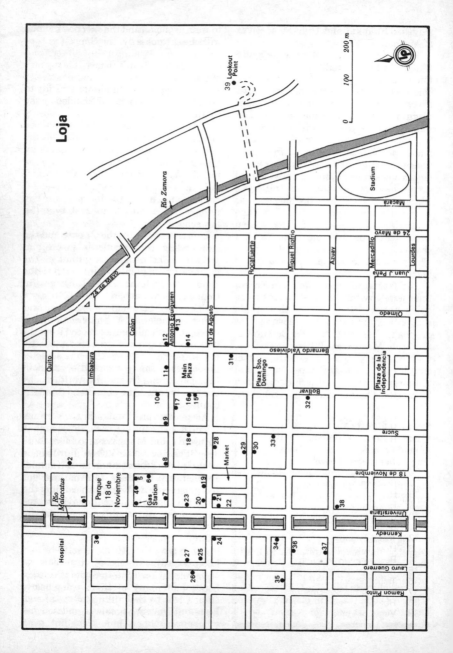

travelled route through the coastal towns of Machala and Huaquillas.

Information

The Post Office is in the municipal building on the north side of the main plaza. It is not very obvious, so ask. The IETEL office is a block away. There are no

1	Centinela del Sur (buses)
2	Viajeros (buses)
3	Transportes Sarguaro (buses)
4	Turismo Oriental (buses)
5	Hostal Don Juan & Residencial Sta Marianita
6	Hotel Metropolitan
7	Restaurant Rey Neptuno
8	Hotel Mexico
9	Banco Central
10	Restaurant Andaluz
11	Post Office
12	TAME
13	ITEL
14	Cathedral
15	Chifa 85 & Pescadería 200 Millas
16	Cine Velez
17	Cafetería Glacier
18	Hotels Acapulco, Londres, Cuxubamba
19	Hotel Paris
20	Hotel Miraflores
21	Hotel Americano
22	Hotels Quinara, Riviera, Inca
23	Hotel Saraguros Internacional
24	Hotel Río Amazonas
25	Transportes Loja Terminal & Pensión
26	Pensión Guayaquil demis Amores
27	Restaurant Suizo-Lojano
28	Hotels Austral & Internacional
29	Hostal Crvstal & Hotel Loja
30	Residencial Caribe
31	Cine El Dorado
32	Teatro Popular
33	Hotel Imperial
34	Restaurant Americano
35	Restaurant San Andres
36	Transportes Cajanuma
37	Transportes Sur-Oriente
38	Hotel Ejecutivo
39	Virgin of Loja

exchange houses and the only bank which will change dollars is the Banco Central, whose rate was almost 20% lower than exchange houses in Cuenca. They won't change sucres into dollars. Peruvian soles are also difficult to negotiate and a bad rate is given. It is better to change money in Macará.

Two local newspapers, *El Mundo* and *El Siglo*, carry only local news. Guayaquil and Quito newspapers are available by about 8 am.

Things to See

A short but pleasant walk east from the centre and across the River Zamora, where washerwomen can sometimes be seen at work, and then up the small hill to the statue of the Virgin of Loja, which is protected by a caged (stone) lion. Here there is a rather damaged lookout with good city views.

The cathedral is on the main plaza, and from September to November it contains the miraculous Virgen del Cisne (Virgin of the Swan), carved in the late 1500s by Diego de Robles. During other months of the year the statue is kept at the village of El Cisne, some 70 km away. Both the cathedral and the church of Santo Domingo have interesting painted interiors and elaborate statues.

The weekly market is on Sunday, but Saturdays and Mondays also seem to be busy. The day of the Virgen del Cisne is celebrated on 8 September, and an annual international produce fair is held for about four or five days on either side of the 8th. (It's called 'international' because Peruvians attend it.)

Places to Stay

Loja appears to have an excess of accommodation. I counted over two dozen hotels and many of them were nearly empty. Maybe they fill up for the annual fiestas. Some of the hotels were closed and others were open but I couldn't find anyone to show me a room. The lack of guests may well mean that the owners will be willing to bargain. The hotels are close together so wander around until you find one that appeals to you.

Places to Stay – bottom end
One of the cheapest places is the *Residencial Santa Marianita*, which is clean and secure but has only cold water. They charge US$1.20 per person. Similar prices are charged at the *Hotel American, Hotel Mexico* and *Residencial Caribe*. The last two have hot water.

For US$1.50 each try hotels *Londres, Acapulco* and *Cuxubamba*. These are next to one another and are clean, pleasant and have hot water. The *Cuxamba* also has some rooms with private baths for US$2.50 each. The *Hostal Don Juan* also charges US$1.50.

For better rooms with hot water and private bathrooms try the *Hotel Metropolitan* for US$2.50 per person, or the friendly *Hotel Miraflores* for US$3 with a private bath and US$2 without.

There are several hotels near the *Transportes Loja Terminal*. The place right above the terminal is cheap but very noisy. Across the street is the unfriendly *Pensión Guayaquil de Mis Amores*, which charges US$2 per person in rooms with private baths but only cold water. I don't like either of them. There are other good hotels near this terminal but they are more expensive.

Places to Stay – middle
There are several very comfortable and reasonably priced hotels. *Hotel Paris* charges US$3 per person for rooms with private bathrooms and hot water. It's been recommended by several travellers but I've heard mixed reports. Good value is the *Hotel Inca*, which charges US$3.50 each for clean rooms with private bath, carpeting and TV (though Loja programming can best be described as lacklustre!).

The *Hotel Ejecutivo* at US$4 single also has clean rooms with private bath and

TV. Even better is the *Hotel Río Amazonas* which offers all the above plus a room phone and a restaurant for US$4.50 a single and US$6.50 a double. It is a block away from the Loja bus terminal. Other clean hotels with private bathrooms in this price range are the *Saraguros Internacional, Riviera* and *Quinara*.

The best place in town is the new *Hotel Imperial*, a few blocks away from everybody else. They charge about US$8 a single and US$12 a double.

Places to Eat
On the west side of the main plaza you have the choice of Chinese or seafood at the *Chifa 85* and the *Pescadería 200 Millas*. Both are good, particularly the chifa. Just up from the plaza is the more elegant *Restaurant Andaluz*, and around the corner the *Cafetería Glacier* is OK for breakfasts and snacks. *Restaurant Suizo-Lojano* by the Loja bus terminal is reasonable and has a variety of food. Also good is the *Restaurant Americano* a few blocks to the south. I couldn't find any outstanding restaurants.

Entertainment
There are three movie theatres, of which the *Cine Velez* on the main plaza usually shows the best films. Above the *Cine El Dorado* there is the *La Rosa* discotheque, open at weekends, but it seems teenage rather than adult oriented.

Getting There & Away
Air Loja is served by La Tola airport, which is in Catamayo some 30 km to the west. At this time, TAME has daily flights (except Sundays) to Guayaquil. You have to leave Loja at 5 am to be at the airport by 6 am for the 7 am flight, which costs about US$9.50. There are no buses at that time, but TAME may help organise shared taxis for about US$1.50 per passenger. Alternatively, spend the night in Catamayo. After the flight to Guayaquil has returned, the same plane leaves for Quito at 9 am; the

fare is about the same. Check with the TAME office at the corner of the main plaza in Loja for up-to-date information.

Bus There are many different bus terminals in Loja but the most important is the Transportes Loja Terminal on Avenida 10 de Agosto and Guerrero. Their buses are often booked up several hours or a day in advance, so you should book early. The booking office is crowded, noisy and intimidating, so be prepared. There are two desks: one for same-day bookings and the other for departures on future dates. Once you've sorted out which is which, you can ask the clerk at what times buses are available and buy your ticket.

There are four daily buses to Quito (US$4.50, 18 hours); four buses to Macará (US$1.80, seven hours); eight buses to Zamora (80c, two to three hours); four buses to Machala (US$2.10, eight hours); five buses to Guayaquil (US$3.20, 11 hours); one night bus at 10.30 pm to Huaquillas (US$2.90, 10 hours); and various other departures to intermediate points. It's a very busy terminal.

There are several terminals around the Parque 18 de Noviembre. Centinela del Sur has five daily departures for Machala. The road to Cuenca was being rebuilt in 1987 and delays were common. Co-op Viajeros has seven daily buses to Cuenca (US$2.40, up to 10 hours) and Turismo Oriental has a single night bus to Cuenca. Transportes Saraguro has six or seven buses a day to – you guessed it – Saraguro (60c, two hours). Some of these continue on to remote communities beyond Saraguro, such as Selva Alegre and Manú.

For buses to Vilcabamba you have to go to Transportes Cajanuma or Transportes Sur-Oriente, both of which have four buses a day that take one hour and cost 45c. A few of their buses continue south as far as Valladolid.

There are a few other infrequent buses going to remote and rarely visited villages in the surrounding mountains. Ask around. These are most likely to run at weekends for the Loja market.

VILCABAMBA

A minor road heads due south from Loja and drops steadily through green mountainous scenery to Vilcabamba, some 30 km away. En route you pass through the village of Malacatos, distinguished by a large church with three blue domes visible from a great distance. Malacatos has a Sunday market and there is a basic restaurant, *Salón Estrellita* behind the main plaza.

Vilcabamba has for many years been famous as 'the valley of longevity'. Inhabitants supposedly lived to be 100 or more, and some claimed to be 120 years old. This was attributed to their simple, hard-working lifestyle and the excellent local climate. Scientific investigation has been unable to substantiate these beliefs but the legend persists and gives rise to some minor local tourism. The climate certainly is very pleasant and the surrounding countryside offers lovely walks.

Most of the town surrounds the main square, where there is a church, an IETEL office, a few simple stores and the town's total choice of eating and accommodation possibilities. On Calle Vega just down from the church is an *Artesanías* sign where a few local handicrafts are sold.

Places to Stay & Eat

On the main square there are two basic restaurants and the clean and friendly *Hotel Valle Sagrado*, which charges US$1 per person.

About a km from the main plaza, on the very outskirts of town, is the modern *Parador Turístico Vilcabamba*, which has a restaurant, bar and rooms with private baths for about US$6 per person.

Getting There & Away

There is a Transportes Sur-Oriente bus

office on the main plaza and buses return to Loja every hour or so.

CATAMAYO

Loja was founded twice. The first time was in 1546, on what is now Catamayo; the second time on its present site two years later. Despite its long history, Catamayo is a totally unremarkable town except for its airport, La Tola, which serves Loja 30 km away.

Places to Stay

It is possible to stay here, although accommodation is basic. There are three hotels. *Hotel Lacita* is a few blocks from the central plaza, the *San Marcos* is on the plaza itself, and the *Turis* is on the corner of the plaza. The last is the cleanest-looking at US$1.50 per person. There are several basic restaurants on and near the plaza, and a market as well.

Getting There & Away

There are frequent buses from the plaza to Loja with Transportes Catamayo. There are also slow buses to Quito and Guayaquil. Local buses can take you to explore the small villages to the north and south of Catamayo. A taxi to the airport is about 50c.

About 25 km after Catamayo the road forks. The north fork goes to Machala via the colonial gold-mining towns of Portovelo and Zaruma in the province of El Oro. The south-west fork goes through Catacocha to the border town of Macará.

CATACOCHA

It's a scenic but bumpy seven hour ride from Loja to Macará. Catacocha is the halfway point and the only place you could break the journey. It's a very rural village and on market day (Sunday) it seems as if there are more horses than vehicles in town.

Places to Stay & Eat

There are two basic hotels, both a couple of blocks from the main plaza but in different directions. They are the *Hotel Guayaquil* and *Turismo*. Both charge about US$1.20 each per night. There are a few basic restaurants.

MACARÁ

From Loja at 2225 metres, through Catacocha at about 1700 metres, the road continues to drop steadily to Macará at a hot and dusty 500 metres above sea level. Macará is a small and unimportant town on the Peruvian border. The faster and more convenient coastal route carries almost 100% of the international traffic. The main advantage to the Macará route is the scenic descent from Loja. There are two police checkpoints on this road – no problem if your passport is in order.

Information

Although there is a bank in Macará, it does not have foreign exchange facilities. Because of the low volume of border traffic, there are few people who will change money. If you ask around, however, you will always find someone.

Rates for exchanging soles into sucres and vice versa are inferior to using US cash dollars, so try to arrive at the border with as little local cash as possible. Exchange rates for cash dollars were better with Macará street changers than with the bank at Loja but worse than with the exchange houses in Cuenca. If possible, try to ascertain exchange rates before arrival at the border by talking with travellers going the other way.

There is an IETEL office and a ratty movie theatre.

Places to Stay & Eat

There are four hotels. The best, and the most expensive, is the DITURIS-run *Parador Turistico* on the outskirts of Macará on the way to the border. It has simple, clean rooms with private baths and is excellent value for US$3.50 a single, US$6 a double and US$8.50 a triple. There is a restaurant, which is the best place to eat if you're staying here.

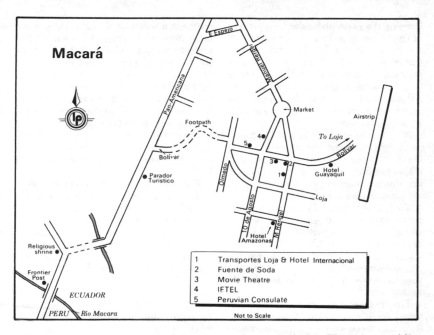

1   Transportes Loja & Hotel Internacional
2   Fuente de Soda
3   Movie Theatre
4   IFTEL
5   Peruvian Consulate

There are three cheap and basic hotels in the town centre. They only have cold water but the weather is warm enough that it isn't a great hardship. *Hotel Internacional* is over the *Transportes Loja* bus terminal; hence it is often full and can get very noisy. *Hotel Amazonas* is on the same street and quieter. *Hotel Guayaquil* is over a store and you should ask the store owners for rooms. It is occasionally closed. All three hotels charge about US$1 per night.

There are a couple of basic restaurants opposite the bus terminal but they are only open at meal times and have limited menus. For mid-afternoon snacks try the *Fuente de Soda*, which isn't very good but at least it's open.

Getting There & Away
Air There are two flights a week to Guayaquil with TAME, using small aircraft such as Twin Otters or Avros. Flights are at 1 pm Monday and Friday and cost US$9.50. There is no airline office; enquire at the airstrip a few minutes' walk from the town centre.

Bus Transportes Loja is the main bus company. The following schedule was in effect recently. Buses are available to:

Loja – 3 am, 1 pm and 4 pm, US$1.80, seven hours
Machala – 6 am, US$2.60, 12 hours
Guayaquil – 6 pm, US$4, 15 hours
Quito – 10 am, US$5.20, 22 hours
Santo Domingo – 1.30 pm, US$4.50, 18 hours

These times are rough estimates. The journeys are tiring and uncomfortable, and you are recommended to go to Loja and break up the journey. If you really must get to the other destinations fast, you should go via the coast.

Crossing the Peruvian Border

Macará is about an hour's walk away from the border at the Río Macará. Pickup trucks leave the market once or twice an hour and charge about 15c. You can take a taxi (usually a pickup truck) for 60c. Vehicles wait at the border to pick up passengers from Peru. Peruvian soles are usually accepted.

At the border there is one fly-blown restaurant where you can get a cold drink. Border crossings are from 8 am to 6 pm daily with irregular lunch hours. Formalities are fairly relaxed as long as your documents are in order.

Travellers entering Ecuador are rarely asked to show exit tickets or money, though a valid passport and tourist card are needed. If arriving, you will be given a tourist card at the border; if leaving, you will be expected to surrender the card you received on arrival to the border authorities.

Travellers entering Peru are occasionally asked for a ticket out of the country, especially those who require a visa. If you don't require a visa you probably won't be asked. If you are, and you don't have an airline ticket out of Lima, you can usually satisfy this requirement by buying a return bus ticket to Sullana, the nearest large town and over 200 km away. The unused portion of the ticket is non-refundable. Most nationalities, however, need only a valid passport and tourist card which is obtainable from the border authorities. 'Gringo' exceptions are Australians, New Zealanders and French citizens who do require visas.

There is a Peruvian consul in Macará – if in any doubt, check. The consulate is open from 9 am to 1 pm Monday through Friday.

Facilities for accommodation, transport and food are inferior on the Peruvian side and it is best to stay in Macará if possible. Trucks leave the border for the first town of Las Lomas when there are enough passengers (usually about 10 am). The road is bad. From Las Lomas to the main town of Sullana the road is paved. A bus leaves the border for Sullana at 2 pm daily. It is difficult to get transport into Peru later in the afternoon and evening; therefore crossing the border in the morning is advisable.

Lonely Planet publishes *Peru – A Travel Survival Kit* for travellers continuing to that country.

The Southern Oriente

Oriente literally means the orient, or east, and is the term used by Ecuadoreans for all of their Amazon basin lowlands east of the Andes. The words *selva* or *jungla* are not used for the area as a whole, although *selva* can refer to a particular part of the forest of the Oriente. Even though the Amazon River itself does not flow through Ecuador, every one of Ecuador's rivers east of the Andean divide eventually empties into the Amazon and hence all of the Oriente can properly be referred to as being part of the upper Amazon basin. The correct term for most of the basin's vegetation is 'rainforest'; popular usage, however, refers to this lush tropical growth as jungle.

A glance at any Ecuadorean map will show its claim to a large section of jungle extending beyond Iquitos. The basis of this claim has a long history. After independence in 1822, the new republic claimed lands as far as the River Marañon in the south, and far eastwards into what is now Brazil. This remote and difficult-to-control area was slowly settled by increasing numbers of Peruvians (as well as a few Colombians and Brazilians). Ecuador gradually lost lands to these countries. In 1941 matters came to a head and war with Peru broke out. Each country accused the other of beginning the aggression. The following year a treaty at Rio de Janeiro ended the war and Peru was allotted a huge section of what had been Ecuador.

The Ecuadoreans have never officially accepted the full terms of this treaty, claiming that it was bulldozed through when most of the world was occupied with WW II; that Peru invaded them; that the limits of the treaty were geographically invalid because a small section in the Cordillera del Cóndor in the south-east was ambiguously defined; and that the land was theirs anyway. Internationally, however, the border as drawn up by the 1942 treaty is accepted. If you should ever fly from Miami to Iquitos on a regularly scheduled jet service, rest assured that you will be landing in Peru!

This dispute affects the traveller in several ways. The south-eastern border region is still very sensitive and there are skirmishes every few years. The last major battles were in early 1981, when several soldiers were killed and aircraft shot down in an area only 20 km from the main road through the southern Oriente. Sabre-rattling continues intermittently. While journeying through the Oriente, even on the well-travelled tourist routes, you should always have documentation on hand, as passport checks at military checkpoints are not uncommon. These are usually quick and hassle-free, assuming your papers are in order.

The dispute also means that crossing the border into the Peruvian jungle is no longer possible for foreign travellers (though various Indian groups do so all the time). So if you were hoping to descend from Ecuador to the Amazon in river boats or canoes, forget it. Finally, try not to wave non-Ecuadorean maps of the region under peoples' noses. One friend had maps of Peru confiscated by customs officers at Quito airport, because the Peruvian maps naturally didn't show the Ecuadorean claim. It should be emphasised that the area is safe to travel in at this time.

The Oriente can be conveniently divided into north and south by the Río Pastaza. The main southern Oriente road begins at Loja and goes through Zamora north to Macas. Beyond Macas the road is unfinished and you have to continue either on foot or by air to Puyo on the north side of the Pastaza.

Most travellers to the Oriente visit the northern region, which admittedly has much more to offer the tourist. Indeed, the southern Oriente is the least-visited part of Ecuador and has a real sense of remoteness. Perhaps that is why I particularly enjoyed travelling through it.

There are two surface routes into the southern Oriente. The most frequently used is from Cuenca through Limón (officially named on most maps as General L Plaza Gutiérrez) to Macas. The other route runs from Loja through Zamora and continues north to Limón, where it joins the first route.

ZAMORA

Although Zamora is only 40 km by road from Loja, the journey takes almost three hours. The road climbs dustily from Loja over a 2500-metre-high pass and then drops tortuously along the Zamora River valley to the town at 970 metres above sea level. The scenery soon becomes tropical, the vegetation thicker, and you begin seeing strange plants such as the giant tree fern. There are good views in either

direction, but the right-hand side of the bus is the best.

Zamora was first founded by the Spanish in 1549, but the colony soon died out because of Indian attacks. It was re-founded in 1800 but remained very small. A local old-timer recalls that when he arrived in Zamora in the 1930s, there were only half a dozen buildings. In 1953 it became the provincial capital when the province of Zamora-Chinchipe was created, although it was still extremely small and isolated. The first vehicle did not arrive in town until 1962.

Zamora is now experiencing a boom since the recent discovery of gold in Nambija, a few km to the north. The sudden influx of miners has strained the resources of the area somewhat, and food costs are relatively high. The present population of Zamora is about 6000.

Saraguro Indians with their typical black shorts are sometimes seen in the Zamora area. They arrive on foot, driving their cattle on the trail from Saraguro,

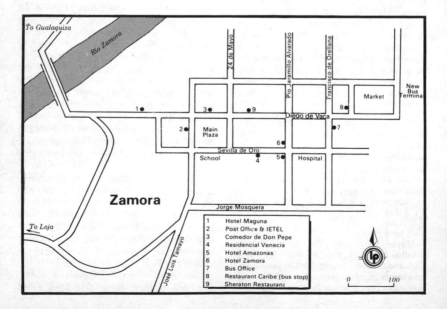

Zamora

1 Hotel Maguna
2 Post Office & IETEL
3 Comedor de Don Pepe
4 Residencial Venecia
5 Hotel Amazonas
6 Hotel Zamora
7 Bus Office
8 Restaurant Caribe (bus stop)
9 Sheraton Restaurant

through 28 de Mayo, to the Zamora-Yanzatza road. North of Zamora, Shuar Indians may also be seen, as well as colonists and miners. The whole area definitely has a frontier feel to it.

Military Checkpoint

The recent conflict with Peru took place close to Zamora. This, combined with the present gold boom, means that there is a high-profile military presence in Zamora. There are military checkpoints on both sides of town. You have to check in and register your passport at the main checkpoint three km from the north-east side of town, on the road to Gualaquiza.

When I arrived from Loja, I had to show my passport at the minor checkpoint west of Zamora. Then I was accompanied into the town itself by an armed soldier who insisted that I go with him to the main checkpoint to register my passport. I couldn't do this at the first checkpoint, nor could I persuade him that I would do it on my way out of town, and I couldn't book myself into a hotel room and get rid of my luggage first. My only (minor) victory was insisting that he paid my bus fare to the main checkpoint three km out of town. This is without a doubt the most intimidating passport check I've had in two years of travelling all over Ecuador. Nevertheless, the armed soldier was polite and friendly (if insistent!), and there were no real hassles.

At the main checkpoint I had to explain my presence – they just aren't used to seeing tourists here. Whatever your feelings are, keep your cool and insist that you are a *turista* visiting the Oriente and taking buses from Loja to Gualaquiza and Cuenca or wherever. This is absolutely not the time to express your interest in the Peruvian border or your fervent hopes to make a fortune in the goldfields. Foreigners are not allowed there anyway. After all this, they didn't even stamp my passport.

Once you've checked in, you're on your own. They don't provide a staff car to take you back into town, so it's a three-km walk, or you can wait for a passing bus (one or two an hour).

Maybe, by the time you read this, it will be possible to register on the Loja side of town, thus avoiding the lengthy hassle described. If you arrive in Zamora from the north on your way out to Loja, it will probably be easier as you will pass by the main checkpoint on your way to town. If you're lucky, you won't get stopped at all. Maybe I just came across a particularly officious official, or some brigadier was passing through and they wanted to impress him. If you're entering the Oriente through Zamora, cheer yourself with the thought that this is the most difficult of all the checkpoints.

Information

There's not much to do. The main plaza is a concrete affair with few trees and little shade. The IETEL and post office are on the plaza. There is a bank but they don't do foreign exchange, and there's a movie theatre on the northern outskirts of town by the river. The town is planning a tree-lined riverside avenue two km long. Most restaurants are closed by 8 pm, so eat early. After dinner on a Saturday, you could try the discotheque over the *Sheraton Restaurant*. The weather is not too hot, with daytime temperatures averaging about 20°C and pleasant evenings with few insects.

Places to Stay & Eat

The three cheap hotels are all clustered together a block away from the plaza. The best and cleanest of these is the *Hotel Zamora*, which charges US$1.50 per person. They have some good balcony rooms which you should ask for. *Hotel Amazonas* and *Residencia Venecia* are not as good and charge US$1.40. None of them have private bathrooms or hot water, but you have to start getting used to that in the Oriente. Anyway, cold showers are refreshing in the hot weather.

A hotel which opened in 1984 provides quite luxurious services. *Hotel Maguna* has rooms with private baths, carpeting, TV and telephone for about US$4 per person. These are 'promotional' prices to advertise the new hotel and may well go up in future. Some of the rooms have excellent balcony views of the Río Zamora.

There are several restaurants on the main street, Avenida Diego de Vaca. *Comedor de Don Pepe* on the main plaza is quite good. *Restaurant Caribe* is full of flies but convenient if waiting for a bus. Menus are sometimes limited and the meal of the day is often the best choice.

Getting There & Away

Bus A new bus terminal is under construction on the east side of the market. Meanwhile, buses arrive and depart from the market; the corner in front of the Restaurant Caribe is the place to wait. There is a bus office but its hours are irregular.

Transportes Loja run about eight buses a day to Loja (90c, three hours). Zamora-Chinchipe buses are open-sided trucks with uncomfortable bench seats designed for midgets. They provide frequent services to nearby villages as far north as Yanzatza. There is no scheduled service from Zamora north to Gualaquiza and beyond. You have to wait outside the Restaurant Caribe for a northbound bus from Loja to pass. Enough passengers normally get off at Zamora that it's not very difficult to get a seat to continue north. Some of these buses go only as far as Yanzatza (50c, 1½ hours); only two or three a day continue as far as Gualaquiza (US$1.30, 4½ hours).

YANZATZA

The northbound road to Yanzatza follows the left bank of the Río Zamora, so the best views are on the right of the bus. There are beautiful vistas of open stretches of the river with heavily forested hills on either side, often with tropical trees flowering in bright reds, yellows and purples. The bus goes through many little Indian hamlets and *fincas* growing a variety of tropical produce such as coffee, sugar cane and citrus fruit. The road also goes near the Nambija mining area, so the journey is enlivened by the various interesting characters getting on and off the bus.

The first village of any size north of Zamora is Yanzatza, 1½ hours away. In 1970 it was only a couple of shacks but since the Nambija gold boom it has become one of the fastest-growing towns in the province. Its population is now in excess of three thousand and there are several restaurants and a couple of basic hotels. These are likely to be full of miners, so it's probably best to continue to Gualaquiza. The hotels *Amazonas* and *Central* are both just off the main square.

GUALAQUIZA

North of Yanzatza the population thins and houses are seen infrequently. The road continues to follow the left bank of the gently dropping Río Zamora, and there are fine tropical views. Sit on the right of the bus. The road crosses the provincial line into Morona Santiago province near the tiny village of Los Encuentros and continues to El Pangui, where there is the basic *Hotel El Cóndor* on the one street. Just north of this village the road drops suddenly and a lovely jungle panorama stretches out below.

A few km before reaching Gualaquiza, the Río Cuchipamba is crossed. A new steel bridge is planned, but meanwhile all traffic must cross the river by a decrepit wooden raft capable of transporting only one vehicle at a time. Most passengers get off the bus – you can cross on a footbridge.

Gualaquiza is a pretty little village of about three thousand inhabitants. The church on the main plaza looks like a toy building, and there are cobbled streets and houses with attractive balconies. The town has a Spanish colonial air. There are also pleasant walks in the surrounding countryside. Gualaquiza closes down early and is definitely *tranquilo*. A new cinema has recently opened.

Places to Stay & Eat

Accommodation is limited as this is a little-visited town. On the main plaza is the simple *Residencial Amazonas*, which charges US$1.50 each. It is probably better than the *Pensión Oriental* on the main street. Recently opened on the main street is the clean *Hotel Turismo* which charges about US$1.50 each. Also on this street is the *Bar Restaurant Gualaquiza*, as good as any of the few restaurants. There is a small market just off the main street.

Getting There & Away

There are several bus companies on the main street, Calle Gonzalo Pezantes Lefebre. Transportes Sucúa, El Cóndor and Oriental each have two or three departures a day for various destinations. Ask around. You can go south (Zamora and Loja), north (Limón, Sucúa and Macas) or west (Cuenca). The next town to the north is Limón (US$1.40, four hours). To Macas it's US$2.80, 8½ hours.

LIMÓN (General L Plaza Gutiérrez)

Limón (population 2300) is a totally unprepossessing town whose main importance is that it lies at the junction of the roads to Cuenca, Macas and Zamora. From Gualaquiza the road passes through pretty but sparsely populated countryside until it reaches the missions of San Juan Bosco and Plan de Milagro (also known as Indanza), about an hour before Limón.

Places to Stay & Eat

Limón is a typical small Ecuadorean jungle town with one main street with two hotels, several simple restaurants and bus offices. Both the *Residencial Paraiso* and *Amazonas* are basic but clean and charge US$1 each. Avoid getting rooms on the street as bus drivers park their buses with engines running while they have a midnight snack or early-morning breakfast. Exhaust fumes fill your room and the noise keeps you awake.

Getting There & Away

Buses from Limón are available to the north, south and west several times a day with various companies who have their offices along the main street. Few buses originate in Limón, however, so departure times are at best approximate. If you have

arrived from the south, this is where you join the road from Cuenca. If you are going to Macas, sit on the right-hand side of the bus, as there are good views of the Río Upano.

MÉNDEZ

This quiet little village of 1250 inhabitants is passed through on the way to Sucúa. It is less than two hours from Limón and 60c a ticket. On the corner of its shady plaza are the very simple pensiones *Miranda* and *Ruiz*, both charging the usual dollar. There are one or two restaurants and the houses have red-tiled roofs and flowery gardens.

SUCÚA

Sucúa, population 4000, is one of the more interesting villages in the southern Oriente. It is the major centre of the Shuar Indians, who were formerly called the Jivaro and were infamous for shrinking the heads of their defeated enemies. This practice still occurred as recently as two generations ago and the *tsantsas*, or shrunken heads, can still be seen in various museums, notably the Municipal Museum in Guayaquil. Most of today's Shuar look very Ecuadorean in jeans and T-shirts, but you still see older Indians with elaborate facial or body tattoos.

There is a pleasant main plaza with shady trees, tropical flowers, cicadas and birds. From the plaza, walk down the main street (Avenida Francisco Orellana) and you'll come to the Shuar Centre on your left, about a km away. Here you can buy booklets and obtain further information about the Shuar. The Shuar have become missionised, as have most of the surviving Oriente Indian groups, so you won't be shown *tsantsas*; other crafts are, however, on display. There is also a mission hospital and a movie theatre.

Places to Stay & Eat

A good hotel is the clean *Hotel Cumanda*, which charges US$2 per night and is on the plaza. Similar is the *Hotel Oriente*, down the main street close to the Shuar Centre. They have a restaurant. The cheapest place in town is the basic *Hotel Colón*, just off the plaza on the main street. There are several restaurants by this corner, including the *Bar Restaurant Rincón Oriental*, probably the best restaurant in the southern Oriente. The waiters wear bow ties and charge about 15c more than the basic places. Definitely worth it.

Getting There & Away

Air For several years, the airstrip at Sucúa provided regular service to Puyo with TAO. In mid-1984, however, the new airport at Macas was opened with a runway capable of taking large planes; that airport has now largely superseded the strip at Sucúa. Light aircraft might take passengers to Puyo on a semi-regular basis so ask at the office by the airstrip. Aircraft can be chartered for flights into the interior of the Oriente; ask at the Shuar centre or the mission. Villages in the interior are for Indians and missionaries; there are no facilities for tourists.

Bus Pickup trucks for Macas (40c, one hour) leave at frequent intervals from 6 am to 5.30 pm every day. Departures are from the corner of the main plaza near the Hotel Cumanda.

Southbound buses pass by the restaurants on the main street at the corner of the plaza. Services are better from Macas.

MACAS

This small (population 6000) but important town is the capital of the province of Morona-Santiago and is the end of the road for most travellers. It has four centuries of history as a Spanish trading and missionary outpost, and an old mule trail still joins Macas with the highlands near Riobamba. A road is planned which will follow this trail, but it is unlikely to be completed in the near future. A road north to Puyo is also projected but it stops about

two hours north of Macas, so the only existing road link with Quito is via Cuenca.

Despite its history, Macas is essentially a modern and developing town. There is a new bus terminal and airport, and the main plaza was completed only in 1983. A new cathedral is being built on a small hill above the main plaza. It's a large, scaffolded, concrete monstrosity at present, but maybe one day ... Almost hidden behind the cathedral is the quaint and simple old wooden church containing some well-carved stations of the cross. From the cathedral hill there's a view of the town and, on a clear day, the often smoking volcano Sangay some 40 km to the north-west. At 5230 metres, it is the seventh highest mountain in Ecuador and one of the most active volcanoes in the world.

Information

There are both IETEL and post offices. The first is new and the second is old. It is likely that a new post office will be built by the main plaza. There is no movie theatre or other entertainment.

Places to Stay & Eat

There are eight hotels in Macas. They all seem to charge a uniform US$1.50 each except the *Pensión Turismo*, which is a few cents cheaper but also the most run down. The *Residencial Upano* is pretty run down too. The best (or at least the most popular) place is the simple *Hotel Encalada*, which also has one of the best restaurants in town. If that's full, the *Hotel Amazonas* is also quite good. There are others marked on the map; none of them are particularly noteworthy. None of these hotels have hot water or private bathrooms.

Macas is a fast-developing town and new hotels are under construction. One, near the bus terminal, and marked on the map, recently opened and charges from US$2 to 4 each, with hot water and some private bathrooms.

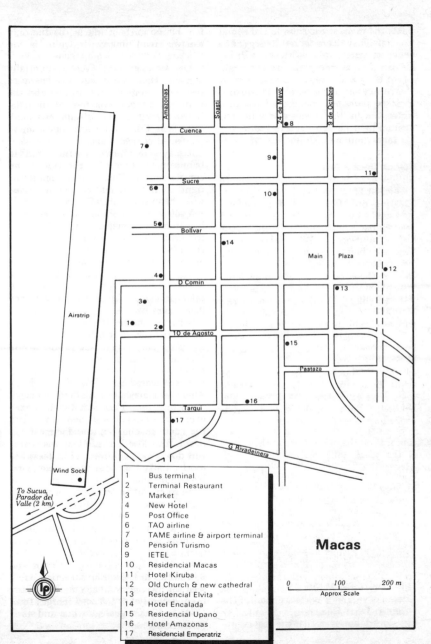

Macas

1	Bus terminal
2	Terminal Restaurant
3	Market
4	New Hotel
5	Post Office
6	TAO airline
7	TAME airline & airport terminal
8	Pensión Turismo
9	IETEL
10	Residencial Macas
11	Hotel Kiruba
12	Old Church & new cathedral
13	Residencial Elvita
14	Hotel Encalada
15	Residencial Upano
16	Hotel Amazonas
17	Residencial Emperatriz

0   100   200 m
Approx Scale

About two km south of town, on the road to Sucúa, is the *Parador del Valle*, which has clean, bungalow-style accommodation for US$7 a double with private bath. There is a restaurant.

Restaurants are generally lacklustre. Most people eat at the *Hotel Encalada*, which has good set meals and a limited menu. There is a reasonable restaurant by the bus terminal and a few others.

Getting There & Away

Air TAME has three flights a week to Cuenca at 11.30 am and three to Quito at 1.30 pm on Monday, Wednesday and Friday. Tickets cost US$11 to Quito and are obtainable from the TAME office in the airport building. The last time I flew out of this town, half the town's population and even people from surrounding villages came to the airport to see the large, four-prop plane land and take off. There was a festive feeling in the air – after all, there's little else to do in Macas. Recently, a 727 jet was also being used for this service.

TAO has flights on most weekdays to Pastaza near Puyo. Pastaza is also known as Shell as it used to be an oil company airstrip. Flights cost US$9 and, because small, light aircraft are normally used, they give a good aerial look at the jungle. Seating is limited and flights are often booked up several days in advance.

Bus All departures are from the new Terminal Terrestre. There are several departures a day for Cuenca (US$2.20, seven hours) and Gualaquiza (US$2.60, 9 hours). Buses and pickup trucks to Sucúa (40c, one hour) are frequent. Transportes Macas runs small buses and pickup trucks to various remote, northern parts of the province, including Chiguaza (US$1, two hours), hourly during daylight hours.

THE JUNGLE FROM MACAS

There are various ways to see more of the Oriente from Macas. It should be mentioned, however, that the best centre for tourism in the jungle is Misahuallí in the northern Oriente.

Many Ecuadorean maps show tracks or trails leading from Macas into the interior. These are usually overgrown as transportation to the Shuar Indian villages and missions further into the Oriente is mainly by light aircraft these days. It is difficult but not impossible to visit some of these villages.

You can hire an *expreso* light aircraft to take you to some of the better-known centres such as Taisha. With luck or the right contacts, flights can be arranged with the mission aircraft.

Visiting nearby Shuar centres on foot or bus is fairly straightforward. There are frequent buses to the mission of Sevilla (Don Bosco), about an hour's walk away on the other side of the Río Upano. A new bridge is being built; at present there is a rickety wooden suspension bridge which takes only one vehicle at a time. All the passengers disembark and walk across the bridge, and the bus follows.

From Sevilla you can head south on foot along a broad track to the village of San Luis, about four hours' walk away. This makes a good day trip and en route you'll pass cultivated areas and Indian huts, where you may be invited to try some yucca *chicha*. This traditional Shuar drink is made by the women, who grind up the yucca by chewing it and then spit it into a bowl where it is left to ferment. If this doesn't appeal to you, bring a water bottle. There are no facilities of any kind beyond Sevilla.

Buses go north along a fairly good gravel road to various destinations up to and including the Río Chiguaza, where the road stops. The bus passes through Shuar territory and you can see a few of their oval-shaped, bamboo-caned, thatched huts on the sides of the road. Most of the Indians riding the bus look unremarkably western, but occasionally a beautifully beaded bracelet or tattooed face is seen.

At the Río Chiguaza the bus returns to Macas but you can continue on foot if you

Top: Colonial Cuenca and Río Tomebamba (RR)
Left: Quito at dusk and Mt Cayambe (RR)
Right: Quevedo river market (RR)

Top: Cofan Indian Children (RR)
Left: Oriente Boy (RR)
Right: Group of Cofan Indians passing under a Breadfruit Tree (RR)

wish. A canoe will ferry you across the river and then you have to ask the way to the villages of 24 de Mayo and Arapicos, where another canoe will ferry you across the Río Palora. There are no facilities at these villages although, if you're lucky, you may find a pickup truck going from Arapicos to Palora where there is a very basic pensión. You may have to walk as far as Palora, as the road is often impassable.

From Palora there are three buses a day to Puyo, in the northern Oriente. Locals say that if you take the first morning bus from Macas to Chiguaza, you can walk to Palora in one long day. I've never tried it.

The Northern Oriente

North of the Río Pastaza are the provinces of Pastaza and Napo, which together form the northern Oriente.

Unlike the southern Oriente, the northern Oriente is well connected with two roads to Quito and hence is the most visited part of Ecuador's jungle. In one long day of bus riding, you can go from Quito to the oil boom town of Lago Agrio in the far north-eastern jungle, or to the tourist centre of Misahuallí in the central Oriente. Various round trips can be made by bus, boat and air. If your time is limited, the quickest of these is the bus journey from Quito through Ambato, Baños, Puyo, Tena, Baeza and back to Quito. This can be done in two long days and gives a good look at the jungle where it meets the eastern slopes of the Andes.

A longer and highly recommended trip can be made by omitting the Tena-Baeza section and going instead via Misahuallí and down the Río Napo to Coca, and then continuing by bus to Lago Agrio and back to Quito through Baeza. Such a trip will give a very good look at many facets of the Ecuadorean Oriente and is not beyond anyone's resources. It is feasible to make the trip in four days, but at least a week or more is recommended. The journey could be broken at either Coca or Lago Agrio, both of which have regular air services to Quito. The trip can be done in reverse but this isn't recommended, as the river portion is against the current and takes over twice as long.

1987 Earthquake

A devastating earthquake in early 1987 caused the loss of hundreds of lives and the closure of the road between Baeza and Lago Agrio. There are now two ways of getting to Lago Agrio. One is to take one of the extra flights from Quito – these are run by the military and an all day wait at the airport is not uncommon. Alternatively,

you can travel by bus to Misahuallí, then by river to Coca, and continue by bus to Lago Agrio. This takes two or three days. The closed road is being worked on and a re-opening in late 1987 is hoped for, but make local enquiry. Be prepared for delays and changes in this region as a result of the earthquake.

THE ROAD TO PUYO

If I were to choose just one stretch of road in Ecuador for the best views of the upper Amazon basin, I would have difficulty in improving upon the drive from Baños to Puyo.

The road follows the Río Pastaza canyon as it drops steadily from Baños at 1800 metres to Puyo at 950 metres. This road has recently been rebuilt, and buses now regularly make the through journey. Just beyond the famous Agoyan waterfall – now site of a new hydro-electric project – the road passes through a tunnel. A few km further, a waterfall splashes from the overhanging cliff onto the road – quite a surprise if you're hitch-hiking in the back of a pickup truck.

Waterfalls frequently cascade into the canyon, and one of the most impressive is by the village of Río Verde, 20 km beyond Baños. You have to walk down a short trail to a suspension bridge to appreciate it properly; ask at the village. As the road drops further, the vegetation rapidly becomes more tropical and the walls of the Pastaza canyon are covered with bromeliads, giant tree ferns, orchids and flowering trees. Near the small community of Mera the canyon walls spread apart, and you see a breathtaking view of the Río Pastaza meandering away to the south-east through the vast, rolling plains of the Amazon basin. The right side of the bus is best for views. There is no higher land between here and the Atlantic, almost 4000 km to the east.

SHELL

Shell is a few km beyond Mera and the two communities together are often called Shell-Mera. At Shell is the Pastaza airstrip, serving Puyo which is about 10 km away. This is the most important airstrip in the province of Pastaza. There is also a military checkpoint here.

Military Checkpoint

All foreign travellers arriving in the Oriente through Shell must register with the army. The procedure is efficient and straightforward. Buses on the way to Puyo stop by the checkpoint and wait while foreigners disembark and register. You have to fill out a form with the usual details (age, nationality, etc) and present your passport and the tourist card which you received on entry into Ecuador. You'll be asked your destination and the purpose of your visit. *Turismo* is the safest and most obvious answer. Your passport will be stamped by the Brigada de Selva No 20 and you'll be free to go.

The whole procedure takes only a minute and the bus drivers are so used to it that they'll wait as a matter of course. The only possible problem is if you only have a few days left on your visa, as they like you to have at least 10 days before going into the Oriente. The stamp is important; it will be inspected by the port captain at Misahuallí before you can take the boat downriver. It may also be inspected at other places in the Oriente.

If you arrive at Puyo by air you should also register. The checkpoint is five minutes' walk east of the airport on the one main street of town. If you are leaving the Oriente through Puyo, you may or may not have to register.

Places to Stay & Eat

There are three basic hotels, of which the *Cordillera* is probably the best. It charges about US$1.20 a night. There are a few simple restaurants. You won't get lost – it's a one-street town with the airport at the west end on the way to Baños, and the

checkpoint near the east end on the way to Puyo. Everything else lies in between.

Getting There & Away

Air There are no regular flights from Shell to Quito. Flights with TAO leave most mornings for Macas aboard light aircraft and cost US$9.50. Seating is limited and tends to be booked up ahead. The TAO office is in the airport. There are various other companies (Condor, ATESA) in Shell which can provide light aircraft for chartered flights to other jungle strips. Shell is also a major US missionary centre and there are schools, churches and hospitals. The missions often have flights into the Oriente and can provide emergency services.

Bus Most people going through Shell will already be on a bus through to Puyo. Should you need a bus to Puyo, wait by the military checkpoint, where pickup trucks leave for Puyo every half hour and charge about 15c. If you want to go to Baños or Ambato, also wait by the checkpoint for buses from Puyo, which will pick you up if they have room.

PUYO

Puyo, with a growing population of about 14,000, is the provincial capital of Pastaza. Until the early '70s it had a real 'frontier' atmosphere, and was the most important town in the Oriente. Since the discovery of oil, however, the frontier has been pushed deep into the jungle and now Lago Agrio vies for the claim of being Ecuador's most important Oriente town.

Information

There are IETEL and post offices marked on the map. Two banks are also marked. The Banco de Fomento doesn't change money but one of the managers will buy cash dollars as a 'favour' at unfavourable rates. The new Banco Internacional was still under construction when I was last in Puyo, but it should be open by now and I've heard rumours that it may exchange

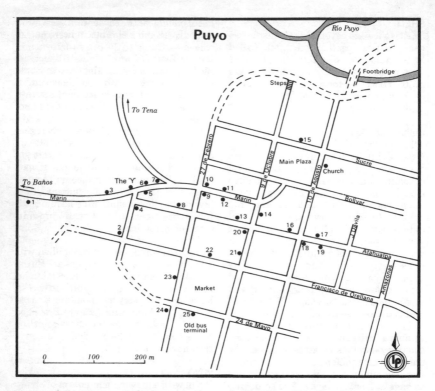

Puyo

Río Puyo

Footbridge

Steps

↑ *To Tena*

●15

Main Plaza

Sucre

27 de Febrero

9 de Octubre

Church

To Baños

The 'Y' 7●

6●

●10

10 de Agosto

●11

3

Marin

Marin

Bolivar

●1

3●

5●

●9

12

●8

4

●13 ●14

Dávila

2

20●

16●

●17

22● 21●

18● 19

Atahualpa

23●

Market

Francisco de Orellana

Amazonas

24● 25●

Old bus terminal

24 de Mayo

0   100   200 m

money. An auto spares dealer near the Banco de Fomento also buys cash dollars at unfavourable rates when he's in the mood. 'Unfavourable' means about 10% or 15% less than in Quito.

Things to See

If you can get up at dawn you'll often see a spectacular view of jagged snow peaks rising up over a jungle covered with rolling morning mists. Later in the morning, the mountains usually disappear into the clouds. The jagged peaks belong to El Altar (5319 metres), the fifth highest mountain in Ecuador, about 50 km to the south-east. Sangay (5230 metres) is also occasionally seen. A good view can be had from the main plaza.

El Tucan gift shop on the plaza has a good variety of handicrafts and functions almost as a museum. It's worth a look and if this is as far into the Oriente as you plan on going, you can buy balsa models, bead and feather necklaces, blowguns and other jungle crafts.

During the day you can go swimming in the river. If you're a bird-watcher you'll see a good variety of jungle species near the river.

For nightlife, there is the Amazonas movie theatre which shows kung-fu movies to the accompaniment of encouraging yells from the local kids. There is a video club on the Tena road, about half a kilometre out of town just past the bridge. They show movies ranging from porno to Oscar winners. You could see how the newly opened Peña Bar is doing; they plan

1	Hostal Turinga
2	IETEL
3	Auto spares store (change money)
4	Residencial Gioconda
5	Hotel Tucan
6	Banco de Fomento
7	Transportes San Francisco
8	Rincon Ambateño Restaurant
9	Teatro Amazonas
10	Residencial El Alamo
11	Pensión Paris
12	Pensión Guayaquil
13	Restaurant Mistral
14	Hotels Europa & California
15	El Tucan gift shop
16	Post Office
17	New Banco Internacional
18	Buses Centinela del Oriente
19	Peña Bar
20	Pensión Susanita
21	Hotel Europa Internacional
22	Residencial Santa & Pensión Georginita
23	Hotel Granada & Pensión Victoria
24	Pensión Tungurahua
25	Residencial Ecuador

on having live music at weekends. Other places open and close sporadically, so ask around.

Places to Stay

There's no shortage of accommodation in Puyo but there are frequent water shortages. During a recent visit, none of the cheaper hotels had any water at all and you had to swim in the river. The water system is currently being repaired. If you need a shower, ensure that there is running water before renting a room.

Places to Stay – bottom end

Hotel Granada at US$1.20 per person, and the very simple *Pensión Victoria* behind it for US$1, have been recommended by budget travellers. They are both by the old bus terminal. There are several other places near here in this price range. These include the very basic *Pensión Georginita* and the somewhat better *Residencial Santa* and *Pensión Tungurahua*. The

Residencial Ecuador is old but well looked after and has pretty flowers in the balconies. Closer to the centre of town are some cheap and run-down hotels such as the *Pensión Guayaquil* and *Paris* and the *Residencial El Alamo* and *Susanita*. I must confess to a no more than cursory examination of these – they don't look up to much.

The *Residencial Gioconda*, near the Transportes San Francisco bus office, looks quite good for US$1.50 per person; some rooms are with private baths. It was full when I tried it – often the sign of good value. *Hotel Tucan* nearby charges US$2 per person for rooms with communal baths. They seem unfriendly. If you want to be fairly sure of a constant water supply and reasonable comfort, I recommend either the hotels *California* or *Europa*, which are next door to one another on 9 de Octubre. They both charge US$2.50 per person with a communal bath and US$3 each for rooms with a private bath. The *Europa* has hot water and a good view from the roof.

Places to Stay – top end

Hotel Europa Internacional (as opposed to the Hotel Europa) is a modern hotel in the town centre which charges about US$6.50 a single and US$11 a double for rooms with a bath. It will have to be seen how it withstands the ravages of time. A similarly priced hotel, which has been a Puyo institution for years and has aged charmingly, is the highly recommended *Hostal Turingia* on the outskirts of town towards Baños. They have accommodation in bungalows with private bath and hot water. The bungalows are set in a tropical garden with a good collection of orchids. There is a good restaurant. Also, there is the *Safari*, about five km away on the road to Tena, which falls in this price range.

Places to Eat

Puyo cannot be recommended to gourmets. One of its better restaurants, and it's by no means fancy, is the *Rincón Ambateño*, which has been here for a long time and has various car-rallying trophies on the walls. The *Mistral* is good for breakfast and OK during the rest of the day. It is decorated with a rather bizarre collection of prints ranging from posters of the Beatles to photographs of local Indian tribes. There are several other places. The better hotels have adequate restaurants, of which the *Europa Internacional* is the best downtown and the *Turingia* is the best overall.

Getting There & Away

Air Pickup trucks providing service to Shell for the Pastaza airstrip leave from the intersection known as the 'Y' (*El Y* is pronounced *el ee*). It's marked with a 'Y' on the map.

Bus The old bus terminal is marked on the map, but few buses depart or arrive there any more. A new terminal to the south-west of town is projected, but is nowhere near completion. Meanwhile, most buses leave from the Transportes San Francisco office. This company has frequent buses to Ambato (US$1, three hours), a few of which continue to Quito (US$1.80, six hours) and Riobamba. The only buses to Tena (US$1, three hours) leave at 6.30 and 8.45 am, so if you want to catch one later in the day you have to wait for a bus passing (*al paso*) from Ambato. These may well have standing space only and during weekends can be completely full. The early morning buses are usually booked the day before.

Centinela del Oriente runs ancient buses to various small villages in the surrounding jungle. The most important of these is Palora, where there is a basic pensión and from where you can continue south by pickup truck (if you are lucky), foot and canoe ferry to Chiguaza near Macas in the southern Oriente. (For more information about this journey, see the section on Macas.) Buses for Palora leave three times a day for the three-hour ride, which involves two river crossings.

PUERTO NAPO

The narrow, gravelled road from Puyo into the Oriente heads almost due north, passing small homesteads and occasional banana plantations until the road crosses the provincial line into Napo. About seven km from Tena, Puerto Napo is reached. There is only one place to stay, *Hotel Palandacocha*. A road fork to the right leads to Misahuallí, 17 km away, or you can continue north to Tena.

You can wait here for a vehicle to take you to Misahuallí. Many buses/trucks to Misahuallí come from Tena and there is often a scramble for seats. It is probably easier, though not necessarily faster, to go into Tena and take a bus back to Misahuallí from there.

TENA

Tena, at about 500 metres above sea level, is the capital of the province of Napo. This province, with an area of over 52,000 square km – almost a fifth of the country – is the largest in Ecuador. Its capital, however, has a population of only 6000.

Tena was founded in 1560, and was the most easterly of Ecuador's early colonial missionary and trading outposts. There were several Indian uprisings in the early days, notably in 1578 when Jumandy, chief of the Quijos, led an unsuccessful revolt against the Spaniards. Tena survived, though many early Oriente towns were completely wiped out by other Indian attacks. Today the area is largely agricultural, with cattle ranches and coffee or banana plantations. It is at the junction of the Tena and Pano rivers and is a minor centre for Ecuadorean tourism. The average year-round temperature is 24°C, with the rivers having a moderating effect on the climate.

The anniversary of Tena's foundation is celebrated on 15 November, and is the time for colourful processions and other festivities. While visiting the town during

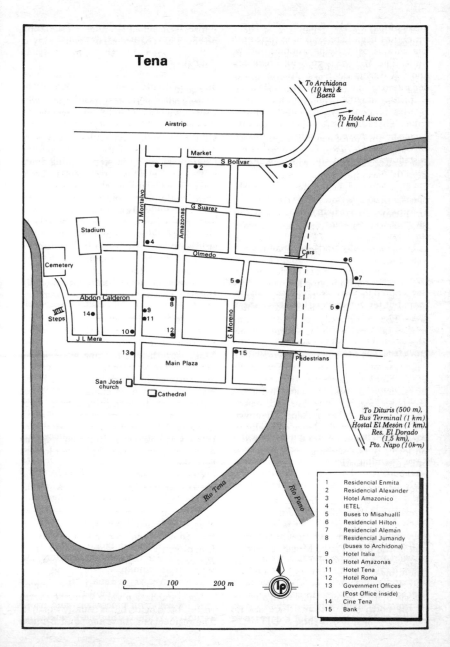

Tena

To Archidona
(10 km) &
Baeza

To Hotel Auca
(1 km)

Airstrip

Market

S Bolívar

● 1   ● 2   ● 3

J Montalvo

G Suarez

Amazonas

Stadium

● 4

Olmedo

Cars

Cemetery

● 6

● 7

5 ●

Abdon Calderon

● 8

Steps   14●   ● 9

● 11

10 ●   ● 12

5 ●

J L Mera

G Moreno

13●   ● 15   Pedestrians

Main Plaza

San José
church

Cathedral

To Dituris (500 m),
Bus Terminal (1 km)
Hostal El Mesón (1 km),
Res. El Dorado
(1.5 km),
Pto. Napo (10km)

Río Tena

Río Pano

0   100   200 m

1	Residencial Enmita
2	Residencial Alexander
3	Hotel Amazonico
4	IETEL
5	Buses to Misahuallí
6	Residencial Hilton
7	Residencial Aleman
8	Residencial Jumandy
	(buses to Archidona)
9	Hotel Italia
10	Hotel Amazonas
11	Hotel Tena
12	Hotel Roma
13	Government Offices
	(Post Office inside)
14	Cine Tena
15	Bank

one of their fiestas, I had one of those unusual experiences which make travelling all the more fun. I was sitting quietly in my hotel room, making notes for the Tena city map, when there was a knock on the door. I opened up, and two officious-looking gentlemen in plain clothes walked in. Perhaps it's the sign of a guilty conscience, but my first thought was, 'Oh, no, what am I in for now?' The gentlemen introduced themselves as the organisers of the Tena beauty pageant which was being held that evening to elect 'Señorita Tena, 1984'. They had heard that a Spanish-speaking foreigner was in town and would I be kind enough to help judge the contest, as they wanted some non-biased judges for a fair vote!

I don't normally hold beauty contests in very high esteem, but I couldn't refuse. The evening turned out to be riotous fun, with each señorita having her own wildly cheering following of relatives, friends and neighbours, and a sound system which screeched maniacally at inopportune moments. Perhaps the most memorable segment of the evening's events was when the MC asked the contestants a question, taken out of a sealed envelope. One of the young ladies, flustered by the rapt attention of several thousand listeners, nervously began to pick her nose before she realised what she was doing. The crowd roared with a mixture of rage and delight. Although I enjoyed myself, I haven't noticed any recent change in my opinion of beauty contests.

Information

There are the usual IETEL and post offices, the latter difficult to find as there are no signs. The post office is inside the provincial government offices at the west end of the main plaza. Money-changing facilities are limited; the bank will sometimes change cash dollars but not travellers' cheques. The mission may be able to help. Although there is an airstrip at the north end of town, there are no regularly scheduled flights. A DITURIS information office is under construction on the main road south of town – maybe it'll be open by the time this is published.

Things to See

There's not much to do in town – one couple wrote to say they didn't think it was worth the extra trip. Most people visit the nearby village of Archidona and the caves of Jumandy. If you're interested in looking for tropical birds, the steps leading down to the Río Tena near the cemetery are a good place for bird-watching. The volcano occasionally seen looming up out of the jungle, roughly 50 km north of Tena, is the 3900-metre Sumaco. Although popularly considered extinct, recent volcanological studies indicate that it is merely dormant so travellers to the region may have a surprise one of these years.

There is one movie theatre. Occasionally the San José mission also shows movies.

Places to Stay – bottom end

The cheapest hotels are in the town centre but they all suffer from water shortages. Make sure there is running water if you don't want to bathe in the river. The most expensive of the 'downtown' hotels is the *Hotel Italia*, which charges US$2 per person in rooms with private bath – not much use if there's no water! It doesn't appear well looked after and the restaurant below was ankle-deep in greasy napkins when I went in for a drink; I didn't look at the rooms.

Cheaper and better is the *Hotel Amazonas* across the street, which is much cleaner and charges US$1.50 each but has only communal showers. The cheapest place in town (and it looks it) is the *Hotel Tena* for about US$1.20. Inexplicably, the *Hotel Roma* and *Residencial Jumandy* were temporarily closed last time I visited Tena; they look as if they're in the US$1.50 price range.

Accommodation away from the centre costs a little more, but is usually worth it. The residencials *Alexander* and *Enmita* and the *Hotel Amazonico* are all at the north end of town. The newest is the clean Alexander, which has pleasant rooms with communal showers for US$2 per person and with private bathroom for US$3 each. The Enmita and Amazonico both charge US$3 per person in rooms with a private bath – both have their own private water supply which normally carries them through any water shortage and they are therefore recommended. The Amazonico has bungalow-style accommodation and the Enmita is run by a friendly lady who also manages one of the best restaurants in town.

Across the bridge in Bellavista is the somewhat unfriendly *Residencial Hilton*, which charges US$4 for a double room and won't give a lower price to singles. They have communal showers. Nearby, the friendly *Residencial Alemán* charges US$3 per person in rooms with a private bath. Similarly priced are the *Hostal El Mesón* and *Residencial El Dorado* which are close to the new bus terminal but a fair walk from downtown.

Places to Stay - top end
The best place in town is the DITURIS-run *Hotel Auca* (tel Tena 161), about two km north-east of the town centre. They have spacious grounds by the river, a restaurant and bar, a discotheque (which they'll open up, they told me, for a couple of paying guests) and a casino! They charge US$6.50 and US$11.50 for singles and doubles with private bathroom.

Places to Eat
There are a number of small and inexpensive restaurants but I always seem to end up eating at the *Residencial Enmita* – some Peace Corps volunteers told me it was the best place in town. It's not expensive.

Getting There & Away
The bus terminal used to be between the market and airstrip at the north end of town but it has recently moved to the south-eastern outskirts of town on the Puerto Napo road. There are several departures a day for Quito (US$2.60, nine hours); both the southern (via Puyo) and northern (via Baeza) routes are used. The latter route is shorter and a little less frequented but you shouldn't have much difficulty in getting a bus out the day after you arrive if you want to make the short Oriente circuit from Quito via Puyo, Tena and Baeza. Flota Jumandy run about four buses a day to Lago Agrio (US$3, nine hours). These times are approximate, as bad roads, old buses and inclement weather make all journey times in the Oriente notoriously unreliable. (Note that the 1987 earthquake has made the road to Lago Agrio impassable – make local enquiry.)

Getting Around
Local buses leave from other places. For Archidona (10c, 15 minutes), buses leave about every half hour during daylight hours from in front of the Residencial Jumandy. Equally frequent services for Misahuallí (30c, 45 minutes) used to leave from the west of the river between the two bridges but according to recent reports they now leave from the east side of the river. Both locations are shown on the map.

ARCHIDONA
Archidona is a small mission village founded in 1560, the same year as Tena, 10 km to the south. Although the village boasts a movie theatre and a couple of basic restaurants, there are no hotels. The main reason for visiting Archidona is to see the main plaza, which is a small but very well laid out forest of tropical palms, vines, ferns, flowers and trees. The plaza is crossed with paths from which you can admire the varied flora.

It comes as a real surprise to see such a beautiful plaza in so small a village; it is probably the mission's work. Their carefully but strangely painted concrete block church is also very colourful. A good day to visit Archidona is on Sunday, when the local Quijos Indians come to their weekly market and to hear mass.

From the plaza you can take a bus to Cotundo and ask to be dropped at the entrance to the Cuevas de Jumandy, about five km north of Archidona. There are three main branches in the cave system, which apparently has not yet been fully explored. There is a cafeteria by the caves but there are no other facilities. You must bring your own lights to see the stalagmites and other formations within. Entry costs 50c.

The next town of any importance to the north is Baeza, about 100 km away. This is at the junction with the Lago Agrio-Quito road and will be described later in this chapter.

1987 Earthquake

In the aftermath of the quake, several dozen US servicemen have been using Archidona as a base for aid operations into the Oriente. In addition, a new road is being built from 14 km north of Archidona to Coca. This also is with US help. As a result, bars, restaurants, gift shops and a cheap hotel have opened in Archidona to cater to the dollar spending gringos – how long these services will last is open to conjecture.

MISAHUALLÍ

This small village is marked on many maps as Puerto Misahuallí and is at the end of the road running from Puerto Napo along the north bank of the Río Napo. It is the best place in Ecuador – indeed, one of the best places on the continent – to see some of the jungle conveniently and cheaply. You can easily get here by bus from Quito in a day, so it is suitable for the traveller with a limited amount of time as well as money.

However, before you grab your hammock and pith helmet and jump on the next bus, you should realise that this isn't virgin jungle. The area has been long colonised and most mammals (monkey, wild pig, jaguar, capybara) have been either hunted

down or had their habitats encroached upon to the point where they cannot survive. What you will see, if you keep your eyes open – or better still, with a local guide – is a variety of jungle birds, tropical flowers, army ants and other insects, and hundreds of dazzling butterflies.

In addition there is a colourful Sunday river market when brightly painted dugout canoes arrive in town with cargoes of jungle produce, and all the nearby inhabitants – from local Indians to hardy gold prospectors – come to buy, sell and trade.

Buses can usually reach Misahuallí in any weather, but extremely high or low water levels can disrupt river services. The 'dry' season – though it can still rain – is November and December. The wettest period is June to August.

If you do want an excursion deep into the jungle, that too can be arranged in Misahuallí. This will require time, patience, flexibility and money – but still it is less expensive than jungle expeditions in other countries. Finally, if you want a reasonable amount of comfort – or even luxury – that is available further downriver, but not at Misahuallí.

Information

Money For shorter trips, sucres are the preferred method of payment. For the 10-day trips, cash dollars are usually acceptable. There are no proper exchange facilities in Misahuallí, although the Hostal Jaguar will often change small amounts of cash dollars at about 5% below the Quito rate. It is best to bring a good supply of sucres from the highlands.

Post There is no post office as such in Misahuallí, and mail takes months to arrive. From Europe to Quito usually takes about two weeks, and from Quito to Misahuallí about two months. If you have the time, you can make postal enquiries and reservations with the guide of your choice by writing to him at Misahuallí, Provincia de Napo, Ecuador. For a long tour, it's best to go to Misahuallí at the beginning of your stay in Ecuador and make arrangements in advance.

Things to See

The various restaurants in Misahuallí are good places to meet potential travelling companions for excursions, or to pick the brains of travellers returning from a trip. Good places are Douglas Clarke's Restaurant Dayuma, Carlos Lastra's bar just off the corner of the main square by the military post, and the El Paisano restaurant just beyond it. It's a small village; you'll be able to 'cruise' the likely places in a few minutes.

There is an 'outdoor movie theatre' near the Residencial El Balcón de Napo which shows movies on dry nights. The picture is projected, or distorted, on a screen consisting of an off-white bed sheet flapping gently in the tropical evening breeze. The generated power supply fluctuates, causing the characters to alternately speak their parts in fast Mickey Mouse fashion or a slow drawl. Seating is on the ground (bring something to sit on). Babies scream, kids yell, teenagers fight, adults gossip, the occasional bat swoops through the projector beam, and everyone has a great time. Don't go for the movie!

If you want to see some of the river without taking a tour, you can take a regularly scheduled boat trip as far as Coca on any day of the week.

Jungle Tours

Even if you don't normally enjoy organised tours, you should consider joining one in Misahuallí if you want to see some of the jungle, particularly if this is your first visit. There are many guides available in Misahuallí, and they offer a variety of tours ranging from one to 10 days in duration. Usually you have to get a group together to make it economical. Travellers pass through Misahuallí every day and it's a small place; if you're alone you'll meet others very soon.

One of the best guides is Douglas Clarke, who has been offering guide services for many years. He used to be a butterfly collector but now works exclusively as a jungle guide. His son Wilfrid and his sister Billy often work with him. He does a simple one-day walk which is a good introduction to the jungle; various plant and insect species are pointed out, and a swim under a hidden waterfall can be included. He also does two-to four-day trips, which include camping in the jungle at his camp where all necessary equipment is provided. Some canoeing in dugouts as well as hiking is involved.

Finally, he will organise a 10-day trip which takes you far down the Río Napo and back up the Aguarico with a chance of seeing wildlife such as macaws, parrots, toucans and rarer bird species; and animals such as caymans, various monkey species and perhaps wild pigs, anteaters, or – with a great deal of luck – a jungle cat. This is a rugged expedition and there is little comfort. It is not for the faint-hearted.

You can find Douglas Clarke at the Dayuma Lodge half a block from the plaza in Misahuallí. He speaks some English (few of the guides in Misahuallí are fluent English speakers), and he has a photo album which will give you a good idea of what to expect on his trips. Everything, including cooked meals, is included in the cost. He charges about US$9 per person for the one-day walk, and about US$15 per person per day on his two to four-day trips. You normally need a minimum of four people at these prices. For the 10-day trip he charges US$1500 for 10 participants (ie US$15 per person per day). If your party is smaller, the per-person costs go up proportionately, and with a bigger party you have to negotiate. Costs tend to vary with fluctuations of the dollar.

Douglas Clarke is but one example of the type of guide services available in Misahuallí. There are many others and you have to shop around to get exactly what you want. Douglas' prices are amongst the highest in Misahuallí and you can find similar tours offered for up to 25% lower. On the other hand, by saving yourself US$3 a day you may find that the standard of guide service, environmental concern, care for the 'client', or quality of the food is other than what you would have liked.

Another outfitter who has been around for a long time is Héctor Fiallos. He runs Fluvial River Tours, which has a little office on the plaza and headquarters at the Residencial Sacha by the river. He is Douglas' main competitor and runs similar but cheaper tours. I've heard very mixed reviews of his operation. Occasionally, I'm told that his guides are not very good or experienced and the food inadequate. Other times I receive glowing reports of an adventurous and enjoyable jungle trip for a reasonable price.

One of Fluvial River Tours main advantages is that you can make reservations in Quito through the Hotel Gran Casino, which enables you to plan your trip in advance. Various itineraries are available and they change from year to year. Discuss them thoroughly before making your choice. In addition to running the standard one to 10-day tours, trips are also made to visit the villages of 'primitive' Auca Indians two or three days' walk into the jungle.

I feel strongly that these kind of tours are not to be encouraged. The guides are rarely sensitive to the needs of the Indians who are undergoing the painful process of integration into 20th-century life. Many guides are just inexperienced local youngsters trying to make a living, and through simple ignorance or sheer bravado the Indians are treated in a degrading or abusive manner.

As often as twice a week, groups of tourists are taken to gawk at 'real' Indians in the 'real' jungle. The Indians stare miserably and with little interest at the frequent hordes of tourists and the parade of goods that to us seems basic: backpacks, not one but two pairs of shoes and a change of clothing, sleeping bag, rain gear, sunglasses, cameras, penknives, cigarette lighters, plastic water bottles, canned food and so on. The tourists expect and demand the basic necessities of water and a place to sleep, but the Indians' thoughts about the matter are ignored and little is given in return.

If you want to see the Indians it is best to wait until they come to you. A few of the more adventurous and acculturated Aucas usually come to the Sunday market in Misahuallí, where you can see them and they can see you in an unstrained and uncompromising atmosphere.

There are many other guides other than Douglas Clarke and Héctor Fiallos. Most of them started working with either Douglas or Héctor and decided to branch off on their own. Carlos Lastra is one such; he is very friendly and does a good job. I enjoyed being with him. Two other outfitters whom I haven't met but who have been recommended are Walter Vasco and Julio Angeles. These, and others, usually have signs or booths up in the corner of the main square.

Make sure that whoever you choose gives you a good deal. Work the details out carefully beforehand to avoid confusion or disappointment. Common sense dictates making sure that costs, food, equipment, itinerary and group numbers are all discussed thoroughly before the tour. The most important matter to settle is the guide; a good guide will be able to show you much you would have missed on your own, particularly if you convey your enthusiasm and interest by asking questions. An inadequate guide will spoil the trip.

A common problem is that a group makes arrangements with an outfitter and then an inferior guide is supplied at the last moment. All the outfitters are guilty of this to a greater or lesser extent and Fluvial River Tours in particular has built up quite a reputation for this. Douglas Clarke obviously can't join every group himself, but at least he tells you so from the beginning and tries to find a suitable guide for you. If you want a specific guide, you may have to wait until he is available.

Make sure you meet with your guide before you leave. Can you communicate adequately? Has he done this before? Can he show you the *achiote* plant (whose red berries are crushed to make decorative body paints)? Can he find the vine which, when cut, provides water fit to drink? Will he take you for a swim by a waterfall or fishing in a dugout canoe or bird-watching or whatever it is you want? What will he cook for dinner and breakfast? Will he hunt for game? – the area is overhunted and a no-hunting policy is encouraged. A few questions like these will soon tell you if you and the guide are going to have a good trip together. Most people have a great time, especially if they plan their excursion carefully.

Places to Stay & Eat

Since the 1987 earthquake, Misahuallí has become an important transport centre for river passage into the Oriente. Prices have temporarily risen and hotels tend to fill early. The situation will probably be alleviated when the Baeza-Lago Agrio road returns to normal. Meanwhile, the prices given reflect the normal ones rather than the temporarily elevated ones.

None of the accommodation in Misahuallí is expensive or luxurious. Water and electricity failures are the rule rather than the exception in all these places. On the plaza you'll find the *Residencial El Balcón de Napo* which has small concrete block rooms, some of them like jail cells. The rooms with a window are OK. The residencial is fairly clean by jungle standards, though the showers are a bit grungy. They charge just over a US$1, as does the rambling old *Residencial La Posada*, which has a hodgepodge arrangement of creaky wooden rooms and somewhat dubious bathroom facilities.

On the corner of the plaza is the nice-looking (from the outside) *Hostal Jaguar*.

They charge US$1.50 per person and some of the rooms are airless cells, but they do have a couple of better rooms with a private bathroom, inexplicably at the same price. They'll probably begin charging more now that the word is out!

Across the street from the Jaguar and a half block from the plaza is Douglas Clarke's *Dayuma Lodge*, behind the restaurant. The lodge is a small, wooden, jungle-style building with four rooms. Two rooms have four bunks each and the other two have six bunks each, dorm-style. One of each of these has a private bathroom and there is also a communal bathroom. If there's two or more of you, you can normally have a room to yourselves, but if you're alone you may have to share. Prices vary from less than a dollar if you use your own sleeping bag in a room without a private shower, to US$2 each if you want bedding and a private shower.

Héctor Fiallos' *Residencial Sacha* is pleasantly located down by the river. It has basic, jungle-cabin-style accommodation for US$1.50 each. During the wet season, especially June through August, the river can be high enough that guests have to wade to this hotel! A canoe is sometimes available.

Finally, the folks at *El Paisano* restaurant have a small hotel which is popular with travellers. Rooms are US$2 a single and US$3.50 a double for clean, simple rooms. There is a garden with hammocks.

All the hotels have some kind of restaurant. The *Dayuma* and *El Paisano* are both good. El Paisano is 100 metres from the plaza on the road past the military post. They serve good vegetarian fare, as well as meat dishes. The *Sacha* has riverside dining but erratic service. *La Posada* serves ice cream.

There are two expensive tourist lodges down the Río Napo. The nearest is *Hotel Anaconda* on Anaconda Island, about an hour from Misahuallí. This is a fairly comfortable jungle-style lodge (bamboo walls and thatched roofs), but there is no electricity. Rooms come with private bathrooms and mosquito screens, and the meals (included in the price) are good. They charge about US$25 per person, per day. Canoe trips and jungle excursions from the island are available at extra cost, and more expensive than from Misahuallí. You'll see pet animals such as monkeys and peccaries.

Further downriver is the much more expensive *Hotel Jaguar*, about 1½ hours from Misahuallí. This is a comfortable modern hotel on the banks of the Río Napo. You can make reservations for it in Quito (agency at Ramírez Dávalos 653, tel 239400), but usually this involves an all-inclusive jungle tour package from Quito lasting three or more days. It is possible to enquire in Misahuallí about shorter or cheaper stays.

Getting There & Away
Boat Motorised dugout canoes leave from the port for various destinations downriver. The port is a block away from the plaza. The major destination is Francisco de Orellana, but everybody calls it by its popular name of Coca. There are daily boats at 11.30 am which hold about 20 passengers, so it is best to try and buy your ticket in advance to ensure a seat. There are two companies, which have departures on alternate days. One has its office under the Residencial La Posada, and the other is across the street, half a block closer to the river. Tickets cost US$5 for foreigners and US$3.50 for Ecuadoreans, so if you have any kind of residency visa, use it.

Arrive early for the departure. First you must register your passport with the Port Captain, a simple formality but you can't leave without it. Ask for the Capitanía; it's on the waterfront. Then find your boat and choose a seat, which are taken on a first-come, first-served basis. The front seats give better forward views but are narrower, the middle seats are wider and more comfortable, the back seats are close to the noise and fumes of the engine. Read

the section on dugout canoes in the Getting Around chapter for more information.

The journey to Coca takes about six hours in normal conditions, but abnormally high or low river levels can disrupt services for days or even weeks. En route to Coca, several points of interest are passed. These are, in geographical order, the village of Ahuano, Hotel Anaconda on Anaconda Island, Hotel Jaguar, the village of Santa Rosa and the village of Bellavista, which is the approximate halfway point to Coca.

Usually two motorised canoes per day leave for these destinations, so it is possible to do a short trip downriver and return on another boat later in the day. There are no facilities at the villages which are mainly inhabited by colonists rather than tribes living in their natural state (although there are Indian colonists). Enquire at the boat offices about times of departure and return.

Even on the second half of the trip down to Coca you won't see much wildlife, as the area is heavily colonised. Little houses on stilts huddle on the bank, prospectors wash sand or pan for gold by the river's edge, colonists wave and whistle for a ride, and impossibly tiny dugout canoes, loaded to the gunwales with an Indian family perched on a pile of bananas, are steadily and gracefully poled upriver. A sudden rain shower can enhance the beauty of the river. The jungle glows greenly in the late afternoon sun, and a few pure white clouds suspended in a perfectly blue sky contrast dramatically with the muddy flowing river. It's worth the discomfort.

If you want to hire your own dugout (with boatman) you can do so from the port of Misahuallí, but it's expensive. To hire a canoe to take you to Coca will for example cost about US$90.

There has been a temporary increase of boat traffic on the river since the 1987 earthquake.

Bus Buses leave from in front of the Residencial La Posada on the plaza, about every 30 minutes during daylight hours. The only destination is Tena, where you can make connections elsewhere. The ride costs 30c and takes ¾ of an hour.

COCA

All Ecuadorean maps show the official name of Puerto Francisco de Orellana, but I've never heard this town referred to by any name other than Coca. It is located at the junction of the Río Coca and the Río Napo (hence its popular name). Its official name derives from the fact that Francisco de Orellana came through here on his way to 'discover' the Amazon in 1542.

The Río Napo is Ecuador's major tributary into the Amazon. Indeed, it is at the point where Ecuador's Río Napo and Peru's Río Marañon meet that the Amazon continues as a single river.

The Coca of today is a sprawling oil town with little to recommend it other than its convenience as an overnight spot after you arrive from Misahuallí. There are no street signs, and every road is unpaved and hence covered with dust, puddles or mud depending on the season. Most of the buildings are just shacks and the place has a real shanty-town appearance – they don't even have a town plaza.

Information

The IETEL office, unlike most of Ecuador, is open only from 9 am to noon and 2 to 5 pm, and 7 to 9 pm Monday to Saturday. On Sunday it is open during the morning and evening hours only. There is a post office but service is very slow. There are no proper money exchange facilities.

All travellers arriving and departing by river must register with the Port Captain at the Capitanía by the landing dock. I was treated extremely courteously here. There's not much to do apart from drink beer, go to the movie theatre or go to bed.

Places to Stay & Eat

The hotel nearest the port is also one of the cheapest and is reasonably clean but often crowded – the *Pensión Rossita* at US$1.20

per night. In the 'town centre' is the best *Hotel El Auca*, which is set in a garden and isn't bad. They charge US$2.20 each or US$3 in rooms with a private bath, and they are often full before nightfall. There are also three basic residencials across the street: the *Tungurahua, Ecuador* and *Lojanita*, in descending order of appearance. They charge about US$1-US$1.50 each. If all else fails, try the very basic *Residencial Turingo*.

Hotel Auca has a halfway decent restaurant although the menu is limited. The next best is *Restaurant El Rey*. It's in a neighbourhood of rather sleazy and questionable bars – but maybe that's what you were looking for anyway. The area is not dangerous. *Restaurant El Costeñito* is new, clean and simple. There are several others.

The *Hacienda Primavera*, two hours downriver (towards Peru) offers simple but clean rooms or camping space. Good, home-cooked meals are available. There are pleasant walks and lakes in the nearby jungle. The hotel and surrounding jungle have been warmly recommended, though I've never been there. They have a representative in Quito for further information – Señor Rodríguez, PO Box 1085, Quito, Ecuador, tel 510387. The street address is Venezuela 1716, Quito. Prices are moderate.

Getting There & Around

Air The runway has been improved and a regular service to Quito has recently been restarted by TAME. Flights leave on weekday mornings. Tickets cost about US$11 and are available from the TAME office by the river, a short way east of the bridge. (Another office is planned in the Hotel El Auca, which has timetables in the lobby.) Flights are not always full and you can sometimes buy tickets at the airport before the flight if the TAME office is closed when you arrive.

It is occasionally possible to fly with an oil company plane, which might be cheaper, or free. You need the usual

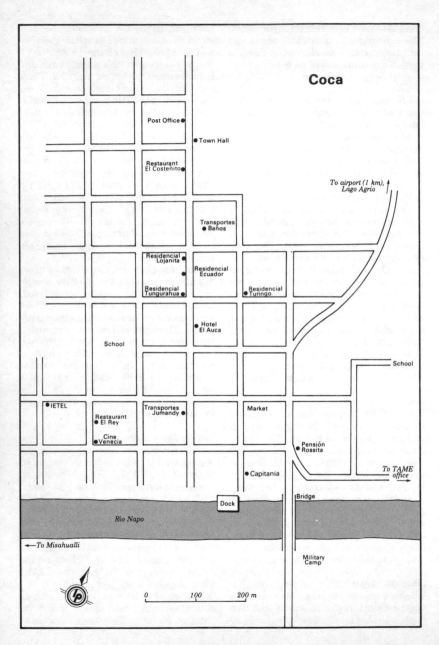

combination of luck, contacts, and being at the right place at the right time.

Boat The trip to Misahuallí takes about 14 hours (though there are some extra fast boats doing it in 10 hours) so you are advised to take the trip in the opposite direction, from Misahuallí to Coca, which takes only six hours. Departures are at 8 am daily and tickets and information are available from the Capitanía. The trip is sometimes broken and passengers camp out by the river – be prepared.

The Capitanía may be able to give you information about getting a boat further downriver. The next destination of interest is the Hacienda Primavera, about two hours downriver. An hour or two further is the ex-American mission of Limoncocha. Nearby is a school and Oriente museum at Pompeya but there is no tourist accommodation. Boat services here are irregular, infrequent and comparatively expensive.

There are very few services to Nuevo Rocafuerte on the Peruvian border. Since the 1981 Peruvian/Ecuadorean war, you need a permit from the military camp in Coca to continue downriver. This is normally refused unless you are travelling with an organised tour group from Misahuallí or on the *Flotel Orellana*. Entering Peru at this point is prohibited. I heard of one traveller who was hassled about being a drug smuggler after asking at the Capitanía about boats to Peru. This is a sensitive region.

Flotel Orellana This large, flat-bottomed river boat has three decks and about two dozen double cabins. It is operated by Metropolitan Touring, Ecuador's biggest travel agency, and the prices are commensurate with this. The tours are fairly good and an English-speaking naturalist guide accompanies the boat to explain the wildlife and surroundings. Day trips to shore are taken in dugout canoes and nights are spent in relative luxury aboard the *Flotel*, which provides good food, a bar and lectures about the jungle. The boat is based in Coca and normally steams downriver, where there is less colonisation and a better chance of seeing wildlife. This is certainly the most comfortable way of seeing Ecuador's Oriente.

Voyages on the *Flotel* last anywhere from three days to a week. These tours are all-inclusive from Quito (normally you arrive and leave by air, included in the price) and the cost is in the region of US$60 per person per day. It may be possible to alter the itinerary to allow you to bus down to Coca and meet the *Flotel* there. Full information can be had from Metropolitan Touring, PO Box 2542, Quito, Ecuador, tel 524400, telex 2482 METOUR ED. The street address is Avenida Amazonas 239, Quito.

Bus Transportes Baños and Transportes Jumandy are the two main bus companies, each with their own office – see map. Baños have five buses a day and Jumandy have two morning buses to Lago Agrio. Most of these continue to Quito and one or two to Tena (when the road is reopened). To Lago Agrio costs US$1 and takes from two to four hours depending on the wait at the ferries (there are two river crossings). To Quito is US$3 and about 12 to 14 gruelling hours. Extra buses to Lago Agrio are available during the road closure between Lago and Baeza.

A road is being built from Tena to Coca and will probably open sometime in the early 1990s.

LAGO AGRIO

The bus ride from Coca to Lago Agrio gives an interesting look at how the discovery of oil has changed the Oriente. Fifteen years ago, this was all virgin jungle and communications were limited to mission airstrips and river travel. Today there are roads and buses, and there are always signs of the oil industry – the pipeline, oil wells or trucks.

A short way north of Coca you have to

Market scene

wait for an ancient car ferry to take the bus across the Río Coca. There are soft drink stands to help you wait. The bus heads east and passes the belching wells of the Sacha oil works. It continues through the small oil town of La Joya de las Sachas, where there are a few restaurants and two basic residencials – the *Carmita* and *Zaruma*. The road is narrow but in good condition and paved in places. It follows the oil pipeline most of the way, and there are several stretches with fine scenery and vistas of the jungle.

You'll frequently see tropical birds; one of the most common is the all-black ani with a long, drooping tail and extremely thick bill. The bus passes occasional small communities and reaches the Río Aguarico. Here another ferry takes the bus across the river. The town of Lago Agrio is a few km beyond.

Lago Agrio is one of the fastest-growing towns in Ecuador. Since the discovery of oil, it has changed from literally virgin jungle to the most important of Ecuador's oil towns. It now has a growing population

of over 8000. A road has been built from Quito and there are daily flights. There are new road links with Colombia and a modern hotel has been opened.

Lago Agrio became the capital of its *cantón* in 1979; the streets are beginning to be paved and a new town plaza has been laid out on the north-western edge of town. Avenida Quito is the main route from Quito to Coca and is still the main street and town centre, but the town is planning to spread around the plaza. Lago Agrio is lobbying to have the province of Napo divided into two, with the southern half keeping the present capital of Tena and the northern half having Lago Agrio as its new capital. It will be interesting to watch Lago Agrio's progress over the next decade.

Although it's the oldest, biggest and 'best' of Ecuador's oil towns, Lago Agrio is still just an oil town, and an oil town is an oil town. Most travellers spend as little time here as possible; it's simply a convenient overnight stop. The drive from the jungle up into the Andes is very beautiful and it's a good idea to rest in Lago Agrio and leave refreshed on a morning bus if you're headed to Quito, so that you can appreciate the scenery. Also, you can use Lago Agrio as a base for further excursions into the jungle on the road which is being pushed ever deeper into the Oriente.

Note that Lago Agrio is often called simply 'Lago' by the locals.

Information
The IETEL office, unlike the rest of Ecuador, is open from 8 am to 10 pm on weekdays, and from 8 am to noon and 8 to 10 pm on Sunday. The post office (closed

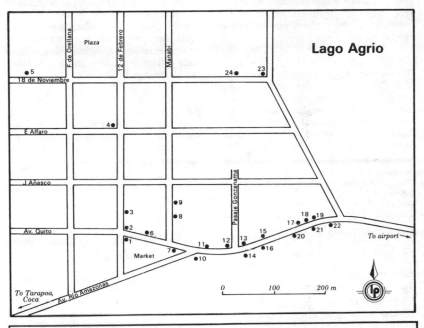

1	TAME Office
2	Hostal El Cofan
3	Banco Internacional
4	Banco de Fomento
5	IETEL
6	Cine Amazonas
7	Hotel Cabaña
8	Residencial Chimborazo
9	Transportes Baños
10	Residencial El Dorado & Hotel Williigram
11	Residencial Baños
12	Transportes Putumayo & Residencial Hilton
13	Transportes Centinela del Norte & Pensión Marsella
14	Transportes Occidentales
15	Hotel Oro Negro
16	Residencial La Mexicana & Hotel Utopia
17	Transportes Zaracay
18	Casa de Cambio
19	Post Office
20	Hotel Machala & Residencial Casino
21	Chifa Rey Coreano
22	Hotel Oriental & Transportes Jumandy
23	Hotel Ambato
24	Cine Oriente

weekends) is up some rickety stairs near the *casa de cambio* and looks like it's in the front room of a private home. Nevertheless, a letter I mailed from there to the USA arrived safely.

The two cinemas sometimes show fairly good English-language films.

The 1987 earthquake has disrupted and changed Lago somewhat and so expect this. I would be interested in recent information about changing facilities in the town.

Money Lago Agrio is only 20 km south of the Colombian border and exchange facilities exist mainly to deal with Colombian pesos, though dollars can also be negotiated. The *casa de cambio* is open irregularly (ie when they have some sucres) and they'll change cash dollars, but travellers' cheques may be refused. Usually you have to wait a few hours for 'authorisation' to change money. The Banco de Fomento normally deals only with pesos. The Banco Internacional sometimes will accept dollars. Expect to pay a commission of at least 5% if you do change money. As usual, it's best to change it in the highlands.

Things to See
There's a Sunday-morning market which can be quite interesting when the local Cofan Indians come into town to buy staples and sell their handicrafts, such as necklaces made of seeds and iridescent beetle wings.

The men often wear a typical one-piece, knee-length smock called a *kushma*, along with a headband around their short hair. This latter may be made of porcupine quills.

The women wear very brightly patterned flounced skirts, short blouses which expose an inch of midriff, bright red lipstick, and have beautiful long, dark hair.

The Cofan Indians are related to the Sequoia people and there used to be tens of thousands of them before early contacts with whites decimated them, mainly by disease. This, unfortunately, is the history of most Amazonian Indian groups. Before the discovery of oil, most Cofans' exposure to non-Indian people was limited to the occasional missionary and they still remain quite shy, as opposed to the Otavaleño Indians for example. They live in several river villages near Lago Agrio but there are no restaurant or accommodation facilities there. Their main village is Dureno and jungle tours can be arranged.

Places to Stay
Lago Agrio is a fast-growing town and new hotels open every year. Some hotels (eg the *Hotel La Mexicana*) are expanding upwards. The top floor has the advantage of being newer and hence cleaner, but then there's the disadvantage of being closer to the roof, the sun and the heat. It's worth looking at different rooms in the same hotel to see what's best for you.

Most hotels provide a mosquito net with the bed. Although spraying keeps the mosquito population in Lago Agrio down to a minimum, you should look for beds with these nets, especially if you're not taking malaria pills.

Places to Stay – bottom end
There are plenty of budget hotels which are cheap, basic and usually look horrible because the rate of deterioration of cheap architecture in the humid jungle is very fast. Some of the oldest and cheapest places are getting a bit rank, so the sensitive might consider it worthwhile staying somewhere more expensive.

The standard budget travellers' hotel seems to be the *Hotel Oro Negro*, which looks like a run-down jail though the rooms are kept clean. They charge US$1.50 each. Similarly priced are the *Residencial Hilton* and the *Hotel Machala*, which both look OK. The following hotels are all about US$1.50 or less and don't look as good: the hotels *Ambato* and *Oriental*; the residencials *Baños, Casino, El Dorado, Chimborazo*; and the *Pensión Marsella*.

Residencial La Mexicana has some rooms for US$1.50 and others for US$3 per person. These have private baths and are fair value. If you stay here, have a good look around, as some of the rooms are definitely better than others. *Hotel Utopia* is basic but cleaner than most and charges US$2 each. *Hotel Cabaña* is similarly priced.

Places to Stay – top end

The best in town is the new and modern *Hostal El Cofan*, which charges about US$8/13 a single/double with private bathrooms (cold water). There is air-con in many of the rooms. It's often full, so get there early.

Places to Eat

Best value meals are in the restaurant of the *Hotel Utopia*, which charges US$1 for a hearty set meal and also has a varied menu. The *Hotel Machala* restaurant is also good, although a little more expensive. The *Hostal El Cofan* restaurant is supposedly the best in town. It is good, and not too expensive, but I found it a bit antiseptic. The *Rey Coreano* is a good *chifa*. There are plenty of other cheap places to choose from if you don't like this selection.

Getting There & Around

Air Lago Agrio boasts the best air schedule from the Oriente to Quito. TAME has a scheduled flight daily (except Sunday) at 11 am which costs US$10 and is often booked well ahead. They have an office downtown which is usually open on weekdays but their hours are quite erratic. Often everyone packs up and goes to the

airport. You can buy tickets at the airport for the extra military flights which leave several times a day while the road is closed – these will stop when the road is reopened.

The airport is about five km east of town and there is a TAME pickup truck which takes people from the office to the airport for 20c about an hour before the flight. Taxis (which are usually yellow pickup trucks) cost up to US$2 but you can go as cheaply as US$1 if you bargain hard.

If you are arriving in Lago Agrio by air, you'll see several buses waiting at the airstrip. Unfortunately, most of these are oil company vehicles picking up workers on the flight and they can't or won't give you a ride. If you ask around, however, you'll eventually find something. One of the buses is usually a public bus, and the TAME people often take passengers back in their truck. There are usually taxis hanging around – see if you can share with someone. The tropically hot or wet five-km walk is not recommended.

The airport is also used by the local oil companies, of which Texaco seems to be the biggest. They can occasionally be persuaded to give travellers a ride, but with TAME's daily flight to Quito, hitching or buying flights on oil planes is often more trouble than it's worth.

I had an amusing experience once, flying from Quito to Lago Agrio. At the Quito airport I ran into an anthropologist I knew. She was accompanying a Cofan couple who had been in hospital in Quito and who were now returning home. She explained that it was the first flight for both of them and they spoke a lot of Cofan and very little Spanish – could I keep an eye on them? Of course; I was delighted to do so, though I couldn't imagine that there would be any problems. And so off I set with my new Cofan friends.

Our first little problem was with the X-ray machine. I convinced them that no harm would come to their little bundles, so they put them onto the conveyer belt and then walked to the waiting plane. They didn't realise that the X-ray machine didn't automatically deliver all hand luggage to the plane – and after all, with all the automated devices to be seen in Quito, why not? So I called the Cofans back for their bundles and they looked at me with some disgust; obviously this fancy machine was no good at all.

We clambered aboard the aircraft and the next thing to deal with were the seat belts. They couldn't quite understand why the stewardess was buckling them in and seemed rather worried when they couldn't unbuckle their belts. A quick demonstration of the fast release device on the seat belts seemed in order. Once we were airborne, they started to complain of an earache. I tried to show them how to equalise the pressure in their ears and there followed a hilarious episode as we held our noses and swallowed and blew and snorted and sprayed. Finally, through the giggles and general uproar, I managed to convey, in sign language, how to get rid of the pain in their ears.

It was a short flight, and soon we were preparing to land at Lago Agrio. I had made sure that the Cofans had gotten window seats, thinking that they would enjoy the views. Instead, as we came in to land, one of the Cofans firmly covered the window with a blanket and then took a couple of very quick, tentative peeks before closing her eyes tightly shut. We landed safely.

Bus Bus services have been temporarily disrupted by the 1987 earthquake which destroyed the Lago Agrio – Baeza road. The following information anticipates the reopening of the road in 1988.

There is no main bus terminal and most bus companies have their offices on or near the main street, Avenida Quito. Buses to Quito cost about US$2.60 and take eight to 11 hours. The following companies have buses to Quito: Transportes Occidentales, Transportes Jumandy, Transportes Centinela del Norte, Transportes Zaracay.

Each company has a variety of buses ranging from slow, noisy old monsters to smaller and faster buses; they all seem to break down periodically so I can't recommend one in particular because you'll only blame me if your bus breaks down! Most of these companies also have services to either Coca (US$1, two to four

hours) or Tena (US$2.50, seven to 10 hours). For some strange reason, Transportes Zaracay has buses to Santo Domingo.

You can continue further into the Oriente with Transportes Jumandy, which have a daily 1 pm bus to Tarapoa (US$1, 2½ hours). Transportes Putumayo also has buses to Tarapoa. Their buses are known as *rancheros* and are open-sided trucks with uncomfortable narrow bench seats. They also run three rancheros every morning to the Río San Miguel, at the Colombian border (40c, one hour). Buses to Shushufindi are also available. The roads into the Oriente from Lago Agrio are constantly being improved and expanded; ask at Transportes Putumayo for the most recent information.

Crossing the Colombian Border

It's certainly possible to enter Colombia from Lago Agrio; the border is less than 20 km to the north and there's always a few Colombians in town. However, gringos should be extremely careful entering or leaving Colombia via this border crossing. The area is notorious for smugglers, and the Colombian side has been called 'dangerous' by Ecuadorean locals. (I wonder if the same is said of Ecuador by the Colombians.) I know of only one gringo who has crossed the border here and he writes that the towns on the Colombian side are so primitive in terms of law and order that it was like being a part of the Gold Rush days. At any rate, if you decide that this little adventure is for you, take care, guard your belongings, and I'd enjoy hearing about your experiences – if you survive!

To get to the border, take a Transportes Putumayo bus to the Río San Miguel and get off at Puerto Colón (about one to two hours). Then take a dugout canoe for the short river crossing to the Colombian side. When you arrive in Colombia, you'll find occasional buses to take you to Puerto Asis (about six hours) where there are places to stay and road, air and river transportation to other parts of Colombia. For more information on getting into Colombia, see under Tulcán.

DURENO

This Cofan village lies on the south banks of the Río Aguarico about an hour east of Lago Agrio by bus or dugout. River transportation is infrequent but Transportes Putumayo have several buses a day to Tarapoa which pass the Dureno turn off. This is marked with a small sign which is not very obvious; it's best to ask the driver. From here follow the path until you reach the Río Aguarico about 200 metres away. From the river bank yell and whistle to attract the attention of the villagers on the other side – somebody will come and get you in a dugout.

Crossing the river costs about 30c per person with a 60c minimum. In the village, you'll be given a roof over your head in an Indian style hut for about 60c each – bring a hammock or sleeping mat as there are no beds. Bring your own food and stove as supplies are rarely available in Dureno.

The Cofans are excellent wilderness guides and know much about medicinal and practical uses of jungle plants. You can hire a guide with a dugout canoe for about US$20 per day. Up to six people can be accommodated in a dugout so it's cheaper in a group. One of the best guides is Emerihildo Criollo. If he's not around ask for Mauricio Mendoa. They speak Cofan and Spanish is their second language but English is not understood. This is off-the-beaten-path tourism and not for those expecting any comfort.

A good one-day trip is from Dureno to the Río Pisuri. Although you won't see much wildlife, jungle plants will be shown and explained to you. Ask questions! For a longer trip ask to be taken to the Río Cuyabeno where there is a National Park, although there has been some colonisation there, too.

One of the villagers is the son of American missionaries – although he doesn't normally arrange trips for travellers he can be of assistance in an emergency.

TARAPOA

This is Ecuador's newest boom town. It's an oil town about 60 km by road east of Lago Agrio and and a few buses go there. At this time there's nothing except a few shacks and the oil works, but already they have two flights a week to Quito, on Wednesday and Friday mornings. Ask at TAME for more information about this service. Apparently there's also a basic place to stay.

Some maps mark a road continuing from Tarapoa to Puerto El Carmen de Putumayo, which is at the junction of the San Miguel and Putumayo rivers and another entry point into Colombia. This road doesn't exist yet, but if Tarapoa continues booming, it may be built one year.

BAEZA

The following description is based on conditions prior to the 1987 earthquake. The road described has been destroyed and it is not known how closely the new road will follow the old one. Many new bridges are being built.

The road west of Lago Agrio roughly follows the Río Aguarico for some 50 km before turning south-west and beginning the long climb up into the Andes by following the valley of the Río Quijos. There are two major landmarks on this ascent. To the right of the road is the 3485-metre volcano Reventador, which means 'the exploder' and which had a period of major activity in the late 1970s. Unfortunately, it's obscured by cloud more often than not. On the left of the road, about 95 km from Lago Agrio, are the San Rafael Falls, about 145 metres high and the biggest in Ecuador.

To see Reventador and the San Rafael Falls properly you can get off the bus just beyond the tiny community of Río Reventador, at a concrete block hut with an INECEL sign on the left of the road. Make sure you get off the bus at Río Reventador and not at the bigger community of Reventador which is about 20 km away. A new metal bridge has been built by Río Reventador and a correspondent writes that the bridge has a plaque proclaiming *Obra de Norman* meaning 'Norman's Work'.

From the INECEL hut it's about 2½ km down a steep track to the falls. There used to be a jeep track but that was destroyed by the earthquake and now there is just a foot trail. You can camp within sight of the falls or go back to Río Reventador, where you can sleep on the floor of the store/bar. Flag a bus down when you want to go on, and be prepared to wait, as the buses are sometimes full.

Beyond Río Reventador the road continues climbing, following both the trans-Ecuadorean oil pipeline and the Río Quijos all the way. There are enchanting views of beautiful cloudforest full of strange species of birds and plants. Several small communities with little to recommend them are passed, and Baeza is reached after 170 km from Lago Agrio and six hours.

Baeza is on the junction with the road to Tena and is the most important village between Lago Agrio and the Quito valley. It was an old, established Spanish missionary and trading outpost, having been first founded in 1548 and re-founded three more times since. The pass from Baeza via Papallacta to the Quito valley was known well before the conquest, but the road from Baeza to Lago Agrio has been opened only by the oil boom, so Baeza is both a historical and geographical junction. It is also a good, quiet spot to stay for walks in the surrounding hills. The low Andean plants and bird life are outstanding.

Places to Stay & Eat
Facilities are very limited. There is only the basic but clean *Hotel Samay*, which charges US$1 a night. There are a couple of simple restaurants. If the Samay is full (very unusual; Baeza is a small town) you can go down to the village of Borja, about four km before Baeza, which also has a basic pensión.

Getting There & Away
There are no bus stations in these villages. You must flag down passing buses and hope that they have room. Buses to Lago Agrio are temporarily not available but services to Tena and Quito continue.

PAPALLACTA
The westbound road from Baeza continues climbing steadily until the village of Papallacta, 40 km beyond. About a km beyond the village, on the right as you head to Quito, are the Aguas Termales or natural hot springs of Papallacta. They're not overly developed and their setting is grand; on a clear day you can see the snow-capped Antisana (5704 metres) about 15 km to the south. The hottest spring is very hot, and there's a refreshing cold plunge pool. It costs about 20c to get in, and changing rooms and toilet facilities are provided, but nothing else.

It's possible to camp by the springs. Otherwise, in Papallacta there is a small, basic, unsigned pensión and a simple restaurant.

Quito is only 60 km away, but the drive is difficult and spectacular. The road climbs over the Eastern Cordillera of the Andes via a pass which is nearly 4100 metres in height, and sometimes snow covered. If you're driving up from the Oriente, be prepared for the cold. Beyond the pass is the valley of Quito.

To get to Papallacta from Quito isn't straightforward. Most bus companies which go to Tena or Lago Agrio won't sell you a ticket unless you are going all the way to the Oriente. You have to wait until departure time and then hop onto the bus and buy a pro-rated ticket from the driver. The problem is that the buses are often full (that's why they didn't want to sell you a ticket for such a short distance in the first place) and even if they're not, some drivers will try and charge you the full price to Lago Agrio, because 'that's what this company does'. One company which can be persuaded to sell you tickets to Papallacta is Centinela del Norte.

Western Lowlands

A physical map of Ecuador shows the country divided neatly into two by the massive range of the Andes. To the east lie the jungles of the upper Amazon basin, and to the west you find the coastal lowlands. The western drop of the Andes is dramatic and steeper than the eastern side. Lowlands of below 300 metres are soon reached; from Ecuador's highest peak (Chimborazo at 6310 metres) it is only 50 km due west to the 300-metre contour, a gradient of about 12%. It does not stay low all the way to the coast, however. After dropping to almost sea level, the land rises again in a barren, scrubby and almost uninhabited range of 700-metre-high hills before dropping to the coast. Thus the coastal lowlands are subdivided into the coast itself, west of the coastal hills, and the flat lowlands lying east of the hills and west of the Andes. It is the latter which are described in this chapter.

Some people's impression of Ecuador is that it is a 'banana republic' – one of those tropical countries that produce bananas and little else. Indeed, until the export of oil began in 1972, bananas were Ecuador's most important product and they remain the country's major agricultural export. The western lowlands were once forested, but much of this has now been cleared to develop agriculture.

Fortunately, the land is fertile and huge banana and palm tree plantations are seen by travellers through this area. It has not been developed much for tourists, and many people rush through it on their way to the coast or highlands. If you're interested in seeing some of the tropical 'banana republic' Ecuador – the kind of countryside that was typically Ecuadorean before the recent oil boom – then it is worth taking a couple of days to travel slowly through this area instead of rushing through.

One of the most frequently used routes from the highlands to the western lowlands is from Quito to Santo Domingo. From here you can head south, through Quevedo and Babahoyo in the lowland province of Los Rios, to Guayaquil on the coast. This is the travellers' route I follow in this chapter.

THE ROAD TO SANTO DOMINGO

From Quito, the bus heads south through the 'Avenue of the Volcanoes' to Aloag, where the Pan American highway is joined by the road into the lowlands. The bus often refuels here and is surrounded by hordes of snack sellers lustily hawking their delicacies. *Aziuuuzias!* seems to be a frequently heard cry as the dry biscuits are usually sold here.

The descent into the lowlands is a spectacular and sometimes terrifying one. You are strongly advised to try and make the journey in the morning, as in the afternoon both the passengers' and the driver's views are often obscured by fog. Despite almost non-existent visibility, the drivers hurtle down the western slopes of the Andes at breakneck speeds. Amazingly, accidents are very rare but near misses somewhat more common.

The road begins in high *páramo*, with views of the extinct volcanoes Atacazo and Corazón to the north and south. The tortuous descent follows the left bank of the Río Pilatón and occasionally waterfalls cascade into the narrow gorge. The road passes the village of Cornejo Astorga (also known as Tandapi) and follows the Toachi River valley. The vegetation starts becoming increasingly tropical and if you're lucky you may see orchids growing on the side of the road. The higher temperatures are noticeable by the time you pull into the village of Alluriquín.

Both Cornejo Astorga and Alluriquín have basic hotels and restaurants; the best of these is the *Hotel Florida* in Alluriquín, but few travellers stay in these villages. They seem to be overnight stops for truck drivers doing the long slow haul from the lowlands up to Quito.

About 17 km before Santo Domingo is a famous hotel run by the aristocratic and very charming Señora Tina Garzón, who emigrated to Ecuador from Russia many years ago. The hotel is called, appropriately enough, *Tinalandia* and is the haunt of bird-watchers and naturalists. There is a nine-hole golf course next to the hotel, but otherwise the extensive grounds have been left largely undisturbed except for a few nature trails. The bird-watching is excellent and Tinalandia boasts a list of over 150 sub-tropical species. It is definitely worthwhile if you have an interest in ornithology.

The accommodation is very comfortable and the food is excellent but you'll have to pay about US$30 per person per day (including all meals). However, I met an Australian/New Zealander naturalist couple who were staying in budget hotels but decided to splurge for a couple of days at Tinalandia. They weren't disappointed. The hotel is sometimes booked by bird-watching groups so you have to take your chances. There is no telephone and if you want to make a reservation you have to write to Tinalandia, Santo Domingo.

Shortly before reaching Santo Domingo you pass an oil pressure station. The road has been following the Trans-Andean pipeline for the last third of its distance. If your bus is continuing beyond Santo Domingo it may avoid the town altogether because there are a couple of by-passes; normally, however, even long-distance buses pull into the town for a break.

SANTO DOMINGO

Santo Domingo de los Colorados, as it is officially known, has a population of 67,000 and is important as a road hub with major roads heading north, south, east and west. At only 500 metres and just 130 km from Quito, this is the nearest lowland tropical town easily accessible from the capital and hence it is a popular weekend destination for Quiteños.

The town used to be famous for the Colorado Indians who painted their faces with black stripes and dyed their bowl-shaped haircuts a brilliant red using achiote. You can buy postcards of them all over Ecuador, but the Indians are now fairly westernised and you are unlikely to see them in their traditional finery except by going to one of their nearby villages and paying them to dress up. Photographers are expected to give 'tips'. The villages are on the road to Quevedo and the best known is Chihuilpe, about 10 km south-west of Santo Domingo. Some of the older Indians, notably the headman Abraham Calazacon and his brother Gabriel, have built up reputations as medicine men and people come from the capital to be cured.

Colorado Indian man

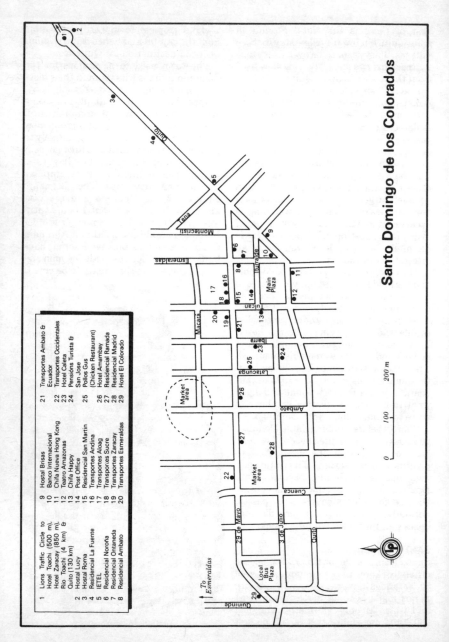

Santo Domingo de los Colorados

1   Lions Traffic Circle to
     Hotel Toachi (500 m),
     Hotel Zaracay (850 m),
     Rio Toachi (4 km) &
     Quito (130 km)
2   Hostal Lucy
3   Hostal Roma
4   Residencial La Fuente
5   IETEL
6   Residencial Noroña
7   Residencial Ontaneda
8   Residencial Ambato

9   Hostal Brisas
10   Banco Internacional
11   Chifa Nueva Hong Kong
12   Teatro Amazonas
13   Chifa Happy
14   Post Office
15   Residencial San Martin
16   Transportes Andina
17   Transportes Aloag
18   Transportes Sucre
19   Transportes Zaracay
20   Transportes Esmeraldas

21   Transportes Ambato &
     Ecuador
22   Transportes Occidentales
23   Hotel Caleta
24   Pensións Turista &
     San Jose
25   Pollos Gus
     (Chicken Restaurant)
26   Hotel Amambay
27   Residencial Ramada
28   Residencial Madrid
29   Hotel El Colorado

Information

Because Sunday is the main market day, the town closes down on Mondays. There are the usual IETEL and post offices, and the Banco Internacional (open Tuesday to Saturday) will exchange US dollars at rates surprisingly close to Quito's.

Things to See

Santo Domingo is a convenient city in which to make bus connections or break a long journey. There are lively street markets (see map) and a busy Sunday market, but otherwise it's not a particularly interesting town. There is one cinema.

The Río Toachi is nearby and city buses go there. Just across the river is a not very well developed and unexciting resort village with a few restaurants, a run-down swimming pool (you may prefer to swim in the river), and some games courts.

Places to Stay – bottom end

There are many extremely basic hotels near the main square and bus terminal areas. There are four on or within half a block of the main plaza: the *Dormicentro, Astoria, Pichinchas* and *Europa*, all of which look very cheap and pretty bad – I didn't even go in. Better are the simple but clean *Pensión San José* and *Turistica*, the latter with hot showers. Almost all the cheap hotels have only cold water, which isn't much hardship in the warm weather. These two places are both US$1 each, as is the *Residencial Madrid*, which is acceptably clean but check the rooms beforehand; many are windowless and apt to be stuffy.

For US$1.20 (US$4 for rooms with private bath) the *Residencial Noroña* is recommended for good-sized, clean rooms close to the buses. The similarly priced *Residencial Ambato* around the corner is OK but the *Residencial Ontaneda* is overpriced at US$2 to US$3 depending on the room (though a few of the rooms aren't bad). Right across from the bus offices is the clean and helpful *Residencial San Martín*, but make sure your room doesn't face the buses. They charge US$1.50, as does the good, clean *Residencial Ramada* near the market.

A little upmarket is the *Hostal Brisas* at US$2, or US$3 with private bath. *Hotel Amambay* also has clean rooms with private bath for US$3 per person but you're still looking at cold water and there are a lot of stairs to climb. *Hotel Caleta* is clean and pleasant but make sure the cold showers work. They charge US$3.50 each in rooms with private baths and have a reasonable restaurant. *Hotel El Colorado* is huge and has spacious rooms with private baths for about US$4 each; worth checking if you want reasonably priced comfort.

If you want to stay away from the town centre, head out on Avenida Quito, where you'll pass a good variety of hotels. Closest to town is the basic *Residencial La Fuente*, soon followed by the *Hostal Roma*, which is good if you want to stay out of town cheaply. They charge US$1.20, or US$2 for rooms with a private bath, and there is a restaurant. Spartan but clean rooms with comfortable beds and private bathrooms cost US$2.20 per person at the *Hotel Lucy*, which also has a good restaurant.

Places to Stay – top end

Continuing out along Avenida Quito, you'll come to the two best hotels in town. First is the *Hotel Toachi*, US$6 per person in rooms with private shower and hot water, a swimming pool and a restaurant. Further out is the well-known *Hotel Zaracay*, which charges US$20 for a double room with bath. The food is excellent and the rooms are in jungle-style cabins with thatched roofs. There are pleasant gardens and a swimming pool.

Places to Eat

The better hotels have reasonable restaurants but otherwise there aren't any particularly noteworthy ones. There are plenty of inexpensive *chifas*; two good ones are on the main square (see map).

A plastic, clean, US-style fried chicken restaurant has recently opened under the name of *Pollos Gus*. There are cheap and basic restaurants next to the bus offices but they don't have much except for the set meal – OK if you're in a hurry.

Getting There & Around

Bus There is no central bus terminal but most companies have offices around 29 de Mayo and Tulcán, with the exception of Transportes Occidentales, which has its office at 29 de Mayo and Cuenca, about five blocks away. If you go to the main bus office area you'll find the drivers' assistants yelling out destinations and it's easy to find the bus you want.

Quito (US$1.10, 2½ hours) and Guayaquil (US$1.90, five hours) are the most frequent destinations with buses leaving at least once an hour with various companies. Make sure you take a small *buseta* if you're in a hurry to get to Guayaquil, as the larger buses can take two hours longer. It's easy enough to get buses to intermediate points such as Quevedo or Daule, but if you want to go to Babahoyo you'll find fewer buses, as most southbound buses take the Daule road beyond Quevedo.

If you're heading south to Peru and don't want to change at Guayaquil, then go with Transportes Occidentales, who have several departures a day to Machala (US$2.60, eight hours). Their buses are fairly slow but are large and reasonably comfortable.

There are buses about every hour to Esmeraldas on the north coast (US$1.50, 3½ hours) with Transportes Esmeraldas and less frequently with Transportes Ambato. This journey could be broken at either La Concordia or Quinindé (officially Rosa Zárate), both of which have simple hotels but otherwise are of little interest.

Buses also go to the central coast but not as frequently as to Esmeraldas. Bahía de Caráquez (US$2.10, six hours) and Manta (US$2.30, seven hours) are both served by Reina del Camino, who don't

seem to have an office in Santo Domingo. Unless they've opened one recently, you'll have to wait for one of these buses to swing through town. They won't stop if they are full. The companies with offices in Santo Domingo don't have many departures to the central coast, so your best bet is Transportes Esmeraldas.

These are general guidelines and you'll find that most of the companies go in most directions to a greater or lesser extent. Just check out the different offices.

There is a local bus plaza at the west end of Avenida 3 de Julio where you can find beat-up old bone-shakers to take you to nearby villages. It can be interesting to take one of these buses just to see the countryside, but make sure that there is a return bus, as these villages often don't have restaurants, let alone a place to stay. You can also find buses here returning to Quito via La Concordia and (San Miguel de) los Bancos, an uncomfortable eight-hour ride, but with beautiful scenery.

Finally, the most useful city bus runs east along Avenida Quito and takes you past the *Hotel Toachi* and *Zaracay* on the way to the Río Toachi swimming area. Take any bus marked 'Río Toachi'.

QUEVEDO

It's a little over 100 km from Santo Domingo to Quevedo on a gently dropping paved road. During the first 15 km you see frequent signs on the sides of the road advertising the homes of Colorado Indian *curanderos* or medicine men. This is where you go if you want to see them, but expect to pay for both cures and photography.

There are little villages about every 20 km along this road. The most important is Buena Fé, about 20 km before Quevedo. Buena Fé has a couple of basic hotels on the main street. The land is agricultural with many banana plantations and, as you get closer to Quevedo, African palm and papaya groves. The palm is important for vegetable oil.

One of the first things I noticed in

Quevedo was a strange smell, rather like stale beer. I thought there was a brewery in town but I was told that it was *tamarindo*, a brown, bean-like fruit popular in fruit juices. Quevedo, with about 70,000 inhabitants, is an important road hub and market town, and *tamarindo* and many other products pass through here. At only 145 metres above sea level, the town is hot but the mountains are not far away.

There are many hotels and it is a good place to break the journey from Latacunga to the coast, if you're going that way. For some reason, the Ecuadorean Chinese community has settled in this bustling and progressive town, so there are many good *chifas* and other Chinese-run businesses.

Information

There are the usual IETEL and post offices, the latter poorly marked and you can't tell it's there when it's closed. The Banco Internacional will change US dollars but at a rate of some 3% less than Quito.

Colorado Indian woman

Things to See

As you might expect in a growing market town, there are markets. The daily early morning produce market on the Malecón by the river is quite colourful and it's pleasant to walk along the river before it gets hot. The market at Septima and Progreso has plenty of plastic junk but also hammocks if you need one.

The coastal influence begins to be felt here and there are some nightclubs. The *Zodiac* is open at weekends and has a 'couples only' rule. The less respectable *El Sotano* looks more like a pick-up joint and is open most nights. There are two cinemas.

Places to Stay - bottom end

There are many cheap hotels in Quevedo but the half dozen or so I visited looked depressingly similar – peeling walls, a lumpy bed, a broken window or no window at all. Some of the rooms were marginally better than others, so it is worth asking to see another room if you don't like the first you look at.

For US$1 each you can stay at the reasonably clean *Hotel Santa*, but they charge an extra 20c for rooms with windows which tend to look out on the noisy main street. For US$1.20 you can stay at the basic *Residencial Mirador, Quito* and *Hotel Guayaquil*, the last with some slightly more expensive rooms with private bath. For US$1.50 there is the *Pensión Vilmita* which is clean but nonetheless just your basic cell. Others in the US$1-US$1.50 range are the *Las Brisas* (broken windows and shabby, but some rooms have river views) and the pensiones *Ideal, Patricia, Nueva Esperanza, Charito, Azuay, Marianela, Guayas* and *Rocxi*, none of which look particularly enticing.

Even if you're on a budget it's worth checking out the *Hotel Imperial* by the river, US$2 each but clean. The rooms all have private bathrooms (cold water) with soap and towel provided, and there are fans. Many of the rooms have river views

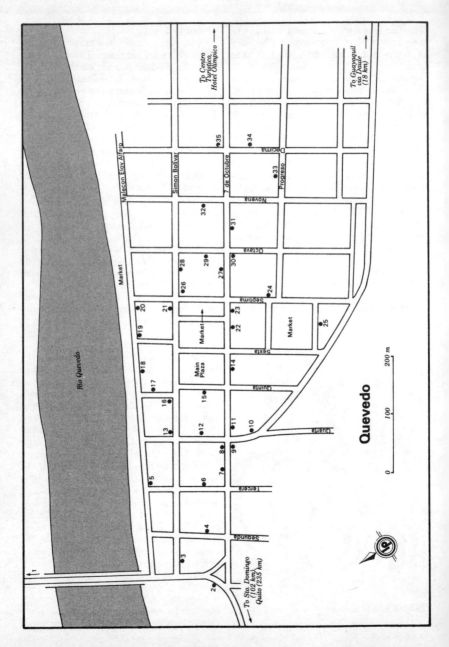

Quevedo

Top: Inca ruins of Ingapirca (RR)
Left: Guayaquil Cathedral and statue of Simon Bolívar (TW)
Right: All Saints Church, Tomebamba River, Cuenca (RR)

Top: Fisherman at work, Atacames (RR)
Left: Balsa fishing boats, Playas (RR)
Right: Fisherman monument, Manta (RR)

(excellent view from the roof). It's very secure and you have to ring the bell to get in.

Places to Stay - top end

There are several slightly more expensive hotels. The *Hotel Orellana* charges US$3 each but doesn't seem much better than the *Imperial*. *Hotel Condado* boasts air-con and private bathrooms for US$3.50 each or a dollar less without air-con. Perhaps the newest and best is *Hotel Ejecutivo Internacional* - all you international executive travellers can get an air-con room for a very reasonable US$4 (with a private bathroom). *Hotel Continental* charges US$4.50 each but not all its rooms are air-con.

Finally, on the eastern edge of town is the comparatively expensive *Hotel Olimpico* tourist complex, complete with swimming pool, restaurant, bar etc.

Many of the cheaper hotels suffer from water shortages so check that the water's running if you want to shower immediately. People often swim in the river.

Places to Eat

With its large Chinese community, Quevedo has plenty of *chifas*. *Chifa Rama Dorada* is one of the fanciest, but still not too expensive, and there are many others along the same street, Avenida 7 de Octubre (Quevedo Day).

Another good place to go is across the river. If you just keep going straight after the bridge, you'll be walking along Avenida Guayaquil which, after half a dozen blocks, makes a large Y. One arm goes to Latacunga and the other to Babahoyo. Between the bridge and the Y are dozens of restaurants, ranging from little street stands to bigger *comedors* and fish restaurants. There's a good choice of places, it's colourful, and it's worth a look.

Getting There & Away

Boat Although the Río Quevedo is wide and deep enough for boats and eventually runs into the Pacific at Guayaquil, there is little river traffic. It is generally cheaper to use the good road connections to the coast.

1	To Latacunga (177km) & Guayaquil via Babahoyo
2	Buses 'de paso' to Quito
3	Hotel Orellana
4	Flota Bolívar (to Portoviejo)
5	Residencial Las Brisas
6	Buses CIA to Guayaquil
7	Residencial Vilmita
8	Hotel Ejecutivo Continential & Buses TIA to Guayaquil
9	Banco Internacional
10	Pensión Ideal
11	Transportes Sucre (to Guayaquil & Sto Domingo)
12	Hotel Guayaquil
13	Transportes Ecuador
14	Church
15	Cine Quevedo
16	Flota Babahoyo Internacional
17	Pensión Patricia
18	Hotel El Condado
19	Post Office
20	Hotel Imperial
21	El Sotano Disco
22	Cine Chan
23	Hotel Santa & Express Sucre (to Cuenca)
24	IETEL
25	Transportes Cotapaxi (to Lataguna)
26	Pensión Nueva Esperanza
27	Hotel Continental
28	Residencial Charito
29	Residencial Quito
30	Pensión Azuay
31	Chifa Rama Dorada
32	Pensións Marianela & Guayas
33	Pensión Rocxi
34	Zodiac Disco & Barra Bar
35	Residencial Mirador

A few dugouts chug up and down and there's usually a raft of bamboo logs floating through, but figure on using the bus to get anywhere.

Bus There is no central bus terminal so you have to roam the streets looking for the various terminals; the main ones are on the map. Quevedo is 180 km from Guayaquil by flat road and 235 km from Quito by mountainous road so it's not surprising that the bus situation heavily favours Guayaquil. In fact, there aren't any direct buses to Quito.

Transportes Ecuador has buses from Guayaquil to Quito several times a day but they are often full by the time they pass through Quevedo. It's better to stand at the town exit at the end of Avenida 7 de Octubre and wait for a bus *de paso* heading for Quito, or to take one of the frequent Transportes Sucre buses to Santo Domingo where you can change to equally frequent buses to Quito. Don't confuse Transportes Sucre with Express Sucre, which has only three daily buses to Cuenca.

Buses to Guayaquil (US$1.30) are very frequent and take from 2½ to four hours depending on the bus. All companies seem to have both large, slow buses and small, fast ones. Ask at Transportes Sucre, TIA and CIA companies. These normally go via Daule. If you want to go via Babahoyo, you should go with FBI – which translates, inoffensively, into Flota Babahoyo Internacional.

Other bus companies you should know about are Transportes Cotopaxi and Flota Bolívar. The first runs seven buses a day to Latacunga, about seven hours by dirt road. The second has an 8 am and a 1 pm bus to Portoviejo, about five hours by dirt road. This route, from Latacunga via Quevedo to Portoviejo, is one of the least frequently travelled and also one of the prettiest highland-to-coast routes. The buses are old, crowded and uncomfortable but the journey more interesting than the standard routes.

SOUTH OF QUEVEDO

If your southbound bus crosses the Río Quevedo bridge, then you are going to Babahoyo; if it doesn't, then you are heading to Daule, which is the most frequent route to Guayaquil and described here.

About 20 km away from Quevedo you reach Empalmé – or Velasco Ibarra, as it's officially called. Here the road forks, westbound on a dirt road to Portoviejo and southbound on paved road to Guayaquil. Empalmé is a busy little junction town with several basic restaurants and pensiones. You're in the heart of banana country here and it continues that way to Balzar, another small market town with a basic hotel.

Near Palestina the good road surface turns to gravel and the going gets slower – evidence of the disastrous floods of 1982/83. Also around Palestina the banana plantations give way to rice paddies, and *piladoras* are frequently seen along the road. These are husking and drying factories with tons of rice spread out on huge concrete slabs to dry in the sun (assuming you're travelling in the dry season). Not everyone can afford the commercial *piladoras* and often you see a poor *campesino* spreading out his few bushels of rice to dry on the tarmac on the side of the road. In other areas, similar *piladoras* are used to dry various crops such as coffee.

About three quarters of the way to Guayaquil, you'll reach Daule. This is another small commercial and agricultural centre with basic hotels. You cross the Río Daule and though you can see a few outboard-powered dugouts, few people travel to Guayaquil that way, as it is prohibitively expensive compared to the bus. Three hours after leaving Quevedo, the bus gets to Guayaquil, Ecuador's major port and largest city.

BABAHOYO

With about 45,000 inhabitants, Babahoyo is the capital of the flat agricultural province of Los Rios. North of it lie banana and palm plantations, south of it are rice paddies and some cattle raising. The ride from Babahoyo to Guayaquil is often made very pretty with huge flocks of white cattle egrets.

Babahoyo, only seven metres above sea level and on the banks of the Río Babahoyo, was badly flooded during the 1982/83 El Niño. To get some idea of what the flood was like, go to the library at the edge of the river. The flood-retaining walls, some six metres high in the dry season, have been completely washed away in places. The water level reached the library entrance, which is on a small patio about half a metre higher than the surrounding streets – all of which were flooded for several weeks. The inhabitants waded knee deep from house to house or used canoes.

An interesting feature of the river is the floating houses which were there before the floods; they just rose and fell with the waters. A few drifted loose but most remained undamaged. You can cross the river for a few cents; there are frequent departures from the dock.

The church on the central plaza has a large modern mural of the Virgin and Child decorating the entire front. The otherwise pleasing effect is marred somewhat by the massive rusty iron doors, which look more like the doors of a maximum security prison than the entrance to a place of worship.

Although it's not exactly exciting, Babahoyo is a bustling and energetic town with much commercial activity. The downtown streets are very busy and, for some strange reason, I found myself liking the place.

Information

The post office is in the government buildings on the central plaza. There is an IETEL office but no money-changing facilities.

Places to Stay

There's plenty to choose from. The *Mesón Popular* rents very basic boxes for US$1.20 per person, but at least it's locked up and looks secure. Similarly priced is the basic *Hotel Zaida*, which has a few rooms with river views. Even cheaper is the *Residencial Babahoyo* – liveable in for US$1.

Other cheap places are the *Pensión Sanchez* (really basic little concrete boxes) and *Hotel Los Rios*, which is next to the fanciest place in town, *Hotel Cachari*. The latter charge from US$4.50 to US$7 per person depending on whether you want air-con, river views, etc. It looks pretty good if you want some comfort.

There's also the *Hotel San Marcos*, with rooms starting around US$1.20 each, though you'll pay twice that for rooms with a private bath. The *Residencial Ensueño* is about US$1.50 each but is next to the FBI bus station and apt to be noisy. *Hotel Dorado Gigante* has fairly clean, spacious rooms with private bath for US$2 each, but when I was there I was asked if I wanted the room for a while or for the night!

Although a little more expensive, *Hotel Riberas* is good value with clean rooms costing from US$2 to US$4.50 each depending on whether you have fan, air-con, private bathroom, river view. Finally, the *Hotel Capitol* is being remodelled but looks as if it's going to be a good, though not very cheap, hotel.

Places to Eat

There are many *chifas* in the town centre, especially on General Barona east of the central plaza. A good one is below the *Hotel Cachari*. Near *El Rosado* is a nice corner café with outdoor tables from which to watch the activity of the plaza. A good cheap place for an outdoor (or indoor) lunch is the *Restaurant Munich*.

Entertainment

There is one cinema. If you're there at the weekend you can poke your head into

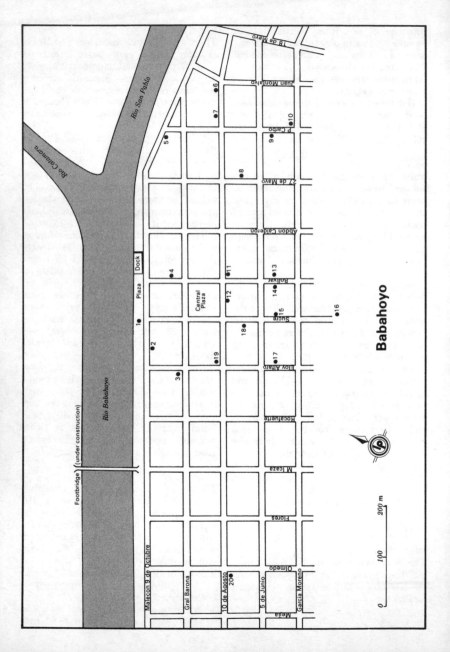

Babahoyo

1	Library	12	Church
2	Hotel Zaida	13	Flota Bolívar
3	Teatro Babahoyo	14	Transportes El Dorado
4	Hotels Cachari & Los Rios	15	Residencial Ensueño & Bus
5	Hotel Riberas del Babahoyo		Companies (Flota Babahoyo,
6	Hotel San Marcos		Interprovincial etc)
7	Pensión Sanchez	16	Hotel Capitol
8	Residencial Babahoyo	17	Residencial Azucena
9	Hotel Reina Maria	18	Mesón Popular
10	Hotel Dorado Gigante	19	Restaurant Munich
11	IETEL	20	Jimmy's Club

Jimmy's Club – I have no idea what it's like or, indeed, whether it is still operating.

Getting There & Away
Bus There is no proper central terminal but most companies have departures from or near the block bounded by 5 de Junio and Bolívar. Most companies have frequent service to Guayaquil (40c, 1½ hours). You can also get buses to most towns in the province.

North Coast

Unlike the coast of Peru to the south, Ecuador has warm water bathing its coast, and swimming is pleasant year round. There are beautiful, palm-fringed, sandy beaches which, unfortunately, suffered greatly during the 1982/83 El Niño floods. Many of the beaches were destroyed (palm trees uprooted, the sand washed away, and ocean front buildings and streets damaged) but are recovering slowly. There are still many scars of the disaster, but hotels are, for the most part, open and functioning normally and it is expected that the beaches will return to their former beauty in the next few years.

There are two definite seasons on the coast. The rainy season is from December to June and the dry season during the rest of the year. The rainy season is hot and humid as well as wet and the climate in the lowlands is uncomfortable. At this time, strangely enough, people flock to the beaches. I suppose the rationale is that if it is hot, humid, wet and stickily uncomfortable, you may as well go to the beach and cool off in the sea. January to March seem to be popular months.

The biggest problem at this time is that the rain can make roads slow or impassable but generally the main roads remain open year round. During the dry season there are often fewer tourists than during the wet!

Travelling along the coast is varied and exciting. If you were to begin in the north and work your way southward, you would travel by motorised dugout, normal bus, *ranchero* bus, poled dugout and on foot.

SAN LORENZO

There are no roads to San Lorenzo and most travellers arrive by train or boat. The train ride down from Ibarra in the highlands is beautiful and takes all day. San Lorenzo itself is not very attractive as there are no beaches; most people use it just as an overnight stop before continuing to Esmeraldas.

San Lorenzo is a small village with a couple of main streets centred around the railway tracks. None of the streets are paved and there are very few vehicles. The town is not very well laid out, but is small and most everyone knows where everything is. *Marimba* music can sometimes be heard in town but there are no special bars or nightclubs; ask around.

Information

There are no proper money-changing facilities. If you ask around you'll find people will change small amounts of Colombian currency or US dollars. It is possible to arrive in San Lorenzo by boat from Tumaco in Colombia, but there is no immigration office and you have to go to Ibarra or Esmeraldas and ask at the DITURIS or police stations there about getting your passport stamped. You may have to go to Quito. There is an IETEL office.

Places to Stay & Eat

None of the few hotels in San Lorenzo are very good, so if you like some comforts you will be uncomfortable here. None of the rooms have private bathrooms, hot water, air-con or other amenities. They should however have a bed and a mosquito net; the mosquitoes can be bad, especially in the wet months. Bring insect repellent or mosquito coils. None of the hotels charge more than US$2 per person.

If arriving by train, it is a good idea to try and find a place to stay quickly because everyone else will be looking. At the train station kids will take you to a hotel (tip expected – about 25c). The nearest hotel is a 10 minute walk straight beyond the train station in the direction that the train was going. This is the

Residencial Las Margaritas which looks OK. Five minutes further into the centre are the *Residencial San Lorenzo* and *Ecuador*, both on the same block and both with simple restaurants which are the best places to eat.

I ate at the *San Lorenzo* where they had beef stew for US$1 and tasty shrimp dishes for US$2. The *San Lorenzo* hotel looks old and run down – they have mosquito netting but you have to ask about a fan. The *Ecuador* is about the same and they charge US$1.25 per person.

I stayed two blocks away in a basic but clean room at the *Residencial Ibarra*. They provided a fan and mosquito netting and charged US$1.70. You'll find the *Hotel Jonny*, which is also OK, conveniently close to the port. There are several other places if these are full – it's a small town so you won't have difficulty in finding them.

Getting There & Away

Rail The *autoferro* leaves daily from San Lorenzo at 6.30 am for Ibarra. Try to book your seat the day before or get to the station early, as the train is usually full. More information on this service is found in the Ibarra section.

Boat General enquiries about boat services are best directed at the Capitanía on the waterfront. They have lists of departing and arriving boats.

There are boats most days to Tumaco in Colombia, but make sure you have all the necessary visas (see Facts for the Visitor). Few people take this route; the journey is done in motorised dugouts, costs about US$7 and takes most of the day. It can get both very wet and sunny so protect yourself and your gear. Border crossing facilities are not geared to foreign tourists and you may have difficulty in entering Colombia.

Other motorised dugouts go to San Pedro (where there is a beach but no accommodation), to Limones (officially called Valdéz), Borbón and to La Tola.

Limones (US$1.25, 1¼ hours) and La Tola (US$2, two hours) are the usual destinations of most travellers and are served by Transportes S L del Pailon with several boats a day. Most boats to La Tola stop at Limones en route but few travellers stop there. If you take an early morning boat to La Tola (services begin at dawn) you can connect with a bus on to Esmeraldas. Tickets are sold in San Lorenzo for the complete journey or you can buy the bus portion when you get to La Tola. The bus portion takes about four or five hours from La Tola to Esmeraldas, so the whole trip from San Lorenzo to Esmeraldas can be done in one day and costs about US$3.50. Accommodation in La Tola is poor and so most travellers make the trip straight through.

Recently, a new route has opened to Esmeraldas from Borbón at the confluence of the Cayapas and Santiago rivers. Motorised dugouts go from San Lorenzo via Limones to Borbón (US$2.20, 2½ hours) and from Borbón there are 'ranchero' buses going to Esmeraldas several times a day (US$1.60, 4-5 hours). Service from San Lorenzo to Borbón is less frequent than to La Tola, although some travellers consider the Borbón route more interesting. Neither will bore you!

It is also possible to take a steamer all the way from San Lorenzo to Esmeraldas, but this isn't highly recommended. You don't see much of the countryside and the boats are cargo vessels that are dirty, hot and uncomfortable. Service is irregular – about twice a week.

The motorised dugout journey via Limones and on to Borbón or La Tola is much more pleasant. The dugouts are small enough to travel through the coastal mangrove swamps and you'll see much more scenery than you will from the larger steamer. Keep your eyes open for the black scissor-tailed frigate birds circling overhead, squadrons of pelicans gliding by, and schools of jellyfish floating past the boat.

LIMONES & BORBÓN

Limones is a small town at the mouth of the Río Santiago and Cayapa delta. It is more important than San Lorenzo, despite the latter's railway connections. Timber is logged in this area and floated down the river to Limones, where there is a sawmill. There are few amenities in town and the two hotels are pretty rough.

The only way into Limones is by boat and you can sometimes see Cayapa Indians here, although more can be seen at Borbón and further up the Cayapa river. The Cayapas are famous for their basket work and there are stores in Esmeraldas and Limones selling their work. The road from Esmeraldas along the coast has a branch to Borbón; a bus service operates during the dry season but delays of days can occur in the wet.

The buses to Esmeraldas are usually 'rancheros' – flat bed trucks mounted with excruciatingly narrow and uncomfortable benches. Try and get an end seat so you can at least stretch one leg. You can get from Limones to Esmeraldas on a twice-weekly boat; ask at the Capitanía. It is easier to go on to La Tola and take the bus.

LA TOLA

This village is the beginning or end of the road, depending on which direction you're headed. There are no hotels, though stranded travellers will be given somewhere to sleep. There are a few stores where you can buy snacks.

Getting There & Away

Buses (usually but not always 'rancheros') with the La Costeñita company take five hours to Esmeraldas and cost US$2. If you take a morning bus from Esmeraldas you will connect with a boat to San Lorenzo and vice versa, so there is no reason to stay in La Tola.

To Esmeraldas The bus journey to Esmeraldas is bumpy and uncomfortable. It is very dusty in the dry season and muddy in the wet. The first half of the

road is very bad and may be impassable during the rainy season. The half way point is the village of Lagarto where there is a basic residencial and a restaurant. A paved road begins at the village of Rocafuerte, also with basic residencial and restaurant. The paved road is intermittent from here.

There are good views of the coastal scenery and I persuaded the driver to let me ride on the roof of the bus, which was better than being squashed inside. I don't recommend this during the rainy season! Watch out for sunburn during the dry. The bird life along the coast is varied and spectacular; I enjoyed looking at trees filled with hundreds of roosting white cattle egrets.

ESMERALDAS

This important city of about 91,000 inhabitants is capital of the province of Esmeraldas. It was near here that the Spanish conquistadors made their first landfall in Ecuador. Esmeraldas has been a major port throughout Ecuador's history. Although fishing and shipping are important, the recent construction of an oil refinery near the terminal of the trans-Andean oil pipeline has provided Esmeraldas with a new source of income and employment.

This is of little interest to most tourists who spend the night and continue southwest to the towns of Atacames, Súa and Muisne, where the best beaches are to be found. Esmeraldas itself also has beaches in the suburb of Las Palmas, but they are not as good.

Information

The unsigned post office is up the stairs from the IETEL office on the waterfront. The IETEL office was extraordinarily efficient when I was last there – they connected me with Quito in two minutes. The market across from the IETEL office is open daily and sells Cayapa basketry among other things.

There is a DITURIS tourist information

office half a block from the main plaza. There is no sign or street number so you find it by going up the stairs of the nondescript office building marked on the map.

Money changers don't exist and last time I was in Esmeraldas the banks told me that it was 'illegal' for them to change money. This was, apparently, a temporary economic measure and has since been lifted. It is best to arrive with enough sucres, however, as the banks remain erratic with their foreign exchange policies.

Places to Stay - Esmeraldas

There are many hotels but the cheapest ones are not too good. Esmeraldas is definitely not the place to come looking for quaint or memorable hotels. There seem to be quite a few travellers in Esmeraldas (especially Ecuadorean holiday-makers and businesss people) and hotels are sometimes full. You may want to stay in Las Palmas.

Places to Stay - bottom end

Many of the cheapest hotels are close to bus terminals and apt to be noisy. They are also not very well looked after. The following are among the very cheapest (less than US$1.50 each) but otherwise have little to recommend them: pensiones *Elsita, Quito* and *9 de Octubre*; residenciales *Paquita* and *Bolívar*; hostals *Isabelita* and *Valparaiso 1*; and *Hotel Suiza*. Of these, the ones not right next to bus terminals are generally a little better.

Slightly more expensive but not much better is the *Nuevo Hotel* at US$1.70. Cleaner, but criticised for being noisy, is the *Residencial Dominguez* at US$2 per person. These are all on the same block of Avenida Sucre, south of the central plaza. There are several other cheap hotels within a couple of blocks. *Hotel Royal* is US$2 each but unfriendly – they wouldn't let me look at a room. 'Take it or leave it.' I left it.

Places to Stay - middle

There is a better selection if you can afford

US$3 to US$4 each, but check your room carefully, as the higher-priced hotels are sometimes no better than the cheapest. Most of the rooms in this section boast private bathrooms, mostly with cold water, but check to see if they are working.

The *Residencial Sulena* (US$3.50 each) is clean, well-lit and secure. There are fans in the rooms but its most commendable feature is the many plants decorating the place. The front yard is a popular evening venue for volleyball. *Hotel Americano* is clean and good value for US$3 a single and US$5 a double. They charge an extra dollar per person for air-con. *Hotel Galeon* is well kept for US$3.80 per person.

The *Hotel Diana* has rooms for US$3.50 per person. The rooms have TV and telephone and the nice little old lady behind the reception desk told me to phone down if the water wasn't running. The place looks as if it has some character. Next door is the new *Hotel Beatriz* which looks quite good for US$3.50 per person or US$4 in rooms with private bath. *Hotel Roma 2* is US$3.50 each, but many of its rooms are without windows and it shouldn't be confused with the better and more expensive *Hotel Roma 1*, which has some good rooms with TV and phone at US$5 a single and US$9 a double. The *Hotel Korea* has good rooms with private bath, fan, and phone for US$4.50 a single and US$8.50 a double or cheaper rooms with fewer amenities.

Hotels *Turismo* and *Chaberrin Internacional* both charge US$4 each. The first is dirty and the second has beds with no sheets. Not all the rooms have private bathrooms. These hotels are not recommended. *Hotel Rita* charges US$10 for a double room and looks sleazy.

Places to Stay - top end

Apart Hotel Esmeraldas charges US$13 a single and US$19 a double and is the best in town.

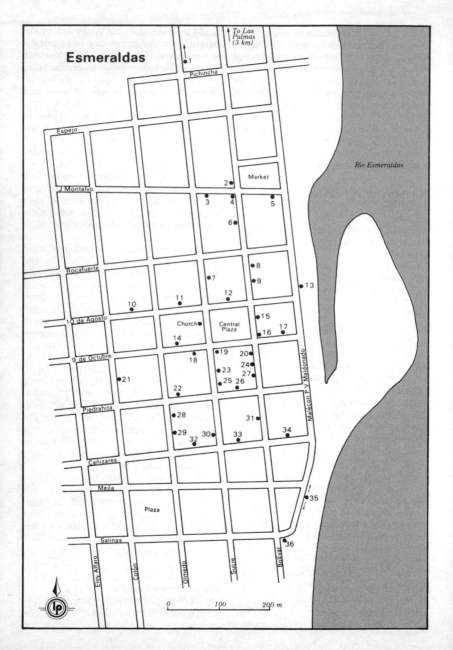

Esmeraldas

To Las
Palmas
(3 km)

Pichincha

Espejo

Río Esmeraldas

Market

J Montalvo

Rocafuerte

10 de Agosto

Church

Central
Plaza

9 de Octubre

Malecon P y Maldonado

Piedrahita

Cañizares

Mejia

Plaza

Salinas

Eloy Alfaro

Colón

Olmedo

Sucre

Bolívar

0   100   200 m

Places to Stay – Las Palmas

There are half a dozen hotels in this beach suburb and most of them are fairly expensive. The two exceptions are the clean, family-run *Residencial Mechita* and the *Hostal Familiar*, both of which charge US$1.50 per person for basic rooms.

The remaining hotels all charge about US$10 a single and US$16 a double and are very comfortable. The *Atahualpa Hotel* is in a large house with a flower garden and the *Hotel Cayapas* also has a pleasant garden. *Hotel del Mar* is closest to the beach. Some rooms have ocean views and US dollars are accepted. *Hotel Hipocampo* has a pleasant patio to sit out on.

Places to Eat

The most expensive hotels have decent restaurants. Although there are no outstanding restaurants in downtown Esmeraldas, the food in the many small *comedors* is often very good. There are many dishes typical of the coast and sometimes found only in this province. Fish and other seafood are more common than meat and are usually served with a mountain of plain white rice, boiled beans and plantains. The plantains are sometimes boiled whole (very stodgy to my taste) or are sliced and fried to make *patacones* – very tasty. Raw seafood is often marinated to make *ceviche*, which is very good, and seafood *cocado* is cooked with coconut to impart a delicate flavour. *Cocadas*, on the other hand, are sweet bars of grated coconut cooked in sugar and sold on bus journeys throughout the province.

In Las Palmas you can find cheap, no-name beach-hut restaurants which have limited menus because they only serve whatever was caught that day. The food is often delicious. There are a few more expensive restaurants near the Las Palmas hotels; some of them quite elegant, such as the *Restaurant Atenas*. *Bayardo's Restaurant* has also been recommended.

Entertainment

The coast is known for its lively African-influenced music. There are no particular places where you can go to listen to shows; you have to catch as catch can because

1	Two Blocks to Apart Hotel Esmeraldas	18	Transportes Occidentales Buses & Pensión Elsita
2	Hotel Chaberrin Internacional	19	Nuevo Hotel
3	Hotel Rita	20	TAME
4	Hotel Turismo	21	Portón 26 Disco
5	IETEL & Post Office	22	Hotel Galeon
6	Banco Central	23	Transportes Zambaro Buses
7	Cita Buses	24	DITURIS (2nd Floor)
8	Hotel Royal	25	Residencial Dominguez
9	Cinema	26	Transportes Esmeraldas
10	Gruta Discoteca & Hotel Valparaiso 1	27	Cine Bolívar
11	Los Lagos & Sudamericano Buses	28	Hotel Roma 1
12	Aero Taxi Buses	29	Residencial Sulena
13	Transportes La Costeñita Buses	30	Hotel Americano
14	Pensión 9 de Octubre	31	Filanbanco
15	Residencial Bolívar	32	Hotel Roma 2
16	Hostal Isabelita	33	Hotels Beatriz & Diana
17	Reina del Camino Buses & Residencial Paquita	34	Hotel Korea
		35	Fish & Vegetable Market
		36	Hotel Suiza

impromptu gatherings are the norm. The best way is to make friends with the locals and ask them. There are discos, but they are usually open only at weekends. Two are marked on the map and the *Porton 26 Disco* has been recommended though I've never danced there. There are a couple of cinemas, of which the *Ciné Bolívar* is the most comfortable.

Getting There & Away

Air There is a flight to Quito every day except Sunday. It leaves at 8 am and costs US$9. There is also a Friday afternoon flight at 4.45 pm. The TAME office just off the corner of the main plaza will sell you a ticket. The major problem is that the airport is about 25 km away from town across the Río Esmeraldas. Passengers and cab drivers gather in front of the TAME office a couple of hours before the flight and four or five passengers are crammed into each taxi at a cost of US$1.80 per person. Incoming passengers get together to do the same thing at the airport.

You can also buy your plane ticket at the airport if the flight is not full. Make sure you get a seat assignment at the airport or you won't get on – there are different windows for ticket buying and seat assignments, so you have to wait in line twice. It's not very organised.

Boat The Capitanía is on the right side of the road linking downtown with Las Palmas, just before you get to Las Palmas. They can give information about which boats are going where, and then you have to talk to the captain of the boat directly. Boats occasionally go to Guayaquil and other coastal ports but the most frequent sailings are for Limones. Boat travel from Esmeraldas is not recommended. It is much more convenient to travel by land and you see more.

There is an immigration office near the Capitanía should you be arriving from Colombia.

Bus There is no central bus terminal. There is a direct road to Quito via Santo Domingo. The fastest service to Quito is with Aerotaxi (US$2.50, five hours) but they drive suicidally fast. Transportes Occidentales and Transportes Esmeraldas are slower and a few cents cheaper. Buses are frequent.

Transportes Occidentales also has frequent buses to Guayaquil (US$2.90, nine hours) and an early evening bus to Machala (US$3.80, 12 hours) if you want to go to Peru the next day. Guayaquil is also served by Transportes Esmeraldas. CITA has four buses a day to Ambato. Reina del Camino has five buses a day to Portoviejo (US$3, nine hours) and a couple to Bahía de Caráquez (US$2.90, eight hours). Transportes Zambaro has slow buses to Santo Domingo.

For provincial buses go to Transportes La Costeñita. Buses for Atacames and Súa (30c, less than an hour) leave every 45 minutes from 6.30 am to 8 pm. There are eight buses a day to Muisne (US$1.10, three hours). Buses to La Tola leave six times a day and the US$3.50 ticket includes the boat to San Lorenzo. Take a morning bus to ensure that you don't have to overnight in La Tola. Many buses also go to other small provincial villages.

Taxi A taxi will take you from Esmeraldas to Atacames for US$10. If arriving at the airport, you can go to Atacames for about the same fare and avoid Esmeraldas completely, which is no great loss.

Getting Around

Take a 5c Las Palmas bus along Avenida Bolívar to get to the port and beaches.

ATACAMES

This small resort town, about 30 km west of Esmeraldas, has built up a reputation among travellers as one of the best places to go for a relaxed and inexpensive beach vacation. It certainly is cheaper and less developed than the beaches in the Guayaquil area, and despite the recent

flood damage remains particularly popular with budget travellers. Inexpensive accommodation can be found right on the ocean front, so you can walk straight out of your room onto the beach. There's not much reason for going into the town centre unless you need to make a phone call at the IETEL office.

Nightlife is variable. I've been here when nothing was happening and other times when every bar was hopping. I can't recommend anywhere in particular; if there's anything going on you'll hear it!

Warning

There is a powerful undertow and no lifeguards. People get drowned every year, so keep within your limits.

Thieves thrive wherever there is a conglomeration of travellers. This is certainly true of beach areas, and Atacames is no exception. Camping is not recommended because thieves cut through the tent material and rob you even if you're asleep inside the tent. It is best to stay in a beach cabin or hotel room and make sure that it has secure locks on the doors and shutters on the windows.

Assaults have been reported by people walking the beaches late at night. If you want a midnight beach stroll, go in a group.

Bring insect repellent or mosquito coils, especially in the wet season. The cheapest hotels may have rats so stay in a medium-priced hotel to minimise the chance of seeing them if it worries you.

Although the chance of being bitten by a sea snake is remote, every once in a while they get washed up on the beaches. Don't pick them up, as they are venomous.

Places to Stay

Atacames can get rather full at weekends, especially holiday weekends, so you are advised to try and arrive midweek. January through March is the high season, when prices tend to rise. At other times you can try bargaining, especially if you arrive midweek and plan on staying a few days.

There are a couple of places close to the town centre near the place where the bus lets you off, but most hotels are on or close to the beach. To get to the beach, you have to cross the footbridge, as vehicles don't go there. New hotels, or old hotels under new management and name, open frequently and there's always a wide choice of places to stay. Always check your room or cabin for security before you rent it.

Most showers have brackish water (which is quite salty) and only the more expensive hotels have fresh-water showers.

Places to Stay – bottom end

For the cheapest accommodation the best selection is to your right after you cross the footbridge. The first cheap place you come to is the *Residencial Bachita*, which was repainted a few years ago but looks rather like a barracks building. They charge US$2 each. It is set back a block from the beach, as are the *Residencial Primavera* and *Hotel Balboa*, both of which charge US$1.50 each and are run down. Further down the beach is the *San Baye*, one of the cheapest places. They charge US$2 for a room with two beds. Some rooms have a private bathroom for US$1 extra.

At the far end of the beach are some quiet and tiny A-frame beach cabins with two beds for US$3 a cabin. They are basic but quite acceptable and they have a little restaurant so you don't have to go back to the main tourist area. Unfortunately, because these cabins are about half a km beyond the other buildings, I have heard reports of people being robbed on the way there late at night.

If you turn left at the footbridge you'll see the *Hotel Paco Foco*, which was temporarily closed recently but doesn't look very expensive. At the other far end of the beach is the *Hotel Eden*, also inexpensive. If all the beach front cheapies are full, you can try the basic and run-down *Hotel Bellavista* near the bus stop.

Places to Stay – middle

There are several good mid-priced hotels. The first place you come to if you turn right at the footbridge is the *Hostería Los Bohíos*, which has pleasant and clean bungalows with private bath for US$7.50 a double. Next door is the *Hotel Atalaya*, which has clean rooms with private bath for US$6 a double. Both places are good

and secure but they aren't right next to the beach.

Closer to the beach is the *Hotel Tahiti*, which has a restaurant, simple but clean cabins and rooms with and without baths. Prices range from about US$4 to US$7 a double, depending on which rooms you get. The staff are friendly and lock up your valuables for you. The private baths have brackish water but there is a communal fresh-water shower too.

A new hotel next to the *Tahiti* is the *Hotel Chavalito* which is run by an ex-merchant marine who has a fund of good stories to keep you entertained. Rooms with private baths cost about US$7.50 a double, there is a restaurant/bar, and the place is secure and friendly. The two best rooms at the front of the hotel have ocean view balconies.

Heading left from the beach, you'll eventually come to *Cabañas Roger*. They charge a minimum US$5 per person and have a bewildering system of taxes and extra charges for rooms with a sea view or with a private kitchen (refrigerator and stove). All the rooms have private showers and some of them are new and look good. Some of the bungalows are suitable for up to six people and you could probably bargain for a better rate. They'll happily explain their prices to you so you won't get slapped with a 'sea view tax' as you're about to leave.

Places to Stay – top end

To the left across the footbridge you'll find the comfortable bungalows of *Cabañas Costa del Sol*, about US$13 a double. They have a good restaurant. Heading in the opposite direction, you'll find the clean and modern bungalows of the *Hotel Juan Sebastian* set in a flower garden. They charge from US$5 to US$10 per person, depending on the room and the season. They also have a restaurant and bar. Similarly priced, but on the main road, is the good *Hotel Las Vegas*.

Places to Eat

There are many simple *comedors* close to the beach near the footbridge. They all tend to serve the same thing – whatever was caught that morning. Make sure you ask the price before you get served or you may be overcharged. All the *comedors* seem to be much of a likeness, so wander around till you find one that you fancy. Many of them double as bars or dancing places in the evenings and their popularity changes with the seasons. Keep your ears open and you'll soon hear where it's happening.

Getting There & Away

Bus All buses stop at the corner of the main road by the Disco La Barca; there is no bus terminal. You pay for your ticket when you board the bus. Buses for Esmeraldas (30c, 45 minutes) normally begin from Súa and there are plenty of seats. Most buses from Esmeraldas to Atacames continue to Súa. Buses for Muisne (90c, two hours further down the coast) are often full when they come from Esmeraldas and you may find it easier to return to Esmeraldas and then retrace your route. Alternatively, be prepared to ride on the roof.

Taxi Taxis from either Esmeraldas airport or downtown Esmeraldas charge about US$10.

SÚA

This is a small fishing village and is rather more bustling than Atacames. It's an interesting place to stay if you'd rather watch the boats and fishermen at work than just hang out on the beach. The fishing industry brings its attendant frigate birds, pelicans and other sea birds but also means that the small beach is dirtier than the one at Atacames. The general setting is attractive. There is an IETEL office with one phone.

Súa is about a six km walk by road from Atacames. I've also heard that you can walk along the beach at the lowest tides, but if you try this be careful not to get cut off. The 1982/83 floods washed out some of the beach and it may no longer be possible.

Places to Stay & Eat

There's much less to choose from than in Atacames. The *Residencia Quito* is a basic hotel on the road into town which charges US$1.50 each. On the waterfront are several cheap places, of which the *Hotel Súa* and *Residencial Proaño* are the cheapest but aren't up to much. The *Residencial España* has a dance floor and is liable to be noisy if it's a party night on the weekend. They charge US$1.50 each. Slightly better is the *Residencial Mar y Sol* for US$2 each. They also have a couple of rooms with private showers for twice that price.

If there is a group of you, try the *Cabañas Las Acacias*, which charge about US$22 for six-bed bungalows with private bath. During the off season they'll be willing to bargain, and they also have some rooms where you can stay for about US$2.50 each. It's the best cheap place in town if you can bargain them down a bit. Finally, there is the pleasant and well looked after *Hotel Chagra Ramos*, where you can get a good double room with fan and private bath for US$8 in the off season. There is a good restaurant here. Otherwise you can try the cheap *comedors* past the *Residencial España*.

Getting There & Away

Buses to and from Esmeraldas run about every 45 minutes and arrive and leave from in front of the Residencial Mar y Sol. It takes 10 minutes to Atacames (10c) and about an hour to Esmeraldas (35c). You pay on the bus.

If you want to go further along the coast to Muisne you have to wait out of town along the main road for a bus passing from Esmeraldas (often full).

MUISNE

This is the end of the road from Esmeraldas. I have always enjoyed this little village because it is relatively remote and not many people come here. The journey is interesting. The old bus (or *ranchero*) drives along a very bumpy dirt road but the scenery is good. I rode on top of the bus and enjoyed the views of rolling green countryside with many species of tropical trees and birds.

At the end of the road you have to take a motorised dugout to reach Muisne, which is on an island. Boatmen will meet the bus and take you to their boat – just follow other passengers. The fare is about 50c depending on how far the bus can get; some of the road was washed out in 1982/83.

When you disembark at Muisne you'll see the main road heading directly away from the pier into the town 'centre'. There are several cheap and basic hotels – solo women travellers should beware of the *Residencial Narcisita*. The others are all unremarkable and charge about US$1 to US$1.50 per person. It's best to continue on the main road, past the town square, and towards the ocean. The main road deteriorates into a grassy lane and it's about a km to the beach.

About 500 metres before arriving at the beach you pass the new and modern *Hotel Galápagos* charging US$2.50 per person in rooms with private bathroom. Closer to the beach are little cabins called *Ipanema* and *San Cristobal*. I've heard that the *San Cristobal* are being torn down and replaced – meanwhile the owner rents rooms with a view of the ocean in his house. The cabins are basic wooden shacks that are clean, have a shower and mosquito nets. They charge US$2 to US$3 per person depending on the season. It's definitely not fancy but is a *tranquilo* place to stay and you have a huge beach to yourself. Bring insect repellent.

There is a basic store by the beach where simple foodstuffs can be bought. There are a couple of basic restaurants (*Comedor Martha, La Moneda*) in town which serve cheap set meals at normal meal times, but don't expect anything after 7.30 pm. There's a lot of driftwood on the beach and some travellers cook their own food.

SOUTH OF MUISNE

There is no road south of Muisne, so if you want to travel further you have to try other options. If you ask around the dock in Muisne you'll find a couple of boats each morning heading down the coast to Bolívar and Cojimíes or occasionally as far as Manta. Boats are usually large motorised dugouts and stay fairly close to the coast, so it is an interesting journey for the adventurous traveller. Fares from Muisne to Cojimíes are about US$4.50 and the journey takes almost two hours

You can also head south on foot and get to Cojimíes in one day if you leave early. At low tide, pickup trucks sometimes act as buses on some sections and you may get a ride, but don't rely on them. There are several rivers to cross but you can find dugouts to ferry you for about 10c or 20c. Bring change. From Muisne, walk south along the beach for about five km; take a dugout across the river and continue seven km along the beach past Mompiche (small store); follow a jeep track over the headland four km to Punta Suspiro; make the dugout crossing to Portete (small store); walk five km to Bolívar.

Although you can sometimes catch rides, be prepared to walk the whole distance if necessary. I've done this walk twice and seen sea snakes, a beached whale, crabs galore, jellyfish, sea birds and other sea creatures along the beach.

Bolívar has a little port and if you wait and ask around you can get a boat ride to Cojimíes for about US$1.50. It may take a few hours to get a passage so leave Muisne at dawn, as there are no hotels in Bolívar. You can rent a boat for about US$15 to take you to Cojimíes if you can't get a ride.

Warning
Rain during the wet season can cause delays.

COJIMÍES

The road begins again here and there are daily *rancheros* south. They run along the coast at low tide so departure times vary. The Costa del Norte bus office is on the main street. Buses to the next village of Pedernales cost US$1 and take about 1¼ hours. Buses sometimes go further.

Across the street from the bus office there is a very basic (wash in a bucket) unmarked hotel which will give you a bed for about US$1.50. There are basic restaurants. Although facilities are limited, people tend to be extra friendly in these out-of-the-way places.

PEDERNALES

There is a Costa del Norte bus office on the main street where you can buy tickets for Cojimíes (northbound) or San Vicente (southbound, US$3, four hours). There are three or four departures a day. There are a couple of basic (again no showers), unmarked *residencials* near the bus offices. The *Residencial Hamacas* is the slightly better one and a bed costs US$1.20 to US$1.50.

The buses usually follow the beach and the ride is very fast on the hard-packed sand, especially between Pedernales and Cojimíes. There are some rougher stretches south of Pedernales.

A correspondent reports that: 'between Cojimíes and Pedernales there is a hotel lost in the coconut groves – the *Cocosolo*. It's for lovers of deserted beaches and the noise of the wind clattering through the palm leaves. About US$5 per person in the cabins – restaurant attached'. Ask your bus driver if he knows of it.

Pedernales has a small airstrip and occasional light aircraft fly to San Vicente by Bahía de Caraquez – about US$5.

JAMA

This is another one-pensión village between Pedernales and San Vicente but buses are often full when they come through.

SAN VICENTE

This resort village is a short ferry ride across the Río Chone from the more important town of Bahía de Caráquez. There are pleasant beaches and a few hotels.

Places to Stay

If you turn right from the pier you'll find two cheap and basic places for US$1 each – the *Residencial San Vicente* and *Lilita*.

Closer to the pier is the more expensive but good *Hotel Vacaciones*, which charges US$8 a single and US$14 a double. They have a pool and decent restaurant. On the northern outskirts of town on the road to Pedernales there are the *Hotel Alcatraz* and *Hotel Las Hamacas*. Both have bungalows with private bathroom, a pool, a private beach, and charge about US$7.50 per person. Three km north of San Vicente on the beach is a resort hotel with family bungalows costing about US$20. They have a restaurant.

Places to Eat

Behind the market there are some cheap and clean *comedors* such as the *Yessenia*. The best place in the San Vicente/Bahía area is the *Restaurant El Internacional* on the main street in San Vicente. The best hotels have restaurants.

Getting There & Away

Air There is an airstrip for light aircraft behind the market. For more information about arranging flights, contact Aerotransporte Bahía in Bahía de Caráquez.

Boat Ferries take 15 minutes to reach Bahía de Caráquez and leave several times an hour all day long. The fare is 10c. After dark it costs about US$1.25 to hire a boat to take you across (four passengers maximum). There is a car ferry. You can hire boats for trips anywhere you want for US$5 an hour.

Bus San Vicente is the main office of the

Costa del Norte company and they have three buses a day to Pedernales – one to Cojimíes and two inland to Chone. The bus office is close to the boat pier.

BAHÍA DE CARÁQUEZ
This is a small (13,000 inhabitants) but nevertheless fairly important port and holiday resort. There are beaches both here and across the river in San Vicente. For some reason it is rarely visited by travellers although the beaches are as good as elsewhere and the hotels adequate. The Río Chone entrance is quite busy and you can laze around at a riverside café and watch the boats go by, or go for a ferry ride.

Information
There is a bank but they don't change foreign currency. There are both IETEL and post offices and two cinemas. To get to the best beaches go north on Avenida Montufar for about 500 metres. The strange-looking corrugated tin church on the main plaza is worth a look if you've nothing better to do.

Places to Stay
There are several cheap places, of which the cheapest and shabbiest is the *Residencial Don Antonio. Pensión Victoria* is also cheap and marginally better. *Pensión Miriam* has been recently repainted (I wonder how long it'll stay looking that way!) but is otherwise not up to much. Some rooms are a little better than others, so look around. Only the few rooms facing the street have windows. *Hotel Palma* looks better on the outside than it is inside. Other basic hotels are the residenciales *San Fernando* and *San José*. None of these is remarkable in any way; you get a bed to sleep in for US$1 to US$1.50 per person. None of them can be recommended for being very clean or well looked after.

Two new hotels have recently opened on Calle Ante. They are the *Residencial Vera* and *Residencial Los Tamarindes*.

Rooms with private bath are US$2.50 per person.

Hotel Americano has rooms with a private bath and air-con for US$8 single which is a little expensive. The most luxurious is *La Herradura*, which has carpeted rooms with private bathroom, air-con and TV for US$16 a double. A good hotel named *La Piedra* has been built by the beach.

Places to Eat
There are some reasonable and inexpensive cafés by the river near the dock. There are a couple of cheap *chifas*. The *Restaurant El Galpón* opposite the market is cheap and good. *La Galería* on Bolívar by the main plaza has been recommended but isn't very cheap. Down by the beach at the end of Avenida Montufar there are some nice pavement restaurants such as *Los Helechos*, which is one of the more expensive but not exorbitantly so.

Getting There & Away
Air Aerotransporte Bahía have light aircraft which leave from the airstrip in San Vicente to various coastal destinations. There are no scheduled flights so make enquiries.

Boat There is a car ferry to San Vicente and a passenger ferry leaves from the dock several times an hour during daylight (10c, 15 minutes). San Vicente has more boats. Although Bahía de Caráquez is a coastal port, passages to other ports are not easily found.

Bus The two bus companies have offices next to one another on the south end of the waterfront. All buses out of Bahía de Caráquez climb a hill which gives good views of the Río Chone estuary; sit on the left when leaving town and look back. Coactur have buses to Portoviejo (85c, two hours) and Manta (US$1, 2½ hours) every hour. Reina del Camino has several buses a day to Portoviejo, Quito (US$3.30, eight hours), Esmeraldas (US$3.10, eight

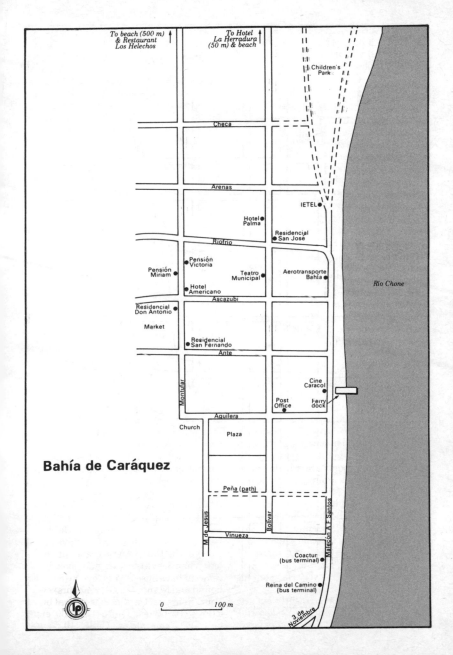

To beach (500 m) & Restaurant Los Helechos

To Hotel La Herradura (50 m) & beach

Children's Park

Checa

Arenas

IETEL

Hotel Palma

Residencial San José

Riofrio

Pensión Victoria

Pensión Miriam

Teatro Municipal

Aerotransporte Bahía

Río Chone

Hotel Americano

Ascazubi

Residencial Don Antonio

Market

Residencial San Fernando

Ante

Cine Caracol

Post Office

Ferry dock

Aguilera

Church

Plaza

Bahía de Caráquez

Peña (path)

Montufar

M de Jesus

Bolívar

Vinueza

Malecón Alfredo Santos

Coactur (bus terminal)

Reina del Camino (bus terminal)

3 de Noviembre

0   100 m

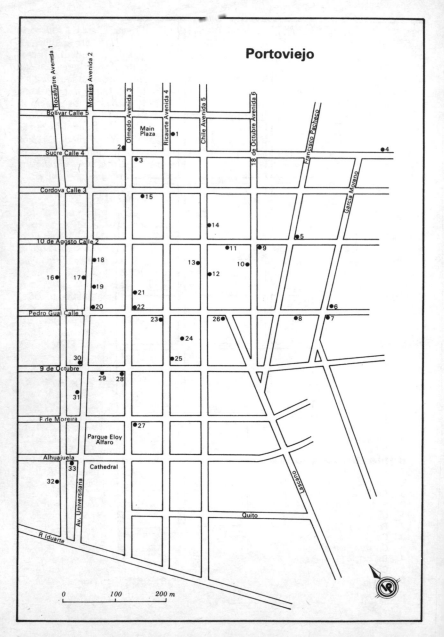

Portoviejo

hours), Santo Domingo and Guayaquil (US$2.70, six hours).

PORTOVIEJO

This large city of 102,000 inhabitants, founded on 12 March 1535, is one of the oldest in Ecuador. It is the capital of Manabí province, which is important for coffee and cattle. Portoviejo has a thriving agricultural processing industry and is an important commercial centre with good road connections with Quito and Guayaquil. It is a bustling town but not visited much by tourists who prefer to head to the coast, especially for the major resort and port of Manta some 37 km away.

Information

The post office is in the government buildings on the main plaza and there is an IETEL office. The Banco Comercial and Banco de Pichincha change money. The streets have both names and numbers but locals tend to use the names more frequently.

Things to See

Despite the town's colonial history, there are few old buildings. There is a **Museo de Casa de Cultura** with an exhibit of traditional musical instruments, but it was closed last time I was there. You can wander down to the pleasant Parque Eloy Alfaro, where you'll find the starkest, barest modern cathedral I've seen in Ecuador. It takes the wind out of the sails of those people who complain that the Catholic church in Latin America spends all its money on gold ornaments. Next to the cathedral is a statue of Francisco Pacheco, the founder of Portoviejo.

Places to Stay - bottom end

The basic *Pensión Cristal* charges only US$1 per night but is often full by mid-afternoon so it can't be too bad. Similarly priced is the *Pensión Guayaquil*, but it looks run down and dirty. The *Residencial Alfaro* is basic but fairly clean and charges US$1.50 each. Many of its rooms are without windows. This seems to be a common problem.

Many of the rooms at the *Residencial Pacheco* are also without windows but they do at least have fans. They charge US$2 per person or US$3.60 in rooms with

1	Cine Central	17	Rutas Ecuatorianas buses
2	Hotel Restaurant Paris	18	Cuidad de Calceta buses
3	Post Office	19	Hotel Portoviejo Plaza
4	Casa de Cultura	20	Carlos A Aray buses
5	IETEL	21	Coactur buses
6	Hotel Cabrera Internacional	22	Pensión Guayaquil
7	Hotel Madrid	23	Pensión Cristal
8	Cine Acapulco	24	Restaurant Oasis
9	Banco Comercial de Manabí	25	TAME
10	Hotel Ejecutivo	26	CTM Aerotaxis buses
11	Cine Roma	27	Residencial Alfaro
12	Peña Bar Wacho	28	Hotel San Marco
13	Co-op 15 de Octubre & Co-op Jipijapa buses	29	Residencial Pacheco
14	Banco de Pichincha	30	Local buses
15	Cine	31	Flota Bolívar buses
16	Reina del Camino buses	32	Hotel Gregorio
		33	Francisco Pacheco statue

a private bath. *Hotel Portoviejo Plaza* is conveniently near most of the bus offices. Unfortunately its nicest rooms look out on the street and so are noisy. The rooms are small but clean and cost US$2 per person or US$3 with a private bath.

A good, clean, old and rather charming hotel is the simple *Hotel Restaurant Paris*, which has rooms with private baths for US$2.75 per person and is recommended. The good, clean *Hotel Gregorio* charges US$3 per person in rooms with private baths and US$2.50 if you use the communal bath. *Hotel Madrid* has clean and spacious rooms with fans for US$3.50 per person.

Places to Stay – middle & top end

Hotel San Marco has rooms with phone, fan and private bath but it's nothing special. They charge US$6/10 a single/double. The best in town is the *Hotel Cabrera Internacional*, which has double rooms from US$9 to US$18 depending on whether you want a room or an air-con suite. *Hotel Ejecutivo* looks about the same.

Places to Eat

My favourite places are the *Peña Bar Wacho* and the *Restaurant Oasis*. The Oasis is a *chifa* on top of a shopping block with outside dining and views of the city. Inside dining is also available and the prices are reasonable, even though it looks quite elegant and the food good. There is an inexpensive *chifa* below the *Hotel Paris*.

Entertainment

If you're looking for some nightlife try the *Peña Bar Wacho*, which is run by a friendly couple with the charming names of Washington Castillo P and Fatima Fernandez C. It's a small place which is open daily for typical food and has shows mainly at weekends. They feature anything from poets to folk music and it's inexpensive. There are also four cinemas in town.

Getting There & Away

Air The airport is about two km west of town (taxi 60c) and there are flights to Quito at 5 pm, Monday to Friday, and 9 am on Sunday. TAME has an office in town and will sell you a ticket for US$13.

Bus There is no central bus terminal but most of the more than 12 bus companies have offices within two blocks of the intersection of Avenida Morales and Pedro Gual.

Coactur has several buses an hour to Manta (35c, 50 minutes) which leave as soon as they are full. They also have buses for Bahía de Caráquez (85c, two hours). CTM Aerotaxi has buses for Manta. Rutas Ecuatorianas has frequent service to Guayaquil (US$2, 3½ hours). Carlos A Aray has many buses to Santo Domingo (US$2.70, five hours) with some buses continuing to Quito (US$3.80, eight hours) or going to Guayaquil. Reina del Camino has buses to Quito, Santo Domingo, Esmeraldas (US$3.30, nine hours), Bahía de Caráquez and Guayaquil. Flota Bolívar has two slow, old buses leaving at 8 am and 1 pm for Quevedo. Ciudad de Calceta has buses to Calceta (known for its sisal industry).

Other small nearby villages, including the beaches of San Clemente and Crucita, are served by small bus companies whose buses depart from near the intersection of Avenida Morales and 9 de Octubre. Co-op 15 de Octubre and Co-op Jipijapa have buses to Jipijapa about every 45 minutes.

MANTA

Manta, with 99,000 inhabitants, is the major port along the central Ecuadorean coast and an important tourist resort and commercial centre.

Manta has a long history. It was founded by Francisco Pacheco on 2 March 1535, 10 days before he founded Portoviejo. But even before its Spanish foundation Manta, named Jocay by the local Indians, was an important port. The Manta culture thrived throughout the whole

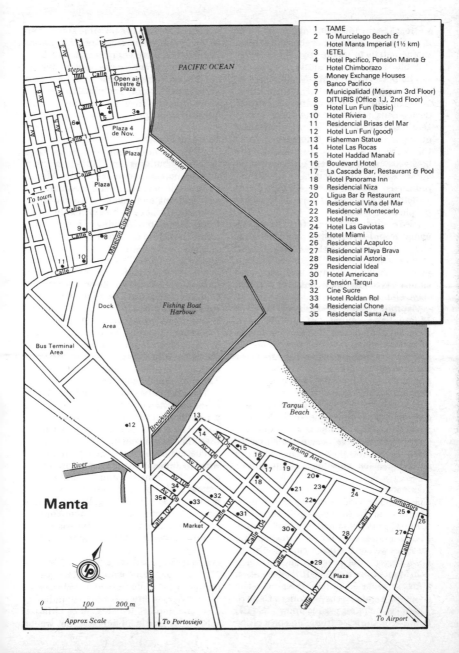

1   TAME
2   To Murcielago Beach &
    Hotel Manta Imperial (1½ km)
3   IETEL
4   Hotel Pacifico, Pensión Manta &
    Hotel Chimborazo
5   Money Exchange Houses
6   Banco Pacifico
7   Municipalidad (Museum 3rd Floor)
8   DITURIS (Office 1J, 2nd Floor)
9   Hotel Lun Fun (basic)
10 Hotel Riviera
11 Residencial Brisas del Mar
12 Hotel Lun Fun (good)
13 Fisherman Statue
14 Hotel Las Rocas
15 Hotel Haddad Manabí
16 Boulevard Hotel
17 La Cascada Bar, Restaurant & Pool
18 Hotel Panorama Inn
19 Residencial Niza
20 Lligua Bar & Restaurant
21 Residencial Viña del Mar
22 Residencial Montecarlo
23 Hotel Inca
24 Hotel Las Gaviotas
25 Hotel Miami
26 Residencial Acapulco
27 Residencial Playa Brava
28 Residencial Astoria
29 Residencial Ideal
30 Hotel Americana
31 Pensión Tarqui
32 Cine Sucre
33 Hotel Roldan Rol
34 Residencial Chone
35 Residencial Santa Ana

PACIFIC OCEAN

steps

Open air theatre & plaza

Plaza 4 de Nov.

Plaza

Plaza

Plaza

To town

Malecon Eloy Alfaro

Breakwater

Dock Area

Bus Terminal Area

Fishing Boat Harbour

Tarqui Beach

Parking Area

River

Breakwater

Manta

Market

Plaza

Lomegas

0   100   200 m

Approx Scale

To Portoviejo

To Airport

western peninsula from about 500 AD until the arrival of the conquistadors, and many artefacts made by these early inhabitants have been found.

The pottery of the Manta culture was well made and decorated with pictures of daily life. Through these pictorial decorations, archaeologists have learnt that the Manta people enhanced their appearance by skull deformation and tooth removal, thus increasing the backward slope of their foreheads and chins and emphasising their large, rounded, hooked noses. This facial structure is apparent in many of the local people even today.

Also evident in their pottery, as well as being recorded in detail by the early conquistadors, was the Mantas' astonishing skill in seamanship. They were able to navigate as far as Panama and Peru, and claims have been made that they reached the Galápagos.

Capitán Bartolomé Ruiz captured a Manta balsa sailing raft in 1526 and recorded that of the 20 crew members, 11 threw themselves overboard in terror, and the remainder were captured for translating purposes and later freed. Similar but smaller balsa rafts can still be seen sailing the coasts today.

Not only were their navigational and ceramic skills well developed; the Mantas were also skilled stonemasons, weavers and metal workers. People wishing to learn more about the Manta culture should visit the museum in the town.

Information

The town is divided into two by an inlet. Manta is on the west side and Tarqui on the east. They are joined by a road bridge. Manta has the main offices and shopping areas, as well as the bus terminal. Tarqui has a bigger hotel selection and beaches.

In Manta there is a DITURIS information office in room 1J on the floor over the shopping arcade at the bottom of Calle 8. There is an impressive new IETEL building on the waterfront. The post office

is difficult to find. It's up some stairs in an office building in front of the Banco Pacifico but there are no signs, so ask.

The Banco Pacifico changes money, as do the exchange houses nearby. Rates vary from day to day and place to place, so shop around. They are usually 2%-5% lower than in Quito.

Things to See

The Municipal Museum on the 3rd floor of the city buildings in Manta is worth a visit to understand more of the Manta culture. Although the exhibit is small, it is well laid out and labelled – but only in Spanish. Although it's officially open from 9 am to 3 pm Monday to Friday, they sometimes close for lunch.

Manta's fishing boat harbour is busy and picturesque. To get over to Tarqui, don't follow the harbour around or you'll have to swim. Cross on the bridge set back from the harbour. In Tarqui there is a huge statue of a Manabí fisherman and beyond it a protected sandy beach. At the end of the beach there are many more fishing boats, which are interesting to watch in the early morning while they unload their cargo. There is a bustling market in Tarqui and a cinema nearby.

The Playa Murciélago beach in Manta is less protected and has bigger waves. It is a couple of km west of the town centre along the waterfront and is less visited than the Tarqui beach.

There is an outdoor theatre in Manta which occasionally has performances, especially during the annual agriculture, fishing and tourism exposition which is held from 14 to 18 October. Portoviejo has a similar event at the same time. You can get more information on what's going on then from the DITURIS office in Manta.

Places to Stay - bottom end

The place to go for cheap accommodation in Manta is Avenida 1 near the Plaza 4 de Noviembre, where there are three hotels near one another which charge US$1 to US$2 per person. They are the hotels

Pacifico and *Chimborazo*, and *Pensión Manta*. The *Hotel Pacifico* looks the best of these and has some rooms with good views. They will give cheaper rates if there is a group of you willing to share a room. Also cheap but really basic are the *Residencial Brisas del Mar* and the old *Hotel Lun Fun*.

In Tarqui, a clean and rambling old budget hotel is the *Residencial Niza*, which is near the beach and has some rooms with ocean views. They charge US$1.50 and have some rooms with up to eight beds which are cheaper per person. Similarly priced but more basic is the *Residencial Acapulco* at the other end of the beach. One of the cheapest of all is the basic *Residencial Chone*, which is reasonably clean and costs US$1 a head.

The *Residencial Playa Brava* charges US$2 for basic boxes which do have private bathrooms. Slightly more expensive but good value is the *Residencial Viña del Mar*, which has simple but clean rooms with air-con and private bathroom for US$5 a double. Similarly priced is the student and youth-group-oriented *Boulevard Hotel*, which might be a good place to meet young Ecuadorean travellers. Other cheap hotels are the residencials *Montecarlo*, *Astoria*, *Ideal* and *Santa Ana*, and the *Pensión Tarqui*.

Places to Stay - middle

Hotel Miami in Tarqui has simple but clean rooms with private bathrooms for US$3 each. Some rooms have good ocean views. *Hotel Roldan Rol* charges US$3.50 in rooms with private bath but is near the market and likely to be noisy. *Hotel Americana* is clean, with double rooms and private baths costing about US$7.50 with a fan. Air-con costs an extra US$1. Some of the upper rooms have good views. *Hotel Inca* has some pleasant rooms with air-con, ocean views and private bathrooms for about US$10 a double. Some rooms are not as good as others, but there is a restaurant.

Hotel Panorama Inn has rooms from US$10 to 14 double depending on the amenities you choose. Rooms are rather worn but spacious, some with good views, and there is a restaurant. They give you pool privileges for *La Cascada* across the street. *Hotel Las Rocas* looks new and charges about the same.

In Manta there is the *Hotel Riviera*, which has rooms with private bathrooms for US$8.50 a double with fan. Air conditioning is US$1 extra.

Places to Stay - top end

The new *Hotel Lun Fun* is good and luxurious and not to be confused with the ratty old hotel of the same name. They charge about US$10 per person and are conveniently located by the bus terminal. Similarly priced is the *Hotel Manta Imperial*, which has a pool and all the modern amenities and is the only hotel near Manta's Playa Murcielágo beach.

In Tarqui there are two luxurious (by Ecuadorean standards) hotels. The modern *Hotel Las Gaviotas* charges about US$23 a double. *Hotel Haddad Manabí* dates from 1931 and is Manta's oldest luxury hotel.

Places to Eat

There are plenty of cheap outdoor *comedors* on the east end of Tarqui beach which serve fresh seafood. The market is also a centre for cheap food. There are several restaurants and bars along the Tarqui waterfront, of which the *Lligua* has large servings of good and inexpensive food. For a night out you can have a rather more expensive but good meal in the more elegant *La Cascada*. The better hotels also have good restaurants.

Getting There & Away

Air Manta is one of the few cities in Ecuador with services to both Quito and Guayaquil. The TAME office on the Manta waterfront will sell you tickets; they are open from 9 am to noon and 3 to 5 pm daily, except Sunday. Flights to Quito cost US$13 and to Guayaquil US$9.

The plane for Guayaquil leaves daily (except Sunday) at 9.30 am, and on Tuesday and Thursday at 6.15 pm. The plane for Quito leaves daily (except Sunday) at 9.15 am. On Sundays there is a 3.30 pm flight to Quito. This service is, as always, subject to change. You can buy tickets at the airport on the morning of the flight but the planes tend to be full at weekends and holidays.

The airport is some three km east of Tarqui and a taxi costs about US$1 if you bargain hard.

Bus There is a large central bus terminal in front of the fishing boat harbour in Manta and almost all buses leave from here, which makes things easy. There are several companies with buses to most major Ecuadorean cities. Journey times and prices are similar to Portoviejo's. Some of the smaller companies running buses to nearby Manabí towns and villages don't have an office in the terminal but their buses leave from there anyway and you pay aboard the bus. An example of this is Coactur to Portoviejo.

MONTECRISTI
This small, interesting village of some 8000 inhabitants can be reached in 15 minutes by frequent buses from Manta's bus terminal. Buses cost 10c and stop running about 6 pm.

Montecristi is an important centre for both the panama hat industry and wickerwork. There are many stores along the main road and along the road leading into the town centre. If you go in towards the centre and ask around, you can see various stages in the manufacture of panama hats.

The town is an old colonial one founded around 1628, when many of the inhabitants of Manta fled inland to avoid the frequent pirate plundering to which the port was subject. There are many unrestored colonial houses left which give the village a rather tumble-down and ghostly atmosphere.

The main plaza has a beautiful church dating back to the early part of the last century. It contains a famous statue of the virgin to which miracles have been attributed, and is worth a visit. In the plaza is a statue of Eloy Alfaro, who was born in Montecristi and was president of Ecuador at the beginning of the century. His tomb is in the town hall by the plaza.

There are no hotels and only a couple of basic *comedors* so it's best to stay in Manta and visit Montecristi on a day trip.

JIPIJAPA
The 'j' is pronounced as 'h' in Spanish, so this town's name is pronounced 'Hipihapa.' Jipijapa has a population of 27,000, and is an important centre for the panama hat industry as well as for coffee and cotton. The town market is a good place to buy panama hats.

You can get to Jipijapa by bus from Portoviejo and Manta. The 1982/83 floods cut off Jipijapa from the west coast and the road is still in bad condition but is being repaired. There are two or three buses a day with Transportes Sur de Manabí, which go to Puerto López. From there you can continue with CITM buses along the south coast to the Santa Elena peninsula.

There are a couple of basic pensiónes.

South Coast

The south coast, consisting of the provinces of Guayas and El Oro, is generally much drier and more barren than the north. The weather pattern changes and the rainy season, which in the north lasts from December to May, lasts only from January to April in Guayaquil. Further west and south it becomes drier still, and by the time the Peruvian border is reached the South American coastal desert begins.

The agriculturally important lands of Los Ríos province continue into Guayas and El Oro. Bananas are the most important crop and irrigation in the dry south means that plantations can continue beyond Machala. Rice, coffee, cacao and African palm are other important crops of the region.

West of Guayaquil is the dry, infertile and scrubby Santa Elena peninsula with not enough rivers for irrigation. Archaeological investigation shows that the land used to be as wet and fertile as it is now in the northern coastal areas, but drought and deforestation over the last 5000 years have wrought severe changes. Pottery decorations and other remains indicate that early farmers living in the area from 3000 to 1500 BC cultivated maize (corn), manioc, beans, squash, chillies, avocados, papayas, pineapples, palms and the bottle gourd. Bananas, Ecuador's most important crop, were introduced after the Spanish conquest.

The heart of the south coast is Guayaquil, Ecuador's most important port and largest city. To the west are the popular beach resorts of Playas and Salinas and to the south another important port city, Machala, which is the normal gateway to Peru.

GUAYAQUIL
Travellers to Ecuador tend to avoid Guayaquil. It has a reputation as a hot and humid port with too many inhabitants and little of interest. It certainly does have many inhabitants, about 1,600,000 of them, and it is oppressively hot, wet and humid from January to April.

I spent over two years travelling in Ecuador before I finally visited Guayaquil and I must admit to having been pleasantly surprised. It does have its attractions. There is a pleasant walk along the river front, shady plazas, colonial buildings, friendly people and interesting museums. It's worth spending a few days.

The province of Guayas is named after the Puna Indian chief of the same name who fought bravely against first the Incas and then the Spanish. The capital of the province, Guayaquil, is named after the same chief and his wife Quill, whom he is said to have killed before drowning himself, rather than allow them to be captured by the conquistadors.

Information
The DITURIS information office is on the waterfront at the Malecón 2321 and Olmedo, up the stairs. They are officially open from 8 am to 4.30 pm Monday to Friday, speak some English, and are helpful. The IETEL and post offices are in the same huge building comprising the block bounded by Avenidas Ballen and P Carbo.

If you want to buy English-language and other books, the best store is the Librería Científica at Luque 223. There is a public library at the Museo Municipal. Use the back entrance on Avenida 10 de Agosto for the library and the front entrance on Avenida Sucre for the museum.

If you need to get your tourist card extended, you can do so at the immigration office in the government building (Palacio de Gobierno) on the waterfront.

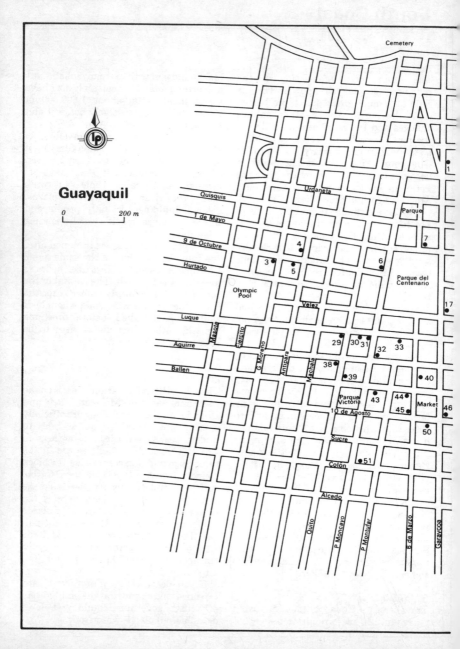

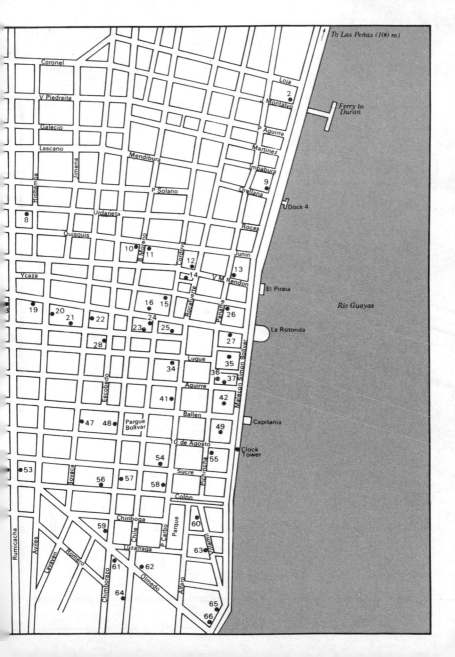

Consulates & Embassies The Peruvian consulate is on the 6th floor of the building at Avenida 9 de Octubre and Chile. It is open from 8.30 am to 1 pm Monday through Friday. Also marked on the map are the Colombian, Argentine and US consulates.

Money Along with Quito, Guayaquil has

1	Hotel Regina
2	La Peña Rincón Folklórico
3	Hotel Oro Verde
4	Machiavello Tours
5	US Embassy & Banco Central Museum
6	Casa de Cultura (Museo & Cine)
7	Cine Centenario
8	Hotel Imperial
9	Hotel Ramada
10	Residencial Pauker
11	Hotel Tourist
12	Church of La Merced
13	Hotel Metropolitan
14	Plaza of La Merced
15	El Camino Vegetariano Restaurant
16	Hotel Casino Boulevard, Teatro Guayaquil, TAME Airline & Galasam Tours (Edificio Pasaje)
17	Hotel Centenario
18	Hotel Londres
19	Cine 9 de Octubre
20	Residencial Imperio
21	Hotel San Juan
22	Cine Metro
23	SAN-Saeta Airline
24	Peruvian Consulate
25	Church & Plaza of San Francisco
26	Hotel Moneda
27	Ecuatoriana Airline
28	La Palma & Cyrano Pavement Cafés
29	Cine Tauro
30	Hotel Alexander
31	Hotel Sanders
32	Hotel Ecuador
33	Cine Presidente
34	Librería Científica
35	Bank of America
36	Metropolitan Touring
37	Colombian & Argentine Consulates
38	Cine Quito
39	Hotel Astoria
40	Cine Imperio
41	Post Office & IETEL
42	Palacio de Gobierno
43	Hotel Delicia
44	Hotel La Buena Esperanza
45	Hotel Marco Polo
46	Residencial Centro
47	Gran Hotel Guayaquil
48	Cathedral
49	Palacio Municipal
50	Hotel El Inca
51	Hotel Colón
52	Hotel Ecuatoriana
53	Residencial Medellín
54	Museo Municipal & Library
55	Hotel Italia
56	Chifa Mayflower
57	Hotel Boston
58	Gran Chifa
59	Residencial María
60	Hotels Santa María, Nacional & Luz de América
61	Residencial El Cisne
62	Hotel Los Angeles
63	Hotel Orquidea Internacional
64	Hotel Residencia Espejo
65	Hotel Humboldt
66	DITURIS

the best foreign exchange rate in Ecuador. The best places to change money are the *casas de cambio*, of which there are over a dozen on the first couple of blocks of Avenida 9 de Octubre by the waterfront and along the first few blocks of Avenida Pichincha. Shop around for the best rate. All *casas de cambio* are closed on Sunday and only a few are open on Saturday morning. There is a *casa de cambio* at the airport which is open at weekends to meet incoming international flights, usually in the morning.

Museums
Most of the museums concentrate on Ecuadorean archaeology and are very good. Unfortunately, two have recently been damaged by fire. The museum of the Banco Pacifico burnt down in 1986 and it is unlikely to reopen for several years. The museum of the *Casa de Cultura* has also been fire-damaged but is still functioning by the latest accounts.

Museo de Arqueologiá del Banco Central
This bank houses a good archaeology museum which is open from 10 am to 6 pm Monday to Friday, and 10 am to 1 pm on weekends. It is free, well laid out, and has a varied and changing display of ceramics, textiles, metallurgy (some gold) and ceremonial masks. The descriptions are good but are only in Spanish.

Casa de Cultura
The archaeology museum in the Casa de Cultura is open from 9 am to 12.30 pm and 3 to 7 pm Tuesday to Saturday. Admission is 20c. There is also a cinema on the premises which shows good movies on occasion.

Museo Municipal
This museum is small but has more varied exhibits. On the ground floor there is an archaeology room, a colonial room and a changing display of modern art. The archaeology room has mainly Inca and pre-Inca ceramics, with some particularly fine pieces from the Huancavilca period (circa 500 AD) and

Gold mask

several figurines from the oldest culture in Ecuador, the Valdivia (circa 3200 BC). The colonial room has mainly religious paintings and a few household items from colonial times.

Upstairs there are modern art and ethnography rooms, inexplicably joined. Here you'll see five of the famous *tsantsas*, or shrunken heads. Other jungle artefacts include beadwork, featherwork, tools and weapons, but unfortunately very few labels. There are also regional costumes and handicrafts. Another room on this floor contains paintings of presidents and famous men, of which my favourite is a wild and eccentric-looking Theodor Wolf, the geologist after whom the highest active volcano in the Galápagos is named. All in all, a varied collection with which to pass the time.

The Museo Municipal is open 9 am to noon and 3 to 7 pm Monday to Friday, 10 am to 3 pm on Saturday, and 10 am to 1 pm on Sunday. Admission is 20c.

Along the Waterfront
The majority of interesting sights are on or within a few blocks of the waterfront. It is a good idea to begin your sightseeing walk near the DITURIS office at Olmedo and the waterfront. Opposite, there is an

imposing statue of José Joaquín Olmedo Maruri, an Ecuadorean poet and politician born in Guayaquil on 19 March 1789. He sits, bardlike, in a colonial armchair.

Heading north along the waterfront road called the Malecón Simon Bolívar, you pass several monuments. One is to the UN, known in Spanish as the ONU (Organización de Naciones Unidas) and another is the famous Moorish-style **Clock Tower** which dates originally from 1770 but has been replaced several times.

Across the street from the clock tower is the **Palacio Municipal**, an ornate grey building which is separated from the simple and solid **Palacio de Gobierno** by a small but pleasant plaza containing a statue commemorating some of the victories of the liberator General Sucre. Both buildings were built in the 1920s, but the Palacio de Gobierno replaces the original wooden structure which was destroyed in the great fire of 1917.

Continuing along the Malecón, you soon come to the famous statue of **La Rotonda**, one of Guayaquil's more impressive monuments (particularly when it is illuminated at night). It shows the historic but enigmatic meeting between Bolívar and San Martín in 1822. Bolívar was the Venezuelan who liberated Venezuela, Colombia and Ecuador from Spanish colonial rule. San Martín was the Argentine liberator who defeated the Spanish in Chile and Peru. After their secret meeting in Guayaquil, San Martín returned to Argentina and exile to France, while Bolívar continued his triumphs in Bolivia.

From La Rotonda there are good views north, along the river front, of the colonial district of Las Peñas at the foot of Cerro El Carmen and, far beyond, the impressive Guayaquil-Duran bridge, the biggest in the country.

Many people like to continue along the waterfront to the picturesque colonial district of **Las Peñas**. Several docks are passed en route, some with restaurant boats and others which are working docks.

Soon after passing the **Duran Ferry** pier you reach the end of the Malecón.

This north end has a reputation for being a poor neighbourhood and tourists are advised to guard their belongings against pickpockets, especially those working the passenger exits from the Duran ferry. The ferry used to be used more by tourists because the railway station for trains to the highlands is in Duran. Now, with the disruption of the train service, almost no baggage-laden travellers come across on the ferry and the number of thieves has dwindled. I felt that the area was quite safe. However, I recently received a letter from a couple of people who were assaulted in the La Peñas district. They wrote: 'someone tried to assault us on Calle Numa Pompillo Llona, at midday on Sunday. Fortunately some locals came out with a shot-gun to protect us, or themselves, I'm not sure which. This halted the two men and we ran off down the street with only bruises. Further down the street, without prompting, we were advised by more than one local that the street was not safe'.

Despite this story, Ecuadorean guide publications continue to describe the Las Peñas area as a 'typical colonial section'. It's worth asking at the DITURIS information office about the area's safety and also to go with some friends.

Las Peñas

Calle Numa Pompillo Llona This street, named after the Guayaquileño (1832-1907) who wrote the national anthem, is one of my favourite sights in Las Peñas. You'll find the street at the end of the Malecón, where you'll see a short flight of stairs leading up to the small **Plaza Colón**, which has two cannons pointing out towards the river, commemorating a battle against Dutch pirates in 1624. The narrow, winding Calle N P Llona begins from the corner of the plaza. Walking up this historic street, you'll see several unobtrusive plaques set into the walls of some houses. These indicate the simple residences of past presidents. The colonial architecture has not been very much restored. Rather, it has been well looked after and is interesting to see.

Several artists now live in the area and there are a few art galleries, of which the one at No 186 is currently the best known and belongs to the painter Hugo Luis Lara. Take your time – it's a short street. At the end of the street is the **National Brewery** which is open from 7 am to noon and 2 to 5 pm Monday to Friday. Brewery tours can be arranged.

Calle N P Llona is a dead-end street, so you retrace your footsteps to the Plaza Colón and, instead of continuing back along the Malecón, you turn right and walk past a small plaza with a brightly painted statue of a fireman (there are two fire stations near by), and past a statue of the conquistador Orellana, to the open-air theatre Bogotá. Behind the theatre is the oldest church in Guayaquil, **Santo Domingo**, which was founded in 1548, restored in 1938, and is worth a visit.

Cerro El Carmen You can continue by climbing the stairs to the right of the church and then heading left up the steep Calle Buitrón (the street of the vulture!) which will soon take you to the top of the hill, **Cerro El Carmen**. From here is a good view of the north section of the river and the impressive **Duran Bridge** which is almost four km long.

Downtown Area

La Merced Return down the hill to the Malecón and walk back to the downtown area along Calle Rocafuerte. The colonial buildings blend into modern ones and after a few blocks you pass the church of La Merced. Although this building is comparatively modern (constructed in 1938), the original wooden church dated back to 1787. It's worth seeing for its richly decorated golden altar. There's a pleasant plaza in front of the church.

San Francisco Two blocks beyond the church you cross the busy Avenida 9 de Octubre, downtown Guayaquil's major thoroughfare. Here Calle Rocafuerte becomes Calle P Carbo and you find the church of San Francisco, originally built in the early 1700s, burnt in 1896, reconstructed in 1902, and now beautifully restored. The plaza in front is notable for containing Guayaquil's first public monument, unveiled on New Year's Day, 1880. It is a statue of the first Ecuadorean president, Vicente Rocafuerte, who held office from 1835-39. Ecuador's first president, Juan Flores, was a Venezuelan.

Parque Bolívar A few blocks further along P Carbo you find the Museo Municipal. A block to the right is **Parque Bolívar**, Guayaquil's most famous plaza. In its small but well laid out gardens live prehistoric-looking land iguanas of up to a metre in length, and of a species different from those found in the Galápagos. They're a surprising sight here, right in the centre of the city. Around Parque Bolívar are most of Guayaquil's first-class hotels.

Cathedral On the west side of the park is the Cathedral. The original building on this site dates from 1547 but, as is common with most of Guayaquil's original wooden buildings, it burnt down. The present structure was completed in 1948 and renovated in 1978. The front entrance is extremely ornately decorated but inside it is cool, simple, high vaulted and modern. High up on the white walls are some fine stained-glass windows.

Parque del Centenario From the Parque Bolívar you can head north a few blocks and walk along the modern Avenida 9 de Octubre to the huge Parque del Centenario, the city's largest plaza. A more colourful walk is along 10 de Agosto to the main market area, which is so crowded with street stalls, people and traffic that your pace slows to a crawl. Watch your belongings; pickpockets are common in market areas. In the Parque del Centenario, which covers four city blocks, there are many monuments. The most important is the great central column topped by Liberty and surrounded by the founding fathers of the country – a monument to patriotism.

Avenida 9 de Octubre continues beyond the park. At its junction with the west side of the park is the museum of the Casa de Cultura. Further along the Avenida you come to the Banco Central museum. If you continue north of the park along P Moncayo, you'll come to the **City Cemetery**, which is well worth a visit. It is a dazzling white and contains hundreds of tombs, monuments and huge mausoleums. A palm tree lined walk leads to the impressive grave of President Vicente Rocafuerte.

The whole walk as described in this section can be done in two or three hours, but if you want to inspect the sights thoroughly, you could spend all day. Keep your eyes open for plaques and signs. Guayaquil is full of them and they give interesting historic information (if you understand Spanish).

Places to Stay

The Guayaquil Tourist Board controls hotel prices and each hotel is required to post their approved prices near the entrance. Perhaps surprisingly, most hotels do have the price list prominently displayed. You may be charged up to 15% tax on the listed price, though some of the cheaper hotels don't bother.

During holiday periods finding a room can be problematical, especially in the better hotels, and prices are usually higher than the listed price. Many hotels, including some of the budget ones, are registered at the DITURIS office where you can complain if you get gouged. Hotel prices seem to change frequently.

For some reason there are not many single rooms to be had. In the cheaper hotels I usually had two or more beds in my room when I was travelling alone. If it's not the holiday season, you can persuade many hotel owners to give you a double or triple at the price of a single. During *fiesta* time, travel with a friend or be prepared to pay for a double.

Places to Stay – bottom end

One of the best cheap hotels is the *Hotel Delicia* – secure and clean. They charge about US$1.60 per person and have rooms with a private bath for US$2.20. Most hotels which charge less than US$2 per person are not as good. Among the cheapest are the *Hotel Residencial Espejo* and the *Residencial Maria* (US$1.20 each), and the *Residencial El Cisne* (US$1.50 each). They are very basic but marginally better than the similarly priced *Hotel Ecuatoriana*, *Residencial Medellin*, *Hotel La Buena Esperanza* and *Residencial Imperio*, which are unsavoury, dirty and generally disreputable. Some of the cheap hotels near the market double as low-class brothels, and female travellers may be improperly treated or molested.

If you can bring yourself to pay between US$2 to US$3, you can do much better. Three basic but reasonably clean hotels are found on one block of Villamil near the waterfront. They are the *Hotel Santa Maria*, *Nacional* and *Luz de America*. Most rooms have fans and you should ask for one if they don't. Some rooms have private baths and some don't have windows, but there's enough variety here that you should be able to find something suitable for US$2 to US$2.50 per person.

This is the waterfront area, however, and when I stopped by the *Hotel Nacional* they asked me,'All night or just a little while?' A few blocks away is the *Hotel Boston*, which charges US$3 a double or US$5 a double with private bathroom. The rooms are tiny, unattractive wooden boxes.

The *Hotel Colón* is out of the way, but looks clean and has rooms for US$4.50 a double with bath. Also rather isolated, but excellent value and recommended, is the *Hotel Imperial*, which has private bathrooms in all its rooms and is very clean and good. Some rooms are a little worse than others because they lack windows. Prices are US$2 to US$2.50 per person. Six blocks away is the similarly priced *Residencial Pauker*, which is secure and friendly. The best rooms are doubles (US$4.50 with bath, US$3.50 without); the few singles are not very good. Across the street is the *Hotel Tourist*, which is not much better. It charges US$4 a single and US$7 a double.

Hotel El Inca has many rooms, most with bathrooms attached, and is fairly clean and secure but basic. Costs are US$2.50, US$4.50, US$6.50 and US$8.50 for singles, doubles, triples and quads. *Hotel Astoria* has very shabby rooms and their water supply is erratic. They charge US$2.20 per person or US$3 in a room with private bath. The *Hotel Marco Polo* is US$2 with bath per person, but I've heard that it's not recommended for single women. Another basic hotel in this price range is the *Residencial Centro*.

Places to Stay – middle
Hotel Centenario charges US$2 to US$5 per person and has some rooms with air-con, phone and private bath but nevertheless remains a basic hotel. The *Hotel Ecuador* is OK although a bit noisy; rooms with bath are US$4 per person. The *Hotel Londres* is a bit shabby but secure, and costs US$3-US$7 per person. The rooms vary a good deal, so see several. Some have private baths, TV and windows, and all have fans.

Hotel Los Angeles is adequate and has rooms with private bathrooms and sometimes air-con. They charge US$3 a single and US$5.50 a double. The *Hotel Sanders*, is a bit run down but still good value for US$3.50 per person in rooms with private bath. Some rooms have air-con. *Hotel San Juan* has rooms with air-con and phone at US$8 a double but is very run down and many of its rooms are windowless.

A good, simple but clean hotel with air-con rooms and private baths is the *Hotel*

Regina for US$6.50 a double. Also very good value is the *Hotel Metropolitan*, which costs US$8.50 a double. Some rooms have river views, the private bathrooms are spotless, and the management is anxious to please. Don't be put off by the fact that it's on the top floor of an office block. Both hotels have a few single rooms for a couple of dollars less. *Hotel Italia* is a little more expensive than this but is not as clean or comfortable. *Hotel Orquidea Internacional* is adequate for US$9 a double with private bath; singles cost the same.

A reader recommends the *Hotel Cervera* at 9 de Octubre and Cordova. Rooms with private bathroom and air conditioning are US$8 a single and US$12 a double.

Places to Stay – top end
Hotel Humboldt is good value for US$11 a single and US$15 a double. They have a swimming pool and restaurant/bar. Also near the waterfront are the more expensive *Hotel Ramada* and the luxurious *Hotel Moneda*. The comfortable *Hotel Alexander* charges US$12 for a single. Other recommended luxurious hotels are the *Gran Hotel Guayaquil*, *Hotel Casino Boulevard* and the *Hotel Oro Verde*. The last-mentioned is the best in town and charges about US$60 for a double.

The area around the *Parque Bolívar* has half a dozen comfortable first-class hotels within one block. You can take your choice and expect to pay US$25 to US$50 a double. Note that the most expensive hotels can be booked in advance and from abroad but then prices are in dollars and more expensive.

Places to Eat
For breakfast I like *La Palma* and *Cyrano* pavement cafés, which are next to one another on Escobedo. They sell good coffee and croissants, and are good places at which to wake up and ease into the day. *La Palma* seems to be the most popular.

One of my favourite places for lunch is

on a boat moored on the riverbank. There are several piers along the Malecón where restaurant boats are moored – these places aren't very fancy. A fairly inexpensive one is *El Pirata*, a couple of blocks from the La Rotonda statue. They have an indoor section and an open top deck with sunshades for when the weather is good.

There are two or three other places like this, mainly north along the river. One is at *Muelle 5* (Pier 5). You can eat seafood and sip a beer while you watch the busy traffic of the Malecón on one side and Guayaquil's river traffic on the other. Fragile craft paddled by banana pedlars bob close inshore and huge ocean-going vessels lumber by in mid-channel. Pleasure craft and fishing trawlers abound, and a constant stream of frigate birds, terns and seagulls fly by.

A *chifa* is always a good choice for the hungry budget traveller and there are several on and around Avenida Colón. One of the very best – elegant and expensive-looking but in fact very reasonably priced – is the *Gran Chifa* on P Carbo near Colón. A few blocks away is the plainer and slightly cheaper *Chifa Mayflower*. There are others to choose from. The most economical meals are to be found in and around the market area.

There are several modern cafeterias on Avenida 9 de Octubre, which sell such delights as hamburgers and French fries and are not very cheap. There's even an authentic *Burger King*. A block away from 9 de Octubre is the *El Camino Vegetariano* where you can eat vegetarian dishes.

The best and most expensive restaurants are in the first-class hotels (normally open to the public). The *Gran Hotel Guayaquil* has a continental breakfast (rolls and coffee) for US$1.50. The coffee is excellent and coffee addicts can get many refills. The *El Parque* restaurant on the fourth floor of the Molicentro building overlooking the Parque Bolívar has been recommended

for dinner – good value but not cheap. Good restaurants are also found in the suburb of Urdesa, a few km to the north-west of downtown and best reached by taxi.

Entertainment

Read the local newspapers *El Telégrafo* and *El Universo* to find out more about what's going on. They give cinema listings of the approximately 18 cinemas in Guayaquil, of which about half are downtown and shown on the map. If you're buying the newspaper for the cinema listings, make sure that the newspaper has them. Occasionally, even the best papers omit the listing if there's been no change. English-language movies with Spanish sub-titles are often shown.

Friday newspapers advertise folk music evenings known as *peñas*, which are normally held at weekends. They are rarely cheap and always start late. A good one is *La Peña Rincón Folklorico* at Malecón 208 and Montalvo. It normally opens at 10 pm for food and drinks, and the show gets under way about midnight and continues until the early hours. Cover is US$3 and drinks aren't cheap.

If you're the athletic type, you can visit the *Olympic Pool*, which costs 30c for a two-hour period. Enquire at the entrance for times.

Guayaquil's Independence Day is 9 October (1820) and, combined with America (or Columbus) Day on 12 October (1492), it is an important local holiday period. More important still is Bolívar's birthday on 24 July (1783), followed by Guayaquil Foundation Day on 25 July (1538). The whole city parties during the last week in July, and hotel rooms may be difficult to find. Banks and other services are also disrupted.

Travel Agencies

Anybody who has anything to do with travel will try and sell you a Galápagos trip. Three agencies are shown on the map. The cheapest is *Galasam Tours*, mid-priced is *Machiavello Tours* and the most expensive is *Metropolitan Touring*. Tours to the Galápagos are generally expensive and these three agencies cover the price spectrum. Further information in the Galápagos section.

Getting There & Away

Air Guayaquil's Simón Bolívar airport is one of Ecuador's two international airports. If you are leaving on an international flight, there is a US$20 departure tax, payable in sucres or dollars. There is a *casa de cambio* at the airport which pays about as much as the downtown rate.

There are many internal flights to all parts of the country. The most frequent are to Quito with both TAME and SAN-Saeta. If you buy your ticket with cash, the two companies will honour one another's tickets so you can arrive at the airport and leave on the next available flight if it isn't full. There are about 13 flights a day Monday to Friday, 10 flights on Saturday, and six flights on Sunday. Tickets cost about US$15. Sit on the right side flying to Quito for the best views.

TAME and SAN-Saeta offer flights from Guayaquil to Cuenca (Monday to Saturday at 10.30 am, Tuesday and Thursday at 3 pm, and Monday and Friday at 4pm, US$9). Only TAME operates flights between Guayaquil and Loja (Monday to Saturday at 8 am, US$9), Machala (Monday to Saturday at 11 am, US$7.50), Manta (Monday to Saturday at 8.30 am, Tuesdays and Thursdays at 5.15 pm, US$9), Salinas (6 pm Friday and 3 pm Sunday during the holiday season), and Macará at irregular intervals. Fares and departure times are subject to change. Flights sometimes leave early – this seems to be a problem with the Machala flight in particular. Get to the airport early.

TAME operates the only scheduled flights to the Baltra airport in the Galápagos. They leave daily except Sunday at 11 am and cost US$312 for the round trip. Cheaper fares are available only to Ecuadorean residents. SAN-Saeta operates the only scheduled flights to San Cristobal airport in the Galápagos. They leave on Mondays, Wednesdays and Fridays at 8.30 am – same fare.

The airline offices are around Avenida 9 de Octubre and Chile; see the map. There are local airlines operating irregular services with light aircraft to nearby coastal towns – enquire at the airport.

Rail Train services from Guayaquil to the highlands were disrupted by the 1982/83 El Niño disaster. No trains have run since then and it is unlikely that services will resume for several years. When they do, the trains will leave from the Duran railway station, which is best reached by taking the Duran ferry from Guayaquil.

Boat The Duran ferry across the Río Guayas leaves three or four times an hour from 5 am to 9 pm daily. The crossing lasts 15 minutes and costs 3c – a great sightseeing trip! The ferry dock is on the Malecón at the foot of Avenida J Montalvo.

The *Pinzón* and *Piquero* for the Galápagos leave from Dock 4 – more information in the Galápagos section. Shipping information can be got from the Capitanía on the Malecón at the foot of Avenida Ballen.

Bus A brand-new bus terminal (Terminal Terrestre) opened in late 1986 just beyond the airport. It is the most modern and efficient bus terminal in Ecuador and boasts many stores, restaurants, tourist information, a bank, hairdresser etc. There are scores of bus company offices and you can get just about anywhere. The following selection gives an idea of what's available – there are many more. For the Santa Elena peninsula you can take Transportes Villamil or Co-op Posorja, which have frequent buses to Playas (70c, 1¾ hours) and Posorja (90c, two hours). Co-op Libertad and CICA have buses to Salinas (US$1.10, 2½ hours).

If you're headed southbound or to Peru,

take CIFA, Transportes Rutas Orenses, Ecuatoriana Pullman or Co-op El Oro to Machala (US$1.70, 3½ hours) and Huaquillas (US$2.20, five hours). CIFA and Rutas Orenses run frequent small buses; the others run larger coaches. Transportes Loja has one bus at 6.30 pm to the border at Macará (US$4.30, 12 hours), and five buses to Loja (US$3.50, 10 hours).

Several companies run buses to Cuenca (US$2.30-US$2.80, five to seven hours). Supertaxis Cuenca and Buses San Luis run faster small buses while Transportes Oriental run larger, slower and cheaper buses. All three companies have buses about every hour.

Babahoyo (50c, 1½ hours) is served by Transportes Urdaneta and Flota Babahoyo Interprovincial (or FBI). Flota Bolívar has eight slow buses every day to Guaranda via Babahoyo.

For Riobamba and Ambato there are many companies taking as little as 3½ hours to Riobamba if the road is OK. These companies include: Transportes Andino, Transportes Patria, CITA, Transportes

Gran Colombia and Transportes Santa. One of the fastest is probably Transportes Andino. Transportes Cotopaxi has slow buses to Latacunga via Quevedo.

Quevedo and Santo Domingo are served by Transportes Sucre and Transportes Zaracay.

Quito (US$2.70-US$3, seven to nine hours) is served by frequent buses with Flota Imbabura, Transportes Ecuador and Transportes Panamericana. All three are close to one another so check around for what's best for you.

Transportes Esmeraldas and Transportes Occidental have about 10 buses a day to Esmeraldas (US$3, nine hours).

Rutas Ecuatorianas has many departures for Portoviejo (US$2.20, four hours), as does Reina del Camino, who also have buses to Manta and Bahía de Caráquez.

It's easy enough to buy tickets in advance if you want to assure yourself of a place.

Getting Around

Airport The airport is on Avenida de las Américas, about four or five km north of the centre of town. A taxi from the airport to the centre will cost about US$2. Taxi drivers are supposed to use meters but many try to charge higher fares from the airport. Bargain. If you cross the street in front of the airport, you can take a bus downtown, and from the centre of town the best bus to take to the airport is the '2 Especial', which costs 5c and takes about a half hour. It runs along the Malecón but is sometimes full, so you should leave yourself plenty of time or take a taxi – often only US$1 from downtown.

Bus City buses are cheap (5c) but are always crowded and the system is complicated. They are mainly designed to get workers and commuters from the housing districts to downtown and back again, and are not much use for riding around the city centre. They never seem to go exactly where you want to go, and what with waiting for them and battling the traffic, you'd be better off walking, which is what I always did. The downtown area is less than two km square so it's easy to walk anywhere.

The DITURIS information office can help you with bus information if you want to go out into the suburbs, though there isn't much to see there except for the suburb of Urdesa which has good restaurants.

Buses to the Terminal Terrestre leave from Parque Victoria.

Taxi If you really must get somewhere in a hurry, you won't get there much quicker on a city bus than on foot. Take a taxi but make sure the meter is working because Guayaquil taxi drivers have the worst reputation in the country for overcharging. You should be able to get between any two points downtown for well under US$1, and to the airport or the Terminal Terrestre for between US$1-US$1.50.

Car Rental If you're feeling affluent, you can rent a car; if you're not, then forget it because it's not cheap. There are several car rental agencies at the airport. Expect to pay at least US$30 per day for a small car. Make sure that insurance, tax and mileage are included. If you find a cheaper deal, ensure that the car you get isn't about to break down.

PROGRESO
Progreso is officially known as Gómez Rendón and is a village about 70 km south-east of Guayaquil. Here the road forks and you head west to Salinas and the Santa Elena peninsula or south to the resort of Playas. The road fork is Progreso's claim to fame; there's no reason to stop here.

From Guayaquil to Progreso the paved road passes through very dry scrubland. It is amazing how quickly the land changes from the wet rice-growing areas in the regions north and east of Guayaquil to the dry lands of the west. Despite the dryness, the scenery is quite attractive and interesting, with strange bottle-shaped kapok trees and bright flowers dotting the hilly landscape.

PLAYAS
From Progreso the road deteriorates into gravel (though it is in the process of being paved) and heads due south for 30 km to Playas, the beach resort nearest Guayaquil.

Playas is also an important fishing village. A generation ago, many of the fishing craft were small balsa rafts with one sail – similar in design to the boats used up and down the coast for many centuries before the Spanish conquest. Now, motor-driven dugouts and other more modern craft are frequently used, but you can still see a few of the old balsa rafts in action. This is one of the most interesting things to look for in Playas. They usually come in at the west end of the beach but this depends on winds and tides.

Because of its proximity to Guayaquil, there are many holiday homes in Playas. It is quite a bustling little resort during the busy seasons (Christmas to Easter and July to September) but feels almost like a ghost town at other times of year.

In the high season all the hotels are open and prices may rise a little; in other months many of the hotels, especially the cheaper ones, close down. Those which are open have few guests and will sometimes lower their prices to have you stay there. Try bargaining.

The Teatro Playas cinema is often closed in the low season too.

Places to Stay – bottom end
The cheapest hotels often don't have running water and are extremely basic – many close during the low season. The best of the cheapies seem to be the *Hotel California* and *Hostería Costa Verde*. They charge about US$1.50 each and have water. Cheaper still are the *Casa de Piedra* (over the Peluquería Oriente hairdresser), the *Hotel Turismo* and the

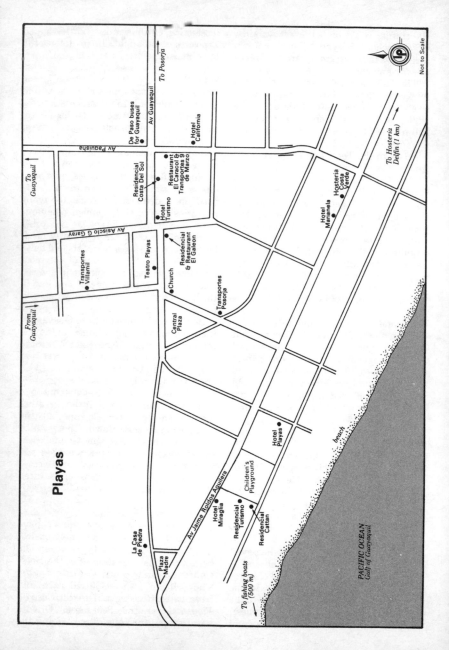

Playas

Residencial Turismo (also known as the *Tropical*). Ask if they have water.

For US$2 per person you can stay at the *Hotel Miraglia*. It's a sprawling old wooden building but the rooms are adequate – some have private bathrooms. *Residencial Costa Azul* has tiny box-like singles for US$2 and better doubles with private bath for US$6.

Hotel Marianela is quite good for US$2.50 per person in rooms with private baths. You can probably bargain for a lower rate if there is a group of you in the low season.

The people at *El Galeon* are friendly, they have an inexpensive but good restaurant, and the place is recommended. Rooms with private bathrooms and mosquito netting are US$3 per person.

Places to Stay – middle

Hotel Playas has simple but clean rooms with private bathrooms for US$7 a single and US$11 a double. They have a restaurant. *Residencial Cattan* provides a bed and three good meals a day for US$11 per person. The rooms have private baths and are clean but the showers have brackish water only. They seem unwilling to provide accommodation without meals but their restaurant is recommended.

If you want to stay out of town you can head roughly east on Avenida J R Aguilera to the *Hostería Delfín* about a km away. Also near here is the *Hostería Gaviota*. These are the best two hotels in the Playas area and have decent restaurants and pleasant rooms which cost a little more than in town.

Places to Eat

The inexpensive beach restaurants, which are all fairly similar, serve fresh seafood. The better hotels have good restaurants; the one below the *Hotel Galeon* is recommended as being good, cheap and open to the public.

Getting There & Away

Transportes Villamil and Posorja are the bus companies with services to Guayaquil (75c, 1¾ hours). Bus schedules tend to be flexible and buses often leave from the store/bar at the corner of Avenida Paquisha and Avenida Guayaquil.

Both these companies usually pick up passengers for Posorja if the bus from Guayaquil is continuing there. Transportes 9 de Marzo has frequent pickup trucks to Posorja (20c, 30 minutes).

Services are normally to Guayaquil, though occasionally a bus will go to the Santa Elena peninsula. You could go to Progreso and change, but buses from Guayaquil to Santa Elena are often full during holidays.

POSORJA

Although the road from Playas to Posorja follows the coast, it is just far enough inland that you get no views of the sea until you arrive in Posorja. The road is good but the scenery not particularly attractive.

A few km out of Playas you go through the old village of El Morro, which is less important than it used to be. There is a huge old wooden church with dilapidated bamboo walls and three white wooden towers; the place is falling into disrepair.

Posorja is an attractive little fishing village with many working boats and hundreds of seabirds wheeling overhead but the beach is dirty and not good for swimming. Posorja is best visited on a day trip.

There are two very basic pensiones. One is literally on the point of disintegrating and the other looks like a particularly sleazy whorehouse – neither are recommended.

SANTA ELENA PENINSULA

As you continue westward from Progreso the land becomes increasingly dry and scrubby, the kapok trees giving way to interminable forests of five metre high cactus. Few people and little animal life is seen, though herds of tough, half-wild

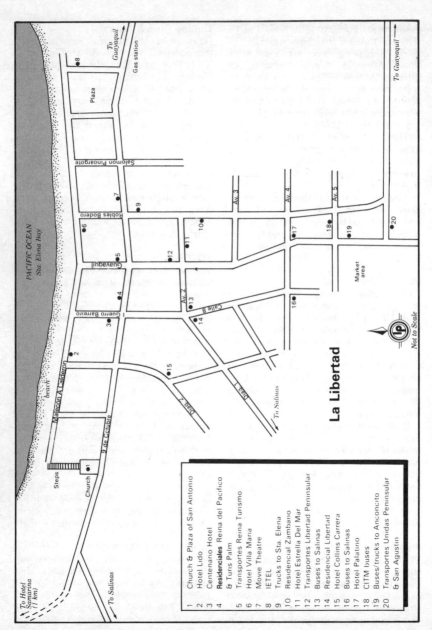

La Libertad

Not to Scale

To Guayaquil
Gas station
Plaza
Salomon Pinoargote
Robles Bodero
Guayaquil
Guerro Barreiro
Malecón A Calderon
9 de Octubre
Av. 3
Av. 4
Av. 5
Av. Z
Calle 8
Market area
To Guayaquil
To Salinas
2 Bend
1 Bend
PACIFIC OCEAN
Sta. Elena Hwy
beach
Steps
Church
To Hotel Samarina (1 km)
To Salinas

1   Church & Plaza of San Antonio
2   Hotel Lido
3   Centenario Hotel
4   **Residenciales** Reina del Pacífico
    & Turis Palm
5   Transportes Reina Turismo
6   Hotel Villa Maria
7   Movie Theatre
8   IETEL
9   Trucks to Sta. Elena
10 Residencial Zambano
11 Hotel Estrella Del Mar
12 Transportes Libertad Peninsular
13 Buses to Salinas
14 Residencial Libertad
15 Hotel Collins Carrera
16 Buses to Salinas
17 Hotel Palatino
18 CITM buses
19 Buses/trucks to Anconcito
20 Transportes Unidas Peninsular
    & San Agustin

goats seem to thrive. Some of the few inhabitants scratch a living from burning the scrub to make charcoal and occasionally you see someone on the side of the road with bags of charcoal.

As you arrive in Santa Elena the landscape changes. Not that it becomes any less dry, it simply becomes built-up. There are three towns on the peninsula and they all seem to run into one another, making the area almost one complete dusty urban zone with few open spaces.

Santa Elena itself is the least important of the towns from the traveller's point of view, though it does have a nearby oilworks and is the home of the peninsula's radio station. *Residencial El Cisne* is a clean, basic hotel on the main square. The other towns on the peninsula are La Libertad and Salinas which is the main resort.

LA LIBERTAD

La Libertad is the largest town on the peninsula, with some 42,000 inhabitants. It is a fishing village and port of some importance and is more interesting to visit (especially in the low season) than Salinas. The El Niño floods caused severe damage to the waterfront and low-lying streets, and many streets are blocked by repair work. A new plaza has been built at the east end of the Malecón and the modern IETEL office is here. There is a bustling market and a cinema.

Places to Stay – bottom end

One of the cheapest hotels on the whole peninsula is the basic but friendly *Residencial Libertad*, which costs US$1.50 per person.

Another cheapie is the *Residencial Reina del Pacifico* which also costs US$1.50 but the rooms are rather horrible little boxes; though they do have a few better rooms with private bath for US$5. Next door is the *Turis Palm* with unfriendly service and basic rooms at US$2 per person or US$3 with private bathroom.

A friendly place on the seafront is the

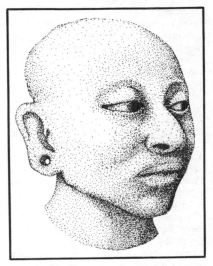

Stone head of La Tolita culture

Hotel Villa Maria, though it's rather the worse for wear since the 1982/83 floods. Rooms with a view are US$2 per person. Other possibilities in the US$1.50 to US$2 bracket include the *Centenario Hotel, Hotel Lido* and the *Residencial Zambano*, none of which look too prepossessing.

Places to Stay – middle

Hotel Palatino is reasonable value though nothing special. Rooms are US$3.50 (US$5 with private bathroom) per person and are cleaner than the rooms with private bathrooms at the grubby *Hotel Estrella del Mar*. The Estrella charges US$3.50 per person but suffers from water shortages and general indifference. It has the potential of improving with better management. The *Hotel Collins Carrera*, also in this price bracket, is worse.

The best place in town is the DITURIS-run *Hotel Samarina* on the waterfront about a km north-west of the town. They have a restaurant, a swimming pool and clean rooms for about US$6 a single and US$10 a double.

Places to Eat

Most restaurants are on Avenida 9 de Octubre or Guayaquil. There are several cheap *chifas* and *comedors* near the *Residencial Reina del Pacifico* and on the way up to the market.

Getting There & Away

La Libertad is the centre of bus services on the peninsula. For Guayaquil (US$1.10, 2½ to three hours) there are several choices. Transportes Reina Turismo has large but slow buses which leave only in the early hours (4.30 to 8.30 am). Transportes Libertad Peninsula has buses about every hour all day long. CICA has no office at this time but has the fastest and most frequent service. Their buses leave from opposite the Residencials Reina del Pacifico and Turis Palm on Avenida 9 de Octubre. The CICA buses from Guayaquil continue to Salinas and then return to Guayaquil from Salinas via La Libertad.

To get to Santa Elena you take one of the pickup trucks which depart frequently from Avenida Robles Bordero near Guayaquil. Frequent buses to Salinas run all day from Calle 8 and either Avenida 2 or 4.

To visit the wild and undeveloped beach of Carnero (with the fishing village of Anconcito and the oil town of Ancón), take one of the frequent buses or pickup trucks leaving from near the market on Avenida Guayaquil and Avenida 5. Near here is Transportes San Agustín, which has *rancheros* running further east along the coast to the fishing village of Chanduy. There is no accommodation in these places.

For going north along the coast to the fishing villages of Palmar, Ayangue, Manglaralto (60c, 1½ hours) and Puerto López (US$1, 2½ hours) you take *rancheros*, buses and trucks with Transportes Peninsulares Unidas or CITM. The first one has departures about every half hour but few of the vehicles make it as far as Manglaralto. Most go as far as Palmar and some go to Ayangue. CITM has two buses a day that go as far as Puerto López and sometimes two more going as far as Manglaralto.

SALINAS

This important resort town is on the tip of the Santa Elena peninsula. About 150 km west of Guayaquil, it is the most westerly town on the Ecuadorean mainland. Unfortunately you cannot go to the very furthest point as there is a naval base there.

Salinas is called the 'best' resort in Ecuador and its casinos, expensive hotels and high-rise condos make it the haunt of affluent Ecuadoreans. It's expensive and quite busy during the season (Christmas to Easter and July to September) and expensive and dead in the off season. The beaches are pleasant but not spectacular and are basically rather spoilt by the high-rise backdrop. I prefer the less-developed beaches of Playas or the north coast.

There is a yacht club and, should you arrive in your own boat, you'll find *Migración* on the waterfront. Also on the waterfront is Pesca Tour, who do expensive deep-sea fishing trips and provide all the equipment.

Places to Stay

There are some very good hotels but they are not very cheap. I visited Salinas in November and found half the hotels closed. The cheapest open place I found was the old and tumble-down *Hotel Tivoli* which had rooms with private bathrooms at US$3.50 per person.

Other hotels in the US$3 to S$5 per person range are the *Hotel Yulee* which is recommended – when it's open; the *Hotel Brisas*, but not in November, it had an open door but no receptionist; and the *Residencial Rachel*, the cheapest-looking of all.

Hotel Cantabrico is good value if you eat all your meals there. They charge US$9 per person in basic but clean rooms with private bathrooms, and all three

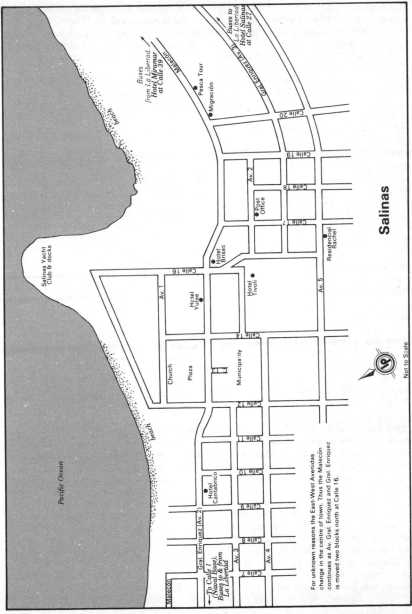

Salinas

Pacific Ocean

beach

Salinas Yacht
Club & docks

beach

Malecón

Buses
from La Libertad,
Hotel Miramar
at Calle 39

Buses to
La Libertad
Hotel Salinas
at Calle 27

• Pesca Tour

• Migración

Gral. Enriquez (Av. 3)

Calle 20

Calle 19

Av. 2

Calle 18

• Post
Office

Calle 7

Residencial
Rachel

Hotel
Brisas

Calle 16

Av. 1

Hotel
Yulee

Hotel
Tivoli

Av. 5

Calle 14

Church

Plaza

Municipality

Calle 13

Calle 12

Calle 11

Calle 10

• Hotel
Cantabrico

Av. 3

Av. 4

Calle 9

Calle 8

Calle 7

Gral. Enriquez (Av. 2)

To Calle 1
(Naval Base),
Buses to & from
La Libertad

Malecón

Not to Scale

For unknown reasons the East-West Avenidas
change in the centre of town. Thus the Malecón
continues as Av. Gral. Enriquez and Gral. Enriquez
is moved two blocks north at Calle 16.

meals are included. If you don't want to eat here you pay US$7 for the room. They have a rather dusty garden with hammocks to lie around in.

The modern *Hotel Salinas* charges US$10 for good and comfortable double rooms with private bathrooms but I would expect to pay a little more in the high season. The most expensive place in town is the *Hotel Miramar*, which boasts air-conditioned rooms, a casino, swimming pool, bar and restaurant. They charge about US$20 for a double in the low season.

Places to Eat
There are various restaurants, bars and discos along the waterfront between Calles 19 and 25 but they're mostly closed in the low season. *Restaurant Caracol* on Calle 6 at the waterfront is good and medium priced.

Getting There & Away
Buses enter town along the Malecón and continue to the naval base, where they turn around and head back to La Libertad along Gral Enriquez. Most buses go only as far as La Libertad. Those that continue to Guayaquil usually stop at La Libertad for up to an hour to pick up more passengers. During the holiday season there are flights from Guayaquil.

NORTH ALONG THE COAST
From La Libertad many buses run north along the coast. Most go only a short way but a few make it as far as Puerto López. The beaches are often very good but there is no accommodation until Manglaralto. There are several fishing villages where Guayaquileños have holiday homes. Palmar and Ayangue are the most popular. The views are good, so sit on the left or ocean side of the bus.

The most interesting sight is the literally hundreds of local fishermen surf-fishing. They catch shrimp with hand nets stretched between a framework of two crossed poles, at the end of which a couple of floats are attached. Wading knee deep in the surf, they push these hand nets up and down the beach. It looks ridiculously like a lawn-mowing convention gone crazy.

The road is quite good until Valdivia, which is the site of Ecuador's oldest culture. There is a small museum there but the best pieces of antiquity are in Guayaquil museums.

North of Valdivia the road deteriorates and the dry landscape begins to get a little wetter. The cactus and scrub give way to stunted trees and the occasional banana plantation.

At Manglaralto there are no hotels, but ask around for accommodation. I managed to find a place to stay, with a friendly local family, for US$1.50. You can do this in the other villages too.

There are a couple of basic *comedors* and an IETEL office on Manglaralto's main square. You can easily do the round trip from La Libertad in a day if you just want to sightsee and swim from some beaches.

Puerto López is the most northerly village reached by bus from La Libertad. It's a busy fishing village and has a clean, basic *residencial* on the waterfront. Transportes Sur de Manabi has a few buses every day which take you to Jipijapa (see North Coast chapter).

MACHALA
South of Guayaquil is the important city of Machala, the capital of the province of El Oro. With about 106,000 inhabitants, it is Ecuador's fourth largest city. It lies in an important banana-growing area and during the 200-km drive from Guayaquil you pass many plantations of bananas, coffee, pineapple and citrus fruits. About halfway to Machala you go through Naranjal, an important agricultural centre but otherwise of little interest.

Despite its economic importance, Machala is not of great tourist interest. Most travellers on their way to and from

Peru pass through here but few people stay more than a night.

It is not totally devoid of interest, however, as the local international port of Puerto Bolívar, only seven km away, is worth visiting. Machala also has a highly touted International Banana and Agricultural Festival during the third week in September which the Ecuadorean tourist authorities assure me is of great interest to tourists. I'm afraid I missed it.

Information

Most streets in Machala are both named and numbered. (I use names.) The DITURIS information office is on the 2nd floor of the office block on Avenida Bolívar at Guayas. It is open somewhat erratically on weekdays.

The IETEL office is several blocks away from the centre on 9 de Octubre. There is a *casa de cambio* at Paez 17-23 which changes both US dollars cash and travellers' cheques at rates about 4% lower than Guayaquil and Quito.

For those who need visas to enter Peru (such as Australian, Kiwi and French travellers, among others), there is a Peruvian consulate open from 8 am to 1 pm Monday through Friday.

Things to See

The international port, Puerto Bolívar, is reached by the No 1 local bus from Machala's main plaza. I've heard claims that it has some coastal nightlife but I couldn't discover any.

There are some seafood restaurants by the waterfront and you can hire motorised dugouts for a cruise among the mangroves to watch the birdlife. For about US$1 you can go as far as the island of Jambelí where there is a beach but no facilities. There is plenty of coastal boat traffic to watch as you sip a beer in a waterfront restaurant.

Back in Machala there are a couple of cinemas, of which the Teatro Tauro is the best.

Places to Stay

Machala has a better variety of hotels than does the border town of Huaquillas, so travellers are better off staying here. The border is not open until 8 am, so by taking a 6 am bus you can still be in Huaquillas by the time the border opens.

Places to Stay - bottom end

Most of the cheap hotels have only cold water but the weather is hot enough that it's not a great hardship. The cheapest and most basic places are the *Residencial Almacha*, which looks very dirty, and the *Residencial Pichincha* which looks a little better.

Somewhat cleaner and better looking is the *Residencial La Internacional* for US$1.50 per person and the *Residencial Machala* for US$2. Also US$2 each is the *Residencial Paula*, which has some rooms with private baths for another dollar.

The *Gran Hotel Machala* is rather run down and has simple rooms for US$2 each or US$3.50 per person with private bathroom. Some of the rooms are OK and some have air-con but others are pretty bad so ask to see another if you don't like the first one you see.

Although the *Hotel Ecuatoriana Pullman* is above the bus terminal, some rooms are surprisingly quiet and some have air-con. It's a bit run down and has rather grubby private bathrooms in the rooms which cost US$2.50 per person. Also in this price range is the *Residencial Mercy* which has improved in the last few years.

Places to Stay - middle & top end

Comfortable rooms with private bathrooms, air-con and sometimes TV are available for about US$9 a single and US$14 a double at the hotels *Encalada, Perla de Pacifico* and *Oro*. They all have restaurants and the *Encalada* has a disco.

The best hotel in town, complete with swimming pool and casino, is the *Rizzo Hotel* which charges about US$13 a single and US$20 a double.

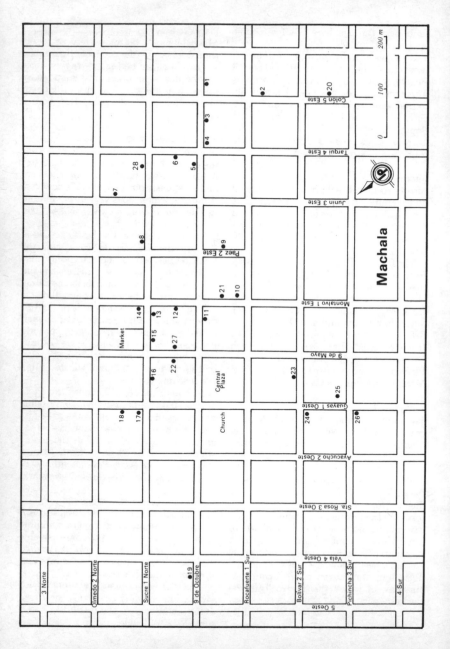

Machala

1	Hotel/Bus Ecuatoriana
2	Cuidad de Piñas Buses
3	CIFA Buses to Guayaquil
4	Encalada Hotel
5	Rutas Orenses Buses
6	Chifa Central Restaurant
7	Residencial Mercy
8	Hotel Perla de Pacifico
9	Money Changer
10	Gran Hotel Machala
11	Residencial Paula
12	Teatro Tauro
13	Residencial Almacha
14	Hotel Oro
15	Residencial Pichincha
16	Cinema
17	Residencial Machala
18	Residencial La Internacional
19	IETEL
20	Panamericana Buses
21	Teatro Municipal
22	Ecuatoriana Airline
23	DITURIS (2nd Floor)
24	CIFA Buses to Huaquillas
25	Rizzo Hotel
26	Peruvian Consul
27	Cinema Central
28	Pullman Express Buses

Places to Eat

There are many *chifas* of which the *Restaurant Chifa Central* is recommended as having a wide variety of good and reasonably priced meals. Budget travellers should try the *chaulafan* which is a cheap but filling rice dish. The best hotels have more expensive restaurants but the food is good.

Getting There & Away

Air TAME flights from Guayaquil to Machala and back leave Machala at 11.45 am every day except Sunday. The fare is US$7.50. You can connect with a Guayaquil-Quito flight to be in the capital the same evening for about US$22.

There isn't a downtown TAME office at this time, so you should go to the airport to purchase your ticket. It is about 1½ km from the town centre and a taxi will cost about 60c.

Lansa also has an office at the airport and they have light aircraft for flights to Guayaquil.

There is an Ecuatoriana airline office if you need information about their international flights from Guayaquil or Quito.

Bus There is no central bus terminal. To get to the Peruvian border at Huaquillas (70c, two hours) it's best to go with CIFA, who leave at very frequent intervals from the corner of Bolívar and Guayas. Ecuatoriana buses also go there at frequent intervals.

Make sure your documents are in order and not packed deep in your luggage as there are two or three passport checks en route. You will be asked to leave the bus to register but the driver is used to this and will wait for you.

CIFA buses also go to Guayaquil (US$1.70, 3½ hours) from their depot on Avenida 9 de Octubre near Colón. There are several other companies in the area. Rutas Orenses has efficient and frequent service to Guayaquil in small buses and Ecuatoriana Buses in larger coaches.

Panamericana has several large coaches a day to Quito (US$3.70, 10 to 12 hours). Ciudad de Piñas has nine buses a day to Piñas, a few of which continue to Loja. They also have one or two buses to Cuenca (US$2.20, five hours). Pullman Express has eight buses daily to Cuenca.

HUAQUILLAS

This dusty one-street town is of importance only because it is at Ecuador's border with Peru. It has a population of about 20,000 (though it doesn't look it) and is 80 km from Machala.

The bus from Machala passes through banana and palm plantations and the dusty market towns of Santa Rosa and Arenillas. There are two or three passport checks en route but these take only a minute (assuming your passport is in order).

There is a busy street market by the border and the place is full of Peruvians shopping on day passes. It's a run-down and dirty town and not a particularly attractive introduction to Ecuador if you're arriving from Peru. Almost everything happens on the one long main street.

Money

There are no banks in Huaquillas or Aguas Verdes, so you have to rely on street moneychangers. They will try to give you a very bad rate but will soon become more reasonable if you can show that you know what the real rate is. Check with other travellers going the opposite way for up-to-date exchange rates.

If you are leaving Ecuador for Peru, it is best to try and get rid of as many sucres as you can in Ecuador and arrive in Peru with dollars. The Peruvian currency is the inti which was created in 1986 by the simple expedient of chopping off the last three zeros from the old currency, the sol. Thus one inti is equivalent to 1000 soles but bills of both currencies are still in circulation.

Peruvian moneychangers will give you more intis for dollars than you'll get in Ecuador and, if you bargain hard and change US$100 or more, you can sometimes get up to 2% better rates than in Lima. There is no black market in Peru but be aware that there are 'official rates' and 'free exchange rates' in Peru. The official rate is used for international transactions such as buying an airline ticket. The free exchange rate is used to change tourist dollars and is usually about 25% higher than the official rate. So don't be fooled by the official rate. Inflation is high in Peru and giving exchange rates is meaningless – ask travellers leaving Peru for the most recent figures.

If you're just arriving in Ecuador you can get within 2% of the Quito rate from street changers if you bargain hard. Again, it is best to use dollars. You can always change sucres to intis and intis to sucres, but the dollar remains king. Other major foreign currencies can be exchanged,

but less favourably, and fewer changers want to deal with them.

Places to Stay

There are several cheap hotels on the main street near the immigration office. None of them are particularly good. One of the cheapest is the basic *Residencial Loja* behind the immigration office. They charge US$1.20 each. Next door is the slightly better *Residencial Bucanero* for US$2 each.

There are several more in this price range down the street but I can't work up much enthusiasm for these either. Hotels tend to be full by early afternoon and you may have to take whatever is available or go to Machala.

There is one good hotel run by DITURIS. The *Parador Turistico Huaquillas* is about 1½ km away from the border on the right side of the main road out of town. You can take a taxi for about 40c or walk. They charge US$5 a single and US$8 a double and have simple but clean rooms with fans and private bathrooms. There is a restaurant.

Places to Eat

There aren't any particularly good restaurants. There is a café behind the immigration office where travellers and moneychangers often hang out. Other places are along the main street.

Getting There & Away

CIFA buses run frequently to Machala (70c, two hours). There is no main bus office but you'll see buses on the main street a block or two beyond the immigration office. A few buses go to Quito (US$4.20, 13 hours) or Guayaquil (US$2.20, 5½ hours), but it's usually easier to go to Machala and change unless you're in a great hurry.

Crossing the Peruvian Border

The border is the Río Zarumilla, which is crossed by an international bridge. As you enter Ecuador from the bridge you'll find yourself on the main road, crowded with market stalls, that stretches out through Huaquillas.

The Ecuadorean Immigration Office is on the left side about 200 metres from the bridge and is identified by the yellow, blue and red-striped Ecuadorean flag. All entrance and exit formalities are carried out here. The Ecuadorean office is open daily from 8 am to noon and 2 to 5 pm. (The Peruvian office is open one hour later.)

You won't have any difficulty in finding the office. Dozens of small boys will offer their services as luggage carriers and guides and the many moneychangers (identified by the ubiquitous black attaché case) will show you the way.

If you are arriving in Ecuador you first need an exit stamp in your passport from the Peruvian authorities. After walking across the international bridge, continue 200 metres to the Ecuadorean Immigration Office. Entrance formalities are usually straightforward. No tourists need visas but everyone needs a tourist card, which are available free at the office.

If you're not entering as a tourist, you need a student, resident, worker or business visa which must be obtained from an Ecuadorean embassy, usually the one that serves your home country. Exit tickets from Ecuador and sufficient funds (US$20 per day) are legally required but are very rarely asked for. You will receive your T3 card (keep it for when you leave) and an identical stamp in your passport allowing you up to 90 days' stay. Usually, only 30 days are given but it is easy to obtain a renewal in Quito or Guayaquil.

Note that you are allowed only 90 days per year in Ecuador. If you've already been in the country for 90 days and try and return, you will be refused entry. If you have an exit ticket from Quito or Guayaquil international airport, you can usually get a 72-hour transit visa just to get you to the airport and out of the country.

If you are leaving Ecuador, the procedure is as follows. Go to the Ecuadorean immigration office and present your passport and T3 tourist card (the duplicate copy of the small document you filled out on arrival). You will receive an exit stamp in your passport and the immigration authorities will keep your T3 card. There are no costs involved. If you

Ecuador's coat of arms

have lost your T3 card, you should be able to get a free replacement at the border, assuming that the stamp in your passport has not expired.

If you have overstayed your permitted time by a few days you can sometimes persuade the immigration official to charge you a fine right there and then – expect to pay no more than US$10. If you get sent back to Guayaquil you will still have to pay a fine, so it's best to get it over with. You can usually get away with a few days over the limit by telling the official how much you loved Ecuador and that you didn't realise how much time had passed.

As you cross the international bridge you will be asked to show the exit stamp in your passport to the Ecuadorean bridge guard. On the Peruvian side (now called Aguas Verdes instead of Huaquillas) you normally have to show your passport to the bridge guard, but full entrance formalities are carried out in the immigration building about three km from the border.

About 300 metres from the bridge there are *colectivo* taxis to take you there.

Most European nationalities (except the French) don't need a visa for Peru, neither do North Americans but Australians and New Zealanders do. Visas are not obtainable in either Aguas Verdes or Huaquillas and you have to go back to the Peruvian consul in Machala if you haven't got one. Other nationalities normally just need a tourist card, available at the Peruvian immigration office.

Although an exit ticket out of Peru is officially required, gringo travellers are rarely asked for this unless they look thoroughly disreputable. Other Latin American travellers are often asked for an exit ticket, however, so if you're a non-Peruvian Latin American (or travelling with one) be prepared for this eventuality. There is a bus office in Aguas Verdes which sells (non-refundable) bus tickets out of Peru. The immigration official will tell you where it is. A bribe may help here.

Galápagos Islands

The Galápagos archipelago is world famous for its incredibly fearless and unique wildlife. Here, you can swim with sea lions, float eye-to-eye with a penguin, stand next to a blue-footed booby feeding its young, watch a giant 200 kg tortoise lumbering through a cactus forest, and try to avoid stepping on iguanas scurrying over the lava. The wildlife is truly phenomenal. The scenery is barren and volcanic and has its own haunting beauty – though some people find it bare and ugly. A visit to the Galápagos is for the wilderness and wildlife enthusiast, not for the average sun-seeker.

Compared to the rest of your travels in Ecuador, the Galápagos are very expensive to visit – mainly because of the airfare. Flying from the mainland and spending a week cruising the islands will cost a minimum of US$500 for even the most thrifty of budget travellers. Therefore the trip is not recommended unless you are really interested in wildlife. The environment is a fragile one, and the islands don't need bored visitors tramping around wondering why they are spending hundreds of dollars to sit on a rocky piece of lava under a searing equatorial sun to watch some squawking sea birds. If you are interested in natural history, however, then visiting the Galápagos will be the highlight of your trip to Ecuador.

This chapter is essentially divided into two sections. The first introduces you to the natural history of the archipelago, describes the wildlife you will encounter and the individual islands. The second section gives you the practical details you will need to know in order to visit the Galápagos.

HISTORY

The Galápagos archipelago was discovered by accident in 1535, when Tomás de Berlanga, the Bishop of Panama, drifted off course while sailing from Panama to Peru. The bishop reported his discovery to King Charles V of Spain and included in his report a description of the *galápago* or 'giant tortoise' from which the islands received their name.

It is possible that the Indian inhabitants of South America were aware of the islands' existence before 1535, but we have no definite record of this.

For over three centuries after their discovery, the Galápagos were used as a base by a succession of pirates, buccaneers, sealers and whalers. The islands provided sheltered anchorage, firewood, water and an abundance of fresh food in the form of the giant Galápagos tortoises, which were caught by the thousands and stacked, alive, in ships' holds. The tortoises could survive for a year or more and thus provided fresh meat for the sailors long after they had left the islands.

The first rough charts of the archipelago were made by buccaneers in the late 1600s and scientific exploration began in the late 1700s. The Galápagos' most famous visitor was Charles Darwin, who arrived in 1835, exactly 300 years after the Bishop of Panama. He stayed for five weeks and made notes and wildlife collections which provided important evidence for his theory of evolution which he was just beginning to develop.

Ecuador officially claimed the archipelago in 1832 and for about a century thereafter the islands were inhabited by a few settlers and were also used as penal colonies. Some islands were declared wildlife sanctuaries in 1934, and the Galápagos became a national park in 1959. Organised tourism began in the late 1960s and an estimated 26,000 people visited the islands in 1986.

GEOGRAPHY

The Galápagos are an isolated group of

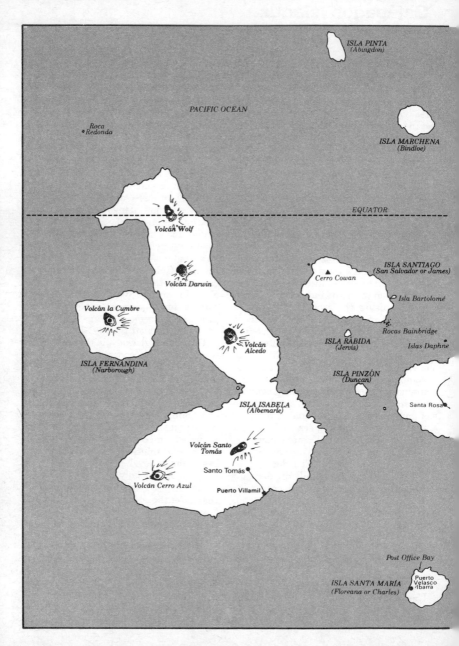

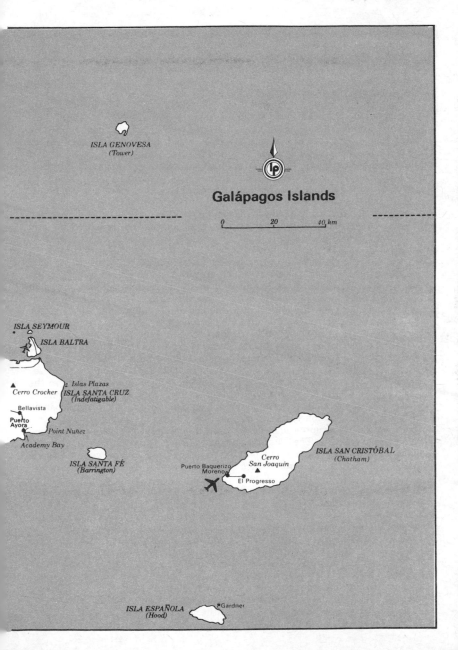

ISLA GENOVESA
(Tower)

Galápagos Islands

0   20   40 km

ISLA SEYMOUR

ISLA BALTRA

Islas Plazas

▲ Cerro Crocker ISLA SANTA CRUZ
(Indefatigable)

Bellavista

Puerto
Ayora
    Point Nuñez

Academy Bay

ISLA SANTA FÉ
(Barrington)

Cerro
San Joaquín   ISLA SAN CRISTÓBAL
(Chatham)

Puerto Baquerizo
Moreno   ▲

El Progresso

ISLA ESPAÑOLA •Gardner
(Hood)

volcanic islands which lie in the Pacific Ocean on the equator about 90° west of Greenwich. The nearest mainland is Ecuador, some 1000 km to the east, and Guatemala, some 1600 km to the north. The land mass of the archipelago covers 7882 square km of which over half consists of Isabela, the largest island. There are 13 major islands (from 14 to 4588 square km), six small islands (from one to five square km) and scores of islets of which only some are named. The islands are spread over roughly 50,000 square km of ocean. The highest point in the Galápagos is Volcán Wolf (1707 metres) on Isabela.

Five of the islands are inhabited with a total (and fast growing) population of about 9000 people who make a living mainly from tourism, fishing and farming.

Most of the islands have two – and sometimes three – names. The earliest charts gave the islands both Spanish and English names, and the Ecuadorean government assigned official names in 1892. Thus an island can have a Spanish, English and official name. The official names are used here in most cases; the few exceptions will be indicated where appropriate.

GEOLOGY

The earliest of the islands were formed roughly four to five million years ago by underwater volcanoes erupting and rising above the ocean's surface. The Galápagos region is volcanically very active and over 50 eruptions have been recorded since their discovery in 1535. Thus the formation of the islands is an ongoing process and the archipelago is a relatively young one compared to the age of the earth (four and a half billion years old – a billion is a 1000 million).

The combination of two relatively new geological theories explains the islands' formation. The theory of plate tectonics holds that the earth's crust consists of several huge tectonic plates, which over geological time move on the surface of the earth. The Galápagos lie on the northern edge of the Nazca plate close to its junction with the Cocos plate. These two plates are spreading apart at a rate of about a km every 14,000 years and thus the Galápagos Islands are slowly moving south-east.

The hot spot theory states that deep within the earth and below the level of the moving tectonic plates there are certain areas which remain stationary and are superheated – these are the hot spots. At frequent intervals (measured in geological time) the heat from the hot spots increases enough to melt the earth's crust and produce a volcanic eruption of sufficient magnitude to cause molten lava to rise above the ocean floor and eventually above the ocean surface.

Whilst the intricate workings of hot spots and tectonic plates are not yet fully understood by researchers, geologists generally agree that this is the way in which the islands were formed. Because the Galápagos are moving slowly to the south-east over the stationary hot spot, one would expect the south-eastern islands to have been formed first and the western islands to have been formed most recently. This has proved to be the case.

The most ancient rocks known in the islands are about three and a quarter million years old and come from Española in the south-east. The oldest rocks known from the western islands of Fernandina and Isabela are less than three quarters of a million years old. The western islands are still in the process of formation and contain active volcanoes such as Volcán Cerro Azul on Isabela, which erupted in 1979 and 1982.

Most of the volcanic rock forming the Galápagos is basalt. Molten basalt has the property of being more fluid than other types of volcanic rock and so when an eruption occurs, basalt tends to form lava flows rather than explosive eruptions. Hence the volcanoes of the Galápagos Islands are gently rounded 'shield volcanoes' rather than the Fuji-like ice-cream cone shape more often associated with volcanoes.

Whilst not every visitor has the time or energy to climb a volcano, a visit to one of the lava flows is within everyone's reach. There are several which can be visited but the one at Sullivan Bay on the east end of San Salvador (also known as Santiago or James Island) is especially rewarding. This lava flow is almost a century old and remains uneroded.

Here you can see *pahoehoe* or 'ropy' lava, formed by the cooling of the molten surface and the wrinkling of the skin into ropy shapes by the continued flow of the molten lava beneath. Impressions of trees can be found in the solidified lava, and some of the first colonising plants – the *Brachycereus* cactus and the *Mollugo* carpetweed – can be seen beginning the slow conversion of a lava field to soil.

COLONISATION & EVOLUTION

When the Galápagos were formed they were barren volcanic islands, devoid of all life. Because the islands were never connected with the mainland, all the species present there now must have been able at one time to have somehow crossed about 1000 km of open ocean. Those that could fly or swim long distances had the best chance of reaching the islands but other methods of colonisation were possible, though more difficult.

These methods include being brought over in animals' stomach contents, or attached to the feathers and feet of birds (as may have happened to plant seeds or insect eggs and larvae), or floating across on vegetation rafts (as may have happened to small mammals, land birds and reptiles as well as plants and insects). Thus the wildlife is dominated by birds (especially sea birds), sea mammals and reptiles.

There are no amphibians because their moist skin is unable to withstand the dehydrating effect of salt water. There are, of course, plenty of tropical fish and marine invertebrates.

Compared to the mainland there are few small land mammals and insects. Large predators never colonised the Galápagos (until the arrival of man). This suggests that the reason the animals of the islands exhibit their well-known fearlessness is because they had no large predators to fear until pigs, goats, cats, donkeys, etc were introduced by man. Escaped domestic animals found little competition and became successful, and now these feral animals create a major problem in the islands.

When the first colonising species arrived millions of years ago they found that the islands were different from the mainland in two important ways. The first was that the islands were physically different from the mainland and the second was that there were few other species to compete with. Some colonisers were able to survive, breed and produce offspring. Obviously, the young were the same species as their parents but they had subtle physiological differences.

A classic example of this in the Galápagos is when a bird produces a chick whose bill is very slightly different from its parent. In the different environment of the islands, some chicks with slightly different bills were better able to take advantage of their environment than others. These are said to have adapted better and the better adapters were more likely to survive to maturity to raise a brood of their own.

These better adapted survivors would pass on favourable genetic traits (in this case a slightly better adapted bill) to the genes of their offspring. Thus over many generations, certain favourable traits were genetically selected for and other less favourable traits were selected against. Eventually the difference between the original colonisers and their distant descendants was so great that the descendants could be considered a different species. This is the essence of Darwin's theory of evolution by natural selection.

Because the earliest colonisers had little competition and a variety of different habitats to choose from, adaptive changes could occur in different ways to take advantage of different habitats or islands. Thus it wasn't only that a longer or broader or smaller bill would be better adapted – it could be that various types of bills could confer adaptive advantages to birds in different ecological niches. One ancestral species could therefore give rise to several modern species in the evolutionary process called adaptive radiation. This explains the presence in the Galápagos of 13 similar species of finches, called Darwin's finches in honour of the founder of evolutionary theory.

WILDLIFE

Dozens of excellent books have been published about the fascinating wildlife of these islands. My aim here is not to compete with them but to provide a brief but comprehensive overview of what the traveller is likely to encounter during their visit. Readers interested in a more in depth account are directed to the following selection.

By far the best general guide to the plant and animal life, with much background information on history and geology, is Michael H Jackson's *Galápagos: A Natural History Guide* (University of Calgary Press, 1985). Also useful is the slimmer volume *Galápagos Guide* by White & Epler, Quito, 1982. Birders should consult *A Field Guide to the Birds of the Galápagos* by Michael Harris (Collins, 1982). Amateur botanists are referred to the pocket-sized *Plants of the Galápagos Islands* by Eileen K Schofield (New York, 1984). Most of these are usually available at Libri Mundi bookstore in Quito.

Maps of the Galápagos are available from the IGM in Ecuador. The best map, full of useful information about wildlife, history and tourism, was published in 1985 by Bradt Publications, 41 Nortoft Rd, Chalfont St Peter, Bucks SL9 OLA, England.

Birds

There are 58 resident bird species on the Galápagos, of which 28 are endemic. A further half a dozen regular migrants are frequently seen and about 25 other migratory species are regularly but not frequently recorded. Several dozen other species are accidental and rarely recorded. Many people are confused between a migrant, resident and endemic species. A resident lives and breeds in the island year round, but the species is also found in

Galápagos hawk

other parts of the world. A migrant is found in the island for only part of the year. An endemic species is a resident which does not normally breed anywhere else in the world (except in captivity or by accident).

During an average week of touring the islands, most careful observers will see over 40 species of birds. If two weeks are spent and some of the more outlying islands are visited, over 50 birds can be recorded. Even the most casual visitor will be able to see 20 to 30 species.

Note that some birds have more than one common name and I mention alternatives in parentheses. Some immature birds have plumage which is markedly different from their parents and makes them difficult to recognise. The naturalist guide on your boat should be able to help you with this problem.

First, the land birds. The 13 species of the famous Darwin's finches are all endemic and everyone sees some of them – although it sometimes takes an expert to be able to tell them apart. All 13 species are thought to have descended from a common ancestor and their present differences in distribution, body size, plumage, beak size and shape, and feeding habits helped Darwin formulate his evolutionary theories. One of the best islands for being able to separate three of the species is Española (Hood). Here, you'll find only the warbler finch (with its tiny warbler-like bill) the small ground finch (with its small finch-like bill) and the large cactus finch (with a massive bill).

The fearless mockingbirds are seen everywhere – these too are endemic. They are thrush-sized, streaked grey and brown, with a long tail and curved bill. There are four species, again varying in bill size but most easily separated by their distribution. Most of the western and central islands are home to the Galápagos mockingbird. The Chatham, Charles, and Hood mockingbirds are limited to those islands only (Chatham is officially

Isla San Cristóbal; Charles is Santa María or Floreana; Hood is Española).

Prettier, and therefore perhaps more interesting to the casual observer, is the Galápagos dove of which there is only one species. It is frequently seen on many of the islands. Other resident land birds include the endemic and frequently seen Galápagos hawk which is the only hawk breeding in the islands.

Other breeding birds of prey include the diurnal short-eared owl found on most islands and the nocturnal (and infrequently seen) barn owl.

The bright red vermilion flycatcher is widespread in the highlands, in particular, the collapsed calderas called Los Gemelos, in the Santa Cruz highlands, is a good place to see this bird. More frequently seen is the drabber Galápagos (large-billed) flycatcher.

The yellow warbler is common, but the dark-billed cuckoo and the Galápagos martin are less frequently seen. The groove-billed ani is a recent introduction to the islands and is now seen regularly in the Santa Cruz highlands where it probably breeds. The most difficult to see of the land birds are the endemic Galápagos rail, paint-billed crake, and common gallinule (moorhen).

It is the sea birds, however, which make the most lasting impression on the visitor. Five of them are endemic and include the Galápagos penguin, which charms visitors with its clown-like antics.

Most penguins are associated with the colder regions of the southern hemisphere but the cool Humboldt current flowing from Antarctica along the South American coast enables the Galápagos penguin to live here – the most northerly penguin in the world. Although they normally breed on the western part of Isabela and Fernandina, a small colony is often seen by visitors to Bartolomé. Their clumsiness on land belies their skill and speed underwater. The best way to appreciate this is to snorkel with them – it is great fun but don't even think about trying to keep up with an underwater penguin on the hunt!

Apart from the penguins, there is only one other flightless sea bird in the world – the endemic flightless cormorant. At over 90 cm long it is the tallest of the world's 29 species of cormorant and the only one which has lost its ability to fly. It is found only on the coasts of Isabela and Fernandina and nowhere else in the world.

At the opposite extreme of the flight occur in the second half of the breeding season, with October being the busiest month, but you may see it anytime that the colony is occupied. The display involves a perfectly choreographed 'dance' of up to 20 minutes of bowing, bill clicking, bill circling, swaying and freezing, honking and whistling. This is one of the most memorable of Galápagos sights.

The remaining endemic sea birds are the two resident gull species. The lava gull

Galápagos penguins

spectrum is the magnificently graceful waved albatross which can spend years at sea without touching land. Apart from a few pairs which breed on the Isla de la Plata off the Ecuadorean coast, the entire world population of some 12,000 pairs nests on Española. Egg laying occurs from mid-April to late June and the colonies are active with parents feeding their single young through December. When the fledged bird finally leaves the nest, it does not return for four or five years. From January to March, all the birds are at sea.

The waved albatross engages in one of the most spectacular ritualised courtship display of any bird. Courtship tends to is the rarest gull in the world – only about 400 pairs are estimated to exist. Despite this, you have a very good chance of seeing one here. They are generally black with white eyelids.

More colourful is the swallow-tailed gull which is grey and white with bright red feet and legs and a crimson eye-ring. This bird feeds at night and is the only nocturnal gull in the world. It is frequently seen perched on cliff tops during the day. Although a few pairs nest on an island off Colombia, almost the entire world population nests in the Galápagos and therefore the swallow-tailed gull is generally considered endemic.

Three species of booby are found in the islands and although they are not endemic, they are still a popular attraction for visitors. It is easy to understand why – their appearance is amusing and their colonies are among the most approachable in the islands. You can often get within a few feet of a nest which will provide you with great photographs.

The boobies belong to the gannet family and look very much like them; they are fast fliers and exceptional plunge divers. The blue-footed booby is often the first one seen. It really does have bright blue feet which it picks up in a slow, most dignified fashion when performing a courtship display. Bowing, wing spreading, and sky pointing (with the neck, head, and bill stretched straight upwards) are also features of courtship.

At first glance, the males and females are almost identical but you can tell them apart: the female has a slightly bigger pupil and honks, whereas the male whistles. Courtship, mating and nesting occur year round – although nesting is a euphemism for a scrape on the ground surrounded by a ring of guano.

The red-footed booby is the only one which nests in trees and it is found in the outlying islands, such as Genovesa (Tower) where there is a sizeable colony. It is found only in the outlying islands because it feeds far out to sea and thus avoids competing with the blue-footed booby which feeds close inshore.

The third booby of the Galápagos is the masked (white) booby which is pure white with a black face mask. Colonies are found on most of the islands.

There are two frigate bird species in the Galápagos – the magnificent and great frigate birds. They are large, elegant and streamlined black sea birds with long forked tails but the two species are not easy to tell apart. They make an acrobatic living by aerial piracy, often harassing smaller birds into dropping or regurgitating their catch and then swooping to catch their stolen meal in midair.

As with many Galápagos sea birds, their courtship display is quite spectacular. The males have flaps of bright red skin hanging under their necks and these are inflated into football sized balloons to attract females. It takes about 20 minutes to fully inflate the pouch and the male normally sits on a tree and displays skywards to passing females. Occasionally, a male is seen flying overhead with his pouch still distended – a strange sight. North Seymour Island has a constantly active magnificent frigate bird colony.

The brown pelican is instantly recognisable with its huge pouched bill. It is one of the most commonly seen sea birds in the Galápagos. It feeds by shallow plunge diving and scoops up as much as 10 litres of water in its distendable pouch. The water rapidly drains out through the bill and the trapped fish (usually quite small) are swallowed. It sounds straightforward but apparently it isn't. Although parents raise frequent broods of two or three chicks, many of the fledged young are unable to learn the scoop-fishing technique and so starve to death.

The pelicans have wide fingered wings and are good gliders. They are often seen flying in a squadron-like formation, flapping and gliding in unison to create an elegant aerial ballet.

The brown noddy tern is, as its name suggests, generally brown with a whitish forehead and is often seen feeding with pelicans. It may catch fish scraps from the water draining out of a pelican's bill and even perch on the pelican's head to better enable it to reach the food. The sooty tern also breeds in the Galápagos, but is restricted to Darwin Island in the far north and so is rarely seen.

The red-billed tropicbird is less frequently seen than most of the sea birds mentioned thus far, but it is no less spectacular. The most noticeable feature of this splendid white sea bird is its pair of long tail streamers – two elongated feathers often as long as the rest of the body. The coral-red bill and black eye stripe are noticeable at closer range. The birds nest in crevices and holes in cliffs or rock piles on most of the islands, but are most frequently seen on Daphne Major and South Plaza.

Other sea birds are more often seen over the water than on the coast. These include three species of storm petrels which are among the smallest of sea birds. They are dark with a white rump. The three species are distinguished by the differences in the shape of the white area. They feed by grabbing scraps from the surface of the sea, which makes them look as if they are walking on water.

The Galápagos (wedge-rumped) and Madeiran (band-rumped) storm petrels breed in huge colonies on Genovesa (Tower). These colonies are estimated to number hundreds of thousands but not much is known about them. Breeding colonies of the Elliot's (white-vented) storm petrel have yet to be discovered.

On sea crossings between the islands you may see the Audubon's shearwater or Hawaiian (dark-rumped) petrel. They are expert fliers and glide close to the surface of the water – it is difficult to approach them closely.

Because the magnificent sea birds dominate the coasts with their huge nesting colonies and acrobatic aerial displays, it is often easy to overlook the shore birds. Some of these are familiar to North and/or Latin Americans – the great blue heron, the yellow-crowned night heron, the American oystercatcher, the black-necked (common) stilt, the common egret and (a recent arrival) the cattle egret all breed in both the Galápagos and North and South America. Two resident shore birds which are of greater interest to visitors are the greater flamingo and the endemic lava heron.

The flamingo is spectacular – especially in flight when its long trailing legs, outstretched neck, and black wing edges contrasting with its overall pink colour make it an unforgettable sight. The Galápagos population is a small and fragile one and harassing the birds in attempts to make them take off is against park rules and strongly discouraged. One of the best places to see a flamingo colony is on Santa María (Floreana).

The endemic lava heron has a dark greenish grey plumage which blends well with its environment. The adults have bright orange or yellow feet and bill which is often what catches your eye first. They are often seen hunched motionless on a lava beach waiting to jab at an unsuspecting passing crab or lizard. The paler but otherwise similar striated heron is also seen. It is not clear whether these two herons are members of different species, or races of the same variable species.

Ducks and geese are not often seen in the Galápagos. If you do see one, it is most likely to be the white-cheeked pintail which breeds in small numbers on salt lagoons and ponds on most of the major islands.

Several dozen other birds have been recorded as migrants or accidentals. Six of these are regular migrants which normally breed during the summer in North America or the arctic and are often seen in the Galápagos between August and April. These are the semi-palmated plover, ruddy turnstone, wandering tattler, sanderling, whimbrel, and northern (red-necked) phalarope.

Bird Check List

The species of birds tabled are listed in standard taxonomic order. Rare migrants and accidentals are not listed.

	Bird Species in the Galápagos			
	Species	**Sighted**	**Date**	**Notes**
*	Galápagos Penguin	☐		
*	Waved Albatross	☐		
R	Hawaiian Petrel	☐		
R	Audubon's Shearwater	☐		
R	Elliot's Storm Petrel	☐		
R	Madeiran Storm Petrel	☐		
R	Galápagos Storm Petrel	☐		
R	Red-billed Tropicbird	☐		
R	Brown Pelican	☐		
R	Blue-footed Booby	☐		
R	Masked Booby	☐		
R	Red-footed Booby	☐		
*	Flightless Cormorant	☐		
R	Great Frigate bird	☐		
R	Magnificent Frigate bird	☐		
R	Great Blue Heron	☐		
R	Cattle Egret	☐		
R	Common Egret	☐		
*	Lava Heron	☐		
R	Yellow-crowned Night Heron	☐		
R	Greater Flamingo	☐		
R	White-cheeked Pintail	☐		
*	Galápagos Hawk	☐		
*	Galápagos Rail	☐		
R	Paint-billed Crake	☐		
R	Common Gallinule	☐		
R	American Oystercatcher	☐		
M	Semi-palmated Plover	☐		
M	Ruddy Turnstone	☐		
M	Wandering Tattler	☐		
M	Sanderling	☐		
M	Whimbrel	☐		
R	Black-necked Stilt	☐		

	Species	Sighted	Date	Notes
M	Northern Phalarope	☐		
*	Lava Gull	☐		
*	Swallow-tailed Gull	☐		
R	Sooty Tern	☐		
R	Brown Noddy	☐		
*	Galápagos Dove	☐		
R	Dark-billed Cuckoo	☐		
R?	Groove-billed Ani	☐		
R	Barn Owl	☐		
R	Short-eared Owl	☐		
R	Vermilion Flycatcher	☐		
*	Galápagos Flycatcher	☐		
*	Galápagos Martin	☐		
*	Galápagos Mockingbird	☐		
*	Charles Mockingbird	☐		
*	Hood Mockingbird	☐		
*	Chatham Mockingbird	☐		
R	Yellow Warbler	☐		
*	Small Ground Finch	☐		
*	Medium Ground Finch	☐		
*	Large Ground Finch	☐		
*	Sharp-beaked Ground Finch	☐		
*	Cactus Finch	☐		
*	Large Cactus Finch	☐		
*	Vegetarian Finch	☐		
*	Small Tree Finch	☐		
*	Medium Tree Finch	☐		
*	Large Tree Finch	☐		
*	Woodpecker Finch	☐		
*	Mangrove Finch	☐		
*	Warbler Finch	☐		

Key: * Endemic
R Resident
M Migrant

Top: Boats off Isla Plaza, Galápagos Islands (TW)
Bottom: Isla Bartolomé, Galápagos Islands (TW)

Top: Boat building in Puerto Ayora, Galápagos Islands (TW)
Bottom: Brachycereus Cactus on Pahoehoe Lava, James Island, Galápagos Islands (RR)

Top: Frigatebird with mating pouch, Galápagos Islands (TW)
Bottom: Marine Iguana (RR)

A: Blue-footed booby (TW)
B: Male magnificent frigate bird & chick (RR)
C: Male marine iguana in breeding colours (RR)
D: Galápagos hawks (RR)
E: Galápagos tortoise (RR)
F: Sea Lion pups (RR)

Reptiles

The prehistoric-looking reptiles found all over the islands are easily approached and observed. The most frequently seen are the iguanas, of which there are three species, all endemic.

The marine iguana is the only sea-going lizard in the world and is found on the rocky shores of most islands. This iguana has a blackish skin, which in the males other islands but hunting and competition with introduced animals (goats, rats, pigs, dogs), which prey on the eggs, has caused their demise on many islands. The similar looking Santa Fé land iguana is limited to that island only.

The preferred food of both species is the prickly pear cactus and the iguanas are sometimes seen standing on their rear legs in efforts to reach the succulent pads and

Male marine iguana

can change to startling blues and reds during the breeding season. They feed mainly on intertidal seaweeds, although mature males have been recorded offshore at depths to 12 metres and can remain submerged for an hour or more. The row of spines along the entire length of their backs, their scaly skins, their habit of occasionally snorting little clouds of salt spray into the air, and their length – which can reach almost a metre – makes them look like veritable little dragons.

There are two species of land iguanas. They are yellowish in colour and bigger than their marine relatives and adults weighing six kg have been recorded. The Galápagos land iguana is found on Isabela, Santa Cruz, Fernandina, Seymour and South Plaza Islands, with South Plaza being the best place to see them. They were formerly found on most of the yellow flowers. Their mouths are incredibly leathery, enabling them to eat the cactus pads whole without removing the spines.

The most famous of the reptiles is, of course, the endemic giant tortoise for which the islands are named. There is only one species but it has been divided into 14 subspecies of which three are extinct. One of the most noticeable ways to distinguish them (apart from geographical distribution) is by differences in the shape of their carapaces (shells). These differences contributed to Darwin's thoughts whilst he was developing his theory of evolution.

Tens of thousands of tortoises were killed by whalers and sealers, particularly in the 18th and 19th centuries, and now only some 10,000 remain. A breeding project at the Charles Darwin Research Station appears to be successful and it is hoped to begin re-introduction of animals into the wild. The easiest way to see both tiny yearlings and full-grown adults is at the research station. Although they are in enclosures, visitors are permitted to enter the enclosures and get a good close look at these giants, some of which can reach a weight of 250 kg. This is one of the few places where you can actually touch the animals. To see the tortoises in the wild you can go to the tortoise reserve on Santa Cruz or climb Volcán Alcedo on Isabela.

The Pacific green sea turtle breeds and lays eggs in the Galápagos, though it is not endemic to them. These turtles are quite promiscuous and during the breeding season, especially November to January, much mating activity can be observed in the water. Black Turtle Cove on the north shore of Santa Cruz is a particularly good place to see them. Nesting occurs at night on many of the sandy beaches of the islands and mainly occurs from December to June.

The Pacific green sea turtles are huge and may reach 150 kg in weight. Snorkellers sometimes see them swimming underwater and it is an exciting sight to watch such a large animal come flapping serenely by.

Less spectacular but also endemic are the seven species of lava lizard which are frequently seen scurrying around the islands. They can reach 30 cm in length but are usually smaller. Their most distinctive behavioural patterns are rapid head-bobbing and push-up stances to defend their territories and assert dominance. The male is usually larger and strongly patterned with yellow, black, and brown. The female is less strongly patterned but makes up for this by a flaming red throat.

It is easy to separate the species by geographical distribution. San Cristóbal, Floreana, Marchena, Española, Pinta and Pinzón all have their own endemic species that are found nowhere else in the world. The Albermarle species (named after the English name of Fernandina) is found on most of the other islands except for Genovesa, Wolf, and Darwin which have no lava lizards.

Less often seen are the small, harmless, nocturnal lizards called geckos, of which there are seven species (five endemic). They are often associated with human habitations and may be seen in the inhabited areas at night. Geckos have adhesive pads on their digits and can climb vertical walls and even walk upside down on the ceilings of houses. Again, geographical distribution helps with separating the species. One species is limited to Santa María and Española; one to Santa Cruz, Isabela, Santiago and Daphne Major; one to Santa Fé; one to Wolf; and three to San Cristóbal. Only one of these last three is endemic.

Finally, you may see the Galápagos snake, which is small, drab and non-poisonous. There are three species, all endemic, all of the constrictor type, and they are difficult to tell apart. The adults reach a length of one metre and they are not dangerous.

Galápagos tortoise

Reptile Species in the Galápagos			
Species	Sighted	Date	Notes
* Giant Tortoise	☐		
R Pacific Green Sea Turtle	☐		
* Galápagos Snake (3 species)	☐		
* Gecko (5 species)	☐		
R Gecko (2 species)	☐		
* Lava Lizard (7 species)	☐		
* Galápagos Land Iguana	☐		
* Santa Fé Land Iguana	☐		
* Marine Iguana	☐		

Key: * Endemic
R Resident

Mammals

The mammals are less well represented because they had greater difficulty in surviving a long ocean crossing. There are two bat species, which probably flew across or were blown over in a storm. The hoary bat is known from North America but the endemic Galápagos bat has been little studied.

Two endemic species of rice rat are found in the Galápagos, one on Fernandina and one on Santa Fé. These mammals probably floated across on vegetation rafts. It is thought that there were once seven species of rice rat, but five have become extinct since the introduction of the black rat by man. No large land mammals made it to the islands until the arrival of man.

The mammal you'll see the most of is the Galápagos sea lion, which is a subspecies of the Californian sea lion and found on most islands. There are an estimated 50,000 individuals in the Galápagos. The territorial bulls, which can reach 250 kg, are quite aggressive and sometimes chase swimmers out of the water. They have been known to bite if harassed so don't approach them too closely. The females and young, on the other hand, are extremely playful and you can often watch them swimming around you if you bring a mask and snorkel.

Less common are the fur seals, which superficially look similar but on closer inspection are quite different from the sea lions. The best place to see them is Puerto Egas on Santiago.

Other marine mammals you may see when cruising between the islands are whales and dolphins. There are seven whale species regularly recorded in the archipelago but they are difficult to tell apart because they are normally glimpsed only momentarily and from a distance. The seven species are the finback, sei, humpback, minke, sperm, killer, and pilot whales.

The bottle-nosed dolphins are often seen surfing the bow waves of the boats. If seen at night, the dolphins cause the ocean to glow with bioluminescence as they stir up thousands of tiny phosphorescent creatures which glow when disturbed. Less frequently seen are the common and spinner dolphins.

Other land mammals are introduced species gone wild and they create a major nuisance to the native species (including the native plants, birds, reptiles, mammals, and invertebrates) by preying on them and by competing for food resources. They

	Mammal Species in the Galápagos			
	Species	**Sighted**	**Date**	**Notes**
R	Sea Lion	☐		
*	Galápagos Fur Seal	☐		
R	Hoary Bat	☐		
*	Galápagos Bat	☐		
*	Santa Fé Rice Rat	☐		
*	Fernandina Rice Rat	☐		
R	Whales (7 species)	☐		
R	Dolphins (3 species)	☐		

Key: * Endemic
R Resident

include feral goats, pigs, burros, cats, dogs, rats and mice.

Fish
Scientists have recorded 307 species of fish from 92 families in the Galápagos and it is expected that more will be discovered. Over 180 of these fish are found in much of the tropical eastern Pacific and about 50 are endemic. Unfortunately, no comprehensive guides to the Galápagos fish exist at this time although work is being done. It is interesting to note that many species of tropical fish can change their colour and shape as they age and a few can even change their sex midway through life. This certainly makes identification confusing!

Snorkelling in the Galápagos is a rewarding experience and schools containing thousands of tropical fish are routinely seen. Some (but by no means all) of the naturalist guides working on the boats can help identify the more common species. These include blue-eyed damselfish, white-banded angelfish, yellow-tailed surgeonfish, moorish idols, blue parrotfish, concentric puffer fish, yellow-bellied triggerfish and hieroglyphic hawkfish – to

name but a few and to give you some idea of the variety in form and colour.

Dive shops and gift shops in oceanographical aquariums and museums in the United States sell plastic waterproof cards illustrating common fish of the Pacific (from Hawaii and the Sea of Cortez, Mexico). These can be taken underwater and help in identifying some of the Galápagos species. Unfortunately, these cards are not available in Ecuador.

The one type of fish that swimmers are often the most interested in is the shark. There are several species found here and the most common are the white-tipped reef shark and the Galápagos shark. Hammerheads are also occasionally seen. For some reason, the sharks of the Galápagos have never been known to attack and injure a human swimmer and so the chances of you getting bitten are so remote as to be not worth worrying about.

I have often seen sharks whilst snorkelling and have never been bothered by them. Instead, I have been most impressed by their speed and grace underwater which is almost otherworldly. In fact, one of the best reasons to snorkel in the Galápagos is the chance of seeing these magnificent animals in reasonable safety. Despite this reassurance, you should leave the water if you cut or graze yourself.

Another kind of fish which provides the snorkeller with a real thrill is the ray. Again, there are several species; all harmless with the exception of the stingray, which sometimes basks on the sandy bottoms of the shallows and can inflict an extremely painful wound to waders and paddlers. Your guide will warn you of the few beaches where stingrays are commonly found. It is a good idea to enter the water by shuffling your feet along the sandy bottom – this gives stingrays the chance to swim away before you step on them.

Other rays are found in slightly deeper water and are often camouflaged on the sandy bottom. My first ray sighting was of a spotted eagle ray which lay on the bottom motionless and almost invisible. As I swam over it, the fish suddenly broke loose of the sand and flapped away giving me a real shock. The sight of a metre wide ray gently undulating through the water is quite mesmerising. Schools of beautiful golden coloured mustard rays are also seen quite regularly.

Less frequently seen is the giant manta ray which is found in deeper offshore waters. You are most likely to catch sight of one as it leaps out of the water and falls back with a loud slap – with a maximum spread of six metres they make a huge splash as they hit the water.

Sally Lightfoot crab

Invertebrates

The animals dealt with so far (birds, reptiles, mammals, and fish) all possess a backbone containing vertebrae and so are collectively called vertebrates. The remaining animals which are encountered in the Galápagos do not possess a backbone and are hence collectively called invertebrates. The most commonly found phyla include the Poriferans (sponges), Coelenterates or Cnidarians (jellyfish, sea anemones and corals), Molluscs (snails, chitons, shellfish, and octopi), Arthropods (insects, spiders, barnacles, crabs, and lobsters), and Echinoderms (starfish, sea urchins, and sea cucumbers). There are other phyla which are less frequently encountered.

The first invertebrate which most visitors notice is the Sally Lightfoot crab. This small crab is bright red above and blue below and ubiquitous on almost every rock beach.

Also present on rock beaches is a small black crab which blends well with the lava background. These well camouflaged small black crabs are young Sally Lightfoots. The adults are far from camouflaged and rely on their alertness to escape predators. If you try and approach them, they will run away and are even capable of running across the surface of the water in tide pools.

The crabs will, however, approach you if you sit as still as a rock. This is the strategy applied by the herons which prey on the Sally Lightfoots. Often you'll see a lava heron standing motionless on a rocky beach. When a crab comes within reach, the bird will lunge forward and, if successful in capturing a crab, will then proceed to shake it and bang it against rocks until the legs fall off before devouring the animal.

Other crabs are found on sandy beaches. These are the pale coloured ghost crabs which stare at you with unusual eyes at the end of long eye stalks. They leave the characteristic pattern of sand balls which are seen on most sand beaches. In tide pools, you may see the hermit crab which lives in an empty sea shell which it carries around. As a young crab outgrows its protective shell, it finds a larger one to grow into. This 'moving house' occurs several times before the hermit crab reaches adult size.

At low tides, tide pools offer a good opportunity to study marine invertebrates. Starfish, sea anemones, sea urchins, marine snails, barnacles, chitons, and limpets are often found.

As you go further into the water with a mask and snorkel, you can see many more species including sea cucumbers, octopi, and corals and, if you care to poke around some of the rocky underwater crevices, lobster.

Be careful where you poke though, because you may encounter the *Diadema mexicana* sea urchin which has beautiful iridescent black spines which are long, brittle and needle sharp.

Less painful encounters with sea urchins can be had with *Eucidaris thouarsii* which has blunt pencil-like spines which often break off and are washed ashore, sometimes forming a large part of a beach.

The endemic green *Lytechnicus semi-tuberculatus* urchin is also common and despite its prickly appearance, can be held quite easily and its tiny tube feet examined.

Sea urchins' prickly ball appearance belies their taxonomic grouping. They are in fact radially symmetrical in five or more planes and are hence members of the same phylum as the starfish and the sand dollar – the Echinoderms. The sand dollar looks like a flattened disc which has a starfish pattern on it. The starfish themselves are immediately recognisable but come in a fascinating array of sizes, colours, shapes, and numbers of arms ranging from five to many. The sea cucumbers are also Echinoderms. They lie on the bottom and look unfortunately similar to turds.

The Coelenterates are represented by sea anemones which are stationary creatures which capture their food by waving stinging tentacles in the water. These tentacles do not create enough sting to hurt you, should you brush against one in a tide pool or shallow area.

Because of their appearance and the fact that they don't move from place to place, they are sometimes nicknamed 'sea-flowers'.

Swimming Coelenterates are represented by jellyfish which also capture prey using stinging tentacles. These can be quite painful should you come into contact with them, but fortunately, jellyfish aren't seen too often in the popular swimming spots.

Corals are also Coelenterates but there are not many in the Galápagos. The 'Devil's Crown' off Isla Santa María is one of the best places to see living coral.

Dead coral is often found washed up ashore and sometimes forms a large part of a beach.

Insects are the most numerous animals in the world and literally millions of species are found in the tropics. A little over 1000 species are described from the Galápagos, and this comparatively small number reflects the difficulty that insects had in crossing almost 1000 km of ocean to colonise the islands.

There are not many colourful species. There are a few species of butterflies, ants, grasshoppers, and wasps, and many more representatives of the beetle and moth groups.

There is one species of bee, one preying mantis, and two scorpions in the Galápagos. The scorpions (which are more closely related to spiders than insects but like them are in the Arthropod phyla) are rarely encountered and though their sting can be painful, they are not normally dangerous.

Of the other biting insects, mosquitoes, horse flies, and midges are found and can sometimes make beach sunbathing unpleasant. Fortunately, these insects do not fly far and nights spent aboard a boat anchored several hundred metres off shore will usually be insect free. And if they're not, just anchor a few hundred metres further off.

Plants

Between 700 and 800 species of vascular plants have been recorded in the Galápagos, of which over 250 species are endemic. In addition, about 500 non-vascular plants (mosses, lichens, and liverworts) have been described. There are six different vegetation zones, beginning with the shore and ending with the highlands. These zones are the Littoral, Arid, Transition, Scalesia, Miconia, and Fern-Sedge. Each zone supports different and distinctive plant species.

The littoral zone contains species such as mangroves, saltbush and sesuvium. These plants are characterised by their ability to tolerate high quantities of salt in their environment.

Immediately beyond the littoral zone is the arid zone where many of the islands' cactus species are found, including forests of the giant prickly pear cactus. Trees such as the ghostly looking Palo Santo, the Palo Verde, and the spiny Acacias are found here as well as the Yellow Cordia shrub (with yellow flowers).

The 'transition zone has decreasing numbers of the arid zone trees and increasing numbers of lichens, perennial herbs, and smaller shrubs. The vegetation is both varied and thick and no particular plants are dominant.

In the higher islands, the transition zone gives way to a cloud forest type vegetation where the dominant tree is the endemic Scalesia. The trees are covered with smaller plants such as mosses, liverworts, bromeliads, ferns, and orchids.

Next is a treeless high altitude layer characterised by dense endemic Miconia shrub, liverworts, and ferns. This Miconia zone is found only on the south slopes of Santa Cruz and San Cristóbal.

Finally, the highest zone contains mainly ferns and grasses, including the Galápagos tree fern which grows to three metres in height.

It is beyond the scope of this book to delve more deeply into the many hundreds of plant species and the reader is referred to Schofield (1984), Jackson (1985), and Wiggins & Porter (1971).

CONSERVATION & TOURISM

As early as 1934, the Ecuadorean government set aside some of the islands as wildlife sanctuaries, but it was not until 1959 that the Galápagos was declared a national park. The construction of the Charles Darwin Research Station on Isla Santa Cruz began soon after, and the station began operating in 1962.

Few tourists had visited the islands before the station opened, but by the mid 1960s organised tourism had begun with a little over 1000 visitors a year. This figure soon increased dramatically. In 1970 an estimated 4500 tourists arrived and in 1971 there were six small boats and one large cruise ship operating in the islands. There were over 12,000 visitors in 1978 and about 26,000 in 1986, using three cruise ships (holding up to 96 passengers) and about 45 smaller boats (holding four to 16 passengers). In the face of this increasing interest and the inevitable human impact accompanying it, the Ecuadorean government granted further protection to the islands by creating the Galápagos Marine Resources Reserve in 1986.

The National Park covers approximately 90% of the islands' 7882 square km land mass – the rest is taken up by urban areas and farms which existed prior to the creation of the park. The Marine Resources Reserve covers the 50,000 square km of ocean and sea bed within which the islands are located plus a further 20,000 square km buffer zone. The function of the park and reserve is to protect and conserve the islands and surrounding ocean and to encourage scientific research and education.

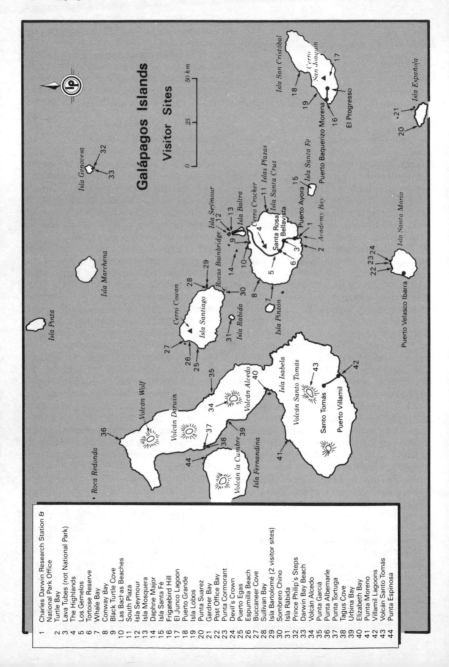

Galápagos Islands

Visitor Sites

1 Charles Darwin Research Station &
  National Park Office
2 Turtle Bay
3 Lava Tubes (not National Park)
4 The Highlands
5 Los Gemelos
6 Tortoise Reserve
7 Whale Bay
8 Conway Bay
9 Black Turtle Cove
10 Las Bachas Beaches
11 South Plaza
12 Isla Seymour
13 Isla Mosquera
14 Daphne Major
15 Isla Santa Fé
16 El Junco Lagoon
17 Frigatebird Hill
18 Puerto Grande
19 Isla Lobos
20 Punta Suarez
21 Gardner Bay
22 Post Office Bay
23 Punta Cormorant
24 Devil's Crown
25 Puerto Egas
26 Espumilla Beach
27 Buccaneer Cove
28 Sullivan Bay
29 Sombrero Chino
30 Isla Bartolomé (2 visitor sites)
31 Isla Rábida
32 Prince Philip's Steps
33 Darwin Bay Beach
34 Volcán Alcedo
35 Punta García
36 Punta Albemarle
37 Punta Tortuga
38 Tagus Cove
39 Urbina Bay
40 Elizabeth Bay
41 Punta Moreno
42 Villamil Lagoons
43 Volcán Santo Tomás
44 Punta Espinosa

Every foreign visitor must pay a US$40 park entrance fee upon arrival and will then be given a full set of park rules and other informative leaflets. The rules are for the protection of the wildlife and environment, and are mostly a matter of courtesy and common sense. Don't feed or handle the animals; don't litter; don't remove any natural object, whether living or dead; do not bring pets; do not buy objects made of sea lion teeth, black coral, tortoise, or turtle shells or other artefacts made from plants and animals; show a conservationist attitude. You are not allowed to enter the visitor sites after dark or without a qualified guide, and a guide will accompany every boat. On all shore trips, the guide will be there to answer your questions and show you the best sites, and also to ensure that you stay on the trails and don't molest the animals.

With 26,000 tourists visiting the islands annually, it is essential to have a system of protection for the islands. The rules are sensible and necessary – they do not infringe on your enjoyment of the Galápagos. Staying on the trails is a good rule unless a sea lion goes to sleep in the middle of the trail and you are then forced to go off trail to avoid the animal! The wildlife is so prolific that you'll see just as much on the trail as anywhere else, and staying on the trails means other areas are properly protected.

VISITOR SITES

To protect the islands the National Park Service limits access to about 45 visitor sites, in addition to the towns and public areas. These visitor sites are found in places where the most interesting features are to be seen and all the wildlife species listed in the previous section can be seen in them. Almost all of the visitor sites are reached by boat and normally landings are made in a *panga* which is the small dinghy that every boat carries for shore trips. (The larger boats carry several pangas.)

Most landing sites are sandy or rocky

beaches as there are few docks. Landings are called 'wet' or 'dry'. During a wet landing you will have to climb out of the panga onto a beach and wade ashore in shallow water, sometimes up to your knees. Dry landings are made onto rocky outcrops or jetties and you'll probably not get wet, unless a rogue wave comes up and splashes you. Boat captains will not take groups to places other than designated visitor sites. Occasionally, a new site is added to the list.

Here follows a brief description of all the islands and their visitor sites. Further information about the towns is given later. More detailed site descriptions and maps are to be found in the *Guide to the Visitor Sites of Galápagos National Park* by Alan & Tui Moore (Galápagos National Park Service, 1980). This book is not easy to find outside of the Galápagos.

Isla Santa Cruz

This island is rarely referred to by its lesser known English name of Indefatigable, and most people call it Santa Cruz. With an area of 986 square km it is the second largest island in the archipelago. A road crosses Santa Cruz from north to south and gives the visitor the easiest opportunity of seeing some of the highland interior of an island. The highest point is Cerro Crocker, 864 metres.

This island has the highest population and the greatest number of tourist facilities. The main town is Puerto Ayora on the south coast and most visitors either stay here whilst arranging a boat, or anchor in the town's famous harbour, Academy Bay, sometime during their cruise. In addition to the tourist facilities, there are nine visitor sites on Santa Cruz.

The **Charles Darwin Research Station** is about a 20 minute walk by road north-east of Puerto Ayora and can be reached on foot or by dry landing from Academy Bay. It contains a National Park Information Centre, a museum in the Van Straelen Exhibition Centre, a baby tortoise house where you can see hatchlings and young tortoises, and a walk-in adult tortoise enclosure where you can meet these Galápagos giants face to face. In addition, there are paths through arid zone vegetation such as prickly pear and other cacti, salt bush, and mangroves. A variety of land birds, including Darwin's finches, can be seen.

A seven km (or three km) trail takes you to **Turtle Bay**, south-west of Puerto Ayora. There is a very fine white sand beach and a spit of land giving protected swimming (there are strong currents on the exposed side of the spit). There are sharks as well as marine iguanas, and a variety of water birds, including pelicans and occasional flamingoes. There are mangroves.

This is one of the few visitor sites where you can go without a guide, and camping is permitted although there is no drinking water or other facilities. To get there, walk north-west of Puerto Ayora on the trans-island road for about a km, and then follow a six km footpath to the left to the beach. A new trail has recently been opened from behind the IETEL office which cuts the trip to about three km. The beach can also be reached by boat. Ask at the park headquarters for up to date information.

There are several sites of interest in the highlands of Santa Cruz and they can be reached from the trans-island road. Access to the sites is through colonised areas so respect private property. These sites can also be visited without guides. From the village of Bellavista, seven km north of Puerto Ayora by road, one can turn either west on the main road or east on a road leading in about two km to the **Lava Tubes**. These are underground tunnels of over a km in length, formed by the solidifying of the outside skin of a molten lava flow. When the lava flow ceased, the molten lava inside the flow kept going, emptying out of the solidified skin and thus leaving tunnels. They lie on private property and are not administered by the Park Service. The owners of the land are happy to let you visit if you pay an entrance fee of about US$1, and provide information and guides if you want. Bring a flashlight.

To the north of Bellavista lie **The Highlands** which are National Park land. A footpath from Bellavista leads towards Cerro Crocker and other hills and extinct volcanoes. This is a good chance to see the vegetation of the Scalesia, Miconia and fern-sedge zones, and to look for the vermilion flycatcher or the elusive Galápagos rail and paint-billed crake. It is about five km from Bellavista to the crescent shaped hill of Media Luna and a further three km to the base of Cerro Crocker.

A part of the highlands which can be visited from the road is the twin craters called **Los Gemelos**. These are actually sink holes rather than volcanic craters and they are surrounded by Scalesia forest. Vermilion flycatchers are often seen here, and short-eared owls on occasion. Los Gemelos is reached by taking the road to the village of Santa Rosa, about 12 km west of Bellavista, and continuing about two km beyond Santa Rosa on the trans-island road. Although the craters lie 25 metres and 125 metres on either side of the road, they are hidden by vegetation and so you should ask your driver to stop at the short trailhead.

Near Santa Rosa there is a **Tortoise Reserve** where you can observe the giant tortoises in the wild. There is a trail from the village (ask for directions) which leads through private property to park land about three km away. The trail is downhill and often quite muddy. The trail forks at the park boundary, with the right fork going up to the small hill of Cerro Chato (three more km) and the left fork going to La Caseta (two km) where camping is permitted. Bring your own water. The reserve is a good place to look for short-eared owls, Darwin's finches, yellow warblers, Galápagos rails and paint-billed crakes (these last two are difficult to see in the long grass).

The remaining four Santa Cruz visitor

sites are reached by boat and with guides. On the west coast are **Whale Bay** and **Conway Bay** and on the north coast are **Black Turtle Cove** and **Las Bachas Beaches**. The first two bays are attractive but infrequently visited.

There is no landing site in Black Turtle Cove, which is normally visited by panga ride. The cove has many little inlets and is surrounded by mangroves where you can see lava herons and pelicans. The main attraction is in the water – marine turtles are usually seen and mating can sometimes be observed. Schools of golden mustard rays are often present and white-tipped sharks may be seen basking in the shallows. It makes a very pleasant change to visit a marine site in a panga instead of walking. This site is occasionally visited by day boats from Puerto Ayora. The nearby Las Bachas beach is popular for sunbathing and swimming, and is often deserted.

Islas Plazas

These two small islands are just off the east coast of Santa Cruz and can be visited by day trip from Puerto Ayora. Therefore visitors on a cruise would do well to visit in the early morning or late afternoon to avoid the day groups. The two islands were formed by uplift due to faulting.

Boats anchor between them and visitors can land on **South Plaza** (the larger of the islands), which is only about 13 hectares in area. A dry landing on a jetty brings you to an Opuntia cactus forest where there are many land iguanas. A one km trail circuit leads visitors through sea lion colonies and along a cliff top walk where swallow-tailed gulls and other species nest. The cliffs are a superb vantage point for watching various sea birds in flight. Red-billed tropicbirds, frigate birds, pelicans, Audubon's shearwaters and others are always seen. Snorkelling with the sea lions is a possibility. Cactus forest, land iguanas, sea lions, sea birds galore – no wonder this is a favourite wild life watching site.

Isla Baltra

Most visitors to the Galápagos arrive by air and land at the Baltra airport. Baltra is a fairly small island (27 square km) off the north coast of Santa Cruz. There are no visitor sites or places to stay here and public and private transport from the airport to Puerto Ayora is available.

Isla Seymour

Separated from Baltra by a channel, Isla Seymour is a small 1.9 square km uplifted island with a dry landing. There is a circular trail (about 1¼ km) leading through some of the best sea bird breeding colonies in the islands. Magnificent frigate birds and blue-footed boobies are the main attractions. There is always some kind of observable activity going on – such as courtship, mating, nesting, or chick rearing – whatever time of year you come.

Swallow-tailed gulls also nest here and other birds are often seen. Sea lions are common and occasional fur seals are seen as well as lava lizards.

Isla Mosquera

This tiny sandy island (about 120 metres wide by 600 metres long) lies in the channel between Baltra and Seymour. There is no trail but visitors can land on the sandy beach to see the sea lion colony.

Islas Daphne

About 10 km roughly west of Seymour two islands of obviously volcanic origin can be seen. Daphne Minor is the one which is very eroded and **Daphne Major** is less eroded, retaining most of its typically volcanic shape which is called a tuff cone. There is a visitor landing site here – a rough scramble onto almost vertical rocks. A short but steep trail leads to the 120 metre high summit of this one third square km island.

There are two small craters at the top of the cone and these contain hundreds of blue-footed booby nests. Masked boobies nest on the crater rims and a few red-billed tropicbirds nest in rocky crevices in the steep sides of the islands.

The only drawback to visiting this island is that the National Park limits visits to one boat per month so either you have to be lucky or arrange your visit well in advance.

Isla Santa Fé

This 24 square km island lies about 20 km south-east of Santa Cruz and so is popular for day trips. Its infrequently used English name is Barrington. There is a good anchorage in an attractive bay on the north-east coast and a wet landing gives the visitor a choice of two trails. A short 300 metre trail takes you to one of the tallest stands of Opuntia cactus in the islands. A 1½ km trail takes the visitor up into the highlands where the Santa Fé land iguana may be seen. This species of iguana is found nowhere else in the world. Other attractions include a sea lion colony, excellent snorkelling, marine iguanas, and, of course, birds.

Isla San Cristóbal

Also known as Chatham, this 558 square km island is the fifth largest in the archipelago and has the second largest population. The provincial capital of Puerto Baquerizo Moreno is found on the south-west coast. Despite being the capital, little tourist activity is found here though the recent introduction of regular flights from the mainland has resulted in an increase in boats and hotels. Nevertheless, most people still use Puerto Ayora as a base.

There are four visitor sites on or near San Cristóbal, but they are not frequently visited by boats from Santa Cruz. The Chatham mockingbird, a species not found elsewhere, is common throughout the island.

Frigatebird Hill is about 1½ km east of Puerto Baquerizo Moreno and can be reached via foot trail without a guide. There is a National Park information office en route. From the hill there is a beautiful view of a bay below and the town behind. Both species of frigate birds nest here and lava lizards can be seen.

A road leads from the capital to the village of El Progreso, about eight km to the east and at the base of the 896 metre high Cerro San Joaquín, the highest point on San Cristóbal. Jeeps can be hired or you can walk on a dirt road going about 10 km further east to **El Junco Lagoon**, a freshwater lake at about 700 metres above sea level and one of the few permanent freshwater bodies in the Galápagos. Here you can see white-cheeked pintails and common gallinules and observe the typical highland Miconia vegetation and endemic tree ferns.

Puerto Grande is smaller than its name suggests. It is a well protected little cove on San Cristóbal's north-western coast. There is a good sandy beach suitable for swimming and the island's fishermen sometimes beach their boats here to work on the hulls. Various sea birds can be seen, but the site is not known for any special colonies.

About an hour north of Puerto Baquerizo Moreno by boat is the rocky and tiny **Isla Lobos** which is the main sea lion and blue-footed booby colony for visitors to San Cristóbal. There is a 300 metre long trail and lava lizards are seen.

Isla Española

This island, often called by its English name of **Hood**, is the most southerly in the archipelago. It is a medium sized island of 61 square km and there are two visitor sites. Because Española is somewhat outlying (about 90 km south-east of Santa Cruz), reaching it requires a fairly long sea passage and captains of some of the smallest boats may be reluctant to go this far. The better boats will often do the long crossing as an overnight passage. The island is well worth visiting from late March to December because it has the only colony of the waved albatross, one of the Galápagos' most spectacular sea birds.

The best visitor site on Española is **Punta Suarez** at the western end of the island. A wet landing is necessary. There is a trail of about two km in length which takes the visitor through masked and blue-footed booby colonies and past a beach full of marine iguanas before reaching the main attraction, the waved albatross colony.

Just beyond the colony is a blow hole through which the waves force water spouts about 20 metres into the air. Sitting on top of the cliffs between the waved albatrosses and the blow hole, you can watch sea birds performing their aerial ballets and their less elegant attempts to land and take off. Other birds to look for are the Hood mockingbird, found nowhere else, swallow-tailed gulls, red-billed tropicbirds, and oystercatchers. The large cactus finch can also be seen, and is found on few other islands. This is one of my favourite visitor sites in the Galápagos.

Gardner Bay is a beautiful white sand beach at the east end of Española. It is reached with a wet landing and there is good swimming and a sea lion colony. An island a short distance offshore provides good snorkelling.

Isla Santa María

Officially known as Santa María but more often called **Floreana** or **Charles**, this is the sixth largest of the islands at 173 square km. It has had an interesting history. The first resident of the Galápagos was Patrick Watkins, an Irishman who was marooned on Floreana in 1807 and spent two years living there, growing vegetables and trading his produce for rum from passing boats. The story goes that he managed to remain drunk for most of his stay until he stole a ship's boat and set out for Guayaquil accompanied by five slaves. No one knows what happened to the slaves – only Watkins reached the mainland.

After Watkin's departure, the island became an Ecuadorean penal colony for some years. In the 1930s, three groups of German settlers arrived on Floreana and strange stories have been told about them ever since.

The most colourful of the settlers was a baroness who arrived with three lovers. There was also an eccentric vegetarian, Dr Friedrich Ritter, who had all his teeth removed before arriving so as to avoid dental problems. He was accompanied by his mistress. The third group was a couple from Cologne, the Wittmers.

Despite their similar nationality, there was a great deal of friction between the groups and mysteriously, one by one, the settlers died. The baroness and a lover simply disappeared and another lover died in a boating accident. The vegetarian Dr Ritter died of food poisoning after eating chicken.

The only ones to survive were the Wittmers, and now Margaret Wittmer, one of the original settlers, continues to live on Floreana with her children and grandchildren. Although several books and articles have been written about the strange happenings on Floreana, no one is really sure of what happened.

The Wittmers live in the tiny village of Puerto Velasco Ibarra on the west coast of Floreana where they run a small hotel and restaurant.

There are three visitor sites on the north coast of Floreana. **Post Office Bay** used to have a barrel where whalers left mail. Any captain of a boat which was heading to where the mail was addressed would deliver it. The site continues to be used, though obviously the barrel has been changed many times. About 300 metres behind the barrel is a lava cave which can be descended with the aid of a short piece of rope. Nearby, there are the remains of a canning factory. There is a pleasant swimming beach. A wet landing is necessary.

Punta Cormorant is also reached with a wet landing. There is a greenish beach; green because it contains crystals of the mineral olivine. There are often sea lions, and swimming and snorkelling are both good.

A 400 metre trail leads across an isthmus to a white sand beach where turtles sometimes lay their eggs. The white beach is also good for swimming, but beware of stingrays and shuffle your feet when entering the water.

Between the two beaches is a flamingo lagoon and this is probably the main attraction of this visitor site. Several dozen flamingoes are normally seen, and this is also a good place to see other wading birds such as the black-necked stilt, oystercatchers, willets and whimbrels. White-cheeked pintail ducks are often seen in the lagoon and Galápagos hawks wheel overhead.

The third Floreana visitor site is the remains of a half submerged volcanic cone, poking up out of the ocean a few hundred metres from Punta Cormorant. Aptly named the **Devil's Crown**, this ragged semicircle of rocks forms one of the most outstanding marine sites in the Galápagos.

A panga ride around the cone will give views of red-billed tropicbirds, pelicans, herons and lava gulls nesting on the rocks, but the greater attraction is snorkelling in and around the crater. There are thousands of bright tropical fish, a small coral formation, sea lions and, if you are lucky, sharks.

Isla San Salvador

The official name is used less often than the old Spanish name 'Santiago', or the English name 'James'. Santiago is the fourth largest of the islands and has four excellent visitor sites within its 585 square km. The best site is **Puerto Egas** on James Bay on the west side of Santiago.

Here, there is a long flat black lava shoreline where eroded shapes form lava pools, caves, and inlets which house a great variety of wildlife. This is a great place to see colonies of marine iguanas basking in the sun. The tide pools contain hundreds of red sally lightfoot crabs which attract hunting herons of all the commonly found species.

The inlets are favourite haunts of the Galápagos fur seal and this is one of the best places in the islands to see them. You can snorkel with the fur seals and there are also many species of tropical fish. I have seen moray eels, sharks, and octopuses during snorkels here – you never know what might show up.

Behind the black lava shoreline is Sugarloaf Volcano which can be reached via a two km footpath. Lava lizards, Darwin's finches and Galápagos doves are often seen on this path. It peters out near the top of the 395 metre summit but from here the views are tremendous. There is an extinct crater in which feral goats are often seen (the wild goats are a major problem on Santiago) and Galápagos hawks often hover a few metres above the top of the volcano. North of the volcano is a crater where a salt mine used to be; its remains can be visited by walking along a three km trail from the coast.

At the north end of James Bay, about five km from Puerto Egas, is the brown sand **Espumilla Beach** which can be reached with a wet landing. Swimming is good. There is a small lagoon behind the beach where various wading birds are often seen, including flamingoes at times. A two km trail leads inland through transitional vegetation where there are various finches and the Galápagos flycatcher.

At the north-western end of Santiago there is a site which is normally visited by cruising past it. This is **Buccaneer Cove**, so called because it was a popular place for 17th and 18th century buccaneers to careen their vessels. Its main attraction today is the beautiful cliffs and pinnacles which are used as nesting areas by several species of sea-birds. This is best appreciated from the sea, but it is possible to land in the cove where there are beaches.

Sullivan Bay is on Santiago's east coast. Here, a huge black lava flow from the turn of the century has solidified into a sheet which reaches to the edge of the sea. A dry landing enables the visitor to step onto the flow and follow a trail of white posts in a two km circuit on the lava. You can see uneroded volcanic formations such as pahoehoe lava, lava bubbles, and tree trunk moulds in the surface. A few pioneer colonising plants such as *Brachycereus* cactus and *Mollugo* carpetweed can be seen. This site is of particular interest to those interested in volcanology or geology.

Isla Bartolomé

Just off Sullivan Bay is the 1.2 square km island of Bartolomé from where you can see the most frequently photographed and hence most famous vista in the islands. There are two footpaths. One begins from a jetty (dry landing) from where it is about 600 metres to the 114 metre summit of the island. There is a good trail which leads through a wild and unearthly looking lava landscape. There are a few pioneering plants but the main attraction is the view towards Santiago which is as dramatic as the photographs suggest and well worth the climb, which is steep but not difficult.

The other visitor site is a small sandy beach in a cove (wet landing). Here there is good snorkelling and swimming and the opportunity to swim with the endemic Galápagos penguins which frequent this cove. Marine turtles and a gaudy variety of tropical fish are also frequent visitors.

The best way to see and photograph the penguins is by taking a panga ride close to the rocks on either side of the cove and particularly around the aptly named Pinnacle Rock to the right of the cove from the seaward side. You can often get within a few metres of the penguins. This is the closest point to Puerto Ayora where you can frequently see these fascinating birds and it avoids the long voyage to the other penguin colonies which are mainly on the west side of Isabela.

From the beach there is a short 100 metre trail leading across the narrowest part of Bartolomé to another sandy beach on the opposite side of the island. The main attraction of this beach is that the marine turtles may nest here between January and March. Both beaches are clearly seen from the viewpoint at the first visitor site described.

Sombrero Chino

This tiny island is less than a quarter of a square km in size and found just off the south-eastern tip of Santiago. It is a fairly recent volcanic cone which accounts for its descriptive name which means 'Chinese Hat'. The hat shape is best appreciated from the north. There is a small sea lion cove on the north shore where you can anchor and land at the visitor site. There is a 400 metre trail around the cove and through a sea lion colony. The volcanic landscape is attractive and there are good views of the cone which gives the island its name. There are snorkelling and swimming opportunities in the cove.

Isla Rábida

Also known as Jervis, this approximately five square km island lies five km south of Santiago. There is a wet landing onto a dark red beach where sea lions haul out, and where there are often pelicans. Behind the beach there is a salt water lagoon where flamingoes and white-cheeked pintails are sometimes seen. There is a three quarter of a km long trail with good views of the 367 metre high volcanic peak covered with palo santo trees.

Isla Genovesa

This island is known more often by its English name of **Tower**. It is 14 square km and the most north-easterly of the Galápagos islands. It is rather an outlying island and so is not always included on a one week itinerary. If you have the time, however, and are interested in sea birds, this island is well worth the long trip. There are two visitor sites and it is the best place to see a red-footed booby colony, as well as giving the opportunity to visit colonies of masked boobies, great frigate birds, red-billed tropicbirds, swallow-tailed gulls, and many thousands of storm petrels. Other bird attractions include Galápagos doves and short-eared owls. Both sea lions and fur seals are present and there are exciting snorkelling opportunities – I have seen hammerhead sharks here.

The island is fairly flat and round, with a large almost land locked cove named Darwin Bay on the south side. Both visitor sites are on Darwin Bay. **Prince Philip's Steps** is on the eastern arm of the bay and can be reached with a dry landing. A steep and rocky path leads to the top of 25 metre high cliffs and nesting sea birds are sometimes found right on the narrow path.

At the top of the cliffs the one km long trail leads inland past dry forest vegetation and various sea bird colonies to a cracked expanse of lava where thousands of storm petrels make their nests and wheel overhead. Short-eared owls are often seen here and it is an excellent hike for the bird enthusiast.

The second visitor site is **Darwin Bay Beach** which is a coral beach reached by a wet landing. There is a three quarter of a km trail along the beach which goes through more sea bird colonies.

A pleasant panga ride can be taken along the cliffs. The panga is often followed by playful sea lions. This excursion gives a good view from the seaward side of the cliffs and of the birds nesting on them.

Isla Isabela

The largest island in the archipelago is the 4588 square km Isabela (occasionally called Albemarle) which occupies over 58% of the entire land mass of the Galápagos. It is a relatively young island and consists of a chain of five fairly young and intermittently active volcanoes, one of which, Volcán Wolf, is the highest point in the Galápagos at 1707 metres (some sources claim 1646 metres). There is also one small older volcano.

Although Isabela's volcanoes dominate the westward view during passages to the west of Santa Cruz, the island itself is not frequently visited by smaller boats because most of the best visitor sites are on the west side of the island. The reverse 'C' shape of the island means that the visitor sites on the west side are reached only after a very long passage (over 200 km) from Santa Cruz, so you either have to visit Isabela without seeing many of the other islands or make a two week cruise.

There are 10 visitor sites on Isabela. One of these is the summit of **Volcán Alcedo** (1128 metres) which is famous for its seven km wide caldera with a steaming fumarole where scores of giant tortoises can be seen, especially from June to December. The view is fantastic.

Reaching this site is quite an undertaking, however, and needs some preparation and effort. A wet landing at Shipton Cove brings you to the start of a steep, rocky, and strenuous 10 km trail to the edge of the caldera, and then it is a further six km to the fumarole. All food and water must be carried. There is a camp site at the beach, another half way up the volcano, and three more on the caldera rim. One of these is at the point where the trail first reaches the caldera, another is at the fumarole, and the third is in between.

You should enquire in the national park office for up to date information and a camping permit. This is a most rewarding trip if you can afford the time, and well worth the hassle and hard work. At the very least it is an overnight trip and two nights are better still.

A few km north of the landing for Alcedo is the **Punta García** visitor site. This consists mainly of very rough aa lava and there are no proper trails though you can land if you want to. Until recently, this was the only place where you could see the endemic flightless cormorant without having to take the long passage around to the west side. Recently, however, these birds have been present only intermittently and visits to this site have declined.

At the northern tip of Isabela is the **Punta Albemarle** visitor site which used to be a US radar base during WW II. There are no trails and the site is known for the flightless cormorants which normally are not found further to the east.

Further west there are several points where flightless cormorants, Galápagos penguins, and other sea birds can be seen, but there are no visitor sites to land in. You can see the birds from your boat, however.

At the west end of the northern arm of Isabela is the small old Volcán Ecuador (610 metres) which comes down almost to the sea. Punta Vicente Roca, at the volcano's base, is a rocky point with a good snorkelling area.

The first official visitor site on the western side of Isabela is **Punta Tortuga** which is a beach at the base of Volcán Darwin (1280 metres). Part of the land here was formed through a recent uplift. Locals report that one day in 1975 the uplift just appeared – no one saw it happen. One day there was nothing and the next day there was an uplifted ledge.

Although there is no trail, you can land on the beach and explore the mangroves for the mangrove finch which is present here, though not always easy to see. This finch is found only on Isabela and Fernandina Islands.

Just south of the point is the visitor site of **Tagus Cove** where early sailors frequently anchored. You can still see some of the names of the vessels scratched on to the cliffs around the cove.

A dry landing will bring you to a trail which you follow for two km past a salt water lagoon and onto the lower lava slopes of Volcán Darwin, where various volcanic formations can be observed. A panga ride along the cliffs will enable you to see the historical graffiti and various sea birds, usually including the Galápagos penguin and flightless cormorant. There are snorkelling opportunities in the cove.

Urbina Bay lies around the middle of the western shore of Isabela and is a flat area formed by an uplift from the sea in 1954. Evidence of the uplift includes a coral reef on the land. Flightless cormorants, pelicans and marine iguanas can be observed. Rays and turtles can be seen in the bay and a wet landing onto a beach brings you to a km long trail leading to the corals. There is a good view of Volcán Alcedo.

Near where the western shoreline of Isabela bends sharply towards the lower 'arm' of the island there is a visitor site known for its marine life. **Elizabeth Bay** is best visited by a panga ride and there are no landing sites. The Mariela Islands are at the entrance of the bay and they are frequented by penguins. The end of the bay itself is a long, narrow and convoluted arm of the sea surrounded by three species of mangroves. Marine turtles and rays are usually seen in the water and various sea and shore birds are present.

West of Elizabeth Bay is the **Punta Moreno** visitor site where you can make a dry landing onto a lava flow where there are some brackish pools. Flamingoes, white-cheeked pintails and common gallinules are sometimes seen and various pioneer plants and insects are found in the area.

On the south-eastern corner of Isabela there is the small village of Puerto Villamil. Behind and to the west of the village there are the **Villamil Lagoons**. This visitor site is known for its migrant birds, especially waders. Harris writes that over 20 species of migrant waders have been reported here and the lagoons are by far the best water-bird area in the Galápagos. The vegetation around the lagoons is dense and there are no trails, although the road to the highlands and the open beach do give reasonable access to the lagoons.

The massive **Volcán Santo Tomás** (1490 metres, also known as Volcán Sierra Negra) lies to the north-west. The tiny settlement of Santo Tomás is on the lower flanks of the volcano and 18 km by road from Puerto Villamil. Trucks or jeeps can be hired for the ride. From Santo Tomás it is nine km further up a steep trail to the rim of the volcano – horses can be hired in the village.

The caldera is roughly 10 km in diameter and is a spectacular site with magnificent views. An eight km trail leads around the east side of the volcano to some active fumaroles. It is possible to walk all the way around the caldera but the trail peters out. You should carry all your food and water. Camping is allowed on the rim. Galápagos hawks, short-eared owls, finches and flycatchers are among the common birds seen on this trip.

Isla Fernandina

At 642 square km, Fernandina (infrequently called Narborough) is the third largest island and the most westerly of the normally visited ones. It is considered the youngest of the main islands and the recently formed volcanic landscapes are most impressive. At least 10 eruptions have been recorded since 1813.

There is one visitor site at **Punta Espinosa**, just across from Tagus Cove on Isabela. The point is known for one of the greatest concentrations of the endemic marine iguanas which are found in their thousands. Flightless cormorants, Galápagos penguins and sea lions are also common.

A dry landing brings you to two trails, a short quarter of a km one to the point and a longer three quarter of a km one out to recently formed lava fields. Here you can see various pioneering plants, such as the *Brachycereus* cactus, as well as pahoehoe and aa lava formations.

Other Islands

The one sizeable island in the central part of the archipelago which has no visitor sites is Isla Pinzón, also called Duncan. It is a cliff bound island, which makes landing difficult, and so it is the least visited of the main central islands. There are two large islands to the north of the archipelago which have no visitor sites. These are Isla Marchena (Bindloe) and Isla Pinta (Abingdon) which are the

seventh and ninth largest Galápagos islands respectively. Both islands have landing sites but visits are infrequent.

The northernmost islands are the two tiny islands of Isla Wolf (Wenman) and Isla Darwin (Culpepper). They are about 100 km north-east of the rest of the archipelago and very seldom visited. Both have near vertical cliffs making landing difficult and Darwin was first visited in 1964 when a helicopter expedition landed on the summit. Various other rocks and islets are present in the archipelago but all are extremely small.

ACTIVITIES
Snorkelling

You don't have to be a great swimmer to be able to snorkel. Donning a mask and snorkel will literally open up a completely new world for you. Baby sea lions may come up and stare at you through your mask, various species of rays come slowly undulating by, and penguins dart past you in a stream of bubbles. The hundreds of species of fish are spectacularly colourful and you can watch the round, flapping shapes of sea turtles as they circle you. This won't, of course, happen immediately you enter the water, but you have a good chance of seeing most of these things if you spend, say, half an hour per day in the water during a week of cruising the islands.

A mask and snorkel also let you observe more sedentary forms of life. Sea urchins, starfish, sea anemones, algae and crustaceans all colourfully combine in an exotic display of underwater life. If I were to give only one piece of advice to someone visiting the Galápagos, I would say, 'Bring a snorkel and mask.' You may be able to buy them in sporting goods stores in Quito or Guayaquil, and they can sometimes be borrowed in the Galápagos, but if you definitely plan on visiting the islands, I would consider bringing a mask from home to ensure a good fit and to enable you to snorkel when you feel like it.

The water temperature is generally

around 21°C from January to April and about 19°C during the rest of the year. If you plan on spending a lot of time in the water you may want to bring a wet suit top with you.

Scuba Diving

Scuba diving is available in the Galápagos but you must have all your own equipment and book a tour in advance, usually through a dive company. Compressed air and tanks are supplied on boats which run dive tours.

PUERTO AYORA

This is the town that most visitors stay in or visit. There is a post office, hotels and restaurants, stores, a IETEL office which works sometimes (radio messages can be sent in an emergency through INGALA), a TAME office, a basic hospital, churches, a movie theatre, and a radio station.

Tourist Information

The TAME office is open from 8 am to noon Monday to Thursday and on Saturday. It is also open from 2 to 5 pm Monday to Friday. Reconfirming your departures is essential. Flights are often full and there is sometimes difficulty in changing your reservation or buying a ticket. Be persistent.

INGALA (Instituto Nacional Galápagos) can give you information about inter-island ferries and the Capitanía can give you information about boats to the mainland. A government run DITURIS tourist information office opened recently but hours are very erratic – it always seemed to be closed when I went there.

Money-changing facilities are not very good and you should change travellers' cheques on the mainland. It is easier to change cash than travellers' cheques but rates are generally poor. The bank usually does not exchange money. A store which changes travellers' cheques (at a poor rate) is shown on the map. Other stores will sometimes also exchange money, and some hotels will do so if you are staying

there. The Casa Blanca Pizzería also changes foreign currency.

The Charles Darwin Research Station and National Park Office is about a km east of town. There is an exhibition hall, an information kiosk, a scientific library, and tortoise-raising pens, but tours are not organised. During the busy seasons, self-styled tour agents set up shop near the Las Ninfas Restaurant.

General Information

Laundry You can get your clothes washed in the house opposite the Residencial Angermeyer. There is a sign 'Clothes Washed Here'. You have to leave them for at least a day.

Shopping You can buy the famous Galápagos T-shirts in several shops; the Fragata Bar & Boutique has one of the best selections. Other souvenirs available include objects made from black coral, turtle and tortoise shell. These animals are protected (coral is considered an animal) and it is illegal to use these animal products for the manufacture of novelties. The practice still continues, unfortunately, and the most effective way of stamping it out is to avoid buying these things.

Most things (T-shirts excepted) are either expensive or unavailable and you are strongly advised to stock up on suntan lotion, insect repellent, toiletries, film and medications on the mainland. Food and drink are available but the choice is limited and comparatively expensive.

A good selection of postcards is available at the post office. Many of these are photographs or drawings by local resident Tui de Roi, famous for her beautifully illustrated books on the wildlife of the islands. Her books are also for sale in various stores and at the Libri Mundi bookstore in Quito. Her mother, Jacqueline de Roi, makes exquisite silver jewellery of the Galápagos animals. The work is not cheap but well worth the money. She lives on the other side of the

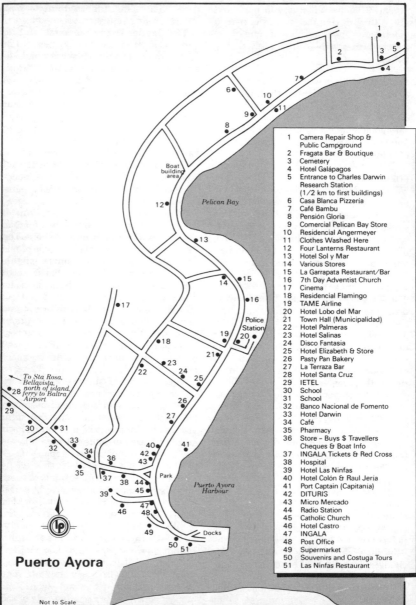

1   Camera Repair Shop &
    Public Campground
2   Fragata Bar & Boutique
3   Cemetery
4   Hotel Galápagos
5   Entrance to Charles Darwin
    Research Station
    (1/2 km to first buildings)
6   Casa Blanca Pizzería
7   Café Bambu
8   Pensión Gloria
9   Comercial Pelican Bay Store
10 Residencial Angermeyer
11 Clothes Washed Here
12 Four Lanterns Restaurant
13 Hotel Sol y Mar
14 Various Stores
15 La Garrapata Restaurant/Bar
16 7th Day Adventist Church
17 Cinema
18 Residencial Flamingo
19 TAME Airline
20 Hotel Lobo del Mar
21 Town Hall (Municipalidad)
22 Hotel Palmeras
23 Hotel Salinas
24 Disco Fantasia
25 Hotel Elizabeth & Store
26 Pasty Pan Bakery
27 La Terraza Bar
28 Hotel Santa Cruz
29 IETEL
30 School
31 School
32 Banco Nacional de Fomento
33 Hotel Darwin
34 Café
35 Pharmacy
36 Store – Buys $ Travellers
    Cheques & Boat Info
37 INGALA Tickets & Red Cross
38 Hospital
39 Hotel Las Ninfas
40 Hotel Colón & Raul Jeria
41 Port Captain (Capitania)
42 DITURIS
43 Micro Mercado
44 Radio Station
45 Catholic Church
46 Hotel Castro
47 INGALA
48 Post Office
49 Supermarket
50 Souvenirs and Costuga Tours
51 Las Ninfas Restaurant

Boat
building
area

Pelican Bay

Police
Station

To Sta Rosa,
Bellavista,
north of island,
ferry to Baltra
Airport

Park

Puerto Ayora
Harbour

Docks

Puerto Ayora

Not to Scale

town harbour and has no store outlet. Ask for directions if you are interested in buying her work.

Studying & Working The Charles Darwin Research Station runs guide courses lasting about six weeks every September. It is necessary to take and pass this course before you can work as a tour guide on the boats. Information on the course is available from Estación Científica Charles Darwin, Puerto Ayora, Santa Cruz, Galápagos, Ecuador.

Some of the main tourist companies, especially Metropolitan (PO Box 2542, Quito) sponsor English-speaking biology graduates to take the course in return for a year's paid work guiding their boats. If you qualify, Metropolitan will obtain visas and work permits for you.

If you are a biologist, it is possible to work as a volunteer with one of the ongoing projects in the islands. Send resumes and work/project suggestions or requests to the Director of the Research Station, currently Dr Gunter Reck. If you are working or studying in the islands you normally qualify for the discounted Ecuadorean airfare to the Galápagos.

Places to Stay

A good range of hotels is available in Puerto Ayora, ranging from cheap and basic to first class, by Galápagos standards at least. There are no luxury hotels. Prices tend to rise with demand and during the heaviest tourist season (December to January and June to August) prices may be higher if the town is full.

It cannot be over-emphasised that a 'tour' based at a hotel and visiting other islands on day trips gives you only a superficial look at the Galápagos. Stay in Puerto Ayora by all means, but make every effort to visit the islands by taking a cruise of at least several days and preferably a full week or more.

Places to Stay - bottom end

There are two cheap hotels in Puerto Ayora and both are basic but clean and friendly, and better value than some of the more expensive places. They are a km north of downtown on the way to the Charles Darwin Research Station.

Pensión Gloria is run by Señora Gloria, whose husband is a guide. They are friendly and will help you organise a tour boat group. They have four double rooms and two triples and charge US$2 per person. They serve a good bread and jam, eggs, juice and coffee breakfast for under US$1. Although facilities are basic, this place is recommended for the friendly service and chances of meeting budget travellers trying to arrange a tour.

Similarly priced and slightly bigger is the *Residencial Angermeyer*, run by members of the family who were among the earliest permanent residents. They are a mine of information and the hotel is in a pleasant garden. It is also popular with budget travellers, but I have received reports that the management is less friendly than at the Gloria. These two places are in my opinion the best in town for travellers who are on a tight budget and are trying to organise their own inexpensive cruise.

It is possible to camp next to the cemetery near the Charles Darwin Research Station but it still costs about a dollar and facilities are almost non-existent. Ask at the Research Station for information about this and other campsites (which are generally difficult to get to and require that you pack in your own water.)

Places to Stay - middle

The *Lobo del Mar Hotel* is popular with Ecuadorean tour groups. Most of their rooms are simple but reasonably clean and with private showers. They charge US$4.50 a single, US$5.50 a double, US$7.50 a triple and US$9 for a quadruple. For about US$3.50 more per person the deal includes three meals a day. The hotel also organises day trips to various islands for about US$20 per passenger.

The *Hotel Las Palmeras* is an excellent mid-range hotel which has received frequent recommendations and so rooms are often full. Prices are around US$5.50 single, US$6.50 double and US$9.00 triple in clean rooms with private bath.

Similarly priced and also clean and modern looking is the *Hotel Salinas*. In this price range are the *Hotel Darwin* and *Hotel Santa Cruz*, which are both fairly new and on the road out of town. Also mid-priced are the *Hotel Elizabeth* and *Hotel Colón*, which I think are overpriced. The *Elizabeth* is particularly unpleasant – dirty, noisy, unfriendly and probably the worst hotel in town.

The new *Hotel Ninfas* charges US$4.50 without and US$10.50 with meals and has private baths in all rooms. The *Hotel Castro* is usually used by tour groups booked with Señor Miguel Castro but you can always try it if you have no luck elsewhere. The recently opened *Residencial Flamingo* is in the mid-price range.

The *Hotel Sol y Mar* is very pleasantly situated right on the waterfront and marine iguanas sunbathe with the guests on the deck or walk over your feet while you're having breakfast. The owner is Señor Jimmy Perez, a rather colourful character who speaks English and runs Trans-Galápagos Tourism. He can also help you get a boat. Clean rooms with private bath are US$9.50 single, US$16 double, US$19 triple, and US$23 quadruple. Good meals are available for US$1.50 (breakfast), US$3.50 (lunch) and US$5 (supper). Similarly priced is the new and pleasant *Hotel Las Ninfas* which also has tours available.

Places to Stay - top end The best hotel in Puerto Ayora is the well recommended *Hotel Galápagos*, which charges US$29/US$52/US$75 for comfortable single/double/triple rooms with private bath and ocean view. They serve excellent meals (about US$5, US$6 and US$7 for breakfast, lunch and supper). A pleasant

bar and a paperback book library are on the premises.

Across the bay from Puerto Ayora is the *Hotel Delfín* with a private beach. You need a boat to get to this hotel from Puerto Ayora.

Places to Eat

There are a number of restaurants and bars in Puerto Ayora and they are good places to meet people. Some of them change hands or names quite often, as places frequented by seasonal influxes of people tend to do. Most of the following have been around for a few years.

Las Ninfas Restaurant by the dock has been the standard meeting place during the day for years. They serve decent meals. The *Pasty Pan* bakery is good for baked goods and also for boat contacts. *La Garrapata Bar/Restaurant* has recently become popular and serves good meals. The bar often stays open until the early hours and is popular with locals and visitors alike. The Garrapata is often closed in the afternoons.

The *Casa Blanca Pizzería* is run by a friendly British couple, and screens videos during weekend evenings for a fee. The *4 Lanterns Restaurant* has also been well recommended for good home cooking. In the evening, the rowdiest action is at *La Terraza Bar*. There are other places.

The restaurant at the *Hotel Galápagos* is good and open to the public, though you should make advance reservation if there is a group of you. This is the only place in Puerto Ayora where all the drinking water is properly filtered and safe. They prepare safe salads too.

Getting There & Away

You can either go by boat or by air – I most definitely recommend air. If you go by boat you will normally waste a lot of time in Guayaquil getting one of the infrequent passages. The money you spend on hotels and food in Guayaquil, plus the hassles involved, means that you really end up saving very little money, if any at all.

Though the air fare is very expensive, there's nothing you can do about it.

Air Rather than spend frustrating days and weeks looking for a ship in Guayaquil, I recommend that you just get on a plane and have done with it. TAME operates morning flights daily (except Sundays) from both Quito and Guayaquil to Baltra Island airport, about four hours away from Puerto Ayora by public transport (see the Getting Around section).

Flights from Guayaquil cost US$324 round trip and take 1½ hours to the Galápagos. From Quito the flight costs US$360 round trip and you have to check in again in Guayaquil and usually board another aircraft.

Because there is a 10% tax on airline tickets in Ecuador, you should be able to get a 10% cheaper ticket if you buy one from a travel agent in the US or some other country where airline tickets are not taxed. This is especially true if you fly to Ecuador with Ecuatoriana, even though the only flights to Baltra are with TAME. (I have received a report that tickets to the Galápagos can be US$100 cheaper if bought in the US but I have not been able to substantiate this.) If you do buy in advance, make sure that you check that your name is on the computer when you get to Ecuador – it usually is but you never know till you check.

Ecuadorean nationals can fly for about US$40. Some foreign residents of Ecuador or workers in the islands are also eligible so if you have a residence visa you should make enquiries.

It used to be that there were military logistic flights which you could wangle your way on to, but this is no longer common and I have not heard of any one who has done this for years. I heard of some travellers who tried to pull a scam by posing as Ecuadoreans and giving an Ecuadorean *cedula* number to purchase cheap tickets. They persuaded the travel agent to sell them the tickets but they were caught at the airport. Security checks in and out of the Galápagos have since been stepped up and now you have to show your identity documents three times, so forget about bluffing your way through with a cheap ticket.

I have heard of some scam which gets you to the Galápagos cheaply, but apparently you have to be an Israeli citizen and the people I talked with were playing their hands very close to their chests! I suppose that as long as the flights are expensive there will be people who will happily waste a month of their time trying to beat the system; if you're not eligible for cheap flights and you think the airfare is too expensive, then maybe you shouldn't be visiting the island anyway.

Flights to the Galápagos are sometimes booked up well in advance but if you go to the airport you'll often find that there are many no-shows. Travel agencies book up blocks of seats for their all-inclusive Galápagos tours. First they sell them to people taking their tours but will release the seats on the day of the flight when there is no longer any hope of selling their tour. If you are tied into a definite itinerary, you should make a reservation; if you're flexible, you can buy your ticket at the airport when you want to fly. You have a better-than-even chance of getting a ticket and it's highly unlikely that you'll be turned away two days in a row.

Some travel agencies will offer you a 'discount' on an airline ticket if you buy their tour of the Galápagos, which is OK if their tour happens to be what you want. Sometimes you can persuade an agency to sell you a discount ticket because they can't fill their tour space.

César Gavela at the Hotel Gran Casino in Quito arranges tours and will sometimes sell you a discounted ticket if you happen to ask on the right day. (Obviously, this is not a reliable way of obtaining a ticket at any time, but it works sometimes.)

So to get a ticket, first go to TAME. If they are sold out, try a travel agent specialising in Galápagos tours, and finally go the airport on the day of the flight if you haven't had any success at TAME or the travel agencies.

Boat If you really insist on avoiding air transport, there are four ways to get to the islands by boat: with the navy, on a cargo boat, on a cruise ship or on your own vessel.

The navy runs the *Calicuchima*, which leaves Guayaquil about twice a month for an 11-day trip. Only about half this time is available for visiting the islands, some naval bases are visited en route, and the accommodation, crew, guides and food have been criticised. The tour costs about US$330 and you can find out more from their office at Transnave on 9 de Octubre and Chile in Guayaquil. (They've moved offices several times in the last few years, so you may have to ask at the Capitanía on the waterfront.)

Cargo ships leave irregularly and charge about US$90 for a one-way trip. Three ships doing this are the *Pinzón, Piquero* and *Iguana*, but the first of these recently broke down and you may well have to wait for up to a month for a departure with one of the others. Conditions are tolerable but basic. The journey out takes about 3½ days and you should be prepared to bring a sleeping bag or hammock. These ships also do round trips but these are mainly for cargo purposes and not for wildlife viewing. You can go if you want to watch cargo being loaded. More information can be had from the Capitanía or at dock No 4 on Guayaquil's Malecón.

The best boats to the islands are the cruise ships which are more comfortable, have a regular schedule, offer better food and guide service, and of course are more expensive. They accommodate 90 passengers in comfortable double cabins. These seven-day tours usually cost about US$1000 inclusive and go one way by boat and return by air. Occasionally, if a tour isn't full, you can wangle a cheaper fare at the last minute.

One cruise ship is the *Bucanero* which

has been recommended for a friendly crew and is operated by Gordon Tours, Baquerizo Moreno 1120 and 9 de Octubre in Guayaquil; and at Juan León Mera 566 and Carrión in Quito. Another is the *Santa Cruz* which is a little more expensive and the 'best' large ship to the Galápagos. Information is available from any major tour agency in Ecuador, especially Metropolitan. Both these boats are relatively luxurious and can be booked via any good travel agent in most countries.

You can travel to the Galápagos in your own boat, but the Ecuadorean authorities give only a 72-hour transit pass to non-Galápagos boats, so you can't normally cruise the islands in your own boat unless you arrange it in advance – a difficult and time consuming process. If you succeed in getting a permit, you must hire a licensed guide to accompany you in the islands.

There is a US$35 port entrance fee charged to visiting yachts. You can moor the boat in Puerto Ayora and hire a Galápagos boat to visit the islands. If you do this you'll also have to pay a US$40 national park fee as well as the boat hire.

Tours The most economical tours are the ones you organise for yourself from Puerto Ayora but if you don't have the time or patience then you can arrange tours from your home country (expensive but efficient) or from Quito or Guayaquil (cheaper but the first places are sold abroad so you sometimes have to wait a few days).

The cheapest prearranged tours that I know of are sold by César Gavela at the Gran Casino hotel in Quito. Departures are on limited dates and getting something suitable is largely a matter of luck – don't expect any luxury. The boats used are similar to those run by Galasam.

A little more expensive and with more frequent departure dates are the tours run by Galasam (Economic Galápagos Tours) and they will often sell you just an air ticket even if you don't want a tour.

Galasam are at Pinto 523 and Amazonas in Quito, and at Avenida 9 de Octubre 424 (11th floor, Edificio Gran Pasaje) in Guayaquil. Their tours are suitable for budget travellers who don't want to organise their own tour once they get to the islands.

They have seven-day tours aboard small boats with six to 12 bunks in double, triple and quadruple cabins. All bedding is provided and the accommodation is clean but spartan, with little privacy. Plenty of simple but fresh food and juice is served at all meals and a naturalist guide accompanies the boat (some guides speak English). There are no extra costs (except for bottled drinks) and the emphasis is on relaxed wildlife-watching and casual cruising rather than luxury. There are toilets, and fresh water is available for washing of faces and drinking. Bathing facilities are often buckets of sea water, though showers are available on some boats. There are pre-set itineraries which visit most of the central islands and give enough time to see the wildlife.

If you want your own itinerary you have to get a group of about six together. A one-week tour costs from US$300 to US$400 per person plus airfare (depending on the time of year). Shorter tours are available. There are weekly departures.

Make absolutely sure that your cruise is not a hotel based one with day trips to various islands. These tours are sometimes offered and it is not clear from the information that the itinerary involves overnights in Puerto Ayora. Ask.

More luxurious tours are also available with other agencies which advertise in Quito and Guayaquil. Their boats are more comfortable, the food is better and they can cost up to US$100 per day or more. If you want this kind of luxury, then a good travel agent in Ecuador or at home will be able to help you with information. I can recommend the Galápagos tours run by Wilderness Travel, 801 Allston Way, Berkeley, CA 94710, USA.

Getting Around

From Baltra Most visitors arrive by air and land on Baltra Island. Have your passport and US$40 visitor fee ready – you won't get out of the airport otherwise. Outside the airport you will be met by a boat representative (if you are on a prearranged tour) and taken by bus on a five minute drive to the boat dock.

If you are an independent traveller heading to Puerto Ayora, do not take the bus to the boat dock. Instead, take the bus to the ferry dock for Isla Santa Cruz. This is a 10 to 15 minute drive. A 10 minute ferry boat ride will take you across to Santa Cruz where you will be met by a bus to take you to Puerto Ayora, almost two hours away. This drive gives you a good look at the interior and highlands of Santa Cruz – dusty and dry in the north and greener and wetter in the highlands and on the south slopes. The ferry and second bus are scheduled to coincide with the departure of the first bus from the airport so there isn't much waiting involved. You should be in Puerto Ayora within four hours of your arrival in Baltra.

The combined bus/ferry/bus trip costs about US$2. There is a ticket booth at the airport in the departure lounge, to your left as you leave the arrival area. You should buy your ticket as soon as you arrive as there is normally only one bus (although a second bus may run if there is enough passenger demand). The journey is often very crowded and passengers sometimes ride on the roof.

Bus Buses from Puerto Ayora to Baltra (via the ferry) leave at 8 am, every morning that there are flights (Monday to Saturday), from in front of the Hotel Colón and Raul Jería Store. The fare is about US$1.50, including the ferry. They return in the afternoon after the plane from the mainland has landed. A second and third bus will run if there is passenger demand. (The flight from Baltra to Guayaquil leaves at 1 pm.)

You can use these buses to be dropped off

at the villages of Bella Vista or Santa Rosa to explore some of the interior. Neither of these villages have hotels and sometimes the return bus is full with passengers from the airport. The most convenient way of seeing the interior and ensuring that you don't get stuck is to hire a bus or truck for the day with a group of other travellers. Ask at your hotel about this.

Boat INGALA can give you up-to-date details of the inter-island passenger boat services. You should buy the tickets a day in advance. Notice that there are two INGALA offices on the map – only one sells tickets. Recently, the following passenger services were in operation from Puerto Ayora:

To San Cristóbal, US$12, Tuesdays and Saturdays.

To Isabela, every other Thursday, US$12, continuing on Friday to Santa María and on Saturday returning to Puerto Ayora.

All these voyages take about four hours. Most inter-island transport is by private boat.

Boat Charters The cheapest way to get around the islands is to charter your own boat in Puerto Ayora. Once in the town, first find somewhere to sleep (especially during the high season when beds can be limited) and then you can start looking for a boat. This normally takes a few days to arrange, though you may be lucky and find a suitable one leaving the next day. If you are alone or with a friend, you'll need to find some more people as even the smallest boats take four passengers. There are always people in Puerto Ayora looking for boats and you should be able to get a group together quite easily in a few days. The busiest and most expensive times are June to August and December to January. You should try to avoid those months if you are economising.

Getting a group together and finding a boat is easier than it sounds. The restaurants and hotels in town will be full of travellers and boat captains will be looking for passengers. Your hotel manager can often introduce you to someone. After all, almost everyone knows everybody else so word will quickly get around.

The cheapest and most basic boats are available for about US$20 per day per person (low season) and this should include everything. The cheaper the boat, the more rice and fish you can expect to eat, and the more crowded the accommodation. The most expensive boats may charge close to US$100 per person per day and are reasonably comfortable, have superb food and excellent crews. Most of these boats run prearranged tours with foreign groups and you are not likely to find these available for budget or independent travel.

The most important thing is to find a boat whose crew you get along with and which has a good and enthusiastic naturalist guide who will be able to point out and explain the wildlife and other items of interest. Owners, captains, guides, cooks, etc change frequently and in addition many boats make changes and improvements from year to year. Generally speaking, a boat is only as good as its crew. You should be able to meet the naturalist guide and captain and inspect the boat before you leave, and you should have an itinerary agreed upon with the boat owner (who may not necessarily be the captain).

It is recommended that you have the itinerary in writing to avoid disagreements between you and other passengers and the crew during the cruise. Be particularly careful to stress what you want. Some tours go out on day trips and return to a Puerto Ayora hotel at night; on these tours you don't get to see the more outlying islands because too much time is spent going back and forth from Puerto Ayora. Make sure that you will sleep on the boat and tour from island to island, unless you prefer staying on dry land. Day trips are available from various hotels.

Boats vary in size from those taking four passengers to those taking 16. (Getting on the 96 berth ships is not normally possible in Puerto Ayora unless you have booked ahead.) Smaller boats are often more cramped but have the advantage of having a smaller group of people landing at the visitor sites. The larger boats have a little more space but you have to tramp around with a dozen or more people.

All land visits must be in a group and accompanied by your guide. A group of about eight is a reasonable compromise. Washing facilities vary from a bucket of sea water on the cheapest boats to freshwater showers (sometimes a freshwater deck hose) on the better boats. If you don't want to stay salty for a week, ask about washing facilities. Also enquire about drinking water – I would recommend treating the water on most of the cheaper boats.

Because a boat is only as good as its crew, it is difficult to make foolproof recommendations. However, travellers have sent me personal recommendations for the following boats, though there are many others which are also good. For around US$25 to US$30 per day, the *El Tiburon* (ask at the Sol y Mar Hotel), the *Golondrina*, the *Fenix*, and the *Flamingo*. For about US$35 to US$40 per day, the trimaran *Windshadow* operated by Ricardo Nuñez.

Mid-priced and for small groups (four passengers) the yacht *Inti* operated by Gil and Anita de Roi is well recommended. A lot of fun is had with Miguel Salcedo on the *Sulidae* which is normally full with 1st class tour groups but is sometimes available off season when he will lower his normal rates. A recommended naturalist guide who freelances is Daniel Fitter – very knowledgeable.

This is just a small selection. If you have a particularly good or bad experience with a boat, please write.

Cruise Itineraries You can go almost anywhere but it takes time to reach the more outlying islands. It is best to visit a few central islands and inspect them

closely rather than trying to cram as many ports of call as possible into your cruise. Inter-island cruising will take up valuable hours of your time and you don't see very much while at sea. If you want to visit the largest island, Isabela, you'll have to allow two weeks.

Assuming you go for a cruise of four to seven days, the islands you should make an effort to visit so that you can see the most are the following: South Plaza, off the east coast of Santa Cruz, has sea lion, land iguana and swallow-tailed gull colonies, a cactus forest and good snorkelling. Seymour, just north of Baltra, has both blue-footed booby and magnificent frigate bird nesting colonies. Black Turtle Cove (or Caleta Tortuga Negra), on the north shore of Santa Cruz, has marine turtles and white-tipped sharks.

Isla Bartolomé on the east side of San Salvador has a small volcanic cone which you can easily climb for one of the best views of the islands. Also there are penguins, sea lions and good snorkelling on Bartolomé. On San Salvador (often known as James) you can walk on a lava flow by Sullivan Bay on the east, and see marine iguanas, sea lions, fur seals, Galápagos hawks and many kinds of sea birds near Puerto Egas on the west. Rabida has a flamingo colony. In addition to the species mentioned, you'll see common species almost everywhere. Masked and blue-footed boobies, pelicans, mockingbirds, finches, Galápagos doves, frigate birds, lava lizards and red sally lightfoot crabs are so frequently seen that they'll become part of the normal surroundings to you.

If you have more time (say a full week) you could visit some of the other islands. The red-footed booby is found only on the more outlying islands such as Genovesa (Tower) and the small islets surrounding Santa María (Floreana). The waved albatross breeds only on Española (Hood) and the flightless Galápagos cormorant is found on the western islands of Isabela and Fernandina, which require a two-week trip.

Day Trips These are a poor alternative to overnight trips but a few people prefer them or find they have no other option. Most days trips cost about US$22 per person (including lunch) and the following islands are visited frequently: South Plaza, Seymour, and Santa Fé. Less frequently visited but still possible on day trips with faster boats are Bartolomé and Santa María. Although you miss the fun, camaraderie, and adventure of a cruise of several days, at least you do get to see a good selection of wildlife and views.

Several hotels and boat companies arrange day trips. One is Costuga which has representatives at the Ninfas restaurant or hotel.

PUERTO BAQUERIZO MORENO

This is the political capital of the Galápagos and is on Isla San Cristóbal. Few travellers came here until recently, when SAN-Saeta started operating a regular jet service. It is still a long way behind Puerto Ayora in interest and facilities however. There is a small museum and a statue of Darwin. Frigate Bird Hill is a short walk from town.

Places to Stay & Eat

The best and most expensive hotel is run in conjunction with SAN airline. This is the *Grand Hotel* which faces a beach at the east end of town. Rooms with private bath are US$19 single and US$23 double.

Cheaper hotels are the *Northia Hotel, Hotel Colón* and *Pension Monica*. This last one is the cheapest at about US$2 per person.

With the new airline services, more hotels are being opened. There are basic restaurants – the best food is at the *Grand Hotel*.

Getting There & Away

SAN-Saeta flights to Puerto Baquerizo

Moreno cost the same as the TAME flights to Baltra. Departures from Quito via Guayaquil are on Mondays, Wednesdays, and Saturdays. The airport is within walking distance of the town.

Getting Around

Bus There are a few buses a day from the capital to the farming centre of El Progreso, about eight km up into the highlands. From here it is possible to rent jeeps for the further 10 km to the visitor site of El Junco Lagoon.

Boat INGALA runs a twice weekly passenger boat service to Puerto Ayora, costing US$12 and leaving on Monday and Wednesdays. The trip takes about four hours. This theoretically enables travellers to fly in to Puerto Baquerizo Moreno with SAN-Saeta and leave from Baltra with TAME. This is not often done, however, and it requires much perseverance to buy one-way tickets and have them confirmed.

Tours

There are a few private boats in Puerto Baquerizo Moreno which can be hired for day trips and overnight trips, but there aren't too many travellers looking to share costs. Galasam is now operating some of its departures from Puerto Baquerizo Moreno. SAN-Saeta are planning on basing the new 120 berth *Galápagos Explorer* at Puerto Baquerizo Moreno and running three or four day trips – I don't know when this will happen.

PUERTO VELASCO IBARRA

This is the only settlement on Isla Santa María, and although there is not much to do here, there is a small hotel and restaurant run by Margaret Wittmer. You can write to her for reservations (Sra Wittmer, Pto Velasco Ibarra, Santa María, Galápagos) or just show up. They are rarely full. There is a black beach near the port where there is a sea lion colony and a flamingo lagoon near by.

INGALA runs a boat every two weeks on Thursday and Friday making the triangular passage Puerto Ayora to Puerto Villamil (Thursday), Puerto Villamil to Puerto Velasco Ibarra and Puerto Ayora (Friday). Each leg is about US$12 and four hours. Rolf Wittmer runs his boat the *Tip Top* from Puerto Ayora to Puerto Velasco Ibarra regularly.

PUERTO VILLAMIL
This is a small port on Isabela, the largest island. There are a couple of hotels and basic restaurants but they are not visited much by travellers. From Puerto Villamil, there is an 18 km road to Santo Tomás where horses can be hired to continue up Volcán Santo Tomás.

INGALA runs a boat service from Puerto Ayora and to Puerto Velasco Ibarra.

Index

MAPS

Temperature

To convert °C to °F multipy by 1.8 and add 32

To convert °F to °C subtract 32 and multipy by ·55

Length, Distance & Area

	multipy by
inches to centimetres	2.54
centimetres to inches	0.39
feet to metres	0.30
metres to feet	3.28
yards to metres	0.91
metres to yards	1.09
miles to kilometres	1.61
kilometres to miles	0.62
acres to hectares	0.40
hectares to acres	2.47

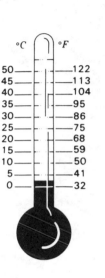

Weight

	multipy by
ounces to grams	28.35
grams to ounces	0.035
pounds to kilograms	0.45
kilograms to pounds	2.21
British tons to kilograms	1016
US tons to kilograms	907

A British ton is 2240 lbs, a US ton is 2000 lbs

Volume

	multipy by
Imperial gallons to litres	4.55
litres to imperial gallons	0.22
US gallons to litres	3.79
litres to US gallons	0.26

5 imperial gallons equals 6 US gallons
a litre is slightly more than a US quart, slightly less
than a British one

Lonely Planet

Lonely Planet published its first book in 1973. Tony and Maureen Wheeler had made a lengthy overland trip from England to Australia and, in response to numerous 'how do you do it?' questions, Tony wrote and they published *Across Asia on the Cheap*. It became an instant local best-seller and inspired thoughts of a second travel guide. A year and a half in South-East Asia resulted in their second book, *South-East Asia on a Shoestring*, which they put together in a backstreet Chinese hotel in Singapore in 1975. The 'yellow book', as it quickly became known, soon became *the* guide to the region and has gone through five editions, always with its familiar yellow cover.

Soon other writers started to come to them with ideas for similar books – books that went off the beaten track and took an adventurous approach to travel, books that 'assumed you knew how to get your luggage off the carousel,' as one reviewer described them. Lonely Planet grew from a kitchen table operation to a spare room and then to its own office. It also started to develop an international reputation as the Lonely Planet logo began to appear in more and more countries. In 1982 *India – a travel survival kit* won the Thomas Cook award for the best guidebook of the year.

These days there are over 60 Lonely Planet titles. Nearly 30 people work at our office in Melbourne, Australia and another half dozen at our US office in Oakland, California.

At first Lonely Planet specialised exclusively in the Asia region but these days we are also developing major ranges of guidebooks to the Pacific region, to South America and to Africa. The list of walking guides is growing and Lonely Planet is producing a unique series of phrasebooks to 'unusual' languages. The emphasis continues to be on travel for travellers and Tony and Maureen still manage to fit in a number of trips each year and play a very active part in the writing and updating of Lonely Planet's guides.

Keeping guidebooks up to date is a constant battle which requires an ear to the ground and lots of walking, but technology also plays its part. All Lonely Planet guidebooks are now stored and updated on computer, and some authors even take lap-top computers into the field. Lonely Planet is also using computers to draw maps and eventually many of the maps will be stored on disk.

The people at Lonely Planet strongly feel that travellers can make a positive contribution to the countries they visit both by better appreciation of cultures and by the money they spend. In addition the company tries to make a direct contribution to the countries and regions it covers. Since 1986 a percentage of the income from each book has gone to aid groups and associations. This has included donations to famine relief in Africa, to aid projects in India, to agricultural projects in Nicaragua and other Central American countries and to Greenpeace's efforts to halt French nuclear testing in the Pacific. In 1988 over $40,000 was donated by Lonely Planet to these projects.

Lonely Planet Distributors

Australia & Papua New Guinea Lonely Planet Publications, PO Box 617, Hawthorn, Victoria 3122.

Canada Raincoast Books, 112 East 3rd Avenue, Vancouver, British Columbia V5T 1C8.

Denmark, Finland & Norway Scanvik Books aps, Store Kongensgade 59 A, DK-1264 Copenhagen K.

Hong Kong The Book Society, GPO Box 7804.

India & Nepal UBS Distributors, 5 Ansari Rd, New Delhi – 110002

Israel Geographical Tours Ltd, 8 Tverya St, Tel Aviv 63144.

Japan Intercontinental Marketing Corp, IPO Box 5056, Tokyo 100-31.

Netherlands Nilsson & Lamm bv, Postbus 195, Pampuslaan 212, 1380 AD Weesp.

New Zealand Transworld Publishers, PO Box 83-094, Edmonton PO, Auckland.

Singapore & Malaysia MPH Distributors, 601 Sims Drive, #03-21, Singapore 1438.

Spain Altair, Balmes 69, 08007 Barcelona.

Sweden Esselte Kartcentrum AB, Vasagatan 16, S-111 20 Stockholm.

Thailand Chalermnit, 108 Sukhumvit 53, Bangkok 10110.

UK Roger Lascelles, 47 York Rd, Brentford, Middlesex, TW8 0QP

USA Lonely Planet Publications, PO Box 2001A, Berkeley, CA 94702.

West Germany Buchvertrieb Gerda Schettler, Postfach 64, D3415 Hattorf a H.

All Other Countries refer to Australia address.

Guides to Latin America

Chile & Easter Island – a travel survival kit
Chile has one of the most varied geographies in the world, including deserts, tranquil lakes, snow-covered volcanoes and windswept fjords. Easter Island is covered, in detail.

Mexico – a travel survival kit
Mexico has a unique blend of Indian and Spanish culture and a fascinating historical legacy. The hospitality of the people makes Mexico a paradise for travellers.

Peru – a travel survival kit
The famed city of Machu Picchu, the Andean altiplano and the Amazon rainforests are just some of Peru's attractions. All the facts you need can be found in this comprehensive guide.

South America on a shoestring
An up-dated edition of a budget travellers bible that covers Central and South America from the USA-Mexico border to Tierra del Fuego. Written by the author the *New York Times* called "the patron saint of travellers in the third world".

Baja California – a travel survival kit
Mexico's Baja peninsula offers a great escape, right at California's back door. This comprehensive guide follows the long road south from raucous border towns like Tijuana, to resorts, untouched villages and deserted villages.

Colombia – a travel survival kit
Colombia is the land of emeralds, orchids and El Dorado. You may not find the mythical city of gold, but you will find an exotic, wild and beautiful country.

Bolivia – a travel survival kit
Bolivia offers safe and intriguing travel options – from isolated villages in the Andes and ancient ruins to the incredible city of La Paz.

Lonely Planet Guidebooks

Lonely Planet guidebooks cover virtually every accessible part of Asia as well as Australia, the Pacific, Central and South America, Africa, the Middle East and parts of North America. There are four main series: 'travel survival kits', covering a single country for a range of budgets; 'shoestring' guides with compact information for low-budget travel in a major region; trekking guides; and 'phrasebooks'.

Australia & the Pacific
Australia
Bushwalking in Australia
Papua New Guinea
Bushwalking in Papua New Guinea
Papua New Guinea phrasebook
New Zealand
Tramping in New Zealand
Rarotonga & the Cook Islands
Solomon Islands
Tahiti & French Polynesia
Fiji
Micronesia

South-East Asia
South-East Asia on a shoestring
Malaysia, Singapore & Brunei
Indonesia
Bali & Lombok
Indonesia phrasebook
Burma
Burmese phrasebook
Thailand
Thai phrasebook
Philippines
Pilipino phrasebook

North-East Asia
North-East Asia on a shoestring
China
China phrasebook
Tibet
Tibet phrasebook
Japan
Korea
Korean phrasebook
Hong Kong, Macau & Canton
Taiwan

West Asia
West Asia on a shoestring
Trekking in Turkey
Turkey

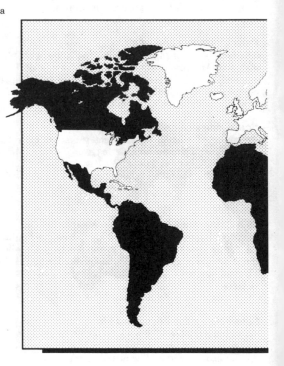

Mail Order

Lonely Planet guidebooks are distributed worldwide and are sold by good bookshops everywhere. They are also available by mail order from Lonely Planet, so if you have difficulty finding a title please write to us. US and Canadian residents should write to Embarcadero West, 112 Linden St, Oakland CA 94607, USA and residents of other countries to PO Box 617, Hawthorn, Victoria 3122, Australia.

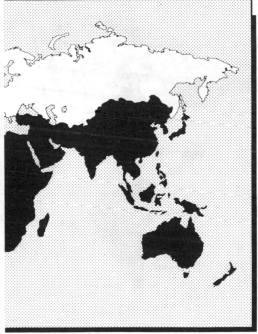

Indian Subcontinent
India
Hindi/Urdu phrasebook
Kashmir, Ladakh & Zanskar
Trekking in the Indian Himalaya
Pakistan
Kathmandu & the Kingdom of Nepal
Trekking in the Nepal Himalaya
Nepal phrasebook
Sri Lanka
Sri Lanka phrasebook
Bangladesh

Africa
Africa on a shoestring
East Africa
Swahili phrasebook
West Africa

Middle East
Egypt & the Sudan
Jordan & Syria
Yemen

North America
Canada
Alaska

Mexico
Mexico
Baja California

South America
South America on a shoestring
Ecuador & the Galapagos Islands
Colombia
Chile & Easter Island
Bolivia
Peru

Lonely Planet Update

We collect an enormous amount of information here at Lonely Planet. Apart from our research there's a steady stream of travellers' letters full of the latest news. For over 5 years much of this information went into a quarterly newsletter (and helped to update the guidebooks). The paperback *Update* includes this up-to-date news and aims to supplement the information available in our guidebooks. There are four editions a year (Feb, May, Aug and Nov) available either by subscription or through bookshops. Subscribe now and you'll save nearly 25% off the retail price.

Each edition has extracts from the most interesting letters we have received, covering such diverse topics as:
- how to take a boat trip on the Yalu River
- living in a typical Thai village
- getting a Nepalese trekking permit

Subscription Details
All subscriptions cover four editions and include postage. Prices quoted are subject to change.

USA & Canada – One year's subscription is US$12; a single copy is US$3.95. Please send your order to Lonely Planet's California office.

Other Countries – One year's subscription is Australian $15; a single copy is A$4.95. Please pay in Australian $, or the US$ or £ Sterling equivalent. Please send your order form to Lonely Planet's Australian office.

Order Form

Please send me

☐ One year's sub. – starting current edition.　　　☐ One copy of the current edition.

Name (please print) ....

Address (please print) ....

....

....

Tick One

☐ Payment enclosed (payable to Lonely Planet Publications)

Charge my　☐ Visa　☐ Bankcard　☐ MasterCard　for the amount of $ ....

Card No .... Expiry Date ....

Cardholder's Name (print) ....

Signature .... Date...

US & Canadian residents
Lonely Planet, Embarcadero West, 112 Linden St,
Oakland, CA 94607, USA
Other countries
Lonely Planet, PO Box 617, Hawthorn, Victoria 3122, Australia